Making Learning REAL

*Reaching and Engaging All Learners
in Secondary Classrooms*

IN THE PARTNERS IN LEARNING SERIES

EDUCATORS FOR **SOCIAL RESPONSIBILITY**

Making Learning REAL: Reaching and Engaging All Learners in Secondary Classrooms
In the Partners in Learning Series
By Carol Miller Lieber
© 2009 Educators for Social Responsibility

esr

Educators for Social Responsibility
23 Garden Street
Cambridge, MA 02138
www.esrnational.org

Cover design by John Barnett/Four Eyes Design
Book production by Erin Dawson

10 9 8 7 6 5 4 3 2 1
Printed in the United States of America

ISBN 13: 978-0-615-28125-4
ISBN 10: 0-615-28125-7

ACKNOWLEDGMENTS

The two new books in the Partners in Learning Series, *Making Learning REAL* and *Getting Classroom Management RIGHT*, represent a lifetime of work in education and twenty years of developing programs and facilitating professional development for the Cambridge, Massachusetts-based Educators for Social Responsibility.

This effort would not have been possible without the support of many people. On a personal note, I would like to thank my mother and late father who nurtured, and at times tolerated, a fiercely independent, curious, and idealistic kid who didn't lose her vision as a grown-up. Professionally, I would like to thank ESR's executive director, Larry Dieringer, who has been a valued thought partner in this process, providing the organizational leadership and support so necessary for the development of new programs and publications.

Over the years, many colleagues have been true partners with me in this work and have served me well as friendly critics and critical friends. In particular, I would like to thank Rachel Poliner, Jennifer Allen, Connie Cuttle, Sherrie Gammage, and Doug Breunlin. I am indebted to Audra Longert and Denise Wolk, my editors, who both have an amazing capacity to fire up my passion while keeping me on track and focused. They don't miss a thing!

There are others who inspire my urgency to write: Thomas Jefferson, whose writings inform my identity as a teacher-citizen; John Dewey, whose work serves as the anchor for my professional practice and compelled me to cofound a progressive secondary school in 1973; Martin Luther King Jr. whose invitation to join the struggle for equity and opportunity changed a young woman's life; Nel Noddings, whose brave and utterly reasonable stance about what's good for children and what's wrong with current reform sheds light in a dark educational moment; and Linda Darling-Hammond, whose life as a teacher educator, researcher, and activist is a model for all educational writers.

Finally, I want to thank all of the school leaders, resident principals, teachers, and students I meet and work with every day here in Chicago, in New York, and across the country. Their needs, requests, and feedback keep pushing me and my ESR colleagues to make our work better.

CONTENTS

PREFACE TO NEW BOOKS
in the PARTNERS IN LEARNING SERIES

Making Learning REAL: Reaching and Engaging All Learners in Secondary Classrooms

Getting Classroom Management RIGHT: Guided Discipline and Personalized Support in Secondary Schools

Why publish two new books instead of a second edition?

We have been gratified by educators' positive responses to the first edition of *Partners in Learning* and have welcomed feedback from teachers, principals, education professors, and professional developers since the book's publication in 2002. Instead of releasing a second edition, ESR has decided to produce two separate books in the Partners in Learning Series:

Making Learning REAL: Reaching and Engaging All Learners in Secondary Classrooms
and
Getting Classroom Management RIGHT: Guided Discipline and Personalized Support in Secondary Schools.

Producing the two new books has provided us the opportunity to incorporate readers' suggestions, add new material that teachers have requested, and make the original content and formatting more user-friendly. Moreover, the new publications enable ESR to turn the spotlight on two equally important areas of classroom practice that are particularly relevant for educators engaged in reform efforts aimed at ensuring that all students experience success in school, achieve at high levels, and graduate ready for college and career.

A decade of supporting hundreds of middle and high schools in their redesign and school improvement initiatives has affirmed our deep commitment to the principles and practices that form the framework for books in the Partners in Learning Series. Three lessons learned from our school change work have stood out for us at ESR:

▶ **Changing school structures without changing classroom practice is not enough.** Merely adding new structures like advisory systems, block schedules, scaffolded academic interventions, freshman academies, and grade-level teaming without changing the practices and relationships within these containers is unlikely to produce the student outcomes that everyone wants.[1, 2, 3] Supporting teachers to change what they actually do in the classroom and how they relate to students remains the most difficult challenge in the reform process.[4, 5, 6] The two fundamental goals for these new publications is to provide new knowledge and "know-how" that builds beliefs and a strong commitment to change classroom practice and to offer a wide array of explicit "how-tos" that enable teachers to do it.

▸ **Changing the quality of instructional practice without attention to personalizing learning and the classroom environment is not enough...** The standards movement and federal mandates of "No Child Left Behind" have put every school on notice to increase academic achievement and reduce the inequality of outcomes among different groups of students. Yet high school dropout and failure rates have hardly budged in recent years, suggesting that the ramping up of instruction and testing will not by itself produce different results—especially for underserved, underperforming students. Many studies have shown, however, that student achievement increases when high expectations and rigorous student work are complemented by efforts to personalize learning, provide higher levels of student support in the classroom, and strengthen positive relationships between and among students and teachers.

> Efforts to respond to the wide range of adolescent students' needs are often approached as add-on components, disconnected from academic achievement, rigorous curriculum, and high teacher expectations for student success. Current calls for reform emphasize the interdependent relationship between personalized learning communities and academic achievement, viewing both as essential to enabling ALL students to meet high standards and create productive futures for themselves. (National High School Alliance)[7]

> Personalized learning is emerging as a response to two notable features of the current high school experience: student apathy and dropping out. Many students see high school as an impersonal experience, forced upon them by an uncaring world at the very moment in their lives when they begin to imagine their independence and yearn for opportunities to expand and express their own talents. (DiMartino, Clarke, and Wolk)[8]

From Lee and Burkam's comprehensive study of school drop-outs, their "most important finding" highlights the impact of student-teacher relationships on students' decisions to stay in school or leave. More than half of students who dropped out claimed that poor relationships with their teachers was a major reason for leaving school. Students who left school characterized many of their teachers as not getting along with students, not interested in their success or failure in school, not caring about them, and not willing to provide extra help when asked. When relationships between students and teachers were perceived as positive, students were much more likely to graduate from high school.[9]

Although much has been written about efforts to personalize the school environment and curriculum, far less has been written about actual techniques for putting personalization into practice. [8, 10, 11] *Making Learning REAL: Reaching and Engaging All Learners in Secondary Classrooms* speaks directly to teachers' requests for concrete tools, strategies, and activities that will personalize their classroom practice; help build better relationships with all of their students; and increase student engagement, effort, and motivation.

▶ **Changing the quality of instruction without attention to improving classroom management and discipline is not enough.** Too many veteran and new teachers cite classroom discipline as a primary reason for leaving the profession. An ASCD teacher poll conducted in December 2008 revealed that the number-one topic about which teachers wanted more information was classroom management and discipline.

> Classroom management skills affect the quantity and quality of the teaching profession. Contrary to popular belief, there is not a shortage of certified teachers in America but rather a shortage of those certified to teach who are willing to either enter or remain in the classroom. The primary reasons why new teachers never enter or quickly leave the profession are based on their inability to manage their classrooms. (Evertson and Weinstein)[12]

Since the implementation of the No Child Left Behind law, a single minded emphasis on instructional leadership, instructional coaching, and content-specific pedagogy may have come at too high a cost. Particularly in urban schools, we encounter teachers who feel overwhelmed and inadequately prepared to manage a supportive and high-functioning learning environment. We believe that effective teachers need to get three things right:

1. High quality instruction and high challenge, highly engaging and meaningful learning

2. Effective classroom management, discipline, and personalized student support

3. Effective interpersonal, facilitation, and group process skills to develop positive, supportive relationships with each student and build a high functioning, high performing group of learners

Contrary to current mythology, high quality instruction and learning are NOT substitutes for #2 and #3. If you can't manage a classroom or negotiate and navigate student relationships with competence and care, quality instruction just isn't going to happen. Making matters even more problematic, research indicates that urban teachers, in particular, report that they receive little or no support when they seek administrators' help with classroom management issues.

Teachers want and need a comprehensive vision of classroom management that will enable them to organize and manage their classrooms for optimal learning; prevent most disruptive behaviors; diagnose and respond to problematic behaviors efficiently; and provide the right kinds of consequences and supportive interventions that will help reluctant and resistant students to turn their behavior around. Equally important, teachers want to feel confident that they can create a safe, welcoming, and supportive learning environment while maintaining order and respect at the same time. No small task! Thus, *Getting Classroom Management RIGHT: Guided Discipline and Personalized Support in Secondary Schools* is devoted entirely to classroom management, discipline, and personalized support.

What's new and different about *Making Learning REAL: Reaching and Engaging All Learners in Secondary Classrooms*

Making Learning REAL is now formatted into three sections.

Section 1: Readings Linking Theory and Research to Core Practices

All of the readings associated with the seven core classroom practices are now located in Chapters 1 through 4 for easy access. Chapter 5 describes how to integrate another critical practice—modeling, teaching, practicing, and assessing life skills—into daily classroom life. Chapter 6 compares a REAL classroom to a more traditional classroom to illustrate how these two classrooms look, sound, and feel for both students and the teacher.

Chapter 1:   Personalize Relationships and Learning in the Classroom
Chapter 2:   Cocreate a Respectful, Responsible, High-Performing Learning Community
Chapter 3:   Meet Adolescents' Developmental and Cultural Needs through High Expectations and Personalized Support
Chapter 4:   Meet Adolescents' Developmental and Cultural Needs by Affirming Diversity in the Classroom
Chapter 5:   Modeling, Teaching, Practicing, and Assessing Life Skills
Chapter 6:   Putting the Practices to Work: A Tale of Two Classrooms

Section 2: Getting Started

Chapters 7 through 10 provide a coherent guide to preparing for the new school year, the first day of class, and the first month of school. The final chapter in this section describes the challenges and opportunities associated with changing classroom practices and offers suggestions for individual and collaborative approaches to professional development.

Chapter 7: Before the School Year Begins
Chapter 8: The First Day of Class
Chapter 9: The First Month
Chapter 10: The Challenges of Changing Classroom Practices

Section 3: The Core Practices

Chapters 11 through 17 present all of the specific strategies and activities associated with each of the core practices for personalizing secondary classrooms and reaching and engaging all learners. Each chapter is devoted to one practice.

Chapter 11: Practice 1—Develop Positive Relationships Between and Among Students and Teachers
Chapter 12: Practice 2—Emphasize Personalized, Student-Centered Learning
Chapter 13: Practice 3—Integrate Multiple Ways of Knowing and Learning
Chapter 14: Practice 4—Establish Clear Norms, Boundaries, and Procedures
Chapter 15: Practice 5—Build a Cohesive Community of Learners
Chapter 16: Practice 6—Provide High Expectations and High Personalized Support
Chapter 17: Practice 7—Affirm Diversity in Your Classroom

Our ongoing work with faculty, leadership teams, and student support staff over the last six years has prompted other significant changes and additions to the book, including:

- A revised and expanded introduction that provides an up-to-date portrait of adolescents in the United States and explores the challenges and dilemmas good teachers face under the mandates of No Child Left Behind

- Sample posters throughout the book that illustrate guiding principles, procedures, and protocols

- Tabs on the right-hand side of certain pages to make it easier to find specific chapters

- A personalization primer in Chapter 1

- More information about adolescent development and the teenage brain in Chapter 3

- More professional development ideas in Chapter 10 that describe how educators have used Partners in Learning in various settings to improve classroom practice

- More strategies for designing and managing student-centered lessons and project-based and independent learning experiences in Chapter 12

- More strategies for differentiating instruction in Chapter 13

- An appendix that includes more than fifty professional development protocols that accompany readings and key topics. They include (1) prereading protocols; (2) while-you-read protocols; (3) small- and large-group dialogue protocols; (4) products, presentations, and report-outs; and (5) planning, assessment, feedback, closings, and final thoughts.

What's new and different about *Getting Classroom Management RIGHT: Guided Discipline and Personalized Support in Secondary Schools?*

Getting Classroom Management RIGHT is a complete revision and expansion of material presented in Chapter 5: Thinking about Discipline in a Partners in Learning Classroom from the first edition of *Partners in Learning*. The expanded content reflects what we've learned through our facilitation of more than a hundred Guided Discipline and Personalized Support institutes across the country over the last five years. The new book also includes more research and evidence-based practices that support our approach to classroom management and discipline. In particular, we show how the explicit practices, strategies, and interventions that inform Guided Discipline and Personalized Support are aligned with the three-tiered framework of Response to Intervention (RTI), a national model for meeting the academic and behavioral needs of three distinct groups of students who inhabit any school. A brief summary of each chapter follows:

- Chapter 1 explores three approaches to classroom management and discipline including ESR's approach, Guided Discipline and Personalized Support; offers sample responses to six familiar problem types; and closes with a glossary of key terms used throughout the book.

- Chapter 2 includes 13 disciplinary case studies that examine the costs and benefits of punitive, do-nothing, and guided discipline responses to typical unwanted behaviors in the classroom.

- Chapter 3 introduces Step 1 of the Guided Discipline and Personalized Support approach—Know Yourself, Know Your Kids, and Know Your School

- Chapter 4 introduces Step 2 of the Guided Discipline and Personalized Support approach—Create Group Norms, Procedures, and Learning Protocols

- Chapter 5 introduces Step 3 of the Guided Discipline and Personalized Support approach—Support Individuals and the Group

- Chapter 6 introduces Step 4 of the Guided Discipline and Personalized Support approach—Invite Students to Engage, Cooperate, and Self-Correct

- Chapter 7 introduces Step 5 of the Guided Discipline and Personalized Support approach—Develop Accountable Consequences and Supportive Interventions

In addition, two appendices contain:

- More than fifteen behavior report forms, problem-solving protocols, conduct cards, and learning contracts that can be used in conjunction with teacher-student conferencing, case conferencing with other faculty, and more intensive interventions

- More than fifty professional development protocols that accompany readings and key topics. These include (1) prereading protocols; (2) while-you-read protocols; (3) small- and large-group dialogue protocols; (4) products, presentations, and report-outs; and (5) planning, assessment, feedback, closings, and final thoughts.

Our team at ESR continues to be inspired by the students and educators we meet. We rededicate these new publications to every teacher who, in difficult times, has been willing to stand up and stand for the kind of challenging, relevant, and personalized education that every adolescent deserves.

Sources:

[1] Allensworth, E. and Easton, J. (2006) *What matters for staying on-track and graduating in Chicago public schools.* Chicago, IL: Consortium on Chicago School Research at the University of Chicago. Accessed online at http://ccsr.uchicago.edu/publications/07%20What%20 Matters%20Final.pdf

[2] Stevens, W. D. (2008) *If small is not enough...the characteristics of successful small high schools in Chicago.* Chicago, IL: Consortium on Chicago School Research at the University of Chicago.

[3] Lee, V., Smith, J., Perry, T., & Smylie, M. (1999). *Social support, academic press, and student achievement: A view from the middle grades in Chicago.* Chicago, IL: Consortium of Chicago School Research at the University of Chicago. Accessed online at http://ccsr.uchicago. edu/content/ publications.php?pub_id=55

[4] Costa, A., and Garmston, R. "Cognitive Coaching: Mediating Growth Toward Holonomy." Chapter 5, pp 52-60 In Strunk, J., Edwards, J., Rogers, S., & Swords, S. (1998). *The Pleasant View Experience.* Golden, CO: Jefferson County Public Schools.

[5] Evans, Robert, *The human side of school change.* Chapter 6, pp. 91-118. "Understanding reluctant faculty".1996. San Franscisco, CA. Jossy-Bass.

[6] Payne, C. *So much reform, so little change: The persistence of failure in urban schools.* 2008. Cambridge, MA. Harvard University Press.

[7] National High School Alliance (2003) Personalization and Social Supports: Site visit protocol and discussion guide. Accessed online at http://www.hsalliance.org/call_action/Protocols/ ProtocolPersonalization.pdf

[8] DiMartino, J., Clarke, J., and Wolk, D. (2003) *Personalized learning; Preparing high school students to create their futures.* Lanham, MD: Scarecrow Education Press.

[9] Lee, V. and Burkam, D. (2003) *Dropping Out of High School: The Role of School Organization and Structure.* American Educational Research Journal, Vol. 40, No. 2, 353-393 (2003) DOI: 10.3102/00028312040002353. University of Michigan.

[10] *Breaking Ranks II: Strategies for Leading High School Reform.* (2004) and *Breaking Ranks in the Middle.* (2006) NASSP. Reston, VA.

[11] The Big Picture Company http://www. Bigpicture.org

[12] Evertson, Carolyn M. and Weinstein, Carol S. (Editors), *Handbook of classroom management: Research, practice, and contemporary issues.* (2006). Philidelphia, PA: Lawrence Erlbaum Associates.

INTRODUCTION

Making School a Place Where Kids Want to Learn and Succeed

I wrote this book from the point of view of a very grateful middle and high school teacher. Although I have served as a principal, professor, curriculum designer, and consultant, my years in the classroom were probably the most memorable and meaningful of my career. It was my good fortune to work in schools that valued all aspects of a young person's growth and development.

For fifteen of those years I worked in a small urban school for seventh through twelfth graders that I co-founded in 1973. The school's students were always a diverse mix who, in another school, might have been labeled the bright and quirky, the sort-of-smart, and the reluctant and resistant. During their six years with us, I watched the students grow more competent and comfortable with the many selves they were trying on and wearing out during their adolescence.

A small school offered opportunities to work with the same students in different settings over many years. It wasn't unusual to teach a student in a seventh grade core class, meet her again in a cross-age elective, become that student's advisor in high school, and then work with her in an advanced-level course. Other curricular structures also enabled us to know our students well. We folded core subjects into cross-disciplinary courses that reduced the number of students we taught by half. Long blocks of time provided students with the space to learn without feeling rushed and the opportunity to investigate the world of texts and the world outside with a rare intensity and purpose. Becoming partners in a learning community was aided by spending long periods of time together.

The faculty were united in wanting to make sure that all our kids had powerful educational experiences, both inside and outside the classroom, in which they cared about what they learned and used their minds well in the process. Quarterly electives and half-day integrated studies allowed students and teachers to pursue individual interests and talents. Each year we expected every student to design and complete an independent learning project and engage in some form of community service. As seniors, students took dual-enrollment courses and participated in month-long internships. We stressed that there wasn't a right way to be a successful learner, although we did insist that students follow through to the finish. (I admit that "last-minute Lucy" and "start-over Sam" made me want to pull my hair out a few times.)

The payoff was witnessing the pride and satisfaction students felt when they met a standard of quality they hadn't thought they could achieve. We wanted students to know what it was like to do a job well. We also hoped they would learn enough about themselves to hold hopeful and realistic expectations about their futures after graduation. Getting all kids into college or getting some kids into the best schools was not our mission. Instead, we encouraged each student to develop a plan or enter a program that would be the best match for advancing his or her personal goals and aspirations—whether it was a community college law enforcement program (Mark is now a city cop), a chef's apprenticeship (Vito is now a famous saucier), or a ticket to the Ivy League (Susan is now a professor at King's College, London).

The other thing we did a lot was have fun—both serious fun that tested kids' pluck and prowess in wilderness and urban adventures, and seriously silly fun that left us tired and happy after a bowling party or an all-night lock-in at the school. We thought playing hard was as important as working hard. During my years in small schools, it was easy to forget that my experience was the exception and not the norm.

At ESR we have worked with thousands of middle and high school educators who are taking steps to build more personalized schools and classrooms. School reform that puts engaging, student-centered learning and personalized classroom practice at the heart of change remains an unfulfilled promise in most schools, large and small. The same questions that framed the research and writing in the original *Partners in Learning* book continue to inform this book, *Making Learning REAL*.

- How do different groups of students experience high school? What can teachers do to help them navigate high school successfully?

- Which students and how many are successful by traditional high school indicators?

- Which students and how many are unsuccessful by traditional high school indicators?

- What factors enable some students to use high school as a gateway to bright futures, while many others experience high school as a dead end?

- How does a faculty get to know all of their students well when too many teachers still teach too many students during any given grading period?

- How do successful teachers personalize student learning for a wide range of learners, especially those who are reluctant and resistant?

- What kinds of learning strategies and tasks are most likely to increase student engagement, effort, and motivation?

- How do good teachers navigate the curricular constraints of standards and content coverage while engaging students in serious work that they find challenging, relevant, and meaningful?

- What kinds of classroom assessment practices and habits of learning actually help students become more self-disciplined and more responsible learners?

- What kinds of practices and routines help build a high-performing group of learners?

Students by the Numbers: A National Portrait

In a book that aims to put students at the center of classroom learning and calls on teachers to know their students well, it's fitting to take a look at some teenage demographics and key statistics that characterize adolescents' high school and postsecondary experiences. The data collected from a variety of sources and presented here should not serve as an excuse for low teacher expectations or make low academic performance acceptable in any classroom. We hope, however, that it does draw attention to a wider and more complex set of factors that influence student well-being and success in school and life.

A Snapshot of U.S. High School Students

In 2008 approximately 16 million teens were enrolled in U.S. high schools. Of these students, 57% were white, 20% were Hispanic, 17% were African American, nearly 5% were Asian/Pacific Islander, and a little over 1% were American Indian/Native Alaskan.[1]

- Nineteen percent children under the age of 18 live in families below the poverty line; 8% live in extreme poverty.[2] Over 60% of poor children are African American and Hispanic. Children under 18 are much more likely than adults to be poor. Being raised in poverty (defined in 2006 as income of $20,444 or less for a family of four with two children) places children at higher risk for a wide range of problems, including exposure to environmental toxins, inadequate nutrition, maternal depression, parental substance abuse, trauma and abuse, violent crime, divorce, decreased cognitive stimulation and vocabulary exposure in infancy, higher risk of negative cognitive and academic outcomes, lower school attendance, higher rates of aggression and violence, drug use, early initiation of sexual activity, mental health problems, failing grades, and early school leaving.[3]

- An additional 22% live in low-income working families.[1]

- Eleven percent of all households are food insecure.[2]

- Thirty-four percent live in families where no parent has full-time, year-round employment; this includes 50% of African American and American Indian/Native Alaskan children.[2]

- Sixty-eight percent of all children live with two parents; 35% of African American children live with two parents.[2]

- Sixty-five percent of African American children live in single-parent families.[1]

- Approximately 160,000 teens are in foster care.[1]

- Six percent live with neither parent.[1]

- Twenty-one percent live in immigrant families, and 20% speak a language other than English at home.[1]

- By age 4, children in professional families hear about 20 million more words than the average child in a working-class family, and about 35 million more words than children in families receiving public assistance.[1]

- Twelve percent do not have health insurance.[1]

- Eight percent have a learning disability as identified by a health care or educational professional.[1]

- Twenty percent of students miss more than three days of school per month.[2]

- Thirty-one percent do not have access to a computer at home.[1]

- African American teens are more than twice as likely to watch more than four hours of television per day than their white and Asian peers.[2]

- Thirty-six percent of 16- to 19-year-olds are employed.[1]

- Fifteen percent of 18- to 24-year-olds neither work nor attend school.[1]

According a recent survey administered by the Centers for Disease Control[4], students in the sixth through tenth grades reported engaging in the following behaviors within the month preceding the survey:

- An estimated 30% had been involved in bullying as a bully, a target of bullying, or both.

- Nearly 8% had been threatened or injured with a weapon on school property.

- Six percent had not gone to school because they felt unsafe at school or on their way to and from school.

- Nearly 36% had been in a physical fight.

- About 9.2% had been hit, slapped, or physically hurt on purpose by a girlfriend or boyfriend.

- About 18.5% had carried a weapon.

- About 5.4% had carried a gun.

- Ten percent had smoked more than 20 cigarettes.

- Forty-five percent of high school seniors had used alcohol.

- Twenty-eight percent had had an episode of heavy drinking (five drinks or more in one setting).

- Eighteen percent had used marijuana, 6% had used methamphetamines, and 6% had used sedatives and stimulants.

- About 28.5% felt so sad or hopeless for two or more weeks in a row that they stopped doing some of their usual activities.

- Nearly 17% had seriously considered suicide. Following a decline in teen suicide rates between 1990 and 2003, the suicide rate for 10- to-24-year-olds increased by 8% in 2004, the largest single-year rise in 15 years.

The percentage of high school students who have had sexual intercourse increases by grade. In 2003, 62% of 12th graders had had sexual intercourse compared with 33% of 9th graders. The median age at first intercourse is 16.9 years for boys and 17.4 year for girls. Approximately one in four sexually active teens contracts a sexually transmitted disease every year. The U.S. teen pregnancy rate decreased 28% between 1990 and 2000, from 117 to 84 per 1000.[5]

In 2004, more than 750,000 young people ages 10 to 24 were treated in emergency departments for injuries sustained due to violence. The leading causes of teen deaths are accidents, homicide, and suicide. In 2003, over 5,000 youth were killed in vehicle accidents, and over 300,000 teens were injured in car crashes. Among 10- to 24-year-olds, homicide is the leading cause of death for African Americans and the second leading cause of death for Hispanics. In 2003, 5,570 young people ages 10 to 24 were murdered, an average of 15 each day. Of these victims, 82% were killed with firearms.[4]

High School Completion and the Dropout Problem

The Harvard Civil Rights Project found that, "Nationally, only about 68% of all students who enter 9th grade will graduate with regular diplomas in 12th grade. While the graduation rate for white students is 75%, only about half of Black, Latino, and Native American students earn regular diplomas alongside their classmates."[6] Equally troublesome is the widening gender gap among high school graduates. Nationally in 2003, 72 percent of female students graduated, compared with 65 percent of male students.[7] Urban districts face the greatest challenges. Two-thirds of the nation's largest fifty cities experience graduation rates of between 30% and 58%.[8]

In a comprehensive study conducted by the Consortium on Chicago School Research, researchers concluded that good attendance and decent grades the first time students take a course are the greatest predictors for high school graduation. When freshmen fall behind in credits, their chances of dropping out are four times more likely. Hence, high schools are providing more attention, resources, supports, and early interventions to help freshman stay on track and graduate in four years. Findings revealed that course passing rates are primarily determined by attendance. In extensive interviews, students cited three factors that affected both grades and attendance: the lack or presence of strong supportive student-teacher relationships, the degree to which school felt important to their future, and the degree to which classwork was relevant and meaningful.[9]

Twenty-five to thirty percent of students drop out of school, a rate that hasn't changed since the early 1980s. *The Silent Epidemic: Perspectives of High School Dropouts*, a report from the Bill & Melinda Gates Foundation, notes that 88% of students have passing grades when they drop out. Boredom, restlessness, and irrelevance were more often associated with school leaving than academic difficulties were.[10]

When high school leavers are interviewed, they have no problem telling adults what factors and conditions would have improved their chances of graduating with their classmates:

- Eighty-one percent of students wanted opportunities for real-world learning to make their courses more relevant.

- Eighty-one percent of students wanted better teachers to make class more interesting.

- Seventy-five percent of students said that smaller classes with more individual instruction would make a difference.

- Seventy-one percent of students thought that better communication between parents and school and more parent involvement would have helped them stay in school.

- Seventy-one percent said that parents should make sure students got to school every day.

- Seventy percent thought that better adult supervision and more vigilance concerning class attendance would improve their chances of graduating.[10]

Student Engagement

Interest in high school among 12th graders has continued to decline since 1983, when 40% percent reported that their schoolwork was often or always meaningful. By 2000, the number stood at 28%. In 2000, 32% of seniors said that most of their courses were very or slightly dull, up from 20% in 1983. Seniors who felt that school learning would be helpful or very helpful in later life dropped from 51% in 1983 to 39% in 2000.[11]

A poll of 9th and 10th graders in California revealed that only 39% said they liked school and felt that their schools and teachers did a good job of motivating them to work hard and do their best. Sixty-one percent of students reported they didn't like school and didn't feel motivated to succeed. Yet 90% of this same group of reluctant learners said they would be more motivated if they could take courses related to future careers and technology. The study found no differences among racial and ethnic groups; possibly surprising is that more girls than boys said they wanted more hands-on learning.[12]

Over the years we have conducted dozens of focus groups about students' experiences of high school.[13] One question we always ask is, "Think about the classes in which you're bored and restless, and now think about the classes that you look forward to everyday, the classes in which you know you're learning something important. What exactly is the difference? What are you doing and what are teachers doing?" In teenage parlance, here's what they said. "We learn more and like it more when...."

- we get to work on our own projects

- teachers make us want to learn—they get excited and want us to get excited too

- she tells us why the work is hard so we can get inside of it

- we have a voice in what we're doing

- we do mock trials and role-plays of real events

- teachers care about what we think—we have opinions too

- we have games and contests that help us study and review before a test

- teachers stay on our case until we get it right

- teachers give us personal time and attention in class and after school

- teachers really know me

- we get to work with real things on real problems

- the teacher tells jokes when we're getting bored and then we get back to work

- teachers respect who we are and we don't have to pretend

- we get to play around with theories in math and apply what we're learning

- we get to make up our own questions and assignments

- teachers don't see you just as students. They try to figure out who you are. They try to always make you go further than what you are capable of.

- teachers make it fun and different—we don't do the same thing everyday

- we read a book that makes it your reality

- we don't just do study packets and read the textbook

- we watch movies that help us understand the culture

- we do Socratic seminar

- the teacher moves around a lot—we don't know what he's going to do next

- the teacher makes us practice individually so we know what we're feeling before we present to the class

- teachers connect stuff to your own experience

- teachers can let it go when we make mistakes—they know we're not perfect

- teachers push you to do what you need to do

- we can retake tests and redo assignments so we can get a better grade

Student Aspirations and Postsecondary Outcomes

In 1990, 90% of sophomores said they expected to continue their postsecondary education, and 80% of this group expected to attain a bachelor's degree. The story seven years later was more sobering. Among this group, only 46% had actually enrolled in a degree or certificate program, and only 26% had earned a bachelor's degree.[14] In 2004, 67% of high school graduates enrolled in college, more than in any previous year.[15] Yet this figure only represents about 50% of the total 2004 student cohort after student dropouts are accounted for. One-third of graduates enroll in community college or certificate programs and two-thirds of graduates enroll in four year colleges. Less than 6 out of 10 college enrollees will actually earn an associate or bachelor's degree by the age of 25.[16]

This may be the first generation of young people in U.S. history that is less educated than their parents. Educational attainment for young adults between the ages of 25 and 34 has declined in comparison to older adults between 35 and 64.[17] Although access to college increased until the mid-1990s, college affordability has declined dramatically, reducing the rate of low- and moderate-income college attendees and imposing a massive burden of personal debt on many of those who do manage to go to college. Two trends have widened the gap between middle-to-upper income and low-income students:[1] Since 1983, the median family income has increased 127%, while college tuition and fees have increased 375%; and [2] The largest pool of money for financial aid comes from colleges, which have reallocated large amounts of financial aid from assisting needy students to attracting the most desirable students (most of whom are middle-to-upper class) through financial incentives.[17]

Although the gap in degree attainment between white and African American college graduates actually declined in the 1970s, during the last 20 years the gap between the percentage of white and Asian college students who graduate and the percentage of African American and Hispanic students who graduate has widened.[18] Among people awarded a bachelor's degree in 1995, 78.7% were white, 7.5% were African American, and 4.6% were Hispanic/Mexican American.[19]

Kenneth Gray, professor of workforce education at Pennsylvania State University, paints a memorable picture of student outcomes after high school by inviting us to imagine a classroom of twenty-five fresh-faced first graders. We'll call them the class of 2021.[20]

- Seven of these first graders won't graduate from high school. Most are destined for poverty-wage jobs, unemployment, or a working life in the illegal underground economy.

- Six of the remaining eighteen don't enroll in college; they go directly into the workforce.

    Three will actively seek jobs that match their career goals and go on to have satisfying work lives that often involve advanced training and study at a later point.

    Three are more likely to drift in and out of low-wage jobs for a lifetime.

- Four will enroll in community college or a certificate program.

    Two will drop out.

One will complete an Associates degree or certificate program that prepares them for a specific career.

One will continue her education after community college and complete a four-year degree.

- Eight will enroll in four year college.

Three will drop out.

Five will complete a Bachelors degree within six years.

It's a good bet that the more successful students in this class of 2021 were those who had a better picture of themselves as learners, knew something about what they liked to do and what they were good at, and probably left high school with at least one potential career goal and a plan for accomplishing it. Rather than brandishing four year college as the ultimate goal for all high school students, we might better measure success after high school by a young person's interest and persistence in following his or her personal goals and career aspirations.

It may surprise you (or not!) to learn that nearly 40% of recent college graduates held jobs that had no connection to their college majors and didn't require a four-year degree.[16] Approximately 2 out of 10 jobs in the U.S. actually require a bachelor's degree (21% in 2006 and 22% projected in 2016), making this part of the job market intensely competitive.[21] "When we look at the actual jobs added to the U.S. economy, we find that 'knowledge worker' professions added only 800,000 new jobs, while minimum-wage jobs (e.g., retail sales, janitors and cleaners, waiters and waitresses, maids, security guards) added 2.5 *million*."[22]

Although good scores on exit tests and college entry exams are commonly viewed as the gateways to college success, recent studies indicate that high school grades and GPA are far better predictors of both degree completion and workforce earnings.[23] Why? Course grades capture a broader range of skills measured over a longer period of time.[9] In addition, nonacademic qualities such as perseverance, personal and career goal orientation, motivation, self-discipline, and self-confidence seem to play a greater role in students' chances of completing a degree or certificate program than previously acknowledged.[24 & 25]

The gap between student ambitions, degree completion, and career attainment has been well documented, but seeking reasons and remedies for the gap produces no simple answers. A large body of research identifies students' inadequate academic preparation to meet the rigor and challenges of entry-level college work as the biggest roadblock to college access for underrepresented students.[26 & 27] At least 40% of students take at least one remedial course in college. ACT and the College Board have published major reports recommending that all students take courses that better reflect the challenges of entry-level college work: the pace, difficulty, and quantity of reading; the quantity and precision of analytical writing; and familiarity with the big ideas and systems of thinking that inform different academic disciplines.[28]

Yet it may be just as accurate to conclude that many leave college because the work is difficult or tedious and they've never developed a career goal or other compelling reason to tough it out. Every September, millions of teens face the challenges of college work with the flimsiest of goals to stick with it: "I want a good job. I want to make money. My parents would kill me if I dropped out." Many labor and higher education experts argue that a push for more college readiness skills in high school course work must be accompanied by an equal push for high school students to explore possible career pathways and courses of study that match their interests, assets, abilities, and future aspirations.[29 & 30] Students not only need to know what's expected of them in the place they choose to continue their education; they need to know why they're there.

Moreover, high school educators should be asking, "What is it exactly that differentiates highly successful, high-performing workers from their colleagues? What attributes should we be cultivating in students that expand their possibilities and increase their chances of experiencing a successful and satisfying career?" Two interdependent qualities are closely linked to high performers in their chosen careers: passion, a compelling interest that drives curiosity, motivation, and personal aspirations; and perseverance, the capacity for sustaining a disciplined effort over time to excel and achieve a goal.[31]

Finally, there are risks to insisting on a four-year college preparatory curriculum as the gold standard for high school achievement and making a bachelor's degree the gold standard for postsecondary success. First and foremost, this approach devalues the legitimate pursuit of other learning and work opportunities. Too many students feel pressured to say they want to enter a four-year college or university program before they've even considered whether this choice is a good match for how they learn, what they'd like to study and experience, and what kinds of work might interest them.

Second, the current emphasis on college readiness comes at the cost of teaching, practicing, and assessing the 21st-century skills that employers want most in new hires: employability skills (attendance, work ethic, attitude, timeliness); soft skills (cooperation, teamwork, effective communication); presentation and leadership skills (communicating enthusiasm for the task, presenting yourself effectively, influencing others positively, taking personal initiative, and self-advocacy); and applied reading, writing, and math skills (informational literacy and numeracy).[32] High schools continue to ignore calls from business and labor groups to better prepare students for the contemporary world of work.[16] An analysis of the effects of high school students' competencies on their postsecondary attainment and future earnings found that many of these 21st-century skills appear to substantially influence students' later success in college and in work.[33]

Third, for many students the bachelor-degree mantra creates a false choice: "Either I go to college or I go to work." Even though nearly 80% of jobs don't require a bachelor's degree, 90% of all other living-wage jobs in the U.S. require seasoned experience and/or specialized training, a certificate, a license, or an associate degree. Except for poverty-wage "starter jobs" in sales, services, and food preparation, employers do not generally want to hire people until they are well into their 20s. [16] Thus, all students should be graduating from high school with a postsecondary learning plan linked to future career opportunities, whether it's for a two- or four-year college, a certificate program, an apprenticeship or internship, cooperative education, or military training.

Why do so many young people lose their way before the finish line? What happens in high school that contributes to the dismal outcomes for over 40% of our students?

The Unfulfilled Promise of High School Reform

Like society itself, high school reinforces a culture of haves and have-nots, resulting in a widening gap between students who succeed academically, conform to school norms, and feel an attachment to school—and those who don't. During the last 20 years, school-smart kids have become even smarter and more competitive, leaving their less academically prepared peers in the dust.

Since the mid-1990s, new small schools, redesigned schools, and smaller learning communities within large high schools have been created to bridge the gap between groups of high and low achievers and ramp up academic proficiency and graduation rates for underperforming students. Two laudable goals have shaped these initiatives:

1.   Provide *all* students with a rigorous and relevant education that enables them to be career and college ready;

2.   Increase graduation rates to 90%

The new 3 R's of rigor, relevance, and relationships became the driving principles behind these goals. Core strategies to improve academic performance and increase graduation rates stressed more rigorous coursework for all; more real-world learning applications; more exposure and exploration of possible career pathways; stronger student-teacher relationships; and a more personalized learning environment.

On the positive side, a vast majority of students in new and redesigned schools have reported a greater sense of safety and connection, often describing their schools by saying, "We're a family here."[34 & 35] Yet with very few exceptions, reading and math achievement scores, exit test scores, graduation rates, and postsecondary enrollment for the bottom 40% of students has remained flat. What happened?

Too often, new and redesigned schools have replicated the bad habits of their big siblings: too much tracking; too little inspired instruction and too few engaging classes; unequal access to comprehensive guidance and postsecondary planning; not enough early interventions and supports for students who struggle academically; and inadequate services for students at risk or in crisis.

However, the mandates of "No Child Left Untested" have had the most pernicious impact on high school reform initiatives. No one can argue with No Child Left Behind's commitment to raise school accountability for student performance. There is no doubt that we must redress low achievement and low-quality instruction in underperforming schools. And national literacy and numeracy tests would have plenty of merit as one of several measures of student learning and performance. However, the tools and rules of NCLB have made many of the original reform strategies extremely difficult to implement. Much of what we know about making high schools better places to learn has been pushed aside in favor of choosing high-stakes test scores as the sole benchmark of student progress and school improvement.

The result is a distorted definition of rigor that has sidelined relevance and relationships, the other two R's. All too quickly, the concept of rigor morphed into *rigor mortis* as states and districts rushed to mandate ever more instructional constraints in order to produce acceptable pass rates on state exit exams. The four horsemen of NCLB—(1) high-stakes testing, (2) prescribed content standards and course-pacing guides, (3) more restrictive graduation requirements and fewer electives, and (4) one uniform liberal arts curriculum for all—have blunted most efforts to develop more personalized, engaging, and real-world learning experiences inside the classroom and out in the world. Keep in mind that high-school leavers, low performers, and underachievers cite boredom, disconnection, and irrelevance as the deciding factors in choosing whether or not to "do school." We've included a little background on the four horsemen and some questions that might frame a deeper and more hopeful conversation about each one.

1. High-Stakes Testing

What purposes can standardized testing serve that are scientifically valid, ethical, and useful?

What other kinds of evidence and assessments can provide an accurate picture of each student's academic progress; her literacy and numeracy proficiency; and her mastery of the knowledge, skills, and dispositions necessary for living and working in the 21st century?

What might national literacy and numeracy tests look like? What skill sets do we want graduates to able to use and apply competently in life after high school?

There is absolutely no data from high school-age students showing that high-stakes testing improves student effort, increases student learning, or accurately predicts students' future outcomes. High-stakes exit exams do not measure what a student has learned;[36] they only measure how accurately a student answers a sample set of questions that focus on isolated bits of information and a narrow skill set culled from a much larger domain of knowledge and skills. In the 2008 report *Measuring Up: What Educational Testing Really Tells Us*, Harvard's Daniel Koretz sums up the matter nicely: "The goal has become raising scores as an end in itself rather than improving student learning. The system cheats kids of the education they deserve."[37]

Equally troublesome, the emphasis on measuring reading and math skills to the exclusion of measuring other competencies is narrowing the curriculum and compromising the commitment to eight long-standing goals of U.S. education: (1) basic academic skills, (2) critical thinking, (3) arts and literature, (4) preparation for skilled work, (5) social skills and work ethic, (6) citizenship, (7) physical health, and (8) emotional health.[38]

There are other reasons we should be cautious about judging a school's or individual's performance by scores on a single measurement. Timed, multiple choice, and machine-scored standardized tests will always disadvantage a significant percentage of all learners. Format and content biases favor students who navigate more easily through abstract material that is intentionally disjointed and non-sequential. These biases also favor middle class students, who generally put up less resistance to exercises that have no personal meaning or immediate application beyond the test score itself.[39]

Standardized tests also reward students who are superior readers, who can quickly answer superficial questions, or who have a superior capacity to recall arcane information. These qualities can, no doubt, help a person win a game of Jeopardy; they're just not reliable predictors of a person's capacity to learn, connect, and excel in the real-world performance of work and life. A 1958 report from the Rockefeller Brothers Fund presciently warned against an overreliance on standardized test scores in evaluating student progress:

> *Decisions based on test scores must be made with the awareness of the imponderables in human behavior. We cannot measure the qualities of character that are a necessary ingredient of great performance. We cannot measure aspiration or purpose. We cannot measure courage, vitality, or determination.*[40]

Even the Educational Testing Service asserts that using school-mean proficiency (a school's adequate yearly progress towards proficiency) as the only measure of student progress and learning is scientifically indefensible.[41] The twin goals of ensuring reading and math proficiency for all learners as well as reducing the test score gap between student groups by 2014 are, as it turns out, statistical impossibilities.[42] Using the current trajectory of improvement, 8th graders would reach the required level of proficiency in NEAP tests (National Educational Assessment Progress) in math in 2067, and 12th graders would do so in 2169. For seniors to reach NCLB targets by 2014, improvement would have to accelerate by a factor of 12.[43]

As Richard Rothstein reminds us, the test score gap among racial and income groups is more attributable to the total variability of individual student performance within a group than to differences between groups; "disparities within any race or social group are greater than the disparities between these groups."[38] In other words, within any group, the performance distribution remains relatively constant, so dramatic gains for any one specific group are highly improbable within a decade. Simpson's Paradox is also at work here; "test scores within all groups are rising at the same time that lower-scoring groups are making up a larger proportion of the total [number of students tested]."[43] The paradox reveals itself when you combine data from groups of different sizes composed of different proportions of low-scoring students—the trend line will indicate a test score decline when in fact test scores are rising.

In addition, improving the test scores of the lowest performers within all racial and income groups is more problematic and requires more resources and interventions than policymakers have counted on. Koretz puts it this way: "How do we put pressure on underperforming schools serving low-achieving students to increase the equity of educational outcomes between groups while still sensibly and realistically acknowledging the large variability that will persist within groups?"[42]

Finally, in the name of equity and eliminating "the soft bigotry of low expectations"[44] for poor and minority students, many supporters of high standards and high-stakes testing dismiss differences in income, families, neighborhoods, health care, and housing as poor excuses for the achievement gap.[45] This is a cruel joke. The Educational Testing Service has concluded that over 60% of large statistical differences in test scores between states, among groups, and between individuals are attributable to differences in family structure, family finances, early literacy development before students enter school, and educational resources at home.[2]

2. Prescribed Content Standards and Course-Pacing Guides

Do we only want to develop standards associated with academic knowledge and skill sets?

Should public schools have an obligation to think about developing standards that articulate the kinds of knowledge, skills, and dispositions required to be...

- *an engaged citizen who can sort through competing claims and interests to make informed judgments about the issues of the day?*

- *a good neighbor, family member, and active participant in the local community?*

- *a lifelong learner who has the tools and skills to pursue personal and professional aspirations?*

- *a physically and emotionally healthy member of society who can take on the personal, social, and fiscal responsibilities of adulthood?*

- *a valued, productive member of the U.S. workforce?*

- *a responsible steward of the environment?*

After the 1983 publication by the federal government of *A Nation at Risk*, a fire-and-brimstone attack on U.S. public schools, university professors got very busy developing hundreds of finite academic content standards that, collectively, no one human being can possibly master during four years in high school. There is absolutely no evidence that narrowly prescribed content standards and the curriculum-pacing guides that go with them will improve student learning in high school or better prepare more students for college or the world of work, particularly for the underperforming 30%.

Even though schools now encourage teachers to focus on a few select "power standards," the alignment of exit exams to content standards has resulted in a renewed emphasis on what students know over what students can do. The testing industry has also influenced this trend; it's easier and far cheaper to test knowledge than to measure students' demonstration and mastery of applied skills. Unfortunately, the pressures to cover more and more content conflict with the desires to devote adequate attention to mastery learning and inspired instruction. The temptation to backslide into the "lecture, read, recall, review, and test" mode of teaching is hard to resist, even in advanced-level courses. In his article "Rigor on Trial," Tony Wagner observes how often Advanced Placement instruction overrelies on teacher presentation and recall at the cost of deliberative discussion and analysis in order to prepare students for achievement tests that require more memorization than thinking. He concludes, "Increasingly in our schools, what gets taught is only what gets tested."[46]

In the classroom, the tensions between these completing claims can sound like this:

In one ear you hear...	In the other ear you hear...
"Use the prescribed curriculum-pacing guide to ensure that you are teaching to the standards and that you're on track to teach the complete curriculum. Make sure students are ready for the end-of-course test prepared by the department for your course. And be sure to review specific facts and concepts and practice specific skill sets that will be on the state exit exam next spring."	"Provide differentiated instruction, multiple assessments, and personalized support to push completion of quality work for all of the learners in your classroom—the high achievers, the repeaters, English language learners, and special education students. Allow time for reteaching and regular monitoring of student learning. Engage students in rigorous, relevant learning that ignites their interest and motivation."

Today's high school teachers are more likely to teach students with a wider range of ability levels and learning styles within any given class than they did a decade ago. Capturing the hearts and minds of such a variety of learners calls for a special kind of tour-de-force teaching that involves:

- daily check-ins, immediate feedback, formative assessment, and personal conferencing and coaching

- student self-reflection, self-assessment, and self-monitoring of academic progress

- reteaching for some students and more advanced independent work for others

- content linked to students' experiences, real-world applications, problem-based learning, and authentic assessments (especially if we want to capture students who cite boredom and irrelevance as the reasons for their disengagement)

- student-chosen or student-designed assignments, projects, and investigations that build on their interests and provide opportunities to take responsibility for their own learning

- teaching and practicing procedures and routines that build a high-functioning, high-performing group

- learning protocols and experiential activities that maximize participation and engagement

- dialogue protocols from pair-shares to Socratic seminars in which students practice accountable talk[47] (see page 147, 362), habits of mind and deliberative discussion (see page 344–358)

All of these learning activities require more curricular flexibility, more practice time for students to master key learning protocols and processes, and extended work time to complete high-quality products and presentations. Yet policy experts and administrators alike would have teachers believe that it's a reasonable and realistic expectation to engage in a learner-centered pedagogy at the same time as one continues to march through prescribed course content. Who are they kidding? Classroom instruction, like most other endeavors, is a zero-sum game: "If I choose to do A, I will not be able to do B." Too often, teachers find themselves in the terrible position of choosing whether to teach the curriculum or teach the student.

3. More Restrictive Graduation Requirements and Fewer Electives

How might diploma and exit requirements more accurately reflect the multiple missions of public schooling: mastery of essential academic skills; development of good character; demonstration of good citizenship; development of the attributes of a lifelong learner; preparation for college and the world of work; and acquisition of habits and skills that foster self-discipline, healthy well-being, and good relationships?

How might course requirements more accurately reflect the diverse needs, abilities, interests, and aspirations of all young people, not just some? What kinds of requirements will entice the 30% of students who drop out to show up everyday and stay to earn their diplomas?

How do graduation requirements balance the importance of a common knowledge base and critical skill set with options for students to pursue their interests and cultivate their strengths in advanced academic studies; career and technical education; and fine, practical, and applied arts?

More restrictive graduation requirements are not likely to entice potential dropouts to stick around for more of the same. In Washington, D.C., for example, where fewer than 60% graduate, students must pass 22 required courses—including two years of a foreign language, three years each of abstract math and lab science, a full year of British literature, and music—to earn a diploma. Efforts to get tough have fast-forwarded us to our educational past. Many states and large cities have adopted graduation requirements that share much in common with the college preparatory course of study endorsed by the Committee of Ten in 1893.[48] These recommendations rolled out when about 5% percent of Americans attended high school and 3% of all 14- to 17-year-olds graduated.[49] Do we really think that one overly restrictive set of graduation requirements is the only road to quality education and life success for 16 million teenagers? Let's look at one example of how the new-old rules change what it takes to get a diploma.

The American Diploma Project, initiated in 2005, advocates that students be required to take a year each of Algebra I, Algebra II, and geometry.[50] These recommendations mirror those of the Committee of Ten, which called for all high school graduates to have mastered plane and solid geometry as well as algebra through quadratic equations. Seventeen states have recently adopted these requirements, and some have gone beyond them—Texas, for example, now mandates a fourth year of abstract mathematics for every student. Who decided that a young person's future is at risk if he or she doesn't pass the endurance test of three or four years of abstract mathematics? Even Nel Noddings, a former calculus teacher and Professor of Education, Emerita, at Stanford University, raises doubts about the prudence and efficacy of requiring every student to pass two or three years of rigorous abstract mathematics.[51]

Manufactured fears over the loss of U.S. competitiveness in math and science and worries about students not being prepared for all those nonexistent high-tech manufacturing jobs have led policy experts to swap common sense for silliness. According to the Department of Labor, only 4 out of 44 occupational categories require more than ninth-grade proficiency in math.[16] Jobs that do require higher levels of math (including algebra) are held by fewer than 5% of all full-time employees.[52]

The new benchmark of three or four years of abstract math for everyone ignores more compelling and relevant course configurations that would place the study of mathematics in this century instead of the previous one: applied mathematics in engineering, construction, public policy, industry, and health sciences; integrated math that incorporates statistics, probability, and discrete mathematics; math credits earned in CTE courses (career and technical education); or interdisciplinary courses that combine science and math into intensive studies of the physical or natural world. Even Cathy Seeley, past president of the National Council of Teachers of Mathematics, has raised the question of whether simply requiring more courses is enough to raise student achievement in math: "We need to look carefully at the mathematical content of our high school courses and the way that content is presented to students... In order to improve student achievement and learning at the high school level, we are going to have to teach in different ways than we have for the past 30 years."[53]

As the number of required credits increases, course failure rates rise. More F's mean more time in repeat classes and even fewer opportunities to explore a variety of arts, technology, career, and applied-learning courses. The role that self-selected courses play in students' decisions to leave high school or graduate should not be underestimated. These are the classes where many students identify interests and skills they will keep for life, where they find a supportive mentor, or where they discover potential career possibilities.

In the meantime, many budget-strapped districts have reduced the number of instructional periods in the schedule (thereby reducing the number of electives a student can take in any given grading period) or eliminated many hands-on, learning-by-doing courses altogether. The elective shortage is not just a result of faculty reductions; it can also be traced to an increase in the number of required classes that must be taught and an increase in the number of faculty course assignments devoted to reteaching students who failed required courses. In more schools than ever, learning activities that were once part of the school day—such as the school newspaper, drama, yearbook, and musical performance groups—are now the province of after-school clubs, unfairly discriminating against students who work or have other after-school responsibilities.

4. One Uniform Liberal Arts Curriculum for All

How might we imagine courses and learning opportunities that integrate the knowledge and skills of academic disciplines with relevant content, practical applications, and concrete experiences that link what students should know and learn to the world they live in?

What kinds of attributes and qualities make any learning experience or student work in any area of study meaningful, rigorous, and engaging?

There is absolutely no evidence that a uniform college preparatory liberal arts curriculum for all increases graduation rates, better prepares students for college, or promotes more engaging and rigorous learning in the classroom. In fact, the only comprehensive study and evaluation of secondary curricula in the U.S. completely contradicts this premise. Conducted and documented between 1930 and 1942, the Eight-Year Study aimed to investigate whether the traditional liberal arts curriculum was the only road to college success and preparation for work and life. What made this research groundbreaking was the cooperation and support of over 300 colleges and universities that agreed to waive strict curricular requirements and accept college applicants from all participating schools and school districts.[54]

The thirty schools and districts that signed on were committed to testing out how they might reimagine the high school curriculum and develop instructional strategies that would most effectively support student engagement and academic success. The project was driven by the following core principles:

- "First, every student should achieve competence in the essential skills of communication—reading, writing, oral expression—and in the use of quantitative concepts and symbols.

- Second, inert subject-matter should give way to content that is alive and pertinent to the problems of youth and modern civilization.

- Third, the common, recurring concerns of American youth should give content and form to the curriculum.

- Fourth, the life and work of the school should contribute, in every possible way, to the physical, mental, and emotional health of every student.

- Fifth, the curriculum in its every part should have one clear, major purpose. That purpose is to bring to every young American his great heritage of freedom, to develop understanding of the kind of life we seek, and to inspire devotion to human welfare."

What they learned is especially prescient given the current national commitment to boosting achievement, graduation rates, and college enrollment and completion.[54]

- College success is not determined by a uniform set of curriculum requirements. Departure from the traditional content and pattern of curricular organization did not lessen students' readiness for college.

- Students from all thirty schools were academically equivalent or superior to the matched control group of their peers at every college.

- Students from the most experimental schools were academically superior to students from the six most conventional high schools in the study.

- Involving students in the planning of new curricula at their respective high schools seemed to have two big payoffs: increased achievement and engagement in school life during high school; and a higher level of connection to college life, the arts, and civic culture than their matched peers in college.

- Students were far more engaged and academically successful in high school when teachers used an integrated, interdisciplinary approach to the curriculum.

- Teachers were energized by their work and cited their collaboration with colleagues as an experience that broke down barriers from teacher to teacher and subject to subject.

Too often, a traditional liberal arts curriculum is viewed as the only legitimate course of study that can promote excellence; provide rigorous student work; and help students develop higher levels of literacy, numeracy, and complex reasoning. This assumption propagates the belief that no other subject matter, work-based learning experiences, or curricular configurations involve precision of thought or sophisticated use of skills. What kind of snake oil are we selling here? Any learning experience in any course in any subject meets the rigor test when

- the task is purposeful;

- students engage in the experience wholeheartedly;[55]

- students generate new knowledge or apply knowledge to practical problems; and

- students use an array of high-level intellectual, expressive, artistic, and manual skills and processes to produce or present a piece of quality work that successfully achieves the goal of the activity.[56]

More than 50 years ago, the report on education from the Rockefeller Brothers Fund cogently expressed the truth about rigor: "Our conception of excellence must embrace many kinds of achievement at many levels….There is excellence in abstract intellectual activity, in art, in music, in managerial activities, in craftsmanship, in human relations, in technical work."[57] Even Chester E. Finn Jr., conservative education commentator and former assistant secretary in the Department of Education under President Reagan, concedes that "it's important to strike a balance here. It's not unreasonable for society to want *all* of its children (at least all who are capable of this) to acquire many of the same skills and body of knowledge. Which doesn't mean they all can or should be taught those things the same way—or that the 'common' part is the entirety of a child's education."[58]

Is it so difficult to imagine a high school education that honors the need to master essential skills and a core of common knowledge *and* respects the variability among real adolescents who learn differently, hold different interests, have different talents and abilities, and want to learn different things?

What Should 21st-Century Learning Look Like?

Here are a baker's dozen of suggestions that might actually increase graduation rates, dramatically improve literacy and numeracy, better prepare students to be career, college, and life ready, and bring learning into the 21st century. Every idea on the list has already been done and done well in exemplary American high schools.

1. Broaden the variety of content courses that students can take to meet literacy, numeracy, science, and social studies requirements for graduation, and create a better balance between required academic core courses and electives in which students can pursue advanced academic studies; career and technical education; and fine, practical, and applied arts.

2. Develop a core set of tests, tasks, problems, projects, and exercises from which students must complete a specified number to earn proficiency in literacy, numeracy, and citizenship.

3. Ensure that every student has an advocate or mentor who helps him or her develop a personal learning plan during high school that culminates in the completion and defense of a postsecondary plan that matches his or her interests, talents, strengths, and aspirations.

4. Encourage dual enrollment at college campuses so that all seniors can test their capacity to handle college work and explore potential courses of study and training.

5. Repackage compartmentalized liberal arts classes into cross-disciplinary courses that more accurately reflect the interdependent systems that shape a postmodern global society.

6. Get kids out of the school building! The lack of place-based learning experiences contributes to an appalling ignorance of students' own communities and potential career opportunities.

7. Balance textbook study with more virtual learning; more direct methods of acquiring knowledge; and more information sources from the community, the workplace, the marketplace, and the media.

8. Rethink schedules in ways that can incorporate extended blocks of time for labs, shops, studios, and off-site learning. Offer more quarter and semester colloquia, seminars, and workshops centered on a specific topic, applied skill, or career domain. Although kids like and need routine, they also love the anticipation of something new and different.

9. Decouple learning and earning course credit from "seat time" in a classroom. The Carnegie unit (120 hours = one unit of study) was created in 1906 as a way to standardize both college admission criteria and the reporting of the high school experience. There's no reason beyond precedent that schools must remain attached to a formula that equates seat time with learning or presumes that all students require the exact same amount of time to achieve proficiency in a specific course of study.

10. Insist that students complete at least one exemplary work sample and at least one independent or applied learning project (to be placed in their exit portfolios) in every course.

11. Provide more cooperative education, internships, service-learning projects, and apprenticeships—but supply stiffer academic criteria for earning credit and more coaching and supervision.

12. Invite students (from the "hard to reach" to the "gifted and talented") to design their own independent courses that can incorporate students' work experiences, their study and practice of a particular discipline outside of school, teacher mentoring and feedback, and online and off-site learning.

13. Develop a strand of courses that examine adolescents and adolescence through literature, nonfiction, expository research, and personal accounts; a biological, psychological, and health study of adolescent development; and a sociological and historical investigation of adolescence during the 20th and 21st centuries.

The Costs of Not Changing Current Practices

High Achievers at Risk

Even high-achieving students, who appear to navigate effortlessly through their classes, experience conditions that may put them at risk for difficulties either during or after high school. Relentless pressure to perform academically can leave lots of students anxious, overly competitive, fearful of taking intellectual risks, obsessed with grades and test scores, and less than enthusiastic about learning for its own sake. School becomes a different kind of burden.

Moreover, high schools may unwittingly reinforce attitudes of privilege among high achievers who live in their own universe of honors courses, clubs, and activities that separate them from everyone else. Nearly every message from adults in the school setting tells them that they are the chosen few, that their particular brand of achievement is more desirable than and superior to every other kind of success and personal accomplishment. In an *Atlantic Monthly* article , David Brooks calls these students the "organization kids," the ones who describe themselves as power tools and come equipped with their fully loaded tool bags and overscheduled lives.[59]

They have honed the art of being professional students and see every activity as a means of self-improvement that will carry them "one more step on their stairway to advancement. They are the logical extreme of American's increasingly efficient and demanding sorting-out process." Given their good fortune to be on the receiving end of the best America has to offer, their cheerful compliance and deference to authority were no surprise to Brooks. What puzzled him, however, was what he didn't see—no outrage, no passion, no moral qualms—these students accepted their protected and privileged status and gave little or no thought to the disadvantages of their less privileged peers. The world of the "others" was out of sight and out of mind. Brooks heard no debates among these future leaders about making that other world a more just, decent, and equitable place for everyone.

In their ethnographic study of California youth, researchers Phelan, Davidson, and Yu identified a pattern among middle-class high achievers. This group of adolescents was "particularly at risk for developing spurious ideas and stereotypes about others." Their findings suggest that some successful students "are uninterested in knowing, interacting, or working with students who achieve at different levels, who are culturally or ethnically diverse, or who in other ways are perceived as 'different.'"[60] That high schools officially cultivate such a narrow definition of achievement and self-worth reveals a less-than-winning formula for healthy growth and development. Students who can opt out of knowing and working with those who are different can acquire a smugness that diminishes the importance of empathy in their relationships with others. Intellectually, the result can be a reduced capacity to consider perspectives that challenge their own.

Furthermore, student homogeneity within a classroom may actually discourage teachers from helping high academic achievers develop the skills to communicate, collaborate, and negotiate with groups across the divides of race, culture, gender, and personality. In *Working with Emotional Intelligence*, Dan Goleman reminds us that "in the new workplace, with its emphasis on flexibility, teams, and a strong consumer orientation, this crucial set of emotional competencies is becoming increasingly essential for excellence in every job in every part of the world."[61] Given the future that these young people will inherit, we're shortchanging the very students that high school faculties claim they serve best.

The Invisible Middles

The have-nots of high school include another group we don't hear much about, the students I call the invisible middles. They don't get in big trouble. They don't complain out loud. They don't attract a lot of attention. They cruise from class to class in the "shopping mall high school," dulled from just looking around and never buying anything that has personal value and meaning.[62] It is both remarkable and understandable that the problems and realities of these kids are rarely discussed by administrators and faculty with any sense of urgency.

When school staff are already overwhelmed by the competing needs of kids at the top and bottom of the high school pecking order, who has time to be genuinely curious about students in the middle? How often do adults seek out these students, personally inviting them to talk about how they experience school? We know that for many young people, the quality of their relationships with teachers determines the quality of their engagement in the classroom. Whether a young person feels noticed or not influences her desire to do well. As a high school sophomore put it sadly, "My science teacher didn't even know my name until second semester, and by then I didn't care."

The idea that adolescents come with differing sets of developmental needs, learning profiles, and personal interests runs counter to the prevailing view of teaching teenagers. All of these personal characteristics influence how we reach, teach, treat, and engage each individual. Yet

U.S. high schools have spent a hundred years institutionalizing a culture in which adolescents who are the exception are held up as the norm.

Juanita and Benita: A Portrait of Two Teens

Juanita and her mother had already spent a day visiting Washington High School before she arrived as a freshman. Before the school year began, she and her mom talked about her schedule, and Juanita decided on two electives. She loves to draw, so she will take drawing first semester and introductory drama during second semester because she wants to try something new that might be a little challenging. She already knows she's going to college, like her older brother.

Juanita's favorite class is Honors English. Her teacher encourages students to express their ideas and opinions freely in class, but at the same time students know they will need to defend their points of view. Juanita likes identifying with the characters she reads about, imagining what she would do in their place. She has grown up around books; everyone in the family reads. Juanita has gone to the library since she was three, and the printed word is familiar and comfortable to her. She demonstrates an ease with intellectual tasks that require reflection and analysis. Juanita doesn't like her math teacher very much: he's bossy and boring, so Juanita usually does her math homework first to get it over with. Her mom has talked to her a lot about dealing with setbacks and how to make the best of bad situations. So Juanita has decided to just grind it out and get the satisfaction of doing well in spite of the teacher.

Juanita uses a datebook, just like her mother does, to keep track of assignments, activities, and home stuff so she can look ahead at the crunch weeks and let her mom know when she's going to have to let other things slide to meet her responsibilities at school. When she was out sick for a week, she called her buddies to get the scoop on what was happening at school and in class so she wouldn't fall too far behind. Even though her mom works late, the family schedules time at least twice a week when they all sit down for dinner and share what's going on in their lives.

Classes are tracked at school, so the students Juanita sees all day seem a lot like her. She has two best friends from school that she hangs out with—sometimes they study together, too. She also has a group of friends from church that she sees on weekends. They do stuff together as a whole group, not really dating—they go to movies and spend time at each other's houses, and they do service projects one Saturday each month in the community.

Juanita's teachers describe her in the following terms: "Juanita is a self-starter. She has the determination and discipline to accomplish whatever she wants in life. She's even-tempered, well-liked, and always comes prepared. Her curiosity sparks her desire to learn, and her enthusiasm and active participation make her a joy to have in class."

Juanita is a terrific student and a wonderful kid. Students like Juanita come to class with the drive, self-discipline, and internal motivation to take in whatever teachers dish out. It's true that they're a pleasure to teach. These kids are extremely goal-driven and show an amazing capacity to be ready and willing students seven classes a day, five days a week. They are also very school-smart, academically and socially. More important, they know how to set aside or manage personal needs and feelings with such skill that they can usually adjust or adapt to stresses and difficulties. When they do experience setbacks, they can access resources and attitudes that will help them solve problems and make alternative choices and decisions.

The Juanitas of the world are more likely to live in families where education is valued above most other life endeavors, so guidance and conversation around schooling is a common occurrence. Juanita's family encourages her to plan, persevere, and explore a wider world, qualities that are equally rewarded at school. For Juanita, the kind of person she is encouraged to be at home mirrors whom she's supposed to be in school.

Benita, on the other hand, came in to register for classes the day before school started. She hadn't really thought much about her schedule and let her counselor suggest classes for her. Although her mom expects her to be in school and stay in school, she gives Benita a friendly warning: "What you do is up to you. I'm counting on you to be responsible, just like you are with your sisters." Benita takes great pride in being the older sibling and helping take care of things at home.

For Benita, school is mostly boring and too quiet. It doesn't connect with who she is the rest of the time. She gets tired of sitting and listening and reading and taking notes. She likes to be active in class, and sometimes gets in trouble when she talks too much or is too loud. Being with her friends at lunch is the best thing about the day, which means she's usually tardy for the next class. One other thing that Benita loves to do is work in the after-school program at the local elementary school. She and her best friend use some of the money they get paid to buy extra materials for projects they do with their after-school kids. This is the second year she has been involved in this program.

Benita likes her math teacher, who makes her class do all kinds of crazy competitions. They work in math teams on big complicated problems that are hard, but fun. Even though she doesn't always do her homework, she has worked hard enough to maintain her B. History class, by contrast, just feels like a big blur of stuff that's hard to remember, and it's difficult to take all those notes. A lot of times, Benita chooses to zone out or groan in the back of the class when frustration gets the best of her.

Benita doesn't like to read much, and the first novel for English class is about people from "olden days" that she can't relate to. She gets embarrassed when she's called on and doesn't know what to say. She hates being in the spotlight like that and responds by rolling her eyes and giving back a hard stare. She's put off her reading assignments for a week. Maybe she'll catch up on the weekend, but with a birthday party for her sister, a party she's going to with her boyfriend, and cleaning the house, maybe not.

Benita's teachers have a mixed impression of her, so their comments about her seem to describe two different people. "Benita is very lively in class and drives her math group to really perform. She learned the hard way that being late has consequences. She frequently comes to class moody and hasn't taken any initiative to improve her English grade. She doesn't handle frustration well, sometimes storming out or distracting others. Benita has proven to be a great lab partner in biology, and we've worked out check-ins so she knows what to study and how to study for tests. Her commitment to improve her grade is impressive."

Benita is struggling to find her way. Social relationships are central to her life right now. At school she is discovering what she likes and what she's good at, learning lessons from the choices she makes, and finding out what will motivate her to meet a personal challenge and do well. When she gets support or when teachers notice the effort she's making, Benita responds positively and works to improve her skills. When she's expected to "just do it" and figure it out on her own, she gets surly and often gives up, not knowing where to begin or how to ask for what she needs.

She is also a great kid. Teachers who have taken the time to get to know Benita like her and recognize the assets that she brings as a student. For example, when her math teacher and her after-school supervisor encourage her to use her "mother" skills to help a group get something done, Benita shines. On the other hand, the teachers who expect her to be like Juanita find her uncooperative and unmotivated.

Of course, Juanita and Benita don't represent the full range of adolescent experience. Yet Benita more accurately reflects the behaviors and sensibilities of the vast majority of American teenagers. The years from 14 to 18 are exactly the time when most young people are acquiring the skills and developing the maturity to navigate competently and responsibly through their worlds of peers, school, and community. The saying "If all you have is a hammer, everything looks like a nail" is acutely relevant here: If Juanita is viewed as the expected norm, then everyone else will be seen as a problem and a problem learner.

Who Do High Schools Serve Best?

High schools are designed to serve kids like Juanita, even though her profile characterizes a very small percentage of students. Juanita is the kind of student most high school teachers dream of, and consciously or unconsciously all other students are compared to her. Neither Juanita nor Benita is a problem kid. The problem lies in our perceptions of these two students. High school culture pretends that Juanita is the norm, when in fact she is the exception. She's the student who comes to high school fully equipped. Her developmental needs are met and supported to such an extent that her motivation to learn far outstrips her need for emotional and academic support from teachers. Juanita is the student whom high school educators are trained and prepared to teach.

What a surprise it is (often mixed with frustration and resentment) when most adolescents are more like Benita. By idealizing the exceptional student, school leaders, parents, and the public continue to support the myth that good high school teaching is mostly about presenting subject matter to students with enough passion and panache to engage them in learning it.

I was increasingly curious to know how teachers' understanding of adolescents, culture, and development informed their practice in the classroom. I wanted to hear how teachers described their students and characterized their world. So I began setting aside time in workshops and staff development dialogues for teachers to discuss what they thought about the kids they taught.

The tension and discomfort spiked whenever adult groups struggled to construct an honest portrait of the amazing variety of students they saw every day. It was as if knowing more about kids might interfere too much with the ways of schooling. These conversations left me confused. For many teachers, knowledge about adolescent development and how teens learn seemed to have little impact on their day-to-day teaching or relationships with students. The inner life of adolescents and the world outside school were viewed as the proper domains of guidance counselors and support staff. "That's their job, not ours," teachers would say. To put this belief in perspective, imagine an early childhood educator insisting that she could teach a young child without knowing how cognitive development, socialization, and emotions influence the way a young child learns.

If we hope to help all of our students become successful during their high school years and afterward, we will need to understand the complexity and range of normal adolescent behavior and teach with that understanding in mind. The assumption that students' thinking, feelings, and behavior function independently of each other continues to drive the organizational culture of most high schools, where the myth of the divided self goes unchallenged. Relentless departmentalization sanctions too many specialized roles of adults in high schools—the content expert in the classroom, the child expert in the guidance center, and the discipline expert in the office. When these adult roles harden and fragment our approach to educating young people, students lose.

Linking Learning and Achievement to Healthy Development

Traditionally, when adolescents perform poorly, get into trouble, and engage in risky behaviors, the burden of blame is on students and parents. In place of this blame game, schools might consider addressing, one by one, the barriers many students face that get in the way of learning, achievement, and healthy development. Barriers that put students at risk academically and behaviorally include:

- internal biological and psychological factors;

- external barriers within the family, among peers, and in the larger community;

- school policies and structures that may place already vulnerable students at greater risk; and

- staff attitudes and biases that create barriers to positive relationships and effective teaching

The chart on pages XX–XX provides specific examples of each of these barriers.

Pioneers in prevention and resiliency research concur that positive attachment to school, a positive attitude about achievement, and positive sustained relationships with adults and peers nurture healthy adolescent development and seem to offer the greatest protection against most risky behaviors.[63] We also know that young people are at greatest risk when they experience academic and behavioral difficulties in school and socialize with other peers who engage in risky behaviors. The research of Hawkins, Catalano, and Benard, calls upon educators to embed principles of prevention, resiliency, and youth development into everyday instruction in secondary schools.[64 & 65] Fostering the following principles in the classroom increases the likelihood that we will reach and engage all learners:

1. **Increase pro-social bonding** among peers and develop positive and personalized relationships between adults and adolescents.

2. **Set clear, consistent boundaries, procedures, and accountability.**

3. **Model, teach, and practice life skills** that promote respect, responsibility, self-discipline, effective communication, problem solving, and cooperation.

4. **Provide a saturation of youth development opportunities** through student-centered learning, student leadership, voice and choice in the classroom, and meaningful participation in school life and in the larger community.

5. **Cultivate within youth a positive sense of identity and hope for the future.**

6. **Set high expectations** that promote positive social norms and a culture of excellence and achievement.

7. **Provide caring and personalized support** so that students can thrive emotionally and succeed academically.

These principles already drive school-based prevention programs; the challenge is integrating them into the domain of teaching and learning. When principles of youth development inform instruction and classroom practice, teachers are more likely to view achievement and social, emotional, psychological, and ethical development as interdependent. Teachers are also more likely to form an accurate picture of adolescents, pay more attention to the barriers that impact their learning, and appreciate how much their personal support can make a powerful difference in a student's life. *Making Learning REAL* places these principles front and center in the text readings in Section 1 and in the core practices in Section 3.

Barriers to Healthy Development and Learning

Outside the High School

Based on a review of over 30 years of research, Hawkins and Catalano (1992) identify common risk factors that reliably predict such problems as youth delinquency, violence, substance abuse, teen pregnancy, and school dropout. These factors also are associated with such mental health concerns as school adjustment problems, relationship difficulties, physical and sexual abuse, neglect, and severe emotional disturbance. Such factors are not excuses for anyone not doing their best; they are, however, rather obvious impediments, and ones to which no good parent would willingly submit his or her child. The majority of factors identified by Hawkins and Catalano are external barriers to healthy development and learning.

Internal Factors (biological and psychological)	External Factors *
Differences (e.g., being further along toward one end or the other of a normal developmental curve; not fitting local "norms" in terms of looks and behavior, etc.) **Vulnerabilities** (e.g., minor health/vision/ hearing problems and other deficiencies or deficits that result in school absences and other needs for special accommodations; being the focus of racial, ethnic, or gender bias; economical disadvantage; youngster and/or parent lacks interest in schooling, is alienated, or rebellious; early manifestation of severe and pervasive problems/antisocial behavior) **Disabilities** (e.g., true learning, behavior, and emotional disorders)	**Community** • Availability of drugs • Availability of firearms • Community laws and norms favorable toward drug use, firearms, and crime • Media portrayals of violence • Transitions and mobility • Low neighborhood attachment and community disorganization • Extreme economic deprivation **Family** • Family history of the problem behavior • Family management problems • Family conflict • Favorable parental attitudes and involvement in the problem behavior **School** • Academic failure beginning in late elementary school **Peer** • Friends who engage in the problem behavior • Favorable attitudes toward the problem behavior

*Other external factors include exposure to crisis events in the community, home, and school; lack of availability and access to good school readiness programs; lack of home involvement in schooling; lack of peer support, positive role models, and mentoring; lack of access and availability of good recreational opportunities; lack of access and availability to good community housing, health and social services, transportation, law enforcement, sanitation.

Source: *Center for Mental Health at UCLA. (2001) Enhancing Classroom Approaches for Addressing Barriers to Learning: Classroom-Focused Enabling.*

Barriers to Healthy Development and Learning

Inside the High School

What we rarely examine are the factors inside the high school that may, however unintentionally, create further barriers, intensifying the difficulties our most vulnerable students face. Because high school is such a significant and enduring experience in an adolescent's life (teens spend more time involved in school-related activities than any other activity) barriers inside the school may diminish chances for healthy development and successful learning as much as barriers outside the school.

Structural and Policy Factors	Staff Realities and Attitudes

• Lack of availability and access to good student support programs – too few counselors, social workers, and on-going partnerships with community agencies that support students and their families
 	
• Sparsity of high quality schools
 	
• Schools are not necessarily welcoming to students and families who don't conform to dominant norms
 	
• Schools are too large with too many students per class
 	
• Lack of positive, on-going relationships between students and staff that endure over several years
 	
• Few opportunities for small groups of students and faculty to build relationships with each other
 	
• Too many learning periods in a day that are too short (50 minutes or less) for completion, closure, reflection, and intense learning experiences
 	
• Punitive disciplinary systems without instructional components that can support students in changing their behaviors
 	
• Curriculum that is deadening, fragmented, culturally inappropriate, and disconnected from students' lives and future goals
 	
• School bias that favors courses, activities, and rewards that reflect the preference of dominant culture students who come to school with the fewest barriers
 	
• Punitive grading systems that favor those who are already successful and disadvantage students who come to school with more barriers
 	
• High stakes testing and exit exams as the critical measure of a student's success
 	
• Classroom practice that doesn't meet developmental needs of diverse learners
	• Lack of significant numbers of school personnel whose personal experiences have more parallels with students who experience multiple barriers
	
	• Bias that favors students who come to high school ready to meet the traditional demands of course work
	
	• Bias that favors traditional over non-traditional learners
	
	• Bias that stresses teacher-centered over student-centered learning
	
	• Bias that blames students for life circumstances that are not within their control
	
	• Bias that diminishes the importance of developmental concerns as students get older
	
	• Little awareness of developmental connections between intellectual, social, and emotional development
	
	• Little training to reach, teach, and support students with commonplace learning, behavior, and emotional problems – this includes
	
	  • Teaching that accounts for differences in learner interests, strengths, weaknesses, and initial limitations
	
	  • Approaches that overcome avoidance motivation
	
	  • Structure that provides personalized support and guidance
	
	  • Instruction designed to enhance and expand intrinsic motivation for learning and problem solving
	
	• Little awareness of prevention and resiliency research and the field of youth development
	
	• Most educators do not see their work as political; so reducing the inequality of opportunities among students may not a big priority

Reaching and Engaging ALL Learners

What is engagement? Engagement in learning involves:

- Cognitive behaviors (attention, effort, problem solving, the use of metacognitive strategies like goal-setting, reflection, and accurate processing of information)

- Intellectual behaviors (the use of higher order thinking skills to increase understanding, solve complex problems, and construct new knowledge)

- Emotions (enthusiasm, interest, alertness, confidence, curiosity, pride, excitement, satisfaction)

Engagement in learning is a combination of:

I CAN (students' perceptions of competence and control)

I WANT TO (students' desires, goals, values, and interests)

I BELONG (students' social connectedness)

I SHOULD (students' identification with school learning expectations, norms, and core values)[66]

An Invitation to Enter Students' Worlds

More than 40 years ago, I walked into my first classroom and faced thirty students who projected a gamut of emotions ranging from intense anticipation to total lack of interest. I immediately felt both the excitement and the anxiety that most young teachers experience. The excitement of teaching motivated me to become very good at "teacherly" tasks: I prepared lessons, projects, and tests with Olympian dedication, hoping to create a stimulating learning environment.

Yet the performance jitters that came with my inexperience were never far away. It didn't take kids very long to figure out what made me uneasy. My daily measure of success was whether class went smoothly without incident or disruption. When it didn't—and students relished placing their personal footprints all over my best laid plans—I became stiff, strident, or disconnected. My road to rethinking what I was doing in the classroom began with Marvin, a charming and squirrelly fourteen-year-old who always had the courage to say out loud what a lot of other kids were thinking.

One day Marvin stuck around after a particularly disappointing world history class, where I had inhabited the glories of fifth-century Greece while my students were still residing in the present. He looked at me, cracking a smile that said, "I'm going to give you some inside information, so use it." Marvin proceeded to give me my comeuppance. "Ms. Lieber," he explained, "just because you get excited about this stuff doesn't mean we do. We're just kids, so teach us that way."

Teaching "after Marvin" changed for me. I took the risk to pay more attention to whom I was teaching than what I was teaching. This didn't mean I stopped teaching *The Iliad* or Shakespeare or Hawthorne or Wright. It did mean that I framed what we were reading in my students' language, in their cultural experiences, in their adolescent dramas. As I learned more about my students and what mattered to them, I relaxed and discovered that what happened between the spaces of instruction was often more important than the formal lesson. More and more, how my students learned and what triggered their interest influenced how I taught. They loved listening to good stories; they liked moving around and consulting with each other on projects; they hated answering the questions at the end of a chapter the same way every time; they were very willing to try on roles as writers and historians when their questions were at the center of research and investigation.

As I developed more personal relationships with students, I got more interested in their world and they became more tolerant of mine. They especially liked thinking they were pulling a fast one by maneuvering discussion away from the topic; this, of course, became the game. Could I find the needle in their haystack and use it to sew up my summary points? It became a challenge to find the right pop icon, movie, or current controversy to serve as a catalyst for making connections to historical and fictional figures of the past. Sometimes what I served up hit the mark for most kids, but not always. I had to get over the perfection thing. The only perfect class I was every going to experience was in my dreams.

Making Learning Real

"This school hurts my spirit," remarked one young woman in a national survey of high school students, appropriately titled "Voices from the Inside."[67] Other students have shared similar thoughts with me. The words of one academically successful junior sum up the most poignant comments I hear from a wide range of students: "In a lot of classes, I am my grade point average. If my grade's in the nineties, I'm okay. If it's in the seventies, I'm not worth the time of day."

I'm no longer surprised when I hear a lot of young people describe high school as a coldhearted and unfriendly place. According to nationally normed high school climate studies, nearly half of high school students feel neutral or negative about the curriculum, the learning climate in the classroom, and their relationships with teachers.[68] These feelings are particularly true for students of color, students from lower-income and less educated families, bilingual students, and kids who get in trouble—the very kids for whom high school should be a stepping-stone to a productive and meaningful adult life.[69]

Improving the quality of relationships among and between adults and young people should stand at the center of personalizing classroom practice. These efforts reflect Thomas Sergiovanni's advice to place equal value on two qualities of effective teaching: "You need to know students well to teach them well" and "You need to be passionate about what you teach if students are to value what is taught."[70]

Good teaching not only supports the intellectual development of adolescents—it nourishes their spirits and touches their hearts. Students want teachers who care about them; they want coursework that connects to their lives and the world they live in; and they want to be academically challenged and held accountable for meeting those challenges. This book is an opportunity to showcase proven classroom practices that enable teachers and students to become partners in a community of learners that feels real.

Most high school teachers have to live with constraints of too little time to work with too many kids. Yet, even in this less than desirable reality, teachers notice a positive difference when they become more intentional about personalizing their classroom practice. One teacher leader summed up her experience this way: "The better I got to know my students and placed their needs at the center of my teaching, the more academic improvement I saw from even my most reluctant students."

The Goal and Organization of *Making Learning REAL*

The goal of this book is to explore how our understanding of adolescents and our use of seven core practices can set the stage for establishing classrooms where students feel important and learning feels important. All of the readings and activities are aimed at teachers' efforts to reach and engage all learners.

The book is divided into three sections:

SECTION 1: Readings Linking Theory and Research to Core Practices

Chapters 1 through 4 now place all of the readings associated with the seven core classroom practices into the first section of the book for easy access. Chapter 5 describes how to integrate the eighth core practice—modeling, teaching, practicing, and assessing life skills—into daily classroom lessons. Chapter 6 compares a REAL classroom to a more traditional classroom to illustrate how these two classrooms look, sound, and feel differently for both students and the teacher.

Chapter 1: **Personalize Relationships and Learning in the Classroom**

Chapter 2: **Co-Create a Respectful, Responsible, High-Performing Learning Community**

Chapter 3: **Meet Adolescents' Developmental and Cultural Needs through High Expectations and Personalized Support**

Chapter 4: **Meet Adolescents' Developmental and Cultural Needs by Affirming Diversity in the Classroom**

Chapter 5: **Modeling, Teaching, Practicing, and Assessing Life Skills**

Chapter 6: **Putting the Practices to Work: A Tale of Two Classrooms**

SECTION 2: Getting Started

Chapters 7 through 10 provide a coherent how-to guide for preparation and start-up of the new school year, the first day of class, and the first month of school. The final chapter in this section presents the challenges and opportunities associated with changing classroom practice and offers suggestions for individual and collaborative approaches to professional development.

Chapter 7:   **Before the School Year Begins**

Chapter 8:   **The First Day of Class**

Chapter 9:   **The First Month**

Chapter 10:   **The Challenges of Changing Classroom Practices**

SECTION 3: The Core Practices

Chapters 11 through 17 present all of the specific strategies and activities associated with each of the seven core practices for personalizing secondary classrooms and reaching and engaging all learners. Each chapter is devoted to one practice.

Chapter 11 — **Practice 1: Develop Positive Relationships between and among Students and Teachers**

Chapter 12 — **Practice 2: Emphasize Personalized, Student-Centered Learning**

Chapter 13 — **Practice 3: Integrate Multiple Ways of Knowing and Learning**

Chapter 14 — **Practice 4: Establish Clear Norms, Boundaries, and Procedures**

Chapter 15 — **Practice 5: Build a Cohesive Community of Learners**

Chapter 16 — **Practice 6: Set High Expectations and Provide Personalized Support**

Chapter 17 — **Practice 7: Affirm Diversity in Your Classroom**

Each of the chapters about the seven core practices includes several key strategies that support the goal of the practice. Specific activities provide concrete examples of each key strategy. The life skill connections indicate how each strategy also supports students' practice of specific life skills.

Here's a sample format box from Section 3 that shows how everything connects:

"Create a Culture of Quality and Completion" is a key strategy for Practice 6: Set high expectations and provide personalized support.

"Monitor use of assignment notebooks" is one of the specific activities that supports the use of the key strategy in the classroom and helps students develop Life Skills 14, 16, and 17.

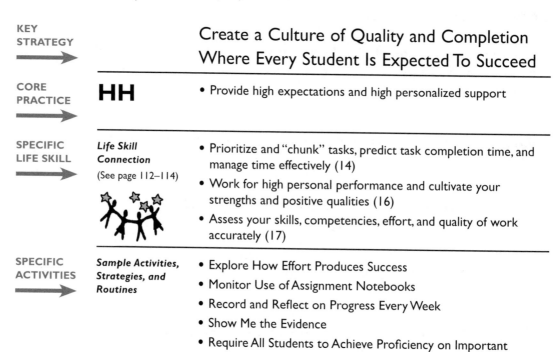

KEY STRATEGY →		Create a Culture of Quality and Completion Where Every Student Is Expected To Succeed
CORE PRACTICE →	**HH**	• Provide high expectations and high personalized support
SPECIFIC LIFE SKILL →	*Life Skill Connection* (See page 112–114)	• Prioritize and "chunk" tasks, predict task completion time, and manage time effectively (14) • Work for high personal performance and cultivate your strengths and positive qualities (16) • Assess your skills, competencies, effort, and quality of work accurately (17)
SPECIFIC ACTIVITIES →	*Sample Activities, Strategies, and Routines*	• Explore How Effort Produces Success • Monitor Use of Assignment Notebooks • Record and Reflect on Progress Every Week • Show Me the Evidence • Require All Students to Achieve Proficiency on Important Assignments • Expect, Insist on, and Support Completion and Quality

Changing Your Practice, Not Your Passions

This book is an invitation to change your practice, not your passions. It is not about giving up high standards, watering down your curriculum, or shortchanging students' intellectual development. Rather, it's about the big and small things you can do and say to help more kids love what you love. All of the information, discussion points, and practices in this guide share a common purpose: to increase the level of motivation, effort, skill, and achievement that students demonstrate in your classroom.

As you read further, I hope you will be thinking about how you can strengthen your own skills as a teacher, mentor, coach, and facilitator. For many of you this guide provides a way to make good practices you already do more intentional. Some ideas may offer new twists on familiar strategies and activities. Others may look and sound very different from your usual routines.

And some suggestions in this guide may serve as a reminder of things you have wanted to do and which you are now ready to try out. It's helpful to note that it can feel awkward to try on a different way of doing things—this is a normal and necessary stage of mastery. Practice will help these strategies become useful tools in your teaching toolbox.

I hope that reading this guide will, at times, feel like a conversation. Talk back to the text. Argue with the ideas presented here. Bring a spirit of open inquiry to what you read. How does your own experience as a learner and a teacher connect with the stories and experiences shared in this book? Notice your reactions to various topics and issues discussed in the book—what grabs your attention and what misses the mark?

Powerful learning and personal insight emerge from struggling with new ideas and new ways of thinking that may feel downright wrongheaded the first time we hear them. The fancy term for this is cognitive dissonance. I expect that some of the things presented in this guide may contradict what you may have always believed about students, learning, and teaching. Writing this book felt a little risky—you might choose to toss it out the first time your eyebrows furrow, your face tightens up, and your mind says, "Wait a minute. I'm not sure about that."

Instead, I invite you to invite in the discomfort. Ask yourself, "What is it that's making me feel confused, uneasy, or resistant to this idea?" Or "How might students benefit from this approach or practice?" Or "How would I feel if I were a student in this situation?" Testing out and grappling with new information and ideas is what learning is all about. Real change is organic—it happens slowly. So take your time reading, picking and choosing pieces of the book that you find most appealing or provocative.

Like the students you teach, each of you brings a unique set of perceptions, knowledge, and experiences to your reading of this guide. I don't presume that everything in this guide will be equally useful to everyone who reads it. My hope is that you will take away what makes sense for you and use what you think will help your students learn and grow.

Endnotes

[1] Annie E. Casey Foundation (2007) *2007 Kids Count Data Book: State Profiles of Child Well-Being.* Annie E. Casey Foundation: Baltimore, MD

[2] Barton, P. and Coley, R. (2007). *The Family: America's Smallest School.* Princeton, NJ: Educational Testing Services (ETS).

[3] Anderson Moore, K. Et. Al. (2009) *Children In Poverty: Trends, Consequences, And Policy Options.* Child Trends Research Brief: Publication 2009:11.

[4] Centers for Disease Control, *Youth risk behavior surveillance summary – United* States, 2003, Morbidity and Mortality Weekly Report, May 2005, 53(2).

[5] Kaiser Family Foundation (2005) *U.S. Teen Sexual Activity* accessed online at http://www.kff.org/youthhivstds/upload/U-S-Teen-Sexual-Activity-Fact-Sheet.pdf

[6] Losen, D., Orfield, G., & Balfanz, R (March 2005) *Confronting the Graduation Rate Crisis in California.* The Civil Rights Project, Harvard University, March 24, 2005 accessed on line at http://www.civilrightsproject.ucla.edu/research/dropouts/dropouts_gen.php

[7] Greene J. and Winters, M. (2006) *Leaving Boys Behind: Public High School Graduation Rates,* Civic Report: No. 48 Manhattan Institute for Policy Research. April 2006

[8] Swanson, C. (2009) *Cities in crisis: closing the graduation gap.* Bethesda, MD. Editorial Projects in Education

[9] Allensworth, E. & Easton, J. (2006) *What Matters For Staying On-Track and Graduating in Chicago Public Schools.* Chicago, IL: Consortium on Chicago School Research at the University of Chicago.

[10] Bridgeland, J., Dilulio, J. & Morison, K. (2006) *The Silent Epidemic: Perspectives of High School Dropouts.* Washington, D.C. Civic Enterprises, LLC.

[11] National Center for Education Statistics. *The Condition of Education 2002, Section 3, Student Effort and Educational Progress.* Accessed online at http://nces.ed.gov/pubsearch/pubsinfo.asp?pubid=2002025

[12] Peter D. Hart Research Associates for the James Irvine Foundation (2006) *California High School Student Engagement Survey.* Washington, DC as reported by Landsberg, M. (2006) *Struggling Students Want Vocational Education, Poll Shows* Los Angeles Times April 2, 2006. Accessed online at http://www.wcpss.net/school_to_career/blog/040606.pdf

[13] Lieber. Unpublished interviews with students in New York City, Des Moines, IA, Oakland, CA, and Chicago, IL.

[14] Schneider, B. & Stevenson, D. (2000). *The ambitious generation: America's teenagers, motivated but directionless.* New Haven, CT: Yale University Press.

[15] Conley, D. (April 2007). The Challenge of College Readiness. *Educational Leadership,* 64(7).

[16] Barton, P. and Coley, R. (2006). *High School Reform and Work: Facing Labor Market Realities.* Princeton, NJ: Educational Testing Services (ETS).

[17] Callan, P. (2008). *Measuring Up 2008: The National report card on higher education*. San Jose, CA: The National Center for Public Policy and Higher Education. Retrieved May 1, 2009, from http://measuringup.highereducation.org/nationalpicture/nationalpdfspresentations.cfm)

[18] Knapp, L., Kelly-Reid, J., & Whitmore, R. (2006, February) *Enrollment in Postsecondary Institutions, Fall 2004; Graduation Rates, 1998 & 2001 Cohorts*. Washington, DC: National Center for Educational Statistics. US Department of Education

[19] National High School Alliance (2009) Washington, DC. Retrieved from http://www.hsalliance.org/statistics/index.asp

[20] Adapted from Gray, Kenneth. (2004) Is high school career and technical education obsolete? *Phi Delta Kappan*, October, 2004

[21] Redovich, D. (2005) *The big con in education: why must all high school graduates be prepared for college?* iUniverse, Inc.

[22] Hodgkinson, B. (2006) *The Whole Child in a Fractured World*. Alexandria, VA: ASCD)

[23] Geiser, S., and Santelices, M.V. (2006). *The role of Advanced Placement and honorscourses in college admissions*. In P. Gandara, G. Orfield and C. Horn (Eds.), Expanding Opportunity in Higher Education (pp. 75-114). Albany, NY: SUNY Press.

[24] Conley, D. T. (2007a) *Toward a comprehensive conception of college readiness*. Eugene, OR: Educational Policy Improvement Center. Retrieved May, 1, 2008 from http://www.s4s.org/

[25] Muraskin, L. & Lee, J. (2004). *Raising graduation rates of low-income college students*. Washington, DC: The Pell Institute for the Study of Opportunity in Higher Education.

[26] Tierney, W.G. & Hagedorn, L. S. (Eds.). (2002). *Increasing access to college: extending possibilities for all students*. Albany, NY: State University of New York Press.) and Kirst, M. & Venezia, A. (May 2003).

[27] *Undermining student aspirations: The frayed connections between K-12 and postsecondary education set students up for failure*. National CrossTalk, 11(2). Retrieved May 7, 2008, from http://www.highereducation.org/crosstalk/ct0203/voices0203-undermining.shtml National Center for Public Policy and Higher Education.

[28] ACT, (2005) *ACT National Curriculum Survey 2005-2006*. Iowa City, IA: American College Testing (ACT))

[29] Swanson, C. (2008, April). *Cities in crisis: A special analytic report on high school graduation*. Bethesda, MD: Editorial Projects in Education Research Center.

[30] Engle, J., Bermeo, A., & O'Brien, C. (2006). *Straight from the source: What works for first-generation college students*. Washington, DC: The Pell Institute for the Study of Opportunity in Higher Education.)

[31] Doskoch, P. (2005, November/December). The winning edge. *Psychology Today*, 38(6), 42-52.

[32] Partnership for 21st Century Skills. (2007). *Framework for 21st century learning: life and career skills*. Tucson, AZ: Partnership for 21st Century Skills. Accessed online at: http://www.21stcenturyskills.org/index.php?Itemid=120&id=254&option=com_content&task=view)

[33] Deke, J, and Haimson, J. (2006). *Expanding beyond academics: Who benefits and how?* Princeton, NJ: Mathmatica Policy Research, Inc. (ERIC Document Reproduction Service No. ED496293) Retrieved from ERIC Database.).

[34] Darling-Hammond, L., Ancess, J, Ort, S. W. (2002) *Reinventing high school: Outcomes of the coalition campus schools project.* American Educational Research Journal, Vol. 39, No. 3 (Autumn, 2002), pp. 639-673

[35] Stevens, W. D. (2008) *If small is not enough...the characteristics of successful small high schools in Chicago.* Chicago, IL: Consortium on Chicago School Research at the University of Chicago.

[36] Henry, P (2007) *The Case Against Standardized Testing.* Mankato, MN: Minnesota English Journal, Fall, 2007)

[37] Koretz, D. (2008). *Measuring Up: What Educational Testing Really Tells Us.* Cambridge, Massachusetts: Harvard University Press.

[38] Rothstein, Richard. (2008) Grading education: Getting accountability right. NY: Teachers College Press

[39] Fair Test, 2008 accessed online at http://www.fairtest.org/

[40] Rockefeller Brothers Fund. 1958. The pursuit of excellence: Education and the future of America. *The "Rockefeller Report" on Education. Special Studies Project V.* New York: Rockefeller Brothers Fund.

[41] Raudenbush, S.W. (2004). *Schooling, Statistics, and Poverty: Can we measure school improvement?* The ninth annual William H. Angoff Memorial Lecture presented at Educational Testing Service, Princeton, New Jersey (April 1, 2004)

[42] Koretz, D. (2008) *Holding NCLB Accountable: Achieving Accountability, Equity, & School Reform*, 1. "The Pending Reauthorization of NCLB: An Opportunity to Rethink the Basic Strategy". Thousand Oaks, CA: Corwin Press

[43] Bracey, G. (2003) *On the Death of Childhood and the Destruction of Public Schools: The Folly of Today's Education Policies and Practices* Portsmouth, NH: Heinemann

[44] Bush, George W, speech delivered on July 10, 2000 at NAACP's 91st annual convention, Baltimore, MD. (complete transcript accessed from Washingtonpost.com/wp-srv/onpolitics/elections/bushtext071000.htm)

[45] Rothstein, R. (2004) Class And Schools: Using Social, Economic, And Educational Reform To Close The Black-white Achievement Gap, New York: Teachers College Press

[46] Wagner, T. (2006) *Rigor on Trial*. Education Week. January 11, 2006

[47] Resnick, L., Hall, M. W. (2005) *Principles of learning for effort-based education.* Pittsburgh, PA: Institute for Learning, Learning Research and Development Center, University of Pittsburgh

[48] *Committee of Ten Report to the National Education Association.* (1892) Cambridge, MA

[49] Renyi, J. (1993) Going Public: Schooling for a Diverse Democracy. New York: New Press.

[50] American Diploma Project (2009) accessed from http://www.achieve.org

[51] Noddings, Nel (2007) When School Reform Goes Wrong New York: Teachers College Press

[52] Redovich, D. (2007) *What is the Rationale for Requiring Higher Math and Science for All?* Accessed online at: http://www.jobseducationwis.org/

[53] National Council of Teachers of Mathematics (2005) accessed online at: http://www.nctm.org/news/content.aspx?id=714

[54] Aiken W. The Eight Year Study (1942) Harper & Brothers, New York and London. http://www.8yearstudy.org/6-11-137-138.html

[55] Kilpatrick, W. (1918) The Project Method: Child-centeredness in Progressive Education. New York: Teachers College Record

[56] Dewey, John. (1916) Democracy and education. New York: Macmillan Company

[57] Rockefeller Brothers Fund. 1958. The pursuit of excellence: Education and the future of America. *The "Rockefeller Report" on Education. Special Studies Project V.* New York: Rockefeller Brothers Fund.

[58] Finn, Jr., C.E., Petrilli, M.J., and Julian, L. (2006). *The State of State Standardsb2006.* Washington, D.C.: Thomas B. Fordham Institute.

[59] Brooks, D. (2001) *The Organization Kid.* Atlantic Magazine, April 2001.

[60] Phelan, P., Davidson, A., & Yu, H. (1998). *Adolescents' Worlds: Negotiating Family, Peers, and School.* New York: NY Teachers College Press.

[61] Goleman, D. Working with Emotional Intelligence. (1998) New York: Bantam Books.

[62] Powell, A.G., Farrar, E., & Cohen, D.K. (1985) The Shopping Mall High School. Boston: Beacon Press.

[63] Henderson, N. and Milstein, M. (2002) Resiliency in Schools: Making It Happen for Students and Educators, Thousand Oaks, CA: Corwin Press

[64] Hawkins J D, Catalano R F, Miller J Y (1992). Risk and Protective Factors for Alcohol and Other Drug Problems in Adolescence and Early Adulthood: Implications for Substance Abuse Prevention. *Psychological Bulletin, 112(1), 64-105.*

[65] Benard, B. (2004) *Resiliency: What We Have Learned* San Francisco:WestEd

[66] National Research Council Institute of Medicine (2004) *Engaging Schools:Fostering High School Students' Motivation to Learn*, Washington, DC: National Academies Press

[67] Poplin, M. & Weeres, J., (1992). *Voices From the Inside*. Claremont, CA: The Institute for Education in Transformation at The Claremont Graduate School.

[68] National Association of Secondary School Principals (NASSP) (1995). Summary of normed climate survey data. Reston, VA.

[69] Nieto, S. (2000), pp. 38-45 *Affirming Diversity: The Sociopolitical Context of Multicultural Education* New York: Addison Wesley Longman, Inc.

[70] Sergiovanni, T (1994) Building Communities in Schools. San Francisco: Jossey-Bass.

SECTION ONE
READINGS LINKING THEORY AND RESEARCH TO CORE PRACTICE

CHAPTER 1

Personalize Relationships and Learning
in the Classroom

♥ **Practice 1: Develop positive relationships among and between students and teachers.**

Ⓢ **Practice 2: Emphasize personalized, student-centered learning.**

⌘ **Practice 3: Integrate multiple ways of knowing and learning.**

A Personalization Primer

(1) What Does the Research Say?
"To teach students well you need to know them well."

Personalized learning emphasizes:

- a safe, supportive environment

- strong personal relationships with teachers

- positive peer relationships

- varied learning opportunities that emphasize choice, voice, collaboration, multiple intelligences, and the social construction of knowledge

- learning tasks that have personal meaning and value

- high levels of personalized academic and behavioral support

Research indicates that personalized learning environments foster greater motivation, increase attachment to learning, and improve academic achievement, especially for underserved, under-performing students and young people who find it more challenging to navigate the dominant culture of high school successfully.[1]

For the majority of adolescents, positive connections to peers, school, and learning are also associated with reductions in high-risk behaviors, including acts of violence, drug abuse, and dropping out of high school, as well as lower rates of emotional distress and increases in resiliency and coping skills.[2]

We know that a sense of belonging is crucial to adolescents' sense of well-being. Improving the quality of relationships among and between adults and young people should stand at the center of efforts to personalize schooling. Getting to know each student personally can make the difference between relationships that feel caring and supportive and those that can feel coercive and alienating. Ensuring that students know each other well is the first step toward developing mutual respect and trust, and forms the foundation of a caring community where students feel safe, welcomed, seen, and heard in a positive manner.

Barriers to successful learning become more pronounced when we teach students as if they were all the same. Practices of personalization enable teachers to "meet learners where they are in terms of their capabilities, interests, attitudes, and other intrinsic motivational considerations."[3] Teachers offer more choices for what students learn and how they learn it; they create meaningful links between students' personal interests and experiences and what they are learning in school.

Research also indicates that academic success for more students is directly linked to "high levels of social support *and* high levels of academic press. Lee's meta-analysis of data from schools involved in restructuring and redesign confirms that students who experienced both high expectations *and* high support performed better than students in schools that emphasized one or the other."[4]

(2) Personalized Schools Emphasize

Vision

Voice

Choice

I see you. I want to know who you are. We are partners in co-creating a classroom vision of how we treat each other, how we talk to each other, how we learn and work together. It's OUR classroom, not my classroom. We can negotiate what and how we learn. There's not one way to achieve a goal or complete a task. There are always CHOICES. We will create a high-performing community of learners where everyone has a VOICE.

	Systems and Structures	Classroom Practices and Routines
Personalized Relationships	• Advisory • Teaming • Professional learning communities that meet at least weekly for extended periods	• Meet and greets • Learning everyone's name and sharing who we are during the first few weeks of school • Personal check-ins and conferencing
Personalized Learning and Student Work	• Extended learning blocks and flexible scheduling • Six-year personal learning and post-secondary plans • Advisory • Small schools, grade-level teaming, academies, career pathways • Courses by choice and personal interest: nine-week and semester electives; interdisciplinary courses and topic-focused colloquia; AP, dual enrollment and advanced academic courses; career-related and tech courses; independent learning courses and individually-paced courses; internships; credit recovery	• Gatherings and closings • Negotiated learning (choices about what you learn and how, when, where, and with whom you learn it) • Personal learning contracts • Personal goal-setting, reflection, and self-assessment on a regular basis • Differentiated instruction, products, portfolios, exhibitions, presentations, and assessments • Project-based and problem-based learning; collaborative learning; Socratic seminars • Relevant course work linked to real world, practical applications and student's lived experiences, personal interests and aspirations, and learning profiles
Personalized Climate and Culture	• Comprehensive student orientation and transitions at all grade levels • Youth development, peer education, and leadership opportunities for every student every year	• Group agreements, common expectations and procedures, and group learning protocols • Class meetings • Rituals and routines that recognize and celebrate individuals and the group
Personalized Academic and Behavioral Supports	• School-wide system of discipline and accountable consequences that feels fair, supportive, and enforceable • Advisory • Student intervention teams and a separate set of academic and behavioral interventions and supports for "frequent fliers"	• Classroom supports and interventions that create a culture of quality and completion for every student • Modeling, teaching, practicing, and assessing the behaviors you expect (Life Skills) • Guided discipline that invites cooperation and self-correction and includes accountable consequences and interventions

(3) Principles of Personalization

1. Every student and adult feels safe, welcomed, respected, and connected.

2. Every student has an advocate who knows her well, supports her development of her six-year plan, and can say, "I'm on your side and I'm on your case."

3. Students need both high "academic press" and high caring and support to achieve.

4. Positive relationships form the foundation of effective instruction, discipline, and support for students.

5. Healthy development (principles of prevention, resiliency, social and emotional learning, and youth development) is linked to learning and achievement.

6. Personalizing structures and systems without personalizing classroom practice and assessment will produce the same results you always got.

7. One size does not fit all, and high standards don't mean a single standard of excellence. Personalization is about providing curriculum, learning opportunities, and supports that best fit the different developmental needs, learning profiles, personal interests, and aspirations of every student.

8. Every student should experience a redundancy of youth development opportunities every year. "Redundancy" means more than a variety of random opportunities—it involves intentional efforts to ensure that all students experience multiple "hits" of the same opportunity over time, and multiple opportunities to practice and demonstrate the same skills and competencies over time.

9. Academic rigor can turn into academic rigormortis if students don't experience learning opportunities and work that is relevant and personally meaningful.

10. Personalization enables each student to create an educational learning program that's the right fit. Students are able to make choices about:

    – What they learn

    – How they learn it

    – How they demonstrate their understanding and proficiency

    – What courses they take

    – How they develop their postsecondary plan

    – How they can recover credits and meet graduation requirements

(4) Personalizing Learning and the Learning Environment

STUDENTS are able to meet their developmental and cultural needs, interests, and aspirations for...	RELATIONSHIPS between and among students and adults to build a community of...	ADULTS engage in school-wide and classroom practices that provide...
Physical and Psychological Safety to interact with others without fear of being harmed, hurt, embarrassed, or targeted	**Trust and Attachment**	**Right Regard and Protection** of every student's personal well-being, dignity, and safety
Belonging, Connection, and Affection with peers and adults	**Caring, Acceptance, and Cooperation**	**High Personal, Academic and Social Support and Opportunities to Know Students Well**
Voice to express one's own thoughts, feelings, and perspectives and affirm one's personal and group identities	**Respect and Recognition**	**Open Dialogue and Inquiry, Collaborative Problem Solving, and Democratic Governance**
Freedom and Independence to take risks, discover, explore, experiment, direct one's actions, and control aspects of one's life	**Personal Responsibility**	**Clear Boundaries, Accountable Consequences, and Guided Discipline**
Choice to explore options, make one's own decisions, and engage in learning that is personally relevant and meaningful	**Shared Accountability** to reflect on and assess individual and group performance and behavior	**A Saturation of Opportunities** that support students' academic, social, emotional, ethical, and physical development
Creativity and Imagination to produce, present, or perform something of one's own and activate hope and confidence to build a future of one's own making	**Vision and Clarity of Purpose**	**Passion and Enthusiasm to Inspire, Challenge, and Encourage All Students**
Power and Mastery to achieve, contribute, and succeed in school and life	**Leadership and High Performance**	**High Expectation** and insistence on completion and quality work for every student

(5) Making Learning Personal for Yourself

Read the quotations below. Circle or underline a phrase in each quotation that captures what personalized learning means to you.

"Personalized learning implies an ideal: individual students pursuing personal plans supported by a caring teacher who helps them through a series of increasingly challenging tasks toward a future that grows increasingly clear with each success. Using knowledge to gain personal power is not a fresh idea. Empowerment in this spirit is less about preparing youth for tomorrow and more about equipping them for engagement, connection, and contribution today."[5]

"Personalized learning is essentially active learning, organized to answer questions students recognize as important to their lives. Because students learn to gather information to solve problems they recognize in their own experience, personalized learning is often called 'authentic,' mirroring the processes adults use to solve problems at work, at home, or in community." [6]

"Guided by skilled teachers, students look carefully at what they know, generate questions or set goals, gather more information, then use critical thinking skills to propose solutions to an audience of adults and peers. In all these activities, the student is the center of attention, winning praise and eliciting advice from the students, teachers, parents, and community members who attend a presentation. Personalization is not the same as individualization. Personal learning requires the active direction of the student; individualization lets the school tailor the curriculum to scaled assessments of interest and abilities. The difference between individualization and personalization lies in control."[7]

"High schools that successfully personalize learning provide all students with a means of gaining acceptance from the school community, not for conformity with a norm, but for achievements that are unique, self-organized, and carried out independently, often with other students working as a team."[8]

"The atmosphere must allow the adults the time and support to focus on students as people who have promising hopes and aspirations, even if those are veiled or hard to draw out. The adults need to believe deeply that in those hopes lies all motivation for learning and that by attending to aspirations, teaching becomes ever more powerful. In addition, the adults need a personal toolkit of their own that helps them develop the sensitivities, responsiveness, and vocabulary of personal learning."[9]

"A school ought to be a magical place where you are queen or king, and where what you get to do is to focus on your intellect, and on what you can accomplish as a human being, and you come to understand what your life can be. . . . School is supposed to be full of hope, and it's a place where you go to find out how magical your mind is and how terrific it will be when you develop your mind to its full potential."[10]

Reflect on your own learning as an adolescent. Jot down at least three experiences (in a course, in a school activity, or in your life outside of school) in which the learning was personal, powerful, and permanent.

1. Why is this learning experience memorable? What made this an experience where you would say, "This was a great opportunity to keep me moving on my personal learning pathway"?

2. What did you produce, present, or accomplish that made this experience personally important to you?

3. Where did this learning experience take place? Did the setting matter? Why or why not?

4. What tools, skills, knowledge, or insights did you take away that built foundations for your future life and career?

5. What adults supported your learning? What did they do that helped you persist and achieve your goal?

6. In what ways did this experience match your personal style and learning profile?

On a different note, what do you regret not being able to do, learn, or experience in high school? How would your school have needed to change to meet these personal interests?

(6) Making Learning Personal for Your Students

What does it really mean to know kids well enough to teach them well? Here's one way to think about personalizing learning for a wide range of students. Create a word snapshot for four or five students you've known well who are completely different from each other. Imagine what each of these students needs to make your class a good place for them. What kinds of learning experiences would be a great fit for each student?

Name of Student	Personal attributes, passions, and preoccupations; likes and dislikes; ethnicity, cultural identity, family background; group affiliations and social status; learning profile	What does this student need to make a class a place where she/he can be their own person, a committed learner, and a high-performing member of the group?	What kinds of learning experiences would score an 8, 9, or 10 for this student? (What, where, how, with whom, for what purpose?)

(7) Personalized Learning Demands Personalized Teaching

"Personalization: A learning process in which schools help students assess their own talents and aspirations, plan a pathway toward their own purposes, work cooperatively with others on challenging tasks, maintain a record of their explorations, and demonstrate their learning against clear standards in a wide variety of media, all with the close support of adult mentors and guides."[11]

The purpose of personalized teaching is to provide opportunities for all students to participate in and to take control of their own learning. Student participation and control are necessary to produce measurable student achievement in long-term retention of information, internalization of skills, and understanding of important concepts. They are also necessary to engage students, cause them to persevere, and allow them to grow as problem solvers and critical thinkers.

Personalized teaching thus creates the conditions for students to find productive and fulfilling pathways into adult society. Teachers need opportunities to discover that they, too, learn differently and that their preferred learning styles affect their teaching styles. In turn, teachers must design curriculum, instruction, and assessment that reflect the mission of their school and the standards associated with their learning discipline. Personalized teaching will occur only when teachers see clearly that the students they teach shape how they teach and that the quality of their instruction correlates directly with the quality of student learning.[12]

(8) Personalized Teaching Supports Relevant and Rigorous Learning by...

- Creating a shift from teacher-centered to student-centered learning; from teaching for memorization to learning that stresses in-depth understanding, critical thinking, and problem solving; from direct instruction to more facilitation and coaching.

- Aligning curriculum to learning standards through meaningful student work.

- Fostering each student's strengths while providing "academic press" to learn and apply intellectual tools and skills beyond one's comfort zone.

- Creating a culture of completion and quality driven by high expectations and personalized, differentiated support, so that all students can meet or exceed standards of proficiency.

- Differentiating between first attempts, drafts, practice, revisions, and final products and assessments.

- Emphasizing "habits of mind": [13]

  - **Perspectives** – From whose viewpoint are we reading, seeing, viewing, and hearing?

  - **Evidence** – How do we know what we know? What's the evidence? How reliable is it?

- **Connections** – How are things, people, events, ideas, and systems connected to each other? How do they fit together? What's old? What's new? Have we seen or heard this before?

- **Speculation** – How might we look at this? What if. . . . .? What are alternative possibilities?

- **Significance** – What does it mean? So what? Why does it matter? What difference does it make? Who cares? How does this affect me? What's my impact on. . . . .?

- Co-creating complex, intellectual tasks that invite students to

  - **Formulate questions** that frame an investigation, hypothesis, thesis, or experiment;

  - **Conduct historical research** using primary and secondary sources;

  - **Use mathematics** in civic, consumer, social science, or scientific applications;

  - **Critique and compare** works in the literary, visual, and/or performing arts; and

  - **Complete a project or product of one's own choice** that provides an opportunity to design, plan, invent, revise, reassess, analyze, edit, refine, and present a piece of work using sophisticated tools and techniques.

- Rethinking conceptions of intellectual rigor, curriculum content, and benchmarks of student success that more accurately reflect the interdependent systems, interdisciplinary knowledge, and/or social and cultural demands that drive how we live and work today.

- Reinventing traditional subjects into more meaningful and relevant learning units and interdisciplinary courses linked to career pathways and real-world applications of knowledge and skills.

- Emphasizing product and project-based learning, authentic performances, exhibitions, portfolios, and multiple assessments that become part of the learning process itself.

- Affirming students' multiple talents, intelligences, and ways of knowing and learning by engaging all students in a variety of educational experiences and instructional strategies.

- Offering more collaborative learning opportunities that promote a shared construction of knowledge and more independent learning that allows students to pursue personal choices and interests.

- Building bridges between the curriculum and students' lived experiences that affirm their cultural identities, families, and communities.

(9) Personalization in Small Schools and Smaller Learning Communities

Establishing small schools and smaller learning communities within schools is a major personalization strategy. Learning communities of 200 to 500 students strengthen a school's capacity to:

1. Develop shared responsibility for the learning and healthy development of a group of students over time, so that students are well known by the adults who teach and advise them.

2. Ensure that all students can meet and exceed state proficiency standards and enable all faculty to align the curriculum to state standards and state and district learning outcomes.

3. Provide opportunities for students to explore areas of potential career interest, assess their strengths and interests, and determine what kinds of careers might be the best match.

4. Provide opportunities for students to take courses that connect the curriculum to the real world through project-based and applied learning that is rigorous, relevant, and interdisciplinary in nature, mirroring the complex, interdisciplinary, and interdependent systems that drive the postmodern world.

5. Provide a structure that supports all students to develop a personal learning and postsecondary plan throughout high school that prepares them for postsecondary learning experiences, whether it's college, technical school, an apprenticeship, a job, or community college.

6. Ensure that a group of adults takes responsibility for "shepherding" their students through their graduation requirements; this might include career exploration and personal statements, a two year postgraduation plan, exhibitions of mastery, internships, and other benchmarks.

7. Provide structures, strategies, and specific interventions for students who enter high school with significant literacy and numeracy skill gaps and/or continue to experience skill gaps during high school. All of these efforts provide specific academic support strategies and interventions that encourage and enable all students to engage in rigorous course work.

8. Incorporate broader definitions of academic success and intellectual rigor, and offer more choices for how to complete required course work, and more opportunities for students to pursue their interests through independent projects, independent study, internships, courses at community colleges and universities, research partnerships, and service learning.

(10) What Does a Personalized Learning Environment Look and Feel Like?

What does school feel like when caring relationships and efforts to personalize learning are valued throughout the school? Joe, a hypothetical sophomore, might describe it as follows:

I like this school because it's easy to make friends and there aren't that many cliques. I can be with my buddies on the track team, but I can also hang out with my partner in chemistry. My English teacher makes sure that we all get a chance to work with each other in class, so I'm less scared of being around people who aren't just like me. It's been fun learning more about other kids who come from different neighborhoods than mine. I guess I was surprised that we had more in common than I thought.

My classes are okay. My teachers know me as a person and help me to do my best. My Chem teacher really likes my jokes. And my History and English teachers don't think I'm stupid just because it takes me a long time to read something. When I'm having a hard time, I know I can talk to them and work out how to get back on track. If I mess up, I know it's not going to be held against me for the rest of my life—my grade doesn't just depend on a few big tests.

Classes aren't nearly as boring as I'd thought they'd be because we get to make lots of choices about how we do assignments and about how we're going to work together to learn stuff. Teachers don't just lecture at us the whole time—they want to know what we have to say and listen to our suggestions about how to make class better. Even reading isn't so bad anymore because I've gotten to read stuff that I can relate to and we get to talk about our own opinions.

What I like best is my Math class, because my teacher told us in the beginning of the year if we make an effort everyone will pass. Nobody is allowed to just sit in the back. He's helped us to really be a team so we make sure nobody's left behind. Not everyone gets As, especially not me, but all of us have learned some things really well. After being here for a year, I'm more willing to put in the time to get good grades, because my teachers really notice when I make the effort. I know they're on my side.

I think my teachers are pretty fair—they won't let certain behaviors slide, but they also get that we all don't learn the same way and sometimes we need different kinds of help. For instance, my Social Studies teacher meets with some of us at lunch once a week so we can go over the readings that are hard for me to understand. I'm not so afraid to talk in class now because I've already talked about it beforehand.

I feel safe here at school. I pretty much know I'm not going to get picked on because the school slams down really hard on kids who fight or bully or make fun of other people. Teachers are really good about stopping put-downs and nasty remarks. I notice that a lot. And kids in sports and clubs really make an effort to support the school campaign around respect and diversity. Sometimes, it gets old hearing this stuff over and over, but it does get the point across that everyone has the right to be respected for who they are.

In advisory, I've gotten to know more about myself and how I handle my frustrations and relationships with other people. I know I can bring up almost any issue in my advisory and we can talk about it openly and honestly. I like it when my advisor checks in with me just to see how I'm doing. If I had a really big problem there are lots of people around who can help me. One of my friends just lost a parent and he's been really depressed and gets angry over nothing. He exploded in class one day, but instead of getting suspended, he talked to a counselor and joined a group with other students who have had somebody in their family die. That's been a really good thing.

Many more students would succeed in high school if their experiences were similar to Joe's. Personalizing the high school is about students feeling respected as people and being supported and encouraged to achieve regardless of their academic track. Joe wants to learn because teachers know him well and communicate that they're on his side. Joe has a sense that adults are looking out for him. He feels he can be his own person here because his school makes an intentional effort to promote a friendly atmosphere and a culture of caring.

CHAPTER 2

Co-Create a Respectful, Responsible, High-Performing, and Cohesive Learning Community

 Practice 4: Establish clear norms, boundaries, and procedures.

Practice 5: Build a cohesive community of learners.

(11) What Creates a Sense of Community?

Creating a caring, respectful, and responsible community of learners is the starting point for creating an effective learning environment and reducing adversarial relationships. Creating community helps build cohesiveness, a common purpose, interdependence, and support within the group. As students feel more connected to the group, they are more likely to invest in becoming responsible and productive group members.

Conscious efforts to build a community of learners invite students to practice negotiated decision making, exercise voice and choice, and strengthen their participation and leadership skills.

The soul of a classroom is the psychological sense of community created among and between the students and the teacher. Howard Adelman and Linda Taylor describe community in this way:

"People can be together without feeling connected or feeling they belong or feeling responsible for a collective vision or mission. In school and in class, a psychological sense of community exists when a critical mass of stakeholders are committed to each other and to the setting's goals and values and exert effort toward the goals and maintaining relationships with each other. Such an effort must ensure effective mechanisms are in place to provide support, promote self-efficacy, and foster positive working relationships.

A perception of community is shaped by daily experiences and probably is best engendered when a person feels welcomed, supported, nurtured, respected, liked, and connected in reciprocal relationships with others, who is contributing to the collective identity, destiny, and vision."[1]

A number of factors challenge the rationale for creating community in high school classrooms, making it difficult to achieve. There are the obvious pressures of content coverage and testing. If we spend time building community, that's less time spent on the topic. Short class periods that are long on direct skill instruction may provide few opportunities for students to function as a community or work as a team. High school students are conditioned to view the classroom as a vehicle for demonstrating individual mastery, not a container for holding a vision that's shaped by the collective performance of the whole group.

What may be the greatest barrier, however, is the dynamic of a classroom—there's one teacher and up to thirty kids, many of whom may have no interest in creating community at all. Thus, the initial inspiration and responsibility for establishing a sense of community lies in the hands of one person—the teacher. Students' experience of community or noncommunity will hinge on their teachers' beliefs. Teachers who believe that building community can result in increased student motivation and learning, will make it happen. If they don't see the connection, they won't.

Thomas Sergiovanni, who has written extensively on school culture and school leadership sees building community (in and outside the classroom) at the heart of school improvement. He suggests that, first and foremost, a community must have a sense of vision and purpose.[2]

1. **Vision, Purpose, and Intentionality**

    Do we give students compelling reasons for why we're doing what we're doing that make sense to them, not just us or the local school board or department chair? How do we construct a vision of we, not just I? How can we go about developing a sense of shared goals that all of us value? How do we plan ahead, set the stage, seed the ground so students will do what we'd like them to do? If students come without the skills and attitudes we expected, what can we do to help them strengthen their academic and social competencies? What kinds of meaningful opportunities do we provide for students to feel positive about themselves as individual learners and as members of a group?

Three other conditions support the development of a genuine community.

2. **Trust**

    It's all about the relationships we create with students and that students create among themselves. Trust emerges when relationships are supported and maintained through dependability, predictability, genuineness, honesty, competence, integrity, consistency, and personalization. A sense of trust deepens when we feel safe and know that if the boundaries of safety are broken, violations won't be ignored. What can kids count on from us time after time after time? What can kids count on from each other day in and day out?

2

3. **Respect**

   Respect begins by developing an appreciation for each other's uniqueness and what we each bring to the classroom. It's nurtured by cultural sensitivity. (The classroom will be a place where I will be conscious of positively welcoming, noticing, and learning about the diversity of my students and teach to their differences.) A respectful classroom is a place where students aren't embarrassed, insulted, belittled, or humiliated. A climate of mutual respect is supported through the courtesy of asking, inviting, requesting, and by listening before judgment or punishment. Teachers model respectfulness by focusing on the issues—not attacking the person. They are mindful of using a tone of voice and words that communicate that each person has dignity and each student has something important to contribute.

4. **Optimism**

   Optimism begins by holding a positive image of human beings as able and capable. We convey our optimism by valuing an individual's efforts, not just his or her ability. We hold high hopes in life for every student. From smiles, to immediate feedback, to personal conferencing, we let students know that we are confident in their capacities to learn, grow, and change. We believe that students can succeed and don't downplay small successes. (The lesson wasn't perfect, the students weren't perfect, and still it was successful!) In fact, we encourage students to see mistakes, missteps, and setbacks as opportunities to imagine different choices and possibilities. Above all, we do everything we can to let young people know they have the power within them to choose the kind of human beings they want to be in a future of their own making.

Consider out-of-classroom experiences that offer a compelling sense of community and require exemplary practice of effective teamwork—a basketball team, a drama production, or a school newspaper. In each of these arenas, high performance or quality production are dependent on each individual's skills and the collective efforts and skills of the whole group. No coach or sponsor would diminish the role that inspiration, motivation, and attitude play in helping kids to think like a team. Nor would they neglect to teach and assess the specific skills that help a group behave like a team.

(12) Is Your Classroom a Learning Community?

How would your students assess their relationship with you on a scale of 1 to 5?
(1 = never; 2 = rarely; 3 = sometimes; 4 = most of the time; 5 = always)

TRUST

____ My teacher is predictable. I know what will happen in class from day to day.

____ I know what will happen in class when I mess up.

____ My teacher is genuine. She's for real and means what she says.

____ My teacher brings her own passion and personality into the classroom.

____ My teacher is honest and direct. He tells me where he stands and lets me know what I'm doing wrong, so I can correct it.

____ My teacher is fair and consistent and doesn't play favorites. No one is allowed to "get over" on her or "get away with stuff" that's really not okay.

____ My teacher is clear about his roles and boundaries. He keeps confidences when he says he will, isn't two-faced, and doesn't pretend to be a kid.

____ My teacher is competent. She knows her stuff, cares about what she teaches, makes what matters worth learning, and cares about whether I learn it.

____ My teacher is personal with me and gets to know me and cares about me as a person.

____ My teacher is dependable and doesn't give up on me. I can count on my teacher time after time to support and encourage me to do my best and be my best.

RESPECT

____ My teacher calls me by my name and has learned how to pronounce it correctly.

____ My teacher notices me. I'm not invisible. I'm appreciated for my own uniqueness, even if my style and personality are not like my teacher's.

____ My teacher acknowledges and appreciates my culture. If my experience, my race, or my culture is different from his, his words and actions let me know that I'm not bad or inferior.

____ My teacher doesn't embarrass, humiliate, or insult people in class.

____ My teacher doesn't allow others to embarrass, humiliate, or insult people in class.

____ My teacher doesn't demand respect; he sees respect as a two-way street where each person gives respect to get respect; he asks and invites me to learn.

____ My teacher listens to me before she judges or punishes me.

____ When kids mess up, my teacher focuses on the problem and doesn't attack the person.

___ My teacher assumes that students have something to contribute; she values my thoughts, feelings, and opinions.

___ My teacher uses words and a tone of voice that communicate dignity and right regard for each student.

OPTIMISM

___ My teacher holds a positive image of students as able and capable.

___ My teacher values effort, not just ability.

___ My teacher believes that I can succeed and do well in his class.

___ My teacher is friendly, and smiles.

___ My teacher gives positive verbal and written feedback about what I do or what the group does well.

___ My teacher doesn't hold grudges or drag up the past. She gives me a chance to learn from my mistakes and will help me get "back on track."

___ My teacher notices small and big successes for the group or individuals.

___ My teacher gets excited when the class or individuals "get it!"

___ My teacher has high expectations for everyone in class and gives us the academic support we need to meet those expectations.

___ If I'm being negative or having trouble in class, my teacher will talk with me about it and help me get back on track.

PURPOSE AND INTENTIONALITY

___ My teacher gives us reasons for what we're doing that make sense to me.

___ My teacher asks us to do assignments and projects that help me learn; there's not a lot of "busy work."

___ My teacher connects what we're learning to the real world and our own experiences.

___ My teacher plans ahead and makes sure we have the resources, instructions, and help we need to do the work.

___ My teacher involves us in deciding what we learn and how we learn it.

___ My teacher makes us aware of the academic and social skills that we are learning and practicing from day to day.

___ I can explain to someone who's not in my class what I'm learning and why I'm learning it.

___ I can name five things I know I will be expected to accomplish, demonstrate, or complete successfully before the grading period is over.

(13) When Is a Group Not a Community of Learners?

Two school visits brought the issues of community and group identity to my attention, front and center. I was working with a charter school that structured their academic program so that no teacher had more than fifteen students per class. I observed a math class of twelve students for several class periods during the same week. I walked into the room thinking, "What a great opportunity to build a supportive environment for kids who have struggled with math in the past. Kids can get lots of individual attention and the group is small enough to get them excited to tackle problems together and experience the support that everyone can "get it" and the satisfaction that everyone "got it."

What I saw did not match my hopes. The same routine happened during every visit. The teacher posted the math assignment for the day, gave clear "how-to" instructions using a model problem, and proceeded to check in with students who wanted help for the rest of the period. About half the group managed to focus on their assignments most of the time, while the other half found more interesting things to do. Nothing seriously awful happened while I was there; in fact, nothing much happened at all. The teacher paid no attention to the group as a group, and consequently couldn't use the power of the group to ignite the classroom and make things come alive. From course to course, I observed the same phenomenon—students at their seats slogging through lessons alone, except for the teacher's one-to-one interactions with individuals. This picture paints the extreme version of absence of community and missed opportunity.

In fact, another set of observations raised more interesting and subtle questions about the differences between teaching individuals and teaching to the group. The first thing I noticed in Ms. Johnson's art class were the instructions for solving a design problem, written as a giant invitation to her students. Students had a number of options for how to go about this project; it was a class where kids had a lot of latitude to pursue what interested them and express themselves creatively. Most students focused immediately, got their materials, and began to work. It was clear that everyone knew the routine and knew that Ms. Johnson would check in with each of them personally during the period. She began a series of animated one-to-one conversations, asking questions, making observations, and providing encouragement as she moved around the room. This undivided attention went a long way toward building positive relationships between the teacher and each student.

As students worked independently, one noticed an impressive degree of self-discipline and motivation. Ms. Johnson had worked hard to create an atmosphere of focused energy and purpose, pushing each student to think beyond the obvious and experiment with different solutions so they could get the most out of the course and the most out of themselves. But 40 minutes later, when Ms. Johnson wanted the whole group to gather in a circle and discuss their work, they fell apart before they even began. Some students were still working at their tables while others were scraping chairs across the floor mumbling, "Why do we have to do this?" When they began the discussion, few kids were listening to each other or showing much interest in what was going on. The group didn't yet have a sense of itself as a learning community; nor were students using the skills they needed to function effectively as a group.

Ms. Johnson figured that if students work well individually in her class, they would get it together as a group. It was a surprise to her when they didn't. Her students' sense of self-direction and individual accomplishment was a direct result of the guided instruction, clarity of purpose, and personal feedback that she had provided. By contrast, Ms. Johnson had never given much thought to developing a vision of a community of artists in the classroom or thought much about the kind of deliberate instruction, practice, and coaching that would help her students get good at being a group.

Ms. Johnson's lack of attention around community goals and group skills isn't all that unusual in secondary classrooms. It's easy to assume that high school kids know why and how a classroom of 25 students is different from a space occupied by 25 students in separate cubicles, each working on her own. As teachers, we often hold out the wish that a group will just get better on its own—that over time students will come to know each other better, care about each other more, and gradually become more skillful at working together as a whole group. Yet, everything we know about working well as a team or mastering any skill contradicts a laissez faire approach to establishing a sense of community and developing effective group skills in the classroom.

(14) What Are the Benefits of Building a Learning Community?

We expect students to respect each other, listen to each other, cooperate with each other, learn from each other, and support each other's efforts. But what do we actually do or say that gives them a clear message that working effectively as a whole group or in small groups really matters? When it comes to working in a group, it's perfectly reasonable for students to want a reasonable answer to their favorite questions: "Why should I?" or "What's in it for me?" or "Why are we doing this?" or the all-purpose question honed by years of schooling, "Are we getting a grade for this?"

Our response to kids falls short. From a student's point of view, what's not graded may not have a lot of value. If we assess students only on their performance as individuals, why should they care about the quality of their skills or their contributions as members of a group? Second, even if we do change how we assess student performance, it would be nice to offer students a rationale more compelling than, "You're getting a grade for how you perform as a group."

It's impossible to support students' development of effective group skills if we don't have good reasons for helping students become a group. Here are a dozen reasons that make the case for establishing a more intentional community of learners:

1. Students experience a sense of belonging and satisfaction from developing a common vision and making a collective effort to achieve group goals or solve problems success-fully. When the bottom line is "sink or swim together" students have a genuine stake in supporting each others' successes.

2. Students take greater responsibility for establishing and maintaining positive norms for classroom behavior, resulting in fewer disruptions and discipline problems and greater cooperation and collaborative work habits.

3. Students get to know each other better. The better they know each other, the more likely they are to work together successfully, acknowledge each other's strengths, and accept each other's limitations.

4. A friendly, relaxed atmosphere is a result of a group seeing itself as a group, making it easier for everyone to learn. A state of relaxed alertness promotes high performance; if we're worried about being ridiculed or humiliated, we are less able to focus and concentrate on the learning task at hand.

5. Adolescents engage in a social construction of their reality. They learn from interacting with each other, and how they interact with each other will either enhance or diminish the learning experience.

6. Teachers and students who become partners in establishing a learning community are less likely to be adversarial, and are more likely to maintain positive relationships when kids are experiencing difficulties.

7. Students are recognized for their use of effective group skills—skills that might go unrecognized if they function only as individual learners.

8. Students experience opportunities where their efforts are appreciated by their peers.

9. In a group, students practice civic participation skills for living and working in a pluralistic, democratic society—the arts of negotiation, compromise, and consensus; listening to other points of view; and exercising public voice and choice through responsible decision making.

10. Students can develop skills to counter and reduce bias, prejudice, and stereotyping within and across groups.

11. Navigating and negotiating successfully within a group fosters skills and attitudes that promote effective relationships with family, friends, colleagues, and co-workers.

12. Participating in effective group experiences helps students transition from high school to work and postsecondary education, where knowing how to function well in different groups increases opportunity, choices, and options for being successful; in contrast, poor intergroup skills diminish one's life chances for success.

(15) What Does It Take to Build a High-Performing Group?

High-performing groups are able to demonstrate a set of discrete skills regularly and without prompting. (See "Habits of Learning," page 147, "Participation Assessment" Log, page 321. In *Getting Classroom Management RIGHT*, see "Create Group Procedures" Chapter 4.) Learning and mastering any academic or behavioral skill requires lots of practice—six to eight "hits" to get it right. Here's the sequence of steps students need:

1. Give me a reason to learn this. (When we're not very clear about why being a skillful group member is important, we're less likely to engage students in the rest of the steps necessary for habitual and competent use of effective interpersonal and group skills.)

2. Show me how to do it; model it for me.

3. Let me practice it multiple times in multiple contexts.

4. Assess how I'm doing and give me feedback and coaching.

5. Let me practice some more so I can get really good at this and assess how I'm doing on my own.

6. Recognize and acknowledge when I'm doing it regularly and skillfully.

7. Give me opportunities to demonstrate my competency.

8. Let me lead by modeling and encouraging others to use this skill.

Assessing Social Skill Proficiencies and Emotional Competencies:

(4) I do it competently on a regular basis without prompting and encourage and support others to do it.

(3) I do it competently most of the time with a little prompting.

(2) I do it competently some of the time. I still need a lot of prompting and feedback.

(1) This is still a growing edge for me. I hardly ever do it. I always need prompting and I need a lot more practice and feedback.

(0) I won't do it and/or I don't know how to do it.

CHAPTER 3

Meet Adolescents' Developmental and Cultural Needs

HH | **Practice 6: Provide high expectations and high-personalized support.**

(16) Some Benchmarks of Adolescent Development

If we are really serious about improving student achievement, we will need to be as attentive to adolescents' social, cultural, and emotional needs as we are to their intellectual growth and academic performance. Knowing more about the developmental and cultural needs of diverse learners is the basis for creating a classroom and curriculum that understands who your students are, what they know, what motivates them, and how they learn.

One of the most curious aspects of writing this guide was discovering just how vast the chasm proved to be between the day-to-day practice I witnessed in high schools and the current research and thinking that illuminate the world of adolescents and how to teach them. In the last two decades we have learned a lot more about how young people experience schooling, how they learn, and what they need to grow up healthy and become good students, good people, and good citizens. This gap between research and practice is all the more astonishing because national leaders and scholars in the fields of education, prevention, youth development, and learning and behavioral sciences have given us a rich picture of adolescents and their needs.

In her book *The Right to Learn*, Linda Darling-Hammond suggests that knowledge of adolescent development is a critical competency for secondary teachers. This understanding should include "knowing how adolescents think and behave; appreciation for the vast range of normal adolescent thinking and behavior; awareness that each student's cultural identity influences their development; and the awareness that an adolescent's intellectual, social, emotional, and ethical development are inextricably linked, although these aspects of development may reach maturity at different times within a single adolescent."[1]

The four major tasks of adolescence are:

1. **Establishing one's own identity.** Identity has two components—self-concept (the set of beliefs one has about one's attributes and assets) and self-esteem (how we evaluate our self-concept/how we feel about our perceived self as a whole or a specific aspect of ourselves—student, son, gang member).[2] Healthy identity also involves a balance between being with and identifying with others and being comfortable being alone and thinking and acting on one's own.[3]

2. **Becoming more intimate with peers.** As students get older they spend increasing amounts of time with friends and develop new forms of relationships based on sexual attraction. Peer groups serve as powerful reinforcements that validate popularity, status, prestige, and acceptance.[4]

3. **Developing a mature relationship with one's family.** Older adolescents see themselves as equals of their parents, and parents tend to recognize that the power balance in family relationships is shifting.

4. **Achieving a growing sense of autonomy, control, and mastery in the world.**

Early Adolescence: Ages 10–14, Peer Acceptance

There are big individual and gender differences in the timing and results of puberty. Early-maturing girls seem to be especially at risk of emotional, behavioral, and adjustment problems. While most girls have gone through the major transitions of puberty by the time they reach 9th grade, a small minority may lag behind their peers. Most boys entering high school will be in the midst of their developmental transition. Boys who lag far behind are likely to have the most difficulty adjusting and finding acceptance with their peers.

Gaining a sense of their "maleness" and "femaleness" is an important part of their development. Pre-teens are curious about sexual matters. They develop new feelings about their own bodies rather than developing sexual relationships with the opposite sex.

Young teens have a huge need for privacy that emerges from what David Elkind calls the imaginary audience—the notion that everyone is watching you all the time. [5] Kids are very self-conscious at this age and "almost die" from fear of embarrassment. This is the stage when children begin to develop their self-awareness, thus feeling more in control of themselves. With this newfound control come greater challenges to adult authority.

Early adolescents need time to engage in same-gender activities. Membership in groups is important to the pre-teen. "Heroes" to look up to are important. This may include special people outside the family.

Special athletic, artistic, academic, or musical talents may emerge at this time. Adults should encourage areas of potential success as a means of building the child's self-esteem.

Middle Adolescence: Ages 14–17, A Time of Change

Teens struggle with rapid growth, sexual maturation, and desire for independence from their parents. Adults need to keep in mind that their child's hormones have more control over their moods than they do.

Changes in personal habits, manners, dress, and hair, and a preoccupation (or lack of it) with personal hygiene are normal ways for teens to try on their teenage selves. Adults need to choose their battles on this front very carefully.

Young people value both primary same-gender friendships and mixed-gender social groups. Students who have difficulties making and keeping friends don't have access to the social buffers that can make school tolerable and even fun.

Teens have a strong sense of fairness and are judgmental of adults and peers who do not do what is "fair." Teens have a deep need for love and acceptance by parents and peers. Adults should be aware that such a need is often hidden in an effort to act mature.

It's normal for adolescents to:

- Argue for the sake of arguing. (Although this annoying habit gets on adults' last nerves, it is one of the ways that adolescents test their reasoning abilities.)

- Jump to conclusions. (Logical thinking comes and goes. Trying to correct a student's faulty logic or arguing back will only corner a student and make the conversation even more adversarial. Listen, appreciate the point of view, share your perspective, but don't try to convince students to change positions when their feelings are charged.)

- Constantly find fault with an adult's position. (A newfound capacity to think critically ignites the fire to find discrepancies and contradictions.)

- Be overly dramatic. (This is mostly a style of presenting oneself and does not usually foreshadow an extreme action.)

A physical need for extended periods of rest is normal. Adults often mistake this for laziness. Too little rest can result in moodiness. Adults should depersonalize these ups and downs and look beyond them as much as possible.

Opportunities for drug and alcohol experimentation are common. And once teens become sexually active, they remain sexually active.

Different social influences on boys' and girls' behavior often show up in school settings. For instance, girls are more likely to believe that they are not capable of handling challenges and retreat into helplessness, whereas boys are more likely to feel confident about their problem solving abilities. Girls also seem more likely to see failure as a personal flaw. On the other hand, on almost every academic measure girls excel more than boys.

Although in childhood girls are more resilient than boys, this flip-flops during adolescence, and girls appear to be at more risk psychologically. Most boys and girls experience negative feelings about physical changes and body image.

Teens find security in structure, although few ever admit it to adults. Adults need to be firm and consistent around a few "bottom-line" rules and expectations. The rules you state need to be enforced, so don't make too many. Adolescents tend to be much more responsible when the consequences are spelled out ahead of time.

By middle adolescence most kids develop what Elkind calls a personal fable, the belief that no one has ever experienced what they're going through or can possibly understand them (except maybe their best friend). This sense of uniqueness goes hand in hand with feelings of invincibility and wanting to be center stage for attention.

Teens' sense of self is increasingly shaped by how they see themselves as different from others and where they fit in the social network. Most teens experience more internal conflict than social conflict and don't identify themselves as belonging to just one group of peers. The average teen spends 22 hours a week with friends. Adolescents who have friends report more positive self-images and appear to have better relationships with parents and teachers. Attributes of well-liked teens include spontaneity, willingness to try new things, cheerfulness, liveliness, and interest in others. Lonely and shy teens feel more self-conscious, which results in a reluctance to speak, so these kids tend not to be noticed. Shy kids may feel they are perceived as undesirable and may retreat from most social situations.

Late Adolescence: Ages 17–19, Decisions

Mature appearance and behavior may be misleading on all fronts. We may assume that students who "look grown" may be more emotionally, socially, or intellectually mature than they really are. Adults need to acknowledge that most adolescents experience some feelings of frustration and depression during this period due to fears about facing adulthood, school pressures, social life, first-time employment, and college planning.

Career choices can be difficult. Schools should help teens explore careers that are suited to them rather than careers their parents wish they would pursue.

One of the challenges of late adolescence is the ambiguity surrounding the passage to adulthood. There are few rituals that help teens mark their coming of age. And the decision whether to go to work or to college can lead to very different transitions.

(17) 25 More Things You Should Know That Influence Adolescents' Success in School and Life[6]

1. The diversity among adolescents is staggering. In the human lifespan, the period we define as adolescence (ages 13–19) is characterized by the widest range of differences between one human being and another.

2. Timing and pacing of adolescent maturation is uneven and unpredictable. Although social, emotional, physical, intellectual, and identity aspects of development influence each other, they each have a different timetable within the same individual. In addition, sudden changes and shifts in kids' personalities, behaviors, attitudes, and habits are normal.

3. The second most significant growth spurt in the brain (the first is between birth and age three) occurs during adolescence. The synapses in the brain can double in number in one year of adolescence. The overproduction of synapses can also make it difficult to keep track of multiple thoughts and retrieve information quickly. The good news is that teens can re-pattern behavior, learn new skills and habits, and make significant changes in how they operate day to day. The bad news is that habits, preferences, and patterns of behavior get hardwired as kids move through adolescence. If you're a couch potato at age 15, you're likely to be a couch potato for the rest of your life unless there is a compelling, dramatic, transformative experience that motivates and inspires you to change an ingrained habit.

   Think of the teenage brain from a "use it or lose it" perspective: by age 18 the brain starts losing neurons that aren't hardwired by experience—it's called "pruning," and it allows the brain to function more efficiently. The brain nourishes what it uses and tosses away what it doesn't. You can't retrofit the brain in adulthood.

4. The frontal cortex (frontal lobe) is one of the last parts of the brain to mature. It's the CEO of the brain, in charge of executive functions like planning, organizing, setting priorities, making sound and informed judgments, assessing risk, managing and defusing intense and out-of-control emotions. The brain's circuit board is not completely installed until the midtwenties. There's a good reason why adolescents do not gain full adult status until they are 21. For most adolescents, the cortex is asleep at the switch some or even most of the time. Consequently, adolescents' judgment is highly erratic and they are capable of making both extraordinarily good judgments and really bad ones.

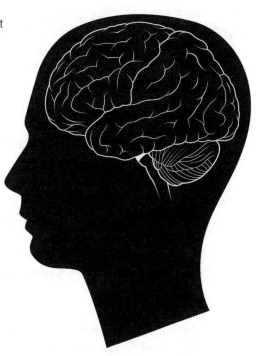

5. The corpus callosum, which is linked to self-awareness and intelligence, continues to develop until the midtwenties, hence a lot of kids are late bloomers.

6. Serotonin (a neurotransmitter) is responsible for inducing relaxation, regulating moods, and regulating sleep. Generally, women have 20–40% higher levels of serotonin than men. However, during the teen years, levels of serotonin decline for both sexes, creating conditions that can increase impulsive behavior.

7. Under the influence of enormous hormonal changes, teenagers rely more on the emotional center (amygdala) in the limbic system than on the reason center in the cortex. The amygdala is revved up, in hyperdrive, and intense feelings like anger, fear, and elation are normal and frequent. This center gets activated when "your button gets pushed," and it captures and stores emotionally intense memories. This is one reason why trauma can impede and interrupt learning.

8. Kids learn best in a state of "relaxed alertness" or "unanxious anticipation." Emotional turmoil can hijack kids to the land of "not-learn." Transitions that help students shift gears and get "brain ready" for learning are crucial.

9. Strong emotional connections with the teacher, the subject, or the task (whether positive or negative) generate learning with more "sticking power" related to memory, retention, comprehension, and application. The good news is that tapping into students' excitement, anticipation, laughter, surprise, and sense of well-being and competency increases learning. The bad news is that negative feelings about a teacher or specific type of learning task will stay with students way beyond the initial event and influence all future experiences in a similar setting or context.

10. Learning preferences (students' likes and dislikes, their fears and passions, what comes easy, what's hard) tend to harden and narrow during adolescence, especially if students' educational experience includes more of the same old, same old.

11. Challenging and complex human contact and relationships stimulate the brain. Teens watch an average of 23 hours of TV per week, more time than they spend interacting with friends, teachers, and family. Unlike previous generations, adolescents today spend far more time alone (with their separate phones, TVs, computers, etc.) and far less time with adults outside school.

12. New experiences with an element of risk, thrill, uncertainty, or danger stimulate neurons that release dopamine, which produces feelings of intense pleasure. So how can we package the intense experiences that kids crave minus the life-threatening price tag? Physical play, sports, dance, and movement of all sorts harness and release positive emotions and serve as a healthy outlet for emotional and sexual energy.

13. Between 10% and 15% of adolescents experience mild to severe depression. This means that at any given time three to four kids might be walking into the classroom depressed. There does appear to be a higher incidence of mild depression (dysthemia) among under-

served students who live in families who experience poverty or serial family crises. Fewer than one in five depressed adolescents receive treatment.

14. Teens' biological clocks are different. Melatonin levels are elevated in the early part of the school day—the brain is saying, "It's nighttime." At the end of the day, teens are not chemically ready for sleep until around 11pm. Yet teens require more sleep than adults (eight to nine hours) and hormones critical to growth and maturation are released during sleep. Sleep is brain food. Sleep deprivation reduces REM sleep and can result in memory and judgment impairment, irritability, and mild depression.

15. Researchers have arrived at some questionable conclusions about girls being shortchanged in schools. During adolescence, increasing numbers of girls do struggle with issues of self-image, assertiveness, and social pressure and acceptance. Yet, on almost every measure, girls do better in school and experience better life choices during young adulthood than boys. Boys tend to have more positive images of themselves, greater assertiveness, and higher perceptions of social acceptance. Yet, on every measure of success in school except one (percentage of students who score in the top percentiles on SATs), boys are less success-ful than girls. It's also important to note that different subsets of boys and girls appear to be more vulnerable to school failure, teen pregnancy, dropping out of school, other high-risk behaviors, and some mental illnesses, like eating disorders and self-mutilation.

16. Both sexes experience surges of testosterone during adolescence—ego, aggression, hostility, and irritability increase. This is normal.

17. Kids' social skills and interpersonal effectiveness actually decline in early and middle adolescence before they become increasingly competent at navigating new social settings, new kinds of relationships, and new social expectations. Modeling, teaching, practicing, and assessing social skills is essential for thirteen- to fifteen year-olds, so students don't lose so much ground.

18. Kids who behave aggressively over a long period of time share four things in common:

    • They are unable to identify their own emotions, "read" the feelings of others, or empathize with the target of their aggression;

    • They have difficulty predicting the consequences of their actions;

    • Aggression, whether verbal, psychological, or physical, is the only tool in their conflict toolbox—they don't know alternative responses; and

    • They tend to attribute hostile or aggressive intentions to new people they encounter.

19. The job description of all adolescents includes questioning and challenging authority. In particular, students of color, low-income students, newcomer students, and English-language learners may be more likely to distrust adult authority and the intentions of adults in general. Authoritarian (as opposed to authoritative) teachers who demand, command, and use their power over students are more likely to trigger responses of hostility and defiance than efforts to cooperate.

20. Adolescent "frequent fliers" (kids who experience chronic academic and behavioral difficulties) are least likely to respond positively and productively to punishment. In fact, a punitive approach to discipline (without opportunities for reflection, self-correction, instruction, support, and meaningful consequences and interventions) usually escalates feelings of anger, hostility, alienation, and rejection in already troubled students.

21. Reluctant, resistant, and failing students who "turn around" cite two factors that enable them to get back on track:

    • A long-term, positive relationship with an adult

    • Learning experiences that are personally meaningful and involve multiple ways of knowing, understanding, and demonstrating what they learn

22. The self-esteem movement didn't do adolescents any favors. Self-esteem cannot be taught or developed through a bunch of activities that encourage students to like themselves. High self-esteem results from genuine attachment to others, a sense of control and power in crucial areas of one's life, and experiences of mastery and competence. It's that simple and that daunting. It's also important to note that students of color who have a strong, positive, ethnic identity tend to have higher self-esteem. We have to expand the opportunities in school where students can experience these essential building blocks of self-esteem.

23. The most significant factors that determine the frequency of high-risk behaviors among adolescents (i.e., violence, substance abuse, pregnancy, etc.) are

    • Their degree of attachment to school

    • Their level of academic achievement

    • The friends with whom they hang out

24. Students who work fewer than 20 hours a week or participate in some personally significant school activity do better academically than those who don't. However, kids who work more than 20 hours a week tend to underperform at school.

25. By 9th grade the majority of adolescents see themselves as "losers" in the game of school. To be sure, there are developmental factors at work here, as well as years of negative labeling (by self and others), and years of navigating in a very harsh win-lose culture that communicates that "Some of you matter and some of you don't." Distressingly, the gap between successful and unsuccessful students actually increases between 9th and 12th grades.

(18) Factors Associated with Resilience and Positive Life Chances

Resiliency is the capacity to achieve positive outcomes and life chances despite personal set-backs and adverse circumstances. Communities, families, schools, and classrooms can all create conditions that provide youth with a redundancy* of these opportunities.

- Stable, positive relationships with at least one caring adult ("I'm on your side and on your case.")

- High, realistic academic expectations and high levels of personalized support

- Experiences of personal competence and team mastery

- Positive family environment that reflects a warm, nurturing parenting style and includes both limit-setting and respect for the growing autonomy of adolescents

- Development of emotional intelligence and the ability to cope with stress and frustration effectively

- Religious or spiritual anchors that nurture meaning, altruism, and a larger purpose in life

*"Redundancy" means more than a variety of random opportunities. It involves intentional efforts to ensure that students experience multiple "hits" of the same opportunity over time and multiple opportunities to practice and demonstrate the same skills and competencies over time.

From their work with young people on the margins, Martin Brokenleg and Larry Bendtro have a created a framework for "reclaiming youth" based on four basic needs:[7]

3

How the drive to meet basic needs affects the individual

Basic Need	When need is met in positive ways, students feel...	When need is met in negative ways, students feel...	When need is unmet, students feel...
Belonging A sense of strong ties and bonding with the family and the larger community; a sharing of mutual acceptance and mutual concern	Attached Loving Friendly Intimate Gregarious Cooperative Trusting	Loyal to gang A craving for attention A craving for acceptance Promiscuous Clinging Attracted to cults Overly dependent	Unattended Guarded Rejected Lonely Aloof Isolated Distrustful
Mastery Competence; achievement; control over self and environment	Achievement oriented, successful, creative Problem solving-oriented Motivated Persistent Competent Adequate	A over-inflated sense of competence and control Arrogant Risk-seeking Overworked with workaholic tendencies The urge to cheat Skillful when engaging in delinquent behavior	Nonachievement oriented Oriented to failure Risk-avoiding Fearful of challenges Unmotivated Easily discouraged Inadequate
Independence Autonomy combined with responsibility and self-control; self-reliance; empowerment and control over one's self and one's own destiny	Autonomous Confident Assertive Responsible Internally controlled Self-disciplined Capable of leadership	Dictatorial Reckless, Urge to bully, intimidate Sexually exploitative Manipulative Rebellious Defiant of authority	Submissive Lack of confidence Inferior Irresponsible Helpless Undisciplined Easily led and influenced
Generosity Caring, empathy, and altruism; acceptance of responsibility for the welfare of others	Altruistic, caring Opent to sharing Loyal Empathetic Prosocial Supportive	Condescending Over-involved A sense of martyrdom Servile Exploited and used	Selfish, narcissistic Lack of affection Disloyal Hardened Antisocial Exploitative

(19) What Should We Know about How Adolescents Learn?

1. Adolescent learning should merge the concrete and abstract (formal operational thinking) as much as possible. It's important to remember that most adults and adolescents spend very little time engaged in abstract thought that is divorced from living and working in the concrete world. Thus critical thinking, an abstract ability, should be taught in a concrete context as much as possible. We also need to remember that text is abstract until and unless a student makes meaning of it by connecting it to what he knows and what he has experienced.

2. Students' learning preferences and styles become even more distinct as they get older. Struggling readers find it more and more difficult to slog through texts. Kids who thrive on "hands-on" learning but don't get the chance to learn this way may become restless, resistant, and reluctant. Only 23% of kids are linear-sequential learners.[8] These are the learners who are "book smart" and "test smart," with the ability to process large amounts of information quickly. This 23% of students becomes even more savvy at "doing school," while the majority of students find formal, abstract learning (if presented without a real-world context) boring and disconnected from their lives.

3. Knowledge needs to be relevant; hence student-centered learning (where students have more choices about what they learn or how they learn it, and more opportunities to link their own interests and experiences to classroom learning) becomes even more important for adolescents, who are always going to ask, "What does this have to do with me? Why do I need to know this? How can I personally express myself in this assignment?"

4. Knowledge is constructed socially and mediated conversations with adults are essential to move learning beyond what one already knows and can do. There is a need to process information and check it out with others, so cooperative, experiential, interactive learning works for a majority of kids.[9]

5. Adolescents get better at multitasking but sometimes overreach their capacity. ("I can listen to music, cruise the net, and do my homework at the same time!")

6. Adolescents are immersed in their own culture – they truly live in the here and now of their own lives. This is why history, for example, if it's not connected to their own world or feelings, is a challenging subject for most students. Inserting students' worlds into academic content gives you a better shot at reaching and teaching more kids effectively.

7. Adolescents question adult norms and beliefs—their radar is ultrasensitive to hypocrisy. They can make good arguments and examine the arguments of others critically. It is natural for young people to challenge rules and assumptions.

8. Young people gravitate toward controversy. They enjoy a thoughtful argument and like to discuss issues that don't have just one answer. Adolescents' thinking becomes more complicated. They can handle issues that have gray areas; in fact, kids like being challenged to dig around if the digging around makes meaning for them. Moral dilemmas, ethical questions, "big ideas" about life-and-death issues are extremely interesting to young people.

9. Students develop the capacity to hold multiple perspectives; they can use more sophisticated powers of reasoning to examine several perspectives at once rather than looking at problems as an either/or proposition.

10. Students like to create their own theories and test the theories of others.

11. The more "intelligences" students use in a learning experience, the more they will retain. Howard Gardner has defined these intelligences as verbal/linguistic, logical-mathematical, musical, spatial, kinesthetic, interpersonal, intrapersonal, and naturalist.[10] This principle also applies to the senses—the more multisensory the experience, the more students take in.

12. Activities that combine cooperation and healthy competition grab most kids' attention and focus. Thus team competition using small groups is an ideal learning structure.

13. Most adolescents love contests, games, puzzles, mysteries—most anything that begins as a problem. Whenever possible, try to "problematize" the curriculum.

14. Authentic assessment that has an audience is compelling to most adolescents. Think about sports, drama, band, chorus, the newspaper, art shows, peer education, tutoring, service learning—all of these activities have a real audience and involve a definite product or performance. Kids like to demonstrate what they know and can do.

15. Kids want and need to express themselves—to put their personal stamp on things. This is why courses we call electives are critical to a balanced curriculum.

(20) Developmentally Appropriate Practice—Teaching to Adolescents' Developmental Realities

Although educators win as many bad jargon awards as any other group of specialized professionals, "DAP" is actually a useful term, one that should become commonplace among high school staff. DAP means developmentally appropriate practice. Emerging from the field of early childhood education, this phrase is a way of describing the relationship between instruction and the specific stage of intellectual, physical, social, emotional, and ethical development within an individual child.

In other words, DAP is about linking appropriate learning experiences to the developmental stage that indicates what and how a student thinks and feels, what a student can do physically, and how she perceives and engages with people and the world around her. An important reminder about DAP is that a developmental stage of learning and readiness is informed by a child's chronological age and his life experience in his family, culture, immediate environment, and the school.

Good teaching is occurring when developmental considerations guide decisions about the appropriate learning environment and instructional activities for a particular child or children of a particular age. DAP devotees would say that developmental ages and stages should shape how teachers talk to kids, how teachers respond to various behaviors, and how teachers guide children through simple and complex learning experiences.

Here are a couple of examples that illustrate what developmentally appropriate practice is all about. Young children cannot recognize letters of the alphabet until they've had plenty of experiences discriminating one shape from another. Consequently, an early childhood teacher provides lots of opportunities for children to explore, identify, and sort two- and three-dimensional shapes. Other reading-readiness activities help children develop their imaginations and share stories about life beyond the immediate visible, physical space they can see and touch. This capacity to imagine something that cannot be seen is crucial for making meaning of the abstract symbols on a written page.

On the social side of things, young children need guided practice that helps them experience how to share, how to play fair, or how to sit in a circle quietly and listen to other children. These are all learned behaviors that become habits only when teachers notice, encourage, and talk with children about how they practice these behaviors on a daily basis. High school educators could learn a lot from watching the interactions between a preschool teacher and a four-year-old.

Why is any of this relevant to secondary education? Development doesn't stop when a child becomes fourteen. Rather, the opposite occurs. The intensity and pique of adolescence might, in fact, inspire us to be even more mindful of how we design learning environments and curricula that are more responsive to young people's intellectual, physical, social, emotional, and ethical development. When we overlook asking whether and how we engage in developmentally appropriate practice, we risk making high school students endure a lot of things that verge on the developmentally ridiculous. A few examples will suffice.

FROM DEVELOPMENTALLY QUESTIONABLE TO DEVELOPMENTALLY APPROPRIATE: A FEW EXAMPLES

School Start Time

Most high schools begin classes between 7:15 and 8:00 A.M. because of bus schedules and adult preferences to start early and leave early.

> **What's developmentally inappropriate?** Adolescents' biological clocks are different – their physiological rhythm of waking and sleeping is later to bed and much later to rise and be fully present.

> **What's more developmentally appropriate?** School start time would be closer to 9 A.M.

Emphasis on Teacher-Directed, Whole-Group Instruction

Teachers often determine most of what is taught and how it is learned, requiring all students to do the same thing the same way at the same time.

What's developmentally inappropriate? The desire for increasing autonomy, choice, and independence dominates the adolescent years just when learning in school becomes the most restricted. Most academic courses offer diminishing opportunities for personal expression and engagement with subject matter at the very time when adolescents are most eager to place a personal stamp on what they do. It is ironic that kindergartners usually have more choices and independent learning experiences in one day than a high school sophomore might experience in a week of 35 classes.

What's more developmentally appropriate? Balance whole group instruction with opportunities for students to pursue personal choices, interests, and independent explorations. Even when learning involves the whole group, provide opportunities for students to help make decisions about curricular content and how they go about learning it.

Treating Adolescents Like Adults

It's normal to fret about how best to prepare students for the harsher realities of life after high school. Our worries about students becoming too dependent on second chances can lead to the following declaration to students: "I need to treat you like adults and hold you accountable to adult standards. Otherwise, I'm not preparing you for the real world out there."

What's developmentally inappropriate? The irony is that we are most tempted to hang the adult label on the adolescents who exhibit the most unadult behaviors, especially when they haven't lived up to academic responsibilities. It's easy to get caught up in the "big scold" that's usually followed by the "adult sanction." It sounds something like this:

"I expect you to be an adult here, so I don't accept late papers. When you have a full-time job, there's no room for excuses. You better figure out now how to manage your time before you're out there in the real world. You're going to have to take a zero on these two assignments." Or, "You play, you pay. Next time study harder. This time it's an F. There are no retakes or second chances in the adult world out there."

The kids who haven't developed the maturity and sense of responsibility we expect of high school students test our patience and best behavior on a good day, much less on a day when we're already stressed. The problem is that the adult sanction of punitive grading reinforces irresponsible behavior—the student gets off the hook because he isn't held responsible for completing, correcting, or putting in more serious time and effort to demonstrate a satisfactory level of competence. The adult sanction sends another potentially damaging message to students who have the most trouble getting their act together; it communicates to these kids that we care more about punishing the irresponsible behavior than about helping them learn how to be better, more responsible students.

What's more developmentally appropriate? Regardless of legal rights, voting status, and increasing responsibilities, there are good reasons why the developmental stage of adolescence spans from age 11 or 12 to about 19 or 20. Maturity is incredibly personal, depending upon an adolescent's genetic predispositions, physical development, birth order, family circumstances, social experiences, cultural background, and life opportunities in and out of school. In addition, physical, emotional, intellectual, social, and ethical maturity develop at different rates within a single individual. It's only in the early to midtwenties that all of these aspects of self become fully integrated into an adult personality. High school is the laboratory where young people are learning how to manage their time and responsibilities; it's just that some students are better at this much sooner than others.

All of which is to say that it's a risky business to treat kids in high school as if they are already full-fledged adults. Adolescents are *becoming* adults; they are not adults yet. Being a teenager means constantly negotiating when you want to be treated like a kid or like an adult to get what you need. One of the biggest challenges for high school teachers is navigating back and forth between adult-to-adult and adult-to-kid learning experiences and communication modes. It's a fine line, and getting this right has a lot to do with knowing when our role is more parental and when it's more like that of a mentor or facilitator.

If we teach with the assumption that students are not adults quite yet, and recognize that the students we teach are at different stages of the maturity continuum, we have another choice. Instead of relying only on grade penalties and punitive responses, we can develop a sequence of consequences and interventions that say we are serious about insisting that students meet their academic responsibilities. Instructional support strategies can include making an academic plan to complete one's work, daily check-ins, learning new organizational and study strategies, revisions and retakes on important assignments and tests, tutoring, or early morning study sessions.

And for the zero completion gang who rarely experience the satisfaction of handing in quality work, there is always the friendly but firm call to arms: "Today's the day you and your mother agreed that you will not leave school until this work is completed. It matters to me that you pass this course. You put in the effort, we'll work on one thing at a time, and you'll get out of the hole. I'm confident you can do it." For kids who are immature, we need to keep asking the question, "What will help this student learn what it takes to become more responsible? More punishment or more guided support?"

High-Stakes Grading[11]

Test grades are final. If homework isn't handed in on time, it's a 0. A student's final grade is the cumulative average of all graded work, regardless of progress or later mastery in the semester.

What's developmentally inappropriate? The current "accountant" approach to grading belongs in the bookkeeper's office, not the classroom. In fact, where else, ever again in a person's life, will an average of test, quiz, and homework grades determine the quality and effectiveness of someone's performance? As a result of high-stakes grading, millions of high school students spend four years never completing a thing or experiencing mastery in the academic realm. High-stakes grading lets a lot of kids live in the land of the shoddy, where on-time behavior takes precedence over completion, where first-time performance is emphasized at the expense of revision and correction, and where the sheer quantity of graded tasks forfeits the deeper satisfaction of learning what it takes and what it feels like to master something difficult or produce quality work. High-stakes grading devalues the very qualities that help adolescents become lifelong learners and support the goal of competency in the workplace.

What's more developmentally appropriate? Eliminating obsessive grade calculations is not likely to happen in our lifetime. However, there are plenty of ways to make grading practices more developmentally appropriate.

- Weigh grades differently according to task and purpose. Give less weight to practice tasks; give more weight to assessments that illustrate working knowledge and understanding of a key set of skills and concepts. Example: When students are learning a new skill, practice tasks indicate that a student has or has not learned proficiently at some point. The purpose of practice tasks is not to give As to students who got it and Fs to students who didn't. Practice tasks give you feedback on where to go next and what to do to maximize learning for all of your students.

- Provide more time to complete fewer projects and assessments during a grading period; but make sure that these are the kinds of projects and assessments that require students to fully demonstrate in-depth understanding and application of what they are learning.

- Assess effort as well as performance—otherwise, many students will disconnect what they did or did not do from the grades they earn.

- Create opportunities for self-correction, revisions, and retakes as part of developing proficiency.

- Don't employ grades as a threat, punishment, or control lever—these tactics never work for kids who are struggling or have chronic problems turning in assignments or reading assigned materials.

- Help students develop their own goal-setting and self-assessment rubrics.

Final Thoughts about DAP

One of the greatest obstacles to successful instruction is treating students as a homogeneous group, rather than appreciating their developmental and cultural differences. By emphasizing differentiated learning strategies and providing differentiated support, teachers can accommodate differences in student interests, learning styles, abilities, and cultural experiences.

Teachers who engage in developmentally appropriate and culturally responsive teaching value the quality of resiliency in young people—the innate "self-righting" mechanism of individuals to transform and change—and believe in each student's capacity and desire to learn and succeed.[12] When we have a better understanding of students' developmental and cultural needs we are more likely to teach, talk, and discipline in ways that increase student motivation and cooperative behavior. Moreover, a greater understanding of what different groups of adolescents need to be successful invites us to take an unsentimental look at traditions, policies, and practices within our schools that may actually hinder rather than support a student's academic success. School faculties who are committed to reducing personal, social, and cultural barriers to learning and development are more likely to implement changes in classroom practice that reduce school failure and narrow the achievement gap among various groups of students.

(21) The Difference between Expectations and Standards

Setting and communicating high expectations that promote positive social norms and a culture of excellence is at the heart of teaching and learning. Ultimately, it is our attitudes toward young people and our beliefs about how they learn and how they can recover and change that will drive instruction and classroom management. Believing that "there's nothing wrong with you that what's right with you can't fix" produces markedly different student outcomes than the beliefs, "many of you won't be able to succeed in here and there's nothing I can do about it." It is our personal interest and support, feedback, encouragement, and inspiration that make the biggest difference for struggling students.

Current research that focuses on reducing problem behaviors and enhancing academic achievement and resiliency confirms the role that high behavioral and academic expectations play in the lives of adolescents. Holding high expectations, however, is about more than having high standards.

High expectations communicate your beliefs about what students are capable of doing and achieving; they convey your confidence in students' ability to be successful and let students know that their efforts will make a difference in their performance. High expectations are student centered; they are linked to the support and encouragement you provide so that all students can achieve some measure of academic success.

High standards, on the other hand, focus on subject matter content and skills, comparing and evaluating a student's performance in relation to that one standard of academic excellence. In addition, high standards presume that only some students will meet them, making stars of a few while many others inevitably fall short. Consequently, a lot of kids perceive standards as barriers that sort and separate them into groups of winners and losers.

Consider, for example, how more emphasis on high standards or more emphasis on high expectations can lead to very different outcomes. When a single standard of excellence drives assessment, students are evaluated on how well or poorly they measure up to that one standard—students get one shot to show their stuff. Students take a test, get a grade, look at the results for thirty seconds, and then move on to the next unit, regardless of how they perform. What message does this give the students who earn the Cs, Ds, and Fs? They might come to any of these conclusions: "I guess it doesn't really matter if I learn this or not;" "If I didn't learn it this time, I guess I never will;" "If I can't get an A or B, why put in a lot of effort?" or "I'm not good at anything in this class."

In contrast, when high expectations are at the center of assessment, teachers are more likely to communicate that all students are expected to achieve an acceptable standard of proficiency, mastering essential skills and competencies. For example, students might be required to complete a certain number of tasks that indicate proficiency or demonstrate mastery of key sections of a test, or polish one essay to high quality every quarter. Thus the big test is not the big marker of achievement. Some students may need more time, practice, or instruction to meet a standard of proficiency that you set for the whole class, but there is a big payoff for refusing to settle for failure or shoddy work. Everyone gets to feel the pride and pleasure of their own accomplishments.

If you believe that all students can succeed through their own efforts, you are more likely to create a learning environment that encourages all students to become successful learners. Expectations don't have to be dramatic or complicated, but they do become the mantras that students know will drive what happens in class.

Here are a few examples:

Expectations:

- I expect everyone to try to do your best and be your best.

- All of you can be successful learners in this class. I know you have what it takes to do well.

- You don't need to be friends with everyone, but I do expect you to be friendly with everyone.

- We all make mistakes and we can learn from them and right them.

- Sometimes you might make poor choices. And I'm confident that you can recover and get back on track.

- I expect all of you to pass this course. If you put in the effort, I can promise you will pass.

- Working with each other collaboratively is a big deal with me. It's something we will spend a lot of time doing, and I expect everyone to get pretty good at it.

- I expect all of us to treat each other with respect and decency.

- There will be times when you'll feel challenged and struggle a bit. That's normal and we'll get through it.

- I'm counting on everyone to encourage and support each other.

(22) Give Students High Support to Meet Your Expectations

High support provides students with a road map and an emotional compass to meet high expectations. It's the catalyst that can trigger an individual's positive motivation and meaningful engagement in learning. Meeting the developmental needs of adolescents is at the heart of support and encouragement.

Developmental Needs

- Physical and psychological safety to interact with others without fear of being harmed, hurt, embarrassed, or targeted

- Belonging, connection, and affection with peers and adults

- Voice to express one's own thoughts, feelings, and perspectives and affirm one's personal and group identities

- Freedom and independence to take risks, discover, explore, experiment, direct one's actions, and control aspects of one's life

- Choice to explore options, make one's own decisions, and engage in learning that is personally relevant and meaningful

- Creativity and imagination to produce, present, or perform something of one's own, and activate hope and confidence to build a future of one's own making

- Power and mastery to achieve, contribute, and succeed in school and life

In fact, the feelings students bring to any learning experience are the greatest determiner of whether they will learn or not. What you do and say has the power to change how students feel and what they choose to do. Think about teacher support in this way:

Adolescents' Developmental Needs	→	**High Teacher Support** When teachers provide support to meet these needs, most kids feel positively motivated	→	**Learning Can Happen**
Adolescents' Developmental Needs	→	**Low Teacher Support** When teachers don't provide support to meet these needs, most kids are likely to feel resistant, angry, hostile, rejected, alienated, invisible, or uninterested.	→	**Lea~~rn~~ing Ca~~n H~~appen**
Adolescents' Developmental Needs	→	**Students with High Motivation** Some students are the exception – their needs are met or unmet in ways that spark so much personal drive that teacher support may not be as crucial for learning	→	**Learning Can Happen**

What You Can Do

Emotional security is the foundation of self-concept and self-efficacy. Teachers can support teens' healthy development by:

- Offering reassurance

- Offering praise and positive feedback and using criticism sparingly

- Encouraging students to share their interests and demonstrate their talents

- Being patient

- Encouraging independence

- Keeping lines of communication open

- Encouraging friendships

(23) What Does High Personalized Support Look Like?

The idea of teaching as delivering content will work most of the time for 30–40% of kids. But for the vast majority of adolescents, it's only half the job. The other half of teaching is about creating the environment and providing the kind of support that young people need in order to learn and mature. For example, student self-efficacy is enhanced when teachers[13]:

- Create opportunities for different kinds of performance accomplishments that students successfully complete. (Every teacher has his own laundry list of verbs that frame various tasks that students do.)

- Model the behaviors that you want students to use in class and do the learning tasks that you expect students to complete.

- Communicate messages of hope and confidence in a student's present and future.

- Maintain a supportive low-stress/low-threat learning environment.

It's understandable that high support might be construed as coddling or viewed as that "touchy-feely" stuff that counselors are supposed do with kids. High school teachers are more inclined to live by a fairly narrow definition of support that's about helping kids in academic trouble; but this misses the mark. All students need to feel supported emotionally.

High support isn't about supplying a little boost here and there or adding something extra once in a while. It's about the hundreds of little things teachers do everyday to:

- Create a learning environment that meets students' emotional needs for safety, belonging, freedom, respect, recognition, and power—this has to be in place before many students will be ready to learn.

- Provide students with the tools and "know-how" that will help them express and manage their emotions and use them productively.

- Develop relationships and personal connections that invite students to see you as their ally and partner who will help them learn and grow.

- Provide the kinds of encouragement and support appropriate for different kinds of kids.

- Provide the tools and "know-how" for every student to become more "school smart."

What would you prioritize as your most important behavioral and academic goals and expectations? What kinds of support will help students meet them? (See chart on following page.)

	What behavioral goals and expectations do you have for every student?	What kinds of support from you will help all students meet these expectations?	What kinds of outside support will help all students meet these expectations?	How would coddling look different from effective support?
BEHAVIORAL	1. 2. 3.	1. 2. 3.	1. 2. 3.	1. 2. 3.
	What academic goals and expectations do you have for every student?	What kinds of support from you will help all students meet these expectations?	What kinds of outside support will help all students meet these expectations?	How would coddling look different from effective support?
ACADEMIC	1. 2. 3.	1. 2. 3.	1. 2. 3.	1. 2. 3.

(24) The Feeling-Learning Connection

"Emotion is very important to the education process because it drives attention, which drives learning and memory. It's impossible to separate emotion from other activities of life. Don't try."
– Robert Slywest, A Celebration of Neurons

Brain-based research confirms the causal relationship between emotions and learning.[14] How students feel will determine whether they choose to be receptive or resistant to learning, whether they use their emotional energy to listen or to draw attention somewhere else.

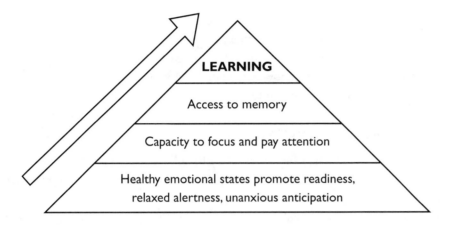

When students feel safe, settled, calm, and purposeful, they are able to balance their feelings with their ability to think. This sense of balance allows them to use emotional energy to focus and pay attention. Students must be able to focus in order to remember. And without access to memory, students are unable to learn. For adolescents, this is no easy task in the best of circumstances, and there's an irony here. By educating their hearts, by welcoming their feelings and emotional energy into the room, we are better able to educate their minds. On the other hand, when students are out of balance and feel emotionally flooded, it's hard for them to focus on anything except the unsettled feelings they're experiencing. When students' emotional needs are ignored or trivialized, their feelings of anger, hurt, hostility, and resistance are going to rule the day.

Embracing this aspect of teaching requires the courage, honesty, and generosity to see adolescents as they really are, not as adults would wish them to be to meet their own needs of comfort and convenience. This also means accepting that adolescence is messy, for both the student who is experiencing it and the adults who are supporting students through this stage in their lives. Students want to believe that you're on their side, that you are there for them, especially when they're having a tough time.

(25) Personalized Learning and Support Increases Motivation

In a society where traditional authority is increasingly ineffective at home, at school, and at work, motivating students in ways that invite their cooperation, good will, and interest in learning is probably the most important and challenging role of educators. Any teacher will tell you that unmotivated students are the toughest kids to reach and teach. Yet, as much as we'd like to, we can't really motivate others. The only person you can motivate is yourself. What you can do is create conditions that help increase a student's desire to learn or persevere when discouraged. (See *Getting Classroom Management RIGHT*, Chapter 7 for tips on conferencing with discouraged and unmotivated students.)

Motivation—the "natural capacity to direct energy in pursuit of a goal"[11]—is an internal quality driven by a person's feelings, thoughts, beliefs, and experiences. However, parents' and teachers' affection, respect, and support are powerful external conditions that can activate and enhance a student's internal motivation.

Students' motivation to learn depends on whether they perceive learning tasks as achievable and important. One of the challenges of teaching diverse learners is designing student work that takes into account students' prior knowledge and developmental learning needs, and at the same time seeks to capture their personal interests.

Think of motivation as a combination of two things:

1. A student's expected outcome (Am I more likely to fail or succeed at accomplishing this goal or task? Will I derive a sense of satisfaction when the goal or task is completed?)

2. The degree to which a student values the goal, the relationship, the task, or the process of accomplishing it.[16]

Here's a handy formula that captures the theory of motivation:

	Student's prediction and capacity to accomplish the task successfully
x	**Student's value and interest in the goal, relationship, task, or process of completing the task**
=	**Student's Motivation**

A couple of examples will illustrate how this works:

> *Shandra is a whiz kid with lots of school smarts. Her capacity to accomplish the task is a ten. But Shandra places no value on and has no interest in this particular science course. She has a hostile relationship with the teacher and has no big goals driving her future plans. At this point, she really doesn't care. Her value and interest in completing the task equals zero. 0 × 10 is 0. There is no way Shandra is going to complete this task successfully.*

> *José, by contrast, wants very much to get a soccer scholarship and knows that he will need to pass his courses, pass the state exit exam, and have an acceptable transcript. He struggles with reading, and writing is downright painful. His capacity to complete a quality essay in English is a four. But his big goal of a*

soccer scholarship and the academic support he's receiving from his teacher help override his struggles with reading and writing. So the value he places on the task, goal, and relationship is a 10. 4 × 10 = 40. José will complete the task and is likely to persevere until the quality of his work is acceptable.

Big goals and hopes for the future are huge internal motivators. Students can tolerate a lot of boredom or tough it out when they've found a compelling reason to "just get it done."

On a lighter note, the movie *Erin Brockovich* brilliantly illustrates the role motivation plays in learning. Imagine Erin Brockovich in high school. (She's the one painting her nails in the back of the room with no books and no homework, the one who can't leave high school fast enough.)

Now fast forward to the scene in which a woman from the larger law firm looks through Brockovich's depositions and tells her that the data required for the lawsuit aren't there. Brockovich promptly begins to recite every client's name, address, phone number, and diseases. She's done the research. She knows the environmental problem inside and out. This work and these clients matter to her and her power as a learner has broken free. Brockovich is finally able to match her wits and intelligence to something she cares about, and that makes all the difference.

From the Collaborative for Academic, Social, and Emotional Learning (CASEL) newsletter comes another key finding related to motivation. A recent study examining predictors of school performance found that a student's "perceived competence" is more influential in boosting achievement in mathematics and reading than "student engagement" is. "Students who are confident about their academic competence—who feel they are up to an academic task—do better than students who doubt their ability, even when actual ability is the same for both." The study suggests that building students' healthy self-awareness of strengths and expressing confidence in their ability to do well can improve students' academic performance.[13]

Kids we describe as "self-motivated" have lots of things going for them.

- They want to please parents and other adults.

- They are very comfortable around teachers; they know how to produce what a teacher wants. Teachers reward them for these behaviors. They like them back.

- They have large and small goals that drive what they do everyday. They can tell you, "I want to succeed at this because. . . ."

- They have already experienced lots of successes in and out of school, so they bring a high level of competence and confidence to their ability to "get it done well."

- Prior successes increase their motivation to fully engage in learning situations—they can play the "WIIFM" (what's in it for me?) game pretty easily and they will keep searching until they find something that sustains their effort and perseverance— whether it's the topic, the task itself, the process, or the people.

Unmotivated students, on the other hand, often experience a combination of failure and disconnection that reinforces an internal message not to try and not to engage. Alan Mendler, author of *Motivating Students Who Don't Care*, shares a set of understandings that can guide our work with unmotivated students.[18]

- All students are capable of learning when they have the academic and personal tools to be successful.

- Students are inherently motivated to learn, but learn to be unmotivated when they repeatedly fail.

- Learning requires risk taking, so classrooms need to be safe places physically and psychologically.

- All students have a basic need to belong, to be competent, and to influence what happens to them. Motivation to learn most often occurs when these basic needs are met.

- High self-esteem should not be a goal, but rather a result that comes from mastery of challenging tasks.

- High motivation for learning in school most often occurs when adults treat students with respect and dignity.

Mendler also suggests some key strategies that can support a positive change in attitude and achievement over time.

1. Emphasize **effort** (ability + effort = achievement).

2. Create **hope** by building the student's expectation of success and communicating your confidence in the student to succeed.

3. Respect a student's desire for **power** and control (choice and voice).

4. Make a **personal connection** with the student every day.

5. **Find out more about the student**, her interests, family background, and learning profile. ("If you can't learn the way I teach, I can teach the way you learn.")

6. **Identify learning gaps** and address them immediately.

7. **Express your enthusiasm, encouragement, and support**. Unmotivated kids rarely experience someone who makes a positive fuss over them or what they're doing. Your cheerleading spirit can rub off.

(26) Different Support for Different Students

Different students need different doses and different kinds of support at different points in time. For highly interested, high-achieving students, support may mean encouraging them to explore careers where people spend a lifetime working in the discipline you teach. You might tap into their enthusiasm by directing them to other resources or suggesting independent projects that give them an opportunity to share their expertise with the class.

For students who struggle academically, support might involve explicit teaching of cognitive strategies that will help them organize, plan, focus, and study. In other words, your support may focus on helping students to become more "school smart."

Developing a trusting and caring relationship is often the most critical first step toward accepting support from an adult at school. When you show that you're interested in getting to know students personally, they may start to believe that they can count on your positive regard for them. If they begin to trust that you will listen first, before judging or disciplining, they are more likely to invest the time and effort to do well.

For students resistant to seeing themselves as successful students, support may first mean validating their life experiences outside of school. Inviting students to tell their stories gives you a way to acknowledge the hard knocks they've experienced and encourage them to tell you things they're proud of in their lives. Time to listen gives you a chance to empathize with their pain and affirm what they care about. Some young people may never have talked with an adult in school who can help them to make connections between the skills they use to manage and navigate their personal lives and ways that they can use these same skills and abilities to succeed at school. Mirror the inner qualities you see in them that reveal their capacity to meet the challenges they face. Resistant students may also need your support in reframing their images of themselves.

This doesn't mean asking students to trade one identity for another as a requisite for academic success. That approach will only intensify resistance and resentment. It does involve giving students feedback and encouragement that can help them build a more inclusive picture of themselves, one in which they can be successful students without giving up loyalty to friends or sacrificing their sense of self and their racial and cultural identity.

For kids who really think school stinks, normalizing the stance of being a reluctant or resistant learner can reassure students that they're not failures for life, just because school is not working for them right now. Share stories about people who hated school but found a lifelong passion despite earlier setbacks. Or bring up examples of people who turned their lives around in early adulthood or who failed many times in life before finally achieving personal success.

Support isn't always easy for you to give or for students to accept—a negative school history can make kids justifiably suspect of any teacher's motives and intentions. Timing and pacing can make a big difference for kids who may be hesitant to believe that you are really there for them. Be conscious of a student's readiness or reluctance to be engaged with you, with other students, and with the subject matter. Small doses of support over a few months can be more effective in the long run than intrusive attempts to get everything out in the open and push too soon. Hard-to-reach students need to see you in action for a while before they will risk making connections and accepting your efforts to support them. Finally, it's good to remind yourself and communicate to these students that every small improvement and every sign of progress spells SUCCESS.

CHAPTER 4

Meet Adolescents' Cultural and Developmental Needs

 Practice 7: Affirm diversity in your classroom.

(27) Affirm Diversity in Your Classroom

Although affirmation, acceptance, and appreciation for diversity are cornerstones of a *Making Learning REAL* classroom, these principles are easier to talk about than to put into practice. Developing the competence, comfort, and sensitivity to teach so many different students effectively can inspire and overwhelm us. For young people, choosing to act on these principles can conflict with the clannishness of adolescent subcultures and the pressures of growing up in a "put-down" society where one student's self-esteem may come at the expense of another's. Adolescents bring equal doses of fear and fascination to their growing awareness of the diversity that surrounds them.

This mix of vulnerabilities and attitudes about diversity can build a wall of stony silence among various groups in the classroom. Or we can make the classroom a safe haven where differences are recognized as resources and assets that can add a richness and vibrancy to any learning experience. Several things can help us better appreciate, learn about, and teach to the differences among our students. First, we need to know ourselves. Teaching is highly personal and subjective. Thus, we need to be aware of the personal and cultural perspectives that shape who we are in the classroom. The more we know about ourselves, the better we can bridge the multiple and different worlds that we and our students inhabit.

Second, we need to know our students and communicate our interest in knowing more about their unique cultural experiences. Knowing our students well also means learning more about how differences of color, culture, class, character, gender, and genes (the physical traits, personality, and intelligences we inherit) influence adolescents' experience of schooling and how they learn.

Third, we need to know the culture of our school, taking a closer look at how the dominant culture of most American high schools continues to benefit some groups of students while disadvantaging others. For students who perceive themselves as culturally different from the high school norm or whom we perceive as culturally different from that norm, high school life can feel particularly discouraging.

Finally, we need to develop a bigger toolbox of strategies and expertise that can help us become more culturally responsive teachers. Specifically, how do we help normalize the vast range of differences among adolescents? How can we teach more effectively to these differences? And how can we help students better understand and "appreciate how individual and group differences complement each other and make the world a much more interesting place?"[1]

(28) Know Yourself and Know Your Students

"To be effective teachers, you must be fully aware of who you are. What baggage (your ideas of race, gender, class, and so on) do you bring to the classroom? Before you can be 'real' with your students, you must 'deal' with yourselves."[2]

Our perceptions of reality—what we take in through all of our senses, what we select to respond to out of everything that comes our way—depend on our identity lenses. Our lenses determine the way we make sense of what we see. Take 60 seconds, and without stopping to think, write down all the words that identify and describe who you are:

_____

_____

_____

_____

_____

Look at your list and look for words or phrases that are associated with any of the following aspects of your identity:

- your race, ethnicity, culture

- your core values—the beliefs, things, and ideas you care about the most

- your gender and sexual orientation

- your physical appearance, abilities, limitations, or illnesses

- your past or current socioeconomic status

- your past or current family roles and status

- your intellectual qualities, interests, and learning preferences

- your past or current educational status

- your sense of humor

- your experiences of personal trauma

- your age

- your general emotional state, personality attributes or temperament

- your friendship or partner relationship

- your avocational passions/hobbies/leisure activities

- your past or current work status/ profession

- your religious affiliation or spirituality

- your country of origin, your regional or community affiliation

- your political affiliation

- any other groups to which you belong by birth, by your family background, by choice

These identity lenses help define who we are to ourselves. They affect how we communicate and interact with students and colleagues. They also influence how others define us. Put simply, these lenses shape what we experience in our lives every single day.

While some aspects of your self-identity are permanent, other aspects may vary according to the privileges, disadvantages, passions, and stressors you experience at any given time in your life. Some lenses may change or shift in importance over time. You might choose to keep some aspects of your identity hidden from others. And there may be some descriptors you didn't list because they don't feel important to you, even though they may be obvious to others.

When you think about your identity lenses, which ones have the most influence on who you are as a person and a teacher? People claim different lenses as part of their core identity and there's nothing right or wrong about valuing any one aspect of your identity over another. No one's unique set of lenses are better or worse than anyone else's. It's also important to remember that every lens carries with it a collection of perspectives and biases that affect the classroom decisions you make every day—from the texts and materials you select, to the learning experiences you value, to the kinds of kids you're most comfortable teaching.

Biases are not all bad—they reflect our passions as well as our prejudices. However, becoming conscious of our biases can help us adjust our teaching practices in ways that foster balance, fairness, and equity. For me, this meant teaching students very differently from the way that I personally learn best. As a school kid, putting a book in my hands was the window to learning just about anything. Yet, through my teacher preparation I became aware that this learning preference is the comfort place for less than a quarter of all learners. So I deliberately set out to learn how to teach in ways that emphasized "hands-on" experiences as well as more reflective learning tasks.

A few examples can help illustrate how biases influence our views of students, teaching, and learning, with the caveat that the particular biases mentioned are not necessarily associated with all teachers who might fit the description in the example. If I'm a math teacher who came to the educational profession after a lucrative business career, I might be more intentional about exposing students to a variety of career paths linked to the world of numbers. By contrast, the algebra teacher down the hall who's spent thirty years in a classroom may not even think about math in a context beyond four walls and a math book.

If I were a very successful honors student who loves high school, I might know very little about young people who hate school and struggle to get through four years of it. On the other hand, if high school were an alienating experience for me, I might go out of my way to make connections with the kids who are labeled as loners, losers, and outsiders.

If I am a social studies teacher with a master's degree in Women's Studies, I might include gender perspectives in all of my courses, while other faculty may never even highlight women in history. If I am a gay man, I might have a keener eye for choosing literature that addresses all kinds of issues around tolerance and exclusion. On the other hand, if I grew up in a culturally conservative community, I might avoid choosing any literary works that might be deemed controversial.

Our identity lenses can also affect the quality of our relationships with different people. When we encounter someone who shares similar aspects of identity (physically, culturally, emotionally, socially, intellectually), we are likely to feel an immediate sense of rapport and affinity with that person.[3] Think about the kids you are drawn to, the kids with whom you feel the greatest affinity. Who are they? What is it about these kids that creates special connections?

Parker Palmer, in his book *The Courage to Teach*, describes good teachers as those who possess "the capacity for connection."[4] Imagine creating a space that welcomes students' whole selves into the classroom—a safe space that invites students to express and share important aspects of their identity without fear of embarrassment, condescension, or rejection. As teachers, the more conscious we are of all aspects of our identity, the more open we can be to seeking many different points of connection with students. We might find ourselves continually asking, "What is it I like about this kid that I see in myself or that I see in those I love and respect?" The connectedness we feel with another person also tends to prompt positive assumptions and images of him or her and elicit more supportive, accepting, and forgiving responses toward this individual.

The opposite is also true. Perceiving others as immutably different from ourselves can trigger negative assumptions and feelings of discomfort, mistrust, and fear. These feelings can lead to physical and emotional distancing, and perhaps even contribute to negative stereotyping of all people whom we perceive to be different in the same way.

Sometimes our lack of awareness can drive obvious differences underground. Teachers will often declare to students and colleagues, "I don't see color in my classroom—I treat all students alike." In school settings, you're also likely to hear, "I don't treat boys and girls any differently" or "I don't care where you're from or who your parents are—when you come into this classroom you're all the same."

However well intentioned, these sentiments deny the fact that students do experience school differently as a consequence of race, gender, class, and other key aspects of their identity. In *Multicultural Education in Middle and Secondary Classrooms*, Rasool and Curtis note that this denial can create psychological walls between students and teachers, making it difficult to connect with students whose identity is culturally different from their own.[5] When teachers neither notice nor appreciate students' multiple identities, kids can easily pick up the message that, "You don't see me for who I really am."

When young people experience messages of invisibility repeatedly in their lives, "You don't see me" can turn pretty quickly into "You don't want to see me—maybe something's wrong with me." During adolescent identity formation, the absence of positive recognition and images of who you are—through direct affirmation or through the faces you see on TV and in the movies, the characters you read about, the people you study, the adults who work with you—can affect your development. What's worse, though, for many young people, is the experience of being bombarded with negative images and stereotypes that target groups with whom students may identify most strongly—racial groups and ethnic cultures, newly arrived immigrant groups, poor people, religious minority groups, or gays and lesbians.

Kids cope with assaults on their identity in different ways at school. Some suffer in silence. Other students create a bifurcated identity that takes on a dominant culture persona at school and replaces it with their home culture identity as soon as they leave school. This strategy often comes at the cost of "always feeling weird and never fitting in anywhere," as one student put it. Poor and working class students are likely to be mistrustful of adult authority, especially when it's heavy-handed, and will often choose defiance as a way of standing up for themselves. Young people who see themselves as members of "out-groups" at school may turn to ridiculing "in-groups."

Sometimes, as a matter of self-protection, a student will reject learning and the values (i.e., being successful at school) of adults and peers within the dominant culture who convey their dislike or disapproval of all things different from conventional white middle class norms and preferences. Herbert Kohl calls this stance, "not-learning."

Not-learning tends to take place when someone has to deal with unavoidable challenges to her or his personal and family loyalties, integrity, and identity. In such situations, there are forced choices and no apparent middle ground. To agree to learn from a stranger who does not respect your integrity causes a major loss of self. The only alternative is to not-learn and reject their world.[6]

More than anything else, adolescents want to feel normal and be seen as normal. They are pre-occupied in the paradoxical search for a unique identity and a sense of connection with others "just like me." A gay colleague shared what his experience was like in high school.

> *I wanted my teachers to respect and appreciate all of me, not just the achiever/leader part of me that I brought to school. I kept asking, 'Am I normal?' It would have meant so much to me if teachers had pointed out, in a positive, joyful way, the remarkable differences among people we read about and talked about, especially people who broke away from the stereotypes of who they were supposed to be and what they were supposed to do. It would have made such a difference if teachers would have shared stories and examples of people who truly represented all of us—men, women, people of all races and cultures, gays and straights, people with different families, religions, jobs, and education. If teachers would have just been a little more conscious of this, I would have felt such relief. I could have said to myself, 'Okay, I can fit in here. There is a place for me with the differences I bring. There are other people like me she finds worth noticing and discussing.'*

> *With my peers, it was the same deal. I wouldn't have felt so alone if teachers had reassured us that being different was normal—that there were lots of ways that kids were different from each other, the same way there were common experiences that we all shared growing up. If we had known a little more about each other—if teachers had let us know more often that the differences we brought to class made us much more interesting and made us all a better group—I think our acceptance of each other would have felt easier and more real.*

(29) Know Your School and The Dominant Culture That Shapes It

Only when we acknowledge that most high schools espouse a fairly narrow set of cultural norms, values, and traditions can we go about creating high school experiences that better serve all of our students. Sometimes it's just a matter of asking some really simple, but critical questions: "Which students get recognized and rewarded? Do the things we teach and do here reflect the needs and interests of all of our students and families, just some of our students and families, or somebody else's students altogether? Do any of our practices and policies favor some groups of students and harm others? Do any of our practices increase separation and divisiveness among student groups?"

Four brief stories illustrate how paying attention can make all the difference between good practices and bad ones.

1. Two teachers in a dialogue group taught the second year of a two-year algebra course for lower-track students. As designed by the department chair, the course was a series of unrelated abstract topics with no practical applications whatsoever. Students who generally performed well in year one (where the curriculum included lots of hands-on experiences and practical problem solving) performed miserably in year two. Only a fraction of these students went on to take geometry.

    As these teachers described their students' frustrations and their own frustrating attempts to change the course, several teachers had a collective "Aha!" One person remarked, "You've been griping about this for four years. How long do you think it would have taken to get this course changed if it was a class full of AP students with involved parents?" The grim contrast between whose needs get attended to and whose needs get neglected sparked a healthy outrage. The group rallied other teachers to the cause, prepared a course change recommendation, met with the principal and department chair, and redesigned the course by the next semester. In the process, they changed how they would teach the course and changed their expectations of students. They took on the goal of preparing every student to take geometry.

2. Another high school was confronting the fact that year after year, student leaders came from the same academic track and the same neighborhoods. So what did they do? Students and teachers personally invited kids attending summer school to be part of their Student Leadership training team. This one decision completely altered the composition of student leaders and led to an annual campaign to recruit student leaders who more accurately represented all groups within the school.

3. I worked with students and faculty in a large urban high school where a majority of students were recent immigrants from Southeast Asia and Central America. For years, the school fielded a losing football team where only a handful of fans showed up. Finally the school spirit squad had sense enough to ask students why they didn't come out in big numbers to field the team or watch the games. A lot of kids shared that they had no interest in football at all. What they wanted were more opportunities to play soccer and ping-pong. The happy solution? The school stopped trying to make square pegs fit into

round holes. They abandoned varsity football, enlarged their soccer program, and established intramural and inter-high school ping-pong leagues.

4. In a high school that takes great pride in its monthly assemblies and celebrations sponsored by various ethnic clubs, the social studies department decided to stage an annual medieval fair that highlighted European life in the 15th century. As it was being conceived, no one raised questions about requiring all world history students to participate in a school-wide event that drew attention to one cultural group at the exclusion of all others. Four years later, there is open discussion and some excitement about making this event one that celebrates the life and culture of groups across the continents during this period of history.

It would be easy to assume that high schools now create opportunity and provide greater access for those who don't belong to the dominant culture. The opposite is true. High schools tend to reinforce low self-worth among students of color and non-native English speakers.[7] Furthermore, the achievement gap between students of higher and lower socioeconomic status is greater by the end of high school than it is for incoming ninth graders.[8] Class remains the most influential determiner of academic success in high school.

(30) How Does Privilege Work in High School?

High schools, in particular, are laden with unspoken rules and assumptions about the right way to behave, the right way to speak, the right way to get respect and power, and the right way to learn and be tested. These rules and assumptions are part of the "hidden curriculum" of every high school, although you won't find most of them in an official school handbook. Rather, these unwritten codes reflect the values and dominant culture of the people who make the rules. Historically, high school rule makers reflect the norms of the educated upper-middle-class families.

Generally, students who reflect these norms physically, socially, and intellectually get more attention, more encouragement, more resources, better teachers, a more engaging curriculum, and more critical and creative learning experiences. Most structures, practices, and activities in high school are designed to support the success and achievement of this group over other groups.

Taken for granted privileges are all too obvious to people who don't have them. Yet, educators and parents from the dominant culture are often reluctant to acknowledge how policies and practices that favor some students will, by definition, disadvantage others.

Advanced Placement courses and the "honors track" illustrate how dominant culture privileges can operate on overt and covert levels. In many high schools, it is assumed that parents are at least familiar with the courses students are taking and will play an active role in helping their children succeed in advanced courses—whether it's editing and proofing a paper, taking time to discuss a project, or ensuring that their kids have the right supplies, books, and gear at their fingertips. Upper-track students are expected to manage multiple tasks seamlessly and "chunk" their work into discrete tasks that build on one another. It's assumed that students can find all

4

the resources they need easily and use them effectively. Most important, when students are experiencing difficulties, it is assumed that they can talk with teachers comfortably or seek other students to study with. All of these behaviors reflect habits, family values, and expectations associated with upper-middle-class educated families.

Over the years, I've talked with hundreds of students and adults who saw themselves as culturally different from the majority of their peers in advanced classes. Here's what they have to say about what it was like for them in advanced and upper-level courses:

From a young man who recently emigrated from Cambodia:

"I didn't know other kids in the class while they all seemed to be friends. If I didn't know something, it was hard to ask them. I didn't want to feel stupid."

From a Mexican young woman:

"My friends thought I was crazy to take this class. In a way I had to pretend I wasn't me. It was like somebody else was taking this class, speaking and acting in a foreign language."

From a white working-class young man:

"I don't have a computer at home so it's hard to keep up. I have a job, too. I had to drop one AP class because I didn't have time to do all the reading. I felt so different from everyone else, like I wasn't really good enough to be here. Sometimes it felt like everyone else knew what the teacher was talking about except me."

From an African-American young man:

"I constantly felt like I had to prove that I belonged in this class even though I knew I was smart. Other kids kept looking at me as if they were waiting for me to drop out. It was hard to speak because I was so afraid of making a mistake. Who needs that? No wonder my friends won't take AP classes."

From a Puerto Rican young woman:

"As soon as people heard my name in class I was different to them—and Spanish wasn't even my first language growing up. What was I doing in advanced science classes? Nobody came right out and said this but I knew that they were thinking it. I hated that I had to wear this label when the white kids didn't have to wear any."

From a young woman from Guyana:

"My parents had to push people at my high school so I could be in advanced classes. English was my first language, but everyone assumed that I couldn't speak English well because I was dark skinned and from a different country. No one ever bothered to ask what my education was like before I moved here."

(31) Countering Hidden Privilege

One absolute about high school is that no student feels confident and on top of things three days in a row. On the other hand, the fears about fitting in and doing well don't feel quite so daunting when kids feel supported by friends and adults at school. When I asked these students what kinds of support from teachers and the school helped them succeed and what kind of support they wished they had had, some common themes emerged:

- It was helpful when teachers made an effort to check in with them instead of assuming that they would go to a teacher and ask for help. Countless students remarked that the rule of thumb in upper-track classes was, "If you have a problem, see me." For many students, this expectation of assertiveness felt awkward and uncomfortable because it was so different from the way they were taught to relate to adults at home. One student said, "When I was having trouble writing essays the way the teacher wanted them written, I was always hoping he would ask me to come in and work with him on my writing. There were times when the written comments on my papers just didn't make sense to me."

- Students say how much they would have liked to hear from former students who were just like them—students who could give them a "heads up" about what to expect and offer tips on how to survive.

- Students of color often expressed sadness and anger when pointing out how seldom they ever had teachers of color who taught them upper-level courses. Students felt frustrated that so many of their teachers couldn't understand why many ethnic minority students see being smart and being "good at school" as a "white thing." One young man remarked, "Take a look around. Most of the teachers, administrators, upper-track students, and parents you see in school are all white. My coach is black—how's that for stereotyping? What I wanted was a black physics teacher." In this discussion, students never ran out of ideas for how to invite a more diverse cross section of men and women into their schools who could share their career pathways and successful lives with young people.

- Words of reassurance that they really could do the work felt particularly crucial to these students. When they felt lost or overpowered by their peers, they longed for words of confidence and a boost of encouragement.

- They wanted teachers to truly understand what it took for them to make it in their classes. None of these kids ever said, "I want my AP teacher to cut me some slack." What they did say is how much it meant to them when a teacher invited them to talk about how it was going for them day in and day out, what was hard to manage, what was getting easier.

Students were deeply grateful when teachers took the time to talk to them privately and acknowledged the sacrifices and efforts they were making to hang in.

- Many students said that they wished they could have taken fewer courses during a semester—fewer, but more difficult classes. Students felt that learning the ropes of doing well took so much longer than they ever anticipated. Many said that they would have learned more if they could have successfully completed fewer more difficult courses than ending up with a mediocre record in six mediocre courses. Kids who worked long hours or were slow readers felt they could have done much better at juggling home, work, and school if they had had more time to study during the school day. Some students said that they never even knew they could take courses in the summer if they hadn't failed anything. Many students would have been willing to adjust summer job schedules to set aside mornings for a course.

- Many students shared stories of not having their academic act together until the second half of high school and didn't want to be written off. "Just because I messed up in the beginning doesn't mean I'm always going to mess up. Sometimes I needed a new start."

Other ways to counter the advantages that some students bring to class include teaching students the explicit codes and rules that are part of being "school smart." This can be as simple as helping a student figure out where to sit to maximize alertness, or as complex as learning how to skim a book or chapter when you don't have time to read the entire assignment carefully.

In some high schools where advanced courses are open to all students, faculty and volunteers facilitate study groups to ensure that all students have access to the resources that will help them learn successfully. Other schools have developed mentoring programs where students of color meet regularly in support groups with a mentor who is from their own cultural background. These groups become a sanctuary where students can share success stories, discuss their difficulties, problem solve together, and support one another.

Recently, while discussing the challenges that some kids experience in upper-level courses, a teacher shared her reservations about providing too much support. She said, "I worry about coddling kids and not making them accountable to real-life expectations. It was good for me when I was in school to feel a little snowed under and have to figure things out for myself. I had to make some hard choices at times and I learned to deal with 'no excuses' deadlines." I invited her (and the rest of the group piped in) to make a list of all the habits, family traditions and routines, resources, special activities, and types of adult-child interactions that had prepared her to meet the challenges of difficult courses with her head up and her feet on the ground. We stopped at item forty-three, stunned at how easy it was to generate an exhaustive list of assets that gifted her with unflagging self-discipline and encouraged her to take on any intellectual challenge. Here's the list:

1. I had to do homework every night after supper.

2. My parents always told me I could accomplish anything.

3. My parents have friends who all have professional jobs.

4. I have always been expected to go to college.

5. I have played the piano and taken lessons for many years.

6. My parents read to me since I was a baby.

7. Everyone in my family reads for pleasure.

8. Being on time was drilled into me as a kid.

9. If I wanted to do something that was a little weird or different, if I could defend it and had a plan, I could do it.

10. Most of my friends took honors and AP classes, so everyone I hung out with did a ton of homework.

11. My parents made sure they met my teachers.

12. People bought me books and educational toys that I could play with—I knew how to have fun playing or just being by myself.

13. I had a regular schedule for doing chores at home.

14. I was not allowed to work on weeknights during the school year.

15. I used a weekly planner during high school.

16. I was on the volleyball team throughout high school.

17. There was a family calendar at home.

18. My parents are big list makers.

19. Both my parents went to college.

20. On vacations we traveled to new places and the kids always got to pick some of the things we did.

21. I watched my mother bring home work from the office.

22.   Almost everyone I knew went to college.

23.   My parents knew my friends' parents.

24.   I had a curfew.

25.   If I was stressed out, I could talk with someone at home about it.

26.   I had two friends who were in all of my AP classes with me.

27.   If I had problems with a class they could help me most of the time.

28.   At least once a week we all sat down to a real meal and talked.

29.   When I was little, if my parents saw mistakes on my papers I had to correct them.

30.   If I didn't do something right the first time I was encouraged to keep trying until I got it.

31.   My parents, my relatives, and other adults in my life always asked me about school, what courses I liked, and what my future plans might be.

32.   My parents showed up at most meetings and events at school.

33.   In high school my job was to do well in school.

34.   I was encouraged to ask questions as early as I can remember.

35.   I was encouraged to ask for what I needed.

36.   I was encouraged to be independent and choose activities I wanted to do when I was a kid.

37.   I was brought up not to leave something unfinished.

38.   Time management was a very big deal—we were always asked about our plans and whether they were realistic.

39.   My parents made me watch the news or public TV sometimes.

40.   My teachers always expected me to do well.

41.   As a kid I knew I could do lots of things well.

42.   I was taught to share and take turns when I was little.

43.   I wasn't allowed to stay out late just hanging out on weeknights.

This experience left all of us confronting some uncomfortable questions. First, we asked ourselves, "So how many kids really come to school with a comparable set of experiences?" This led us to ask, "So how do we view kids who don't come to school with similar experiences?" As our conversation continued, we gathered up the courage to ask the really hard questions that made us all squirm a little. "Why do we get so frustrated when kids aren't as prepared as we were or would like them to be?" Then, we landed in the pit, asking, "Why is it so easy to punish kids for being different, for life situations over which they have no control?"

Our feelings of frustration and inadequacy reflected the dilemmas of trying our best to teach an increasingly diverse student population in "one size fits all" high schools. One teacher's comment said it all: "I want to get to know all of my students, but there's not enough time to give everyone the attention they deserve. I always feel pressured to keep pushing forward even when I know I've left kids behind."

We all took a deep breath and reminded ourselves that we were already doing an awesome job in the face of awesome challenges. Our group couldn't solve all of the problems of schooling, but each of us could begin tomorrow by reaching out a little differently to just one student. That would be enough for one day.

We ended our conversation by trying on the idea of "no-fault learning and teaching." What if we communicated this message to more kids who needed to hear it?

> *"I'm not going to blame you because your starting point may be different from other students. I know you want to learn. Everyone wants to feel smart. Your presence, your voice, and your ideas are important to me."*

> *"I will try meet you where you are. When I miss the mark I want you to understand it's not because I haven't given it my best effort. I can learn more about what you need to feel prepared. I can teach you the hidden rules about what it takes to be successful here."*

> *"If you can't learn the way I teach, I can try to teach the way you learn. I'm on your side. We'll go the distance one step at a time. You can count on me for that."*

If diversity is perceived as an obstacle or deficit, the divide between who succeeds and who doesn't will only get larger. On the other hand, if we see high schools as pluralistic learning communities, acknowledging all of the differences we bring to the mix, we are more likely to change what we do and how we do it to ensure that all students feel welcomed and all students have a fair chance to succeed.

(32) Becoming a Culturally Responsive Teacher
As defined by Raymond Wlodkowski and Margery Ginsberg,

> [Culturally responsive teaching is] "an approach to teaching that meets the challenges of cultural pluralism... it has to respect diversity; engage the motivation of all learners; create a safe, inclusive and respectful learning environment; derive teaching practices from principles that cross disciplines and cultures; and promote justice and equity in society."[9]

As suggested earlier, becoming culturally responsive teachers begins with knowing ourselves, knowing our students, and knowing our school. We are more tuned in to the personal and learning differences that make each student unique, and we are more aware and appreciative of how differences in cultural identity impact students' daily experience of schooling and learning. Culturally responsive teaching "capitalizes on students' cultural backgrounds rather than attempting to override or negate them."[10]

From the perspective of teaching and learning—from the classroom environment we create, the assignments we design, the learning experiences we construct, the support we provide, the consequences we enforce, and the ways we grade—it means we're willing to trade in the mantra of "one size fits all" for "one size fits few."[11] It means knowing the difference between treating kids the same when it comes to setting high academic and behavioral expectations and treating kids fairly but differently when it comes to the kinds of support and assessment tools we use to help all students achieve. Here's a short list of questions that can inform your thinking about how to make your school and your classroom more culturally responsive:

- How does your school define success? How might a definition of success be broadened to better reflect the aspirations of all of your students?

- How have your life experiences as a targeted person and/or as an ally helped you to connect to young people who are targeted or feel excluded from the dominant culture?

- How does your school (and how do you) encourage students' pride in their home cultures and home languages?

- How can families and respected elders in the community play more vital roles in supporting academic excellence at your school and in your classroom?

- What's already going on at your school that makes all groups feel included and welcomed? What changes in courses and activities would help all groups feel more included and welcomed? What new initiatives would you like to see at your school that would affirm to students, staff, and families that a diverse community is supported and valued?

- What changes in policies and teaching practices would do most to ensure that students who are not part of the dominant culture receive the same treatment and opportunities as those who are more advantaged? In what ways can you provide more differentiated support for diverse learners in your classroom?

- What courses, activities, projects, and events seem to involve the most positive interactions across cultures and different groups? What is it about these activities that attracts a real mix of students (ethnic, gender, social class, and academic diversity).

- In what ways can you personally encourage and provide opportunities for kids to cross borders in classrooms and school-wide activities?

- How can you encourage students to draw strength and satisfaction from their capacities to cross borders from one culture to another?

(33) Affirming Diversity in Your High School

- Promote awareness and appreciation of differences within the school community—especially related to race, ethnicity, gender, class, physical ability, sexual orientation, religion, learning abilities and preferences, families, and regional culture.

- Broaden opportunities for less powerful and/or less privileged groups of students to participate, to be heard, and to be understood within the dominant school culture.

- Acknowledge the presence of a dominant high school culture and take steps to change the school culture in ways that all students and parents feel welcomed and feel treated respectfully and fairly; recognize how privileges that may advantage one group are likely to disadvantage other groups.

- Teach students the skills to counter bias, harassment, and stereotyping, and encourage students to become good allies.

- Develop specific opportunities for young people to cross groups and cultures.

- Encourage the use of multiple perspectives and strengthen students' capacities to take on another's perspective.

- Communicate knowledge and appreciation of the history and culture of all ethnic groups that includes a commitment to present divergent interpretations and documentation of historic and current events.

CHAPTER 5

Model, Teach, Practice, and Assess Life Skills

Self-awareness, self-management, and self-expression (personal efficacy);

Interpersonal communication and problem solving (social efficacy);

Cooperation, participation, and leadership (group efficacy).

5

(34) What are Life Skills?

Life skills include the abilities to manage oneself effectively, make responsible decisions, establish positive social relationships, handle interpersonal problems and conflict productively, and strengthen group participation and leadership skills. These competencies are all part of the maturing process and influence all human activity and decision making.

According to CASEL, The Collaborative for Academic, Social, and Emotional Learning, "the aim of social and emotional learning (SEL) programs is to foster the development of students who are knowledgeable, responsible, and caring, thereby contributing to their academic success, healthy growth and development, ability to maintain positive relationships, and motivation to contribute to their communities."[1]

The term "life skills" is used here instead of SEL for several reasons. Social and emotional competencies are often referred to as life skills in the field of youth development. This is also the term used to identify social and emotional competencies in many local, state, and national standards documents. In addition, labeling these competencies as life skills makes sense to adolescents, given high school's emphasis on helping students make successful life transitions to work, college, and other postsecondary learning experiences.

The Life Skills Checklist that follows organizes these competencies in three clusters:

1. Self-awareness, self-expression, and self-management (personal efficacy)

2. Interpersonal communication and problem solving (social efficacy)

3. Cooperation, participation, and leadership (group efficacy)

The checklist provides a quick summary of skills and can be used to prioritize skills that you want to emphasize in your classroom. The checklist can also serve as a self-assessment tool for students to identify:

- Skills they use competently and routinely without prompting

- Skills they want to improve and use more often

- Skills they are not using currently that they want to learn and practice

LIFE SKILLS CHECKLIST

Life skills are the competencies that help you navigate and negotiate your way in the world.

- You need them to be successful students.

- You need them to be responsible citizens.

- You need them to be good life partners.

- You need them to have fun with other people.

- You need them to get a job and keep a job.

- You need them to be a friend and keep a friend.

- You need them to be good parents.

- You need them when life deals you a bad hand.

Assessing Life Skills

Try using a 0–4 scale for assessing life skills competencies.

(4) I do it competently on a regular basis without prompting, and encourage and support others to do it.

(3) I do it competently most of the time with a little prompting.

(2) I do it competently some of the time. I still need a lot of prompting and feedback.

(1) This is still a growing edge for me. I hardly ever do it. I always need prompting and I need a lot more practice and feedback.

(0) I won't do it and/or I don't know how to do it.

Cluster #1: Self-Awareness, Self-Management, Self-Expression (Personal Efficacy)

1. Recognize and name your own feelings.

2. Express feelings appropriately and assess the intensity of your feelings accurately (on a MAD scale of 1 to 10, I feel...).

3. Understand the cause of your feelings and the connection between your feelings and your behavior.

4. Manage your anger and upset feelings (know your cues, triggers, and reducers).

5. Know what you do that bothers others and accept responsibility when you mess up.

6. Reflect on your behavior; be able to learn from it, correct it, redirect it, and change it when you need to.

7. Make responsible choices for yourself by analyzing situations accurately and predicting consequences of different behaviors.

8. Deal with stress and frustration effectively.

9. Exercise self-discipline and impulse control.

10. Say "NO," and follow through on your decisions not to engage in unwanted, unsafe, unethical, or unlawful behavior.

11. Seek help when you need it.

12. Focus and pay attention.

13. Set large and small goals and make plans.

14. Prioritize and "chunk" tasks, predict task completion time, and manage time effectively.

15. Activate hope, optimism, and positive motivation.

16. Work for high personal performance and cultivate your strengths and positive qualities.

17. Assess your skills, competencies, effort, and quality of work accurately.

5

Cluster #2: Interpersonal Communication and Problem Solving (Social Efficacy)

18. Exercise assertiveness; communicate your thoughts, feelings, and needs effectively to others.

19. Listen actively to demonstrate to others that they have been understood.

20. Give and receive feedback and encouragement.

21. "Read" and name others' emotions and nonverbal cues.

22. Empathize; understand and accept another person's feelings, perspectives, point of view.

23. Analyze the sources and dimensions of conflict and use different styles to manage conflict.

24. Use win-win problem solving to negotiate satisfactory resolutions to conflicts that meet important goals and interests of people involved.

25. Develop, manage, and maintain healthy peer relationships.

26. Develop, manage, and maintain healthy relationships with adults.

Cluster #3: Cooperation, Participation, and Leadership Skills (Group Efficacy)

27. Cooperate, share, and work toward high performance within a group to achieve group goals.

28. Respect everyone's right to learn, to speak, and to be heard.

29. Encourage and appreciate the contributions of others.

30. Engage in conscious acts of respect, caring, helpfulness, kindness, courtesy, and consideration.

31. Recognize and appreciate similarities and differences in others.

32. Counter prejudice, harassment, privilege, and exclusion by becoming a good ally and acting on your ethical convictions.

33. Exercise effective leadership skills within a group.

34. "Read" dynamics in a group; assess group skills accurately; identify problems; generate, evaluate, and implement informed solutions that meet the needs of the group.

35. Use a variety of strategies to make decisions democratically.

(35) Why Model, Teach, Practice, and Assess Life Skills?

In his groundbreaking book *Emotional Intelligence*, Daniel Goleman cites numerous studies that show how the degree to which people manage themselves and relate to others effectively influences how well or how poorly they perform the tasks before them. Students who demonstrate high levels of personal, social, and group efficacy are more likely to be academically successful and perform better as independent learners and group participants. Life skills also foster students' internal qualities of motivation, effort, and persistence, thus increasing their capacity to learn.[2]

CASEL points to wide acceptance among education leaders of the following assumptions that support the teaching and practice of life skills:

- Schools are social places and learning is a social process.

- Students do not learn alone but rather in collaboration with their teachers, in the company of their peers, and with the support of their families.

- Emotions can facilitate or hamper students' learning and their ultimate success in school.

- Because social and emotional factors play such an important role, schools must attend to this aspect of the educational process for the benefit of all students.

Insufficient attention to supporting students' social and emotional development can perpetuate barriers to student learning, increasing feelings of disaffection, boredom, inadequacy, hopelessness, fear, and anger. In turn, these feelings can prompt unwanted behaviors ranging from classroom disruptions to dropping out of school. Issues such as discipline problems, disaffection, lack of commitment, alienation, and dropping out frequently limit success in school or can lead to failure not just in school but in life.[3]

Healthy adolescents tend to experience a saturation of opportunities that foster competence, self-determination, and connection with others.[4] These growing capacities are the signs of maturation to adulthood and, in large part, will determine the kinds of relationships a person will experience over a lifetime—as a worker, a life partner, a parent, a friend, and a citizen.

Recent research also shows a positive relationship between habits of self-discipline (personal efficacy) and academic success. "In a comparative study of over 300 8th graders, researchers measured the influence of self-discipline and IQ on school success. Results showed that highly self-disciplined adolescents outperformed their more impulsive peers on every academic performance variable. Self-discipline measured in the fall was a better predictor of gains in academic performance over the school year than was IQ. The researchers suggest that in a culture that craves instant gratification, building self-discipline may be the key to success in learning."[5]

(36) Infusing Life Skills into Daily Classroom Practice

In *Making Learning REAL*, the modeling, teaching, practice, and assessment of life skills are not viewed as a separate practice or "stand-alone" curriculum of SEL or character education lessons.

Our work with secondary school teachers suggests that infusing life skills into student learning opportunities and daily instructional and disciplinary practices is much more effective. Here's what we've learned that informs our approach.

Most high school teachers don't have the time, inclination, or comfort level to teach a prescribed, sequenced set of life skill lessons in their courses. Teacher resistance often arises from two very reasonable objections:

1. Teaching skill lessons in a prescribed sequence gets in the way of teaching and practicing life skills that address an immediate learning goal or meet the immediate needs of individuals or the group.

2. Teaching "stand-alone" lessons can feel phony to both teachers and students when there's no meaningful context. Justifiable complaints ("This is stupid!", "Why are we doing this?") will sabotage the best of intentions.

We have found that teachers prefer to focus their efforts on teaching specific life skills that will enable their students to meet specific proficiency and performance expectations in their courses.

They also want the flexibility to choose the right "teachable moment" for timely instruction and practice of life skills. When life skills practice has a direct impact on a student's grade and success in class, teachers and students perceive the development of life skills competencies as legitimate and purposeful. Here's a success story that illustrates the difference between implementing a prescribed curriculum and using a more developmental approach to teaching and practicing life skills.

A math teacher observed that many of her students were feeling frustrated and angry when attempting challenging assignments in math. She used the concept of escalation to explore how feelings intensify when we are unable to resolve a problem, meet a goal, or complete a task successfully. Groups of students generated a list of strategies they could use to de-escalate their charged feelings and refocus on the task. Students' suggestions were posted and the teacher set aside time for students to reflect on specific situations in which they had used some of these strategies successfully.

LIFE SKILLS CHECKLIST

8.   Deal with stress and frustration effectively.

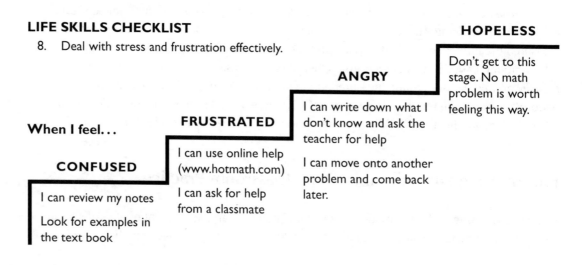

When I feel...

CONFUSED
I can review my notes
Look for examples in the text book

FRUSTRATED
I can use online help (www.hotmath.com)
I can ask for help from a classmate

ANGRY
I can write down what I don't know and ask the teacher for help
I can move onto another problem and come back later.

HOPELESS
Don't get to this stage. No math problem is worth feeling this way.

The research related to learning effectiveness also supports efforts to infuse life skills into daily practice. "According to both social learning theorists and cognitive scientists, it is through modeling—not direct teaching—that most human learning occurs."[6] Young people send us powerful signals every day that they learn more from what adults do than what we say. How and when adults model life skills in their interactions with students will in large part determine whether students actually use these skills in the classroom. Thus it is a teacher's disciplinary and classroom management practices that will have the greatest impact on students' life skill development. It is the teacher's response to a student's behavior that will ultimately shape what skills a student develops and uses in the classroom. When our approach to discipline includes intentional opportunities for students to develop and strengthen life skills, students become more responsible and self-disciplined.

In addition, the field of youth development provides compelling evidence that adolescents' social and emotional competencies improve when these skills are embedded in tasks that they find personally meaningful. Students are more likely to internalize the value of life skill competencies when they experience opportunities to demonstrate these skills in an authentic context. Experiences that involve service and place-based learning, leadership, peer education, an audience for their work, or a performance beyond the classroom will generate greater interest and commitment to learning and practicing life skills.

One more factor should be considered as you develop a plan for infusing life skills into your daily classroom practice. Prevention research suggests that developing a specific skill competency requires six to eight hits—in other words, a one-time experience will not produce a change in behavior. Consequently, teachers need to consider how they incorporate opportunities for:

1. Exposure to and instruction in a new skill;

2. Skill practice in multiple settings and different contexts;

3. Coaching and feedback on students' use of the skill; and

4. Demonstrating mastery of a skill.

Practicing fewer skills will more often generate bigger benefits than trying to practice too many at once.

CHAPTER 6

Putting the Practices to Work

A Tale of Two Classrooms

Two teachers I have imagined represent two different approaches to high school teaching.
Mr. Green and Mr. Brown are experienced social studies teachers. I am also assuming that
there are several features common to both classrooms. Mr. Green and Mr. Brown work in large,
fairly conventional high schools. Students are of mixed ability. Although Mr. Brown's school has
moved to 100-minute block periods for humanities classes and some electives, both teachers
are expected to teach a traditionally sequenced U.S. history course. Both teachers love history and ideas, and they both feel strongly that a big part of their job is providing students with
opportunities to read critically, think deeply, and write clearly. They both expect students to cite
evidence, make informed judgments, and write essays that demonstrate their understanding of
people, events, and ideas that shape important forces in U.S. history.

Welcome to Mr. Green's U.S. History Class (50-minute class period)

As you walk into Mr. Green's room, you notice his desk in front of the blackboard and six rows
of five desks lined up facing the front. There is a bulletin board of student essays and some posters of the U.S. Constitution and Declaration of Independence. There are also several bookcases
of resources that students are free to use. Mr. Green approaches the march of U.S. history
chapter by chapter. The reading assignment from yesterday is written on the board along with
this question: "What events and conditions led the federal government to take a more activist
role in regulating business?"

When the first bell rings and students begin charging in, Mr. Green is sitting at his desk, gathering together a stack of papers to be handed back. He looks up as the second bell rings, and
students quiet down after flinging themselves in their assigned seats rather noisily. Mr. Green
stands up, chats informally with a few kids near his desk, and asks students to review the chapter while he hands out quizzes from yesterday. As he makes his way up and down rows, he has
words of praise for some and stony silence for others. He reminds students who are failing this
quarter that they need to come and see him at lunch on Thursday or Friday of this week to work
out what they can do to improve their grades.

Then Mr. Green says, "Let's get down to business. Your assignment last night was to read about clashes between American industrialists and American labor at the turn of the century." Mr. Green looks at his seating chart and then says, "Monique, please identify some of the conditions that led to conflicts between factory owners and workers." Monique offers an incomplete response to this query, and Mr. Green calls on several other students to summarize the reading assignment and discuss how and why the federal government stepped in to regulate business. He peppers the question and answer conversation with stories, quotations, and old newspaper headlines showing how the growth of industry and the growth of cities transformed the way people lived and worked at the end of the 19th century.

Mr. Green is a good storyteller and captures the attention of some students who begin asking other questions about the factory system, working conditions, and monopolies. Other students are doodling, finishing other homework, or staring at nothing. Long ago, Mr. Green resigned himself to accepting the fact that some students will be with him all the way, while lots of others will get their act together and tune in right before a major assignment is due or the day before a test.

Mr. Green is committed to improving literacy across the curriculum, so most of his assignments and tests involve writing essays. He is dedicated to working with students before and after school on their writing, but he also expects students to make the choice to come to him for help. He hands out a group of essay questions, explaining that the students will each choose one question to write about. He reads several of the questions, each time asking the whole class what issues and evidence they might include if they were choosing this particular question to write about. He points out resources that they might use to complete their essays. A few students pipe in with the usual procedural questions about when the essay is due and how long it has to be. The bell rings and everyone scrambles.

Nine out of twenty-six students have spoken during the 50-minute period. The discussion has emphasized mostly recall questions, with Mr. Green dialoguing with one student at a time while everyone else listens.

Welcome to Mr. Brown's U.S. History Class (100-minute block period)

Mr. Brown's approach to the curriculum is to take a large chunk of time and emphasize one or two themes that reflect key questions that students have generated earlier in the course. His desk is in a corner. Student desks and chairs are clustered in groups of four and chairs can be easily arranged in a circle or square. It's hard to identify the front or the back of the room, because every wall has a special function that's different.

Maps hang from one wall, which also contains photographs of working life at the turn of the 19th century and questions about the present learning unit on change and growth in the industrial age. Shelves by the windows contain resource books and file folders of articles and excerpts on various issues, and student projects and essays are clipped to plastic clothesline rope running from one side of the room to the other.

On another wall, each class has its own space that includes pictures of students, clippings, questions, quotations, and files for assignment instructions, extra handouts, and student papers. Classroom agreements, expectations for the quarter, the big picture plan for the week, and the agenda and goals for today's activities are posted by the blackboard.

When the first bell rings, Mr. Brown is at the door to greet students as they walk in. He says "Hello" to each student by name and hands each student a voting ballot that looks like this:

Referendum on Proposed City Ordinance #132

No employer in the city of _____ may employ 14-to-17-year-olds more than 15 hours a week during any time period when they are enrolled as full time students in middle or high schools.

Please circle Yes or No and jot down at least two reasons for your vote.

YES

NO

Mr. Brown pulls aside a couple of students noting, in a casual way, that he has seen a difference in their participation in class, and he describes specific situations where he noticed their contributions. He checks in with a girl who has been dealing with the pressures of a divorce at home and asks another student how the basketball team is feeling about the loss last night. He reminds another student that they need to set up a time to talk about a plan for finishing some incomplete work.

After the second bell rings, Mr. Brown makes sure that all ballots are in the box and invites students to circle up, moving their chairs from behind their desks so that everyone can see everyone else. He reviews the agenda for the day that's been posted, asks for two volunteers to count the ballots, and takes about five minutes to do a quick go-around with students, encouraging them to speak out, saying, "So what do you think of this proposed city ordinance? Good idea? Bad idea? Not sure?" Some students take a pass, while others eagerly share their opinions. Students announce the vote count and the "No's" win handily.

He pushes a little further, asking, "Why might a community recommend limiting the hours per week that students can work?" Although one student brings up the problem of competing with adults for the same jobs, most students raise concerns about long work hours having a negative impact on school involvement and homework. Mr. Brown notices that the students doing the talking are kids who don't have jobs, and he knows that over a third of the kids in this class work very long hours.

6

He calls for a quick tally of the number of hours various students work per week. To non-working students the number of hours that other students work is shocking. "For those of you who work more than 15 hours a week, how would the passage of this ordinance change your life right now?" As one student responds, two students are already having an intense conversation by themselves; Mr. Brown reminds them about the agreements the class has made about talking and listening in the whole group, asks them to focus on the speaker, and assures them that everyone who wants to will get a chance to speak.

The conversation is intense as students reveal how this ordinance would affect them. What stands out are the kids who talk about how dependent their families are on their income. The group is witness to the anger and concern expressed as these students tell their stories.

"So you can see," he says, "that for many of you this would be a very big deal. If this ordinance were going to be voted on in our community three months from now, what would you want to do?" Now the students are juiced. Kids call out actions they would take, from public hearings, to protests, to getting lists of all eighteen-year-olds to encourage them to vote "No," to mounting a letter writing and phone call campaign to parents.

"The kinds of laws and regulations that governments choose to pass or not pass affect us very personally, even though we might not think about it very much." Mr. Brown closes by saying, "So take a minute and think through your response to this question, 'Should a government have the power to limit the hours that people can work?'" Mr. Brown gives students a minute to think about this and asks students to turn to the person next to them and explain their reasoning. After two minutes he says, "We'll come back to this question later in the week."

"Now let's see what you discovered from your interviews and research."

In the beginning of the year, students brainstormed a huge list of topics and questions that reflected what they thought were truth and lies in the history they had been taught, and what they wanted to learn more about in the North American past and the world that they live in today. This unit is organized around student questions related to the world of work and the power of citizens and governments to change what is unjust. Questions ranged from "Why does the government suck up to business?" to "Why don't all workers have health insurance?" to "Why didn't Reconstruction change the working status of most Black people?" to "Why should government be able to tell a business what to do?"

Last week Mr. Brown asked students what they knew about the working history of people within their families. For the most part students didn't know very much. Mr. Brown admits that he didn't either. He challenged students to think about how they could collect data that will help them understand how the world of work has changed over the last hundred years.

After ideas were tossed out, he gave students a page of job statistics and an excerpt from Studs Terkel's book *Working*, asking home groups to assess how each source brings to light different dimensions of working history. The class agrees on three methods of data collection, and then small groups develop questions and protocols that will help them gather information consistently for each method.

- In extended interviews, find out about the work histories of four family members from four different generations. (Students generate a list of questions to ask in the interviews.)

- Make a chart or graph that shows your family's work history across four generations (more if possible), getting information on at least 20 people in your family. (Students brainstorm various ways that they can present their data to the rest of the class.)

- Find census data and labor statistics that will show you what kinds of work people did, in what numbers, from 1900 to 1990. (Students divide up decades and agree on the kind of data that they want to collect across decades.)

To provide a model for what to do and to generate a little curiosity, Mr. Brown shared the chart he created that presents his own family's work history. Having grown up in a city, he told the class how surprised he was to discover how many of his relatives were farmers in the first part of the century. Students ask more questions about his "work story," and then Mr. Brown sets aside time to discuss any questions or problems related to their research assignment.

Today, the students who collected statistical data make their presentation to the whole class, and the class has a chance to react to the group's findings, looking for trends and changes from one decade to another. Then Mr. Brown divides the class into groups of six that include students who used each different method for collecting data. "As you listen to personal interviews and family work histories, use your journals to note how the world of work seems to change across time and generations and write down other questions that emerge from the presentations you hear."

Mr. Brown asks for a volunteer to be the timekeeper in each group; students will each have about five minutes to present what they have learned. One group seems to have trouble getting started, and Mr. Brown goes over, observes what he sees, asks them what's going on, and discovers that two students don't have their data. He asks the group what feels like the best way to move forward right now and what feels like a fair solution to the missing data problem. The two students agree to pool their data and make a presentation later in the week. In the meantime, a couple of students volunteer to switch groups so that the number of presentations per group balances out.

He continues to roam from group to group, listening and jotting down bits of conversation that can provide bridges to their historical study. He winks and gives a "thumbs up" to a couple of students after they finish speaking. When time's up, Mr. Brown asks students to close their group conversation by each naming something new that they learned or something that they appreciated about a particular presentation.

Then Mr. Brown asks students to go back to their own home groups saying, "Considering what you've heard from all the presentations this morning, discuss what you learned with your home group partners and agree as a group on what you think are 4 or 5 big changes in the world of work over the last century. Here are some starters that might help frame your speculations:"

6

The Changing World of Work in the U.S.

From...	To...
More people who...	More people who...
More jobs that...	More jobs that...
Less opportunity for...	Greater opportunity for...
What conditions, kinds of work, or opportunities did not seem to change over time? Why do you think that is?	

"Take about 15 minutes to do this and post your charts on this board, initialing your chart paper." After their newsprint sheets are posted, students note the most common responses from chart to chart, and Mr. Brown circles the ones that students identify. He asks students to share what they discovered that really got their attention. Finally, Mr. Brown asks the group to speculate on forces and factors that brought about the changes they have described. Students mention unions, the growth of technology, changes in the global economy, more people living in cities, more government regulation, civil rights laws, more educational opportunities.

"So now," Mr. Brown begins, "we have some sense of how work and working conditions have changed. We're going to examine a turbulent period in the last century before these changes kicked in." He points to and reads a couple of the questions written on large strips on the bulletin board:

- What brought about the shift to a more activist role of government? Should governments be able to regulate the places we work, the things we buy, and the services we use? Why or why not?

- How do labor unions help change working conditions for employees? How influential are unions today?

- Should governments have the right to ban products that are harmful to their citizens? Do governments have a responsibility to make sure that businesses operate in ways that are safe, decent, and fair?

- If you put up the money and take the risk, shouldn't you be able to run your business any way you want? After all, you're creating wealth and more jobs!

"These questions emerged from your brainstorm at the beginning of the year. We're going to live with them for a while. In your exhibition you'll be investigating how government laws and regulations affect a particular job or business that interests you. It could be a sports franchise, the sale of guns, the production of Nike shoes, the Internet—you name it. Or you might want to explore how laws and regulations have changed a job that's been part of your family's work history. But first we need to find out more about the conditions that stimulated greater government involvement and citizen activism in labor and business."

Mr. Brown asks students to pick up reading packets, so each home group receives a set of four packets that are blue (urban workers and their families), yellow (industrialists and businessmen and their families), green (organizers, reformers, and activists), and beige (agricultural workers and their families). Some students groan and Mr. Brown says, "I know, I know. Some of you are not exactly thrilled to see a reading packet. But it's hard to judge whether governments and citizens meddle too much or too little in other people's business unless we know what all the fuss was about a 100 years ago."

Students take a few minutes to decide which students will read about which groups. In preparation for work in their home groups later in the week, students review instructions that require them to highlight interesting details, quotations, and images that will help their home group partners get a good picture of their particular group. Each student is to choose one passage to read to their home groups that they think best captures the hopes, fears, and concerns that characterize their group. Mr. Brown encourages students "to keep writing questions and notes in the margins as you read. What do you agree or disagree with? What makes you mad? What makes you say, 'Now that person's speaking the truth!'" This reading packet will go in their portfolios as an example of how students respond critically to other people's words and stories.

Mr. Brown takes a minute to see if anyone has any questions before they begin reading. One student calls out, "I'd rather read my packet with someone else who's reading about the same group of people." This sounds fine to Mr. Brown, who invites others to partner up if that works for them. The reading time gives Mr. Brown a chance to do some personal check-ins with students, especially with those who struggle with reading. When time is called, Mr. Brown asks students to turn to their journals and complete this sentence, "After today's class, I'm left wondering..." He reminds students that they are welcome to come in tomorrow morning if they want to review their readings before class. "I'm counting on all home groups being prepared. On my 1 to 10 scale, this is probably a 9.5."

In closing, Mr. Brown points to the agenda and invites students to say what they liked best or what they would change about class today. As the bell rings, he congratulates the class on persevering through another 100-minute marathon of U.S. history. He talks privately with a few kids, sharing what he noticed about their participation today. To one boy who rarely speaks, Mr. Brown says, "I really appreciated your willingness to talk about your job and your family. It gave other kids a chance to see what it's like to live in your shoes. Thanks."

Every student has spoken in the whole group and every student has shared their research, conclusions, and questions in small groups. Equally important, every student has listened to each other as they contributed new knowledge and perspectives to the issues raised in class today.

So What's the Difference?

Mr. Green is not a bad guy, but he's worn down, having acquiesced to the "game of school" as Robert Fried so aptly describes the deal teachers make: "I'll pretend to teach all of you while most of you pretend to learn."[1] He's willing to settle for quiet compliance and learning that emphasizes memorization. ("I will be reasonable. You don't mess with me, and I won't mess with you. Do your work and I will work with you. It's your choice and your initiative whether you do well or not.") These tacit agreements prop up a system driven by relentless grading

6

(otherwise kids will do even less work) and content coverage (if it's the third week of January, we must be studying _____). Mr. Green still delights in those moments of genuine engagement with a few students; yet, the group comes to life so rarely that these encounters will make Mr. Green's semester, not his day.

Every good teacher knows that you will never engage every student's attention, interest, and seriousness all the time. But a big difference in these two classrooms is Mr. Brown's intentional commitment to construct a learning environment where more of these moments are possible every day for every kid.

(37) An Annotated Description of Key Classroom Practices

The annotated descriptions below illustrate how Mr. Brown incorporates the core practices to create a learning community where he and his students make learning real.

Key Strategy	Examples
Develop personal connections among and between students and teachers.	Mr. Brown meets and greets students at the door.
	Students sit in a circle at the beginning of class as a way to acknowledge that they are a group of learners who are in this together, not just as individuals, rushing in, doing their time, and scrambling when the bell rings.
	Mr. Brown makes personal connections with kids throughout the class period. He also shares something about his own life with students, inviting students to consider this room as a place where people can feel safe to be real instead of going through the motions of faking it.
	Mr. Brown knows these kids pretty well. In journals, they've written about themselves, their goals and hopes, what they need for the classroom to be a good place to learn, and what gets in the way.
Emphasize student-centered learning that is personally meaningful.	Students routinely make choices about what they are learning and how they go about doing their work and accomplishing their goals in the classroom.
	More important, students are responsible for constructing major projects around something that matters to them. In addition, Mr. Brown tries to create opportunities for students to connect what they are learning to the world outside. Each year students work on an action research project that links local community history to current political, cultural, social, or economic issues.

**Emphasize
student-centered
learning that is
personally
meaningful.**

Mr. Brown is only too aware of how boring history is to most students. Although he is required to teach a sequential history course, he chunks larger periods of time into a unit that addresses key questions and themes that students generated in the beginning of the year. He has chosen to make the world of work a linchpin for this unit so that students can bring their own issues and questions around work and careers to their investigation.

He also wants students to have a better understanding of how citizens' efforts, past and present, can spur government to redress injustices and temper the harsher aspects of market capitalism. At the same time, he wants students to struggle with what you get and what you give up in attempting to make laws and regulations that provide the greatest good for the most citizens. So Mr. Brown begins by sparking curiosity about work in their own families and grabbing students' attention with the ballot on limiting student work hours. The controversy over limiting work hours creates a bridge to historical controversies around the length of the work week and the age and hours for child laborers.

The exhibition that each student designs creates a way to explore present business and labor practices in the global marketplace and speculate about the future role that governments might play in regulating multinational corporations.

**Establish clear
norms, boundaries,
and procedures.**

Students and Mr. Brown have negotiated their agreements for classroom norms of behavior, which serve as a daily reminder and tool for group assessment.

**Build a
cohesive
community
of learners.**

The class sinks or swims as a team. Students know that they can't be invisible and that opting out is not an option.

Students have had a voice in choosing their home group partners; they are aware they are responsible to and for each other, especially when they each have responsibility for contributing specific knowledge that will be applied to a task that involves all four of them.

Students participate in generating ideas and questions that form the basis for important tasks and projects.

Key Strategy	Examples

HH
Provide high expectations and personalized support.

Mr. Brown has not sorted his class into those who get it and those who don't. There are important tasks and exhibitions that everyone is expected to complete meeting minimum standards of mastery.

From the first day of class, students know they won't receive Fs but "incompletes" on important tasks. They are responsible for making a plan to complete or re-do major tasks, tests, or projects within three weeks.

On the other hand, Mr. Brown is aware that students come to class with different sets of skills and resistances, and need different kinds of support, especially regarding reading. So he has negotiated with the reading teacher to be available to work with students in study periods, at lunch, and before school.

Mr. Brown also talks privately with some about how they can translate qualities and skills that make them successful "outside" so they can utilize these same qualities and skills to become more successful at "doing" school.

Mr. Brown models the interview assignment before the due date, so students who need a clearer picture of the task have it.

The pacing of the class respects the shifting energy of adolescents; they get to talk, observe, listen, read, discuss, write, and move around.

Students know they can tell Mr. Brown when an activity is a dud, when explanations aren't clear, or when they have a better idea of how to do an activity. They also know that if they mess up, it's not the end of the world. Their grades are determined more by their accumulated efforts toward improvement and mastery and the quality of their performance on projects that they design themselves.

There are a few kids Mr. Brown checks in with every day; noticing what they do, discussing goals they've set, and asking them about their lives. This is a kind of attention that feels different for these kids, who are slowly shifting away from their acquired hostility and indifference about school and learning.

Affirm diversity in your classroom.

Students share personal stories about their lives that provide an opportunity for them to appreciate the differences in their experiences and discover what they share in common.

Mr. Brown is aware that most of his students are descended from families of enslaved Africans who migrated from rural southern communities or families of Europeans who immigrated here three or four generations ago. He has consciously selected readings that explore the lives of northern urban workers and southern agricultural workers between 1880 and 1920. He realizes there will be some discomfort when students confront the racial, ethnic, and class prejudices that influences the treatment of workers and their families. This awareness informs his choice to include writing of important organizers and reformers of the time and also prompts him to search for readings that provide a far more mixed portrait of industrialists and businessmen so students will be less likely to categorize this group as having one monolithic point of view.

Integrate multiple ways of knowing and learning.

Differentiated learning is the norm in Mr. Brown's classroom. Students speak and listen as much as they read and write. Students are used to working individually, as a whole group, and in small groups. There is also more than one way to complete an important project or assignment.

Mr. Brown is also aware that some students are more effective learners when big tasks are "chunked," while others are ready to run with an idea and want to make their own way. Thus, all instructions for major assignments are written with optional space for students to make a plan for how they will complete the assignment.

Life Skill Connections: (Personal Efficacy)

By bringing in the controversy over work hours, Mr. Brown created an opportunity for students to express their feelings and direct their emotional intensity toward constructive problem solving.

Students are cued to respond to the readings critically, and the readings are intended to stir up emotions by describing the lived experience of very different groups.

(Social Efficacy)

Throughout the class, Mr. Brown models attentive listening, serving as witness rather than judge when students share their options and stories in a circle.

Students are also used to giving feedback to each other about the work that they do.

(Group Efficacy)

In home groups, each student has shared observations, defended their thinking, and worked to reach consensus. Students have practiced explaining, summarizing, and responding to questions in their interview groups.

When a group has problems working together, Mr. Brown checks out the situation and expects students to stay with the problem and work it out.

6

A *REAL* Approach to Classroom Practice

This graphic illustrates four simultaneous teacher tasks that are vital elements of any classroom lesson. Guidelines for effective instruction often emphasize "Task 1: Rigorous and Relevant Student Work Aligned with Standards," and "Task 2: Evidence-Based Instruction," while not paying equal attention to "Task 3: Development of a High-Performing Community of Learners" and "Task 4: Guided Discipline, Life Skills, and Academic, Behavioral, and Social Support." Teachers have found this chart a useful reminder to incorporate time and attention to Tasks 3 and 4 in their lesson planning and implementation. (More on Tasks 3 and 4 can be found in *Getting Classroom Management Right: Guided Discipline and Personalized Support in Secondary Schools*.)

1. Rigorous and Relevant Students Work Aligned with Standards

- Curriculum mapping that begins with authentic assessments aligned to standards (8 Ps = products, presentations, performance, projects, proficiencies, participation, problem posting and analysis, portfolios)
- Essential questions that inform the unit of study and key skills and concepts linked to learning standards
- Rigorous student work and ongoing assessment that indicate what students already know; what students have learned; where students are stuck; and how students demonstrate proficiency
- Hooks to students' lived experiences and personal interests
- Applied learning connections to students' lives, the workplace and internship experiences, college and careers, their community, and the world

2. Evidence-Based Instruction that Includes...

- Literacy across the curriculum
- Emphasis on metacognitive development and higher order thinking
- Personalized learning that emphasizes choice and voice
- Emphasis on the social construction of knowledge through collaborative learning strategies
- Differentiated instruction that considers students' readiness and learning profiles, developmental needs and cultural realities, interests, preferences, talents, and aspirations
- Balanced pacing of lessons, incorporating variations in time chunks, learning activities, grouping structures, and noise level within the same class period
- Developmentally appropriate and culturally responsive practice informed by principles of youth development

This is about the individual learners

4. Guided Discipline, Life Skills, and Academic, Behavioral, and Social Support

- High expectations accompanied by personalized support and insistence on quality, completion, and proficiency for every student
- Modeling, teaching, practicing, and assessing the behaviors you expect
- Life Skills development (personal efficacy, social efficacy, and group efficacy)
- Academic and behavioral supports and interventions from the classroom to case management
- Close tracking and monitoring of student progress
- Feedback and coaching loop when students are experiencing academic and behavioral difficulties
- Invitations to cooperate, personal conferencing, and accountable consequences that require students to self-correct, restore one's good standing, learn appropriate behaviors, and make things right

3. Development of a Safe, Respectful, High-Performing Community of Learners

- Building positive relationships among and between adults and students
- Recognition, appreciation, and celebration of individual and group successes
- Development of leadership skills and a positive peer culture
- Development of group norms, procedures, routines and rituals that create community connection:
  "This is how we do things here.
  "This is how we treat each other.
  "This is how we work and learn together."
- Attention to group process and facilitation that support personal growth and group accountability and responsibility

This is about the group

A REAL Classroom Practices Checklist

This checklist provides a quick snapshot of the practices described in Section 3. Individual teachers use this checklist as a guide for choosing a balanced set of practices that they want to introduce in their classrooms. Faculty teams use the checklist to determine shared practices they want to implement across a specific grade level, small school, or smaller learning community.

♥	**Practice 1: Develop positive relationships among and between students and teachers**	— I welcome, meet and greet students at the door. I know and my students know everyone's names by the end of the first couple of weeks — I create multiple opportunities for myself and my students to connect and get to know each other well — I make time to notice individual students; give "10 second hits," and engage in regular conferencing with every student — I make time for meaningful closure activities at the end of the week, quarter, semester, and year
Ⓢ	**Practice 2: Emphasize personalized, student-centered learning**	— I offer students choices from day one — Student goal-setting, reflection, and self-assessment are regular practices in my classroom; students assess their strengths and "growing edges" as learners — I link students' worlds, their preoccupations, and their lived experiences to what I'm teaching
⌘	**Practice 3: Integrate multiple ways of knowing and learning**	— Students get to explore a variety of ways to learn that encourage the use of multiple intelligences — I differentiate instruction, learning opportunities, and assessments to meet the needs, interests, readiness, and learning profiles of different students — Students engage in a variety of collaborative learning strategies to make meaning of what they are learning — Students and I create a vision of what we want our classroom community to be like

6

	Practice 4: Establish clear norms, boundaries, and procedures	— I implement accountable consequences for unwanted behaviors that are clear and consistent — I model, teach, assess, and ensure student practice of classroom procedures and problem-solving protocols — I routinely develop guidelines and agreements for general classroom behaviors and more specific learning tasks
	Practice 5: Build a cohesive community of learners	— Gatherings and closings are weekly routines — I notice, recognize, and celebrate individual and group efforts and accomplishments — There are frequent opportunities for students to negotiate WHAT and HOW they learn — I use class meetings to discuss and resolve classroom issues and to support and maintain a high-functioning group — I use a variety of structures to promote good talk and quality products for pairs, small groups, and the whole class
HH	Practice 6: Provide high expectations and personalized support	— I provide personalized support, feedback, and encouragement so that all of my students can meet my expectations and local and state learning standards — I create a culture of quality and completion by requiring that all students achieve proficiency on some essential learning tasks and assessments — I help students become more "school smart" — I utilize a grading system that assesses students' life skills and habits of learning
	Practice 7: Affirm diversity in your classroom	— I welcome and positively recognize the range of personal and cultural differences that students bring into my classroom — I learn about the cultural backgrounds of my students and their families — Our physical classroom environment celebrates and recognizes my students, their families, neighborhoods, cultures, languages, and personal interests — I incorporate students' cultures and language skills into my curriculum

Life Skill Connections: Model, teach practice and assess Life Skills

Self-awareness, self-management, and self-expression (Personal Efficacy)

Interpersonal communications and problem solving (Social Efficacy)

Cooperation, participation, and leadership (Group Efficacy)

— I let students know what they can do when they're upset and angry, and help them develop self-management skills

— I teach problem solving protocols so students know exactly what they can do when they experience academic, behavioral, or personal problems or intrapersonal conflicts

— I alter the learning environment (considering students' emotional states) in ways that help them settle in, quiet their minds, redirect their energy, and focus

— I use disciplinary strategies that encourage students to take responsiblity for their behavior, invite cooperation and self-correction, offer chances to make a good choice, learn from their mistakes, and make a plan to get back on track

— Students practice a variety of listening and speaking skills during specific learning tasks

— I use one-to-one conferencing to problem solve with students

— I teach the basics of WIN-WIN negotiation and problem solving

— I model, teach, assess, and ensure student practice of specific cooperation, collaboration, and group participation skills

— Students have opportunities to develop leadership skills in small and large groups – taking personal initiative to help, present, perform, teach, share, organize, facilitate, negotiate, and problem solve – and modeling ethical, pro-social behaviors

6

SECTION TWO
GETTING STARTED

CHAPTER 7

Before the School Year Begins

Getting ready for school is a big deal. There's too much to do and never enough time! As you prepare for your classes and incoming students, there are a few things you might want to do that will:

- welcome each student and set the stage for clear communication with students and their families;

- set the tone for what really matters in your classroom;

- organize your classroom space to maximize learning, responsibility, and community; and

- help you create a learning environment that communicates organization and focus and encourages high student participation.

Before the school year begins:

- Write a letter or create a videotape for families of your students.

- Design an assessment and record-keeping system that is standards and learning friendly.

- Stock up on supplies.

- Arrange desks and chairs in a way that makes it easy to see everyone and learn their names.

- Make the classroom "ours."

Write a Letter to Parents or Guardians or Create a Videotape for Families of Your Students

Your first contact with parents and guardians sets the stage for communication the rest of the year. We know that kids do better in school when parents are involved in their children's school. We also know that a parent's influence on their teens is far greater than they think. So you want families to know what's going on in your course. You want families to know how much their support and encouragement can influence both their child's motivation to learn and their academic success.

What do you want parents to know about you, the course you are teaching, and your expectations for yourself and your students? It's likely that you won't see parents at a school open house until several weeks into the school year. Take advantage of "back-to-school" anticipation and anxiety by communicating to parents during the first week of school. Let them know that this is not the last time you will communicate with them. You might want to send a letter home at the beginning of each new quarter, providing a snapshot of last quarter's highlights and a preview of what is coming up. These quarterly communications can also provide the opportunity for students to share their own reflections, self-assessment, and goal setting as part of letters that are sent home.

Compose a letter to send home to parents and guardians on the first day of school. It's one way to let parents know that their support and encouragement are important to you. Give two copies to each student, so parents and guardians can keep one copy and sign the other letter for students to return to you.

Make your letter one page. This is an introduction, and you can always communicate more details later. Choose two or three things that you want to emphasize:

- Describe what your course is about, including requirements, goals, and key learning experiences.

- Describe your hopes and expectations for students.

- Share what might be challenging for students in this class. Have a sense of humor— tell parents if they hear their kids sighing and moaning, it's probably because...

- Let parents know what steps students can take if they are having difficulty meeting class requirements.

- Let parents know how they can communicate with you if they have questions or concerns. Give a school phone number.

- Let parents know what kinds of homework assignments students can expect. Suggest specific ways that they can support and encourage their child's success in this class.

- Emphasize that effort, attitude, and participation really count in your classroom. Identify some of the social skills that you hope will help create a respectful, responsible, and caring classroom.

If some of your students live in families whose parents' or guardians' primary language is not English, you have a couple of options. If all or most of your newcomer families speak the same language, see if someone from your Bilingual or English as a Second Language department can help you translate your letter. If you have students whose families speak a variety of languages, you might invite your students and an English as a Second Language teacher to come in at lunch to work on writing translations of important points in your letter to be sent home with the letter you wrote in English. This activity sends a powerful message to students that you value their family's role in their education and seek their support.

Other Ways to Communicate:

- Create a video to send home.

If you have a communications/video/broadcasting department or your own video cam, introduce yourself by video. Regardless of income, cultural, or social circumstances, most families have a DVD Player. Create a five-to-ten-minute DVD in which you introduce yourself and highlight a few important things that you want parents to know. Make several copies of the DVD so that three or four students per night can take the DVD home, return it, and give it to the next group of families to view.

- Introduce yourself online.

More and more school districts have their own websites. Check to see if there is a place for teachers to post their own communications to families and students on the web.

Design an Assessment and Record-Keeping System That Is Standards- and Learning-Friendly

"We need to move from a testing culture to an assessment culture." — Henry Wong

What Will You Assess?

Political scientists frequently use the phrase, "budget is policy," implying that the amount of money legislators are willing to spend indicates how much a particular policy or project is really valued. Similarly, in education, we can say, "assessment is curriculum." What you choose to assess, how you assess students' learning and performance, how you keep records, and how students participate in assessment all determine what kind of teaching and learning will take place in your classroom. Before the school year begins, you might want to think about your responses to these questions:

- What messages do I want to send to students about assessment and grades? What are my goals for assessment and grading?

- What purpose do grades serve? Do they provide information and feedback so students can improve?

- Do I want to assess what students already know? Am I using grades as a threat or punishment?

- Are grades a means for students to draw comparisons among themselves—who's smart and who's dumb?

- Do grades enable students to assess what they've learned, the quality of their work, their mastery of concepts and skills? Do I want assessment to encourage completion, revision, and correction?

7

- Should assessment help students see the connections between effort and performance?

- Should grades help students monitor their progress and set goals for themselves?

- Should assessment be diagnostic so that I can make instruction more responsive to the needs of diverse learners?

- How involved do I want students to be in assessing their learning experience in my class? (Student involvement can include pre-grading-period conferencing, student-led conferences with parents, development of portfolios, student written reflection and self-assessment, peer assessment, etc.)

- What kinds of assessments do I want students to experience? (For example: criterion-referenced tests, essays, presentations, portfolios, demonstrations, projects, papers, written and verbal feedback, rubrics that indicate the use and proficiency of specific skills, self-reflection activities, informal checking for understanding, conferencing, peer review, exhibitions, etc.)

- What do I want to assess? (For example: students' understanding of discrete subject matter concepts and skills, mastery of academic standards and benchmarks, students' ability to use multiple skills and concepts to complete complex tasks that demonstrate learning, students' application and meaningful use of subject matter knowledge, literacy skills, learning-how-to-learn skills, work habits and self-management skills, communication and problem-solving skills, group participation skills, etc.)

Your responses to these last two questions will shape what you teach and what students learn more than anything else you do. Even though research confirms that students whose goals focus on learning for understanding are more receptive and less anxious learners, high school classrooms are, nonetheless, grade driven. All too often, grading can become a sorting device, turning students into grade point averages and the curriculum into an endless series of graded tasks that may or may not be meaningful. The grade on the paper becomes the end in itself, pushing aside other ways of providing information and feedback that can help students know where they stand and what they are learning.

Nearly a decade of conditioning prompts any high school student to ask, "Are we getting a grade for this?" regardless of the task. Students have already received a loud and clear message throughout their schooling that if it isn't graded, it doesn't really count. Asking teenagers and school decision makers to let go of this assumption is probably unrealistic. However, one way to counter this automatic response is to widen the net of what you assess and expand the tools that you use for assessment.

Name the Tensions and Competing Interests Surrounding Grading and Assessment

Teachers face plenty of dilemmas on the way to constructing effective grading policies and systems of assessment. Think about where you would place yourself on each continuum below. Consider possible costs and barriers to student learning and achievement that can result from the practice on the left-hand side and possible benefits and learning breakthroughs that can result from the practice on the right-hand side. Think particularly about struggling, resistant, and failing students: which practices might help turn around their performance, motivation, and attitudes?

Assessing levels of achievement using one standard of proficiency	⟷	Assessing cumulative progress toward meeting standards of proficiency
An emphasis on **timeliness, deadlines,** and **first-time** results (no credit for late work or incomplete work or later attempts)	⟷	An emphasis on **completion** and **quality** (insistence on completion and a system of credit that incorporates correction, editing, completion of final attempts)
Grading and weighing all student work similarly	⟷	Grading and weighing **practice** and **first attempts** differently from **final products** and **summative assessments**
Assessing **ability** only	⟷	Assessing **ability** and **effort** (habits of learning)
Categorizing all assessments as **tests, quizzes,** and **homework**	⟷	Categorizing assessments by learning task (projects; final products from learning unit; journals/reflections; demonstrations and applications; note taking and other graphic representations of what students read, heard, learn; guided practice; group learning tasks; etc.)
Assessing products only	⟷	Assessing **products, performances,** and **habits of learning**
End-of-term grades based on the total grades on **all student work**	⟷	End-of-term grades based on meeting a selected number of proficiencies/competencies out of a larger total number of proficiencies/competencies
Major learning tasks are graded A through F without expectation or insistence that students correct, edit, redo, or complete with quality	⟷	Grades for major learning tasks are not recorded until student has corrected, edited, redone, or completed task at a proficiency level
Using one uniform assessment or test for all students within a specific learning unit or course that is aligned to what is tested on standardized tests	⟷	Offering a choice of assessments that meet a set of learning standards, competencies, or proficiencies

7

Support Academic Achievement by Assessing the Three L's—Learning How to Learn, Literacy, and Life Skills

Semester grades and report cards mostly measure students' performance on written tests and assignments. What they don't measure are "learning how to learn," literacy, and life skills (competencies related to self-management, interpersonal effectiveness, and group participation) that ultimately determine high or low academic achievement in school, and high or low performance on the job. The result is that most students, especially average and low-performing students, have little awareness of the connections between personal effort and their academic performance.

You have the power to change this by designing an assessment and record-keeping system that includes assessment of the three L's. When you integrate assessment of these skills into daily classroom practice and quarterly and semester grades, you are saying that you value effort and expect students to strengthen skills that will help them become more successful academically. In the bargain, you also provide students and families with more information about who students are as learners. Think about incorporating the following kinds of skills into your grading system.

Assess "Learning How to Learn" Skills

"Learning how to learn" skills, or metacognitive skills as they are sometimes known, refer to one's "self-awareness of cognitive processing strategies and the ability to control them."[1] In other words, how much do we know about how and why we think and learn the way we do; how much do we know about the task and the goal in front of us; and what kinds of tools and strategies can we access to meet our goal and complete the task?

In a summary analysis of research on factors that influence learning, "a student's metacognitive processes had the most powerful effect on his or her learning."[2] What is also interesting is that students whose orientation is toward "task goals" (monitoring progress, acquiring skills, solving problems, gaining knowledge) rather than "ability goals" (caring about how smart or dumb one is in relation to others) "are much more likely to believe that effort can improve skills and knowledge."[3] Yet, these are the very skills that we seldom assess. Here is a short list of learning how to learn skills that lead to student achievement in school:

- following directions and routines

- revising, adapting, and changing learning strategies when one's current strategy isn't working

- discriminating between effective and ineffective learning strategies

- asking questions that lead to deeper understanding

- sustaining effort and persevering until completion of the task

- planning and designing activities that enhance one's learning

- seeking out resources that will enhance one's learning

- thoughtful reflection about what is being learned

- assessing one's effort and performance accurately

More specifically, skills associated with work and study habits fall into this category as well:

- use of multiple strategies to study and prepare for tests

- notebook organization

- bringing necessary materials to class every day

- regular completion of tasks on time

Assess Literacy Skills

For the vast majority of average and low-performing students, reading, writing, speaking, and listening deficits become the biggest stumbling blocks to success in school. Consequently, for many high schools, improving student achievement means emphasizing reading, writing, speaking, and listening skills across the curriculum. Think about your academic discipline and your curriculum—what are the literacy skills that are most relevant to high engagement in learning and high academic performance?

You might want to choose three or four literacy skills that you assess continually throughout the year, or you might want to assess different literacy skills that are emphasized during different marking periods. Here's an example: When I taught a world history/world literature block course, it was critical that students understood that writing coherent paragraphs without run-ons and fragments was a first priority for the first semester, while assessing research skills was a major emphasis during the second semester. On the other hand, students' proficiencies related to double-entry note taking and developing graphic organizers for study and review were assessed during every learning unit throughout the year.

Another example: A friend of mine who teaches math places a huge value on students' ability to talk through their problem-solving processes. Consequently, he assesses this skill in dozens of ways during the first quarter. You might want to look through local and national standards for your content area, highlighting learning standards that relate to literacy skills.

Here are some examples:

Mathematics or Science: ability to write and verbalize clear explanations for solving problems

Social Studies: ability to conduct, organize, and summarize research using a variety of sources, including books, periodicals, the Internet, and other reference materials

7

Across All Disciplines:

- The use of multiple strategies to make meaning of text during the reading of text

- The use of graphic organizers, visual mapping, and written formats to recall and record what one has read, heard, or learned

- The understanding and application of specialized vocabulary related to a specific discipline

Assess Important Life Skills That Demonstrate Personal, Social, and Group Efficacy

PERSONAL EFFICACY

Personal efficacy skills (self-management, self-awareness, self-expression) are closely related to learning-how-to-learn skills, but these skills deserve a category of their own. Besides reflecting a "readiness to learn," this skill set strengthens students' efforts to be self-disciplined and self-regulating. Personal efficacy includes the ability to

- seek help when needed

- tolerate failure, self-correct, and recover from mistakes

- settle in, focus, and attend

- express and manage emotions appropriately, especially feelings of stress, frustration, and anger

- work independently without constant supervision

- manage time effectively

- stay on task amid distractions

SOCIAL EFFICACY

Another rarely evaluated skill set relates to social efficacy. Students' proficiency in basic communication and problem-solving skills influences their capacity to actively engage in learning and to interact with others effectively in the learning environment. These, too, are skills that not only lead to improved performance, but also reflect the kinds of skills that employers seek in their workers. Here again is a brief list of skills you might want to assess:

- effectively uses problem-solving skills to handle personal obstacles and interpersonal conflicts

- understands and accepts differences in perspective, opinion, and experience

- listens to others without interrupting

- uses appropriate language, avoids using profanity, and language that has a negative impact on people and the learning environment

- shows evidence of listening for understanding through paraphrasing, questioning, and summarizing

- communicates needs and feelings assertively, rather than aggressively or passively

- gives and receives feedback effectively

GROUP EFFICACY

Group efficacy involves cooperation, group participation, and leadership skills. You are always teaching individual students and a group of students at the same time. Teachers in high-performing classrooms create learning experiences that help students develop the skills to be both effective individual learners and effective participants and leaders in a group. These skills are also associated with the qualities of good citizenship. They include:

- taking initiative and exercising leadership behaviors within the group

- respecting other voices and encouraging everyone's voice to be heard

- encouraging and supporting others in working productively

- gathering information, discussing issues, generating ideas, and reaching consensus in a group

- doing one's fair share in a group

- completing cooperative learning tasks effectively, with attention to timeliness and quality

- communicating needs and preferences to the group

- engaging in conscious acts of respect, caring, helpfulness, kindness, and consideration toward other group members

- exercising assertiveness and persuasion within a group

- taking on different roles in a group effectively

- expressing appreciation for the contributions of others

- showing sensitivity and appreciation for individual and cultural differences among group members

- interrupting biased, insensitive, and abusive remarks

How to Grade the Three L's

You might try setting aside 15 to 20 percent of your possible grade points for the three Ls. (See sample Student Assessment Form on page 157.) For example, if you choose to assess 20 skills, you assign 10 points to each skill for a total of 200 points. Students would then receive 0 to 10 points, depending upon how regularly and how well they demonstrate a particular skill competency. Here's what it might look like:

Skill Competency	Using a 10-Point Scale for Each Skill
Effective use of intra- and inter-personal problem solving	**10** Student uses the skill naturally on a daily basis and encourages others to use the skill
	8 – 9 Student uses skill regularly and effectively
	4 – 7 Student demonstrates effective use of the skill sometimes, but needs more practice for it to become a natural, everyday behavior
	2 – 3 Student rarely uses this skill and needs to make a more intentional effort to practice it
	0 – 1 Student's inability to use this skill become a major obstacle to learning

Your commitment to teach and model these skills, and the degree to which you encourage and support students to practice these skills, will determine how much students' competency levels improve. At the same time, students also need to develop a greater awareness of how these skills help them become better learners and better people. So you'll need to think about how you and your students assess their use of these skills on a regular basis. Consider these possibilities:

- Students regularly reflect on their use of these skills in their journals.

- You and the students monitor their use of these skills using a checklist.

- You give concrete feedback when you notice exemplary use of a skill or notice how not using a skill is getting in the way of learning.

- Students give each other feedback on the use of specific skills during cooperative learning activities.

- Students choose three or four specific skills to focus on for a quarter, providing an opportunity for you and the student to discuss strategies for improvement and monitor progress.

The more evidence students have that they're using these skills, the more they're likely to continue using them. Self-reflection on their own learning also creates the opportunity to identify and set clear goals from quarter to quarter.

Assessing Habits of Learning

Developing a rubric that assesses students' habits of learning is another way to support the development and practice of critical skills and competencies linked to becoming a successful learner. Here's a sample list of habits to model, teach, practice, and assess. Teachers often expect students to assess habits of learning on a regular basis, and may also invite students to identify specific habits that they want to improve in a given grading term or cycle. Some grade-level teams agree to focus on a few specific habits across the curriculum during the first month of school.

Habits of Learning

Rating Scale:

4. I do it all the time without prompting, and I encourage others to do it

3. I do it most of the time with little prompting

2. I do it some of the time with some prompting

1. I seldom do it and I always need prompting

0. I refuse to do it

Habits of Participation and Communication	Habits of Work	Habits of Self-Discipline	Habits of Mind
— I worked cooperatively with others and did my fair share of the work.	— I followed directions and asked for questions when I didn't understand.	— I sustained my focus and effort even when work was boring or difficult.	— I approached tasks with positive expectations and an open mind.
— I put the goal of the group ahead of my own.	— I attempted and turned in all assigned work.	— I didn't give up and persisted until I got it!	— I accepted challenges and academic risks.
— I volunteered to take on leadership or more responsibility in the group.	— I brought all necessary materials to class and I was ready and organized.	— I handled mistakes, setbacks, stress, and frustration effectively.	— I took intiative to ask questions and probed for deeper understanding.
— I was friendly, helpful, and good humored with others.	— I followed classroom group agreements, routines, and procedures.	— I knew when and how to ask for help when I needed it.	— I used evidence and data to inform and support my thinking.
— I did something positive to make class a good place to learn.	— I addressed each part of the question, task, or assignment.	— I expressed and managed my feelings constructively.	— I made connections between what I'm learning and other knowledge and experiences.
— I shared my thoughts and ideas in small and large groups.	— I edited, corrected, revised, completed all work with accuracy/ proficiency.	— I used positive, non-aggressive language to express myself.	— I explained, restated, and summarized what I learned, read, heard.
— I listened respectfully, without interrupting or engaging in sidebar talk.	— I worked independently and stayed on task without bothering others.	— I was able to solve problems when I experienced personal obstacles.	— I expressed curiosity/ enthusiasm/interest in what I was learning.
— I encouraged everyone to be heard and accepted others' viewpoints.	— I worked silently when it was necessary.	— I did not allow other people's behavior to distract me from the task.	— I organized what I learned and understood through notes, lists, maps, and graphics.

7

Other Alternative Assessment Models

Here are two other ways to rethink what you grade (tests, quizzes, and homework) and how you generate an end-of-term grade (averaging combined grades of tests, quizzes, and homework). Both models generate a more inclusive and balanced system of assessment.

EXAMPLE 1: ASSESSING LEARNING BY TASK AND HABIT

This approach calls for rethinking the assessment categories you use to arrive at an end-of-term grade. There are no artificial homework or quiz categories. Instead, all student work fits within particular types of learning tasks (80% of final grade) and learning habits are assessed separately (20% of final grade).

▶ Major Written Tests, Projects, Products (40% of total term grade)

▶ Practice Work, Editing, Revisions, Corrections (10% of total term grade)

▶ Discussion, Demos, Presentations (10% of total term grade)

▶ Journals, Reflections, Notes, Evidence of Reading/Study (10% of total term grade)

▶ In-Class Labs, Activities, and Group Work (10% of total term grade)

▶ Habits of Learning (see page 147) (20% of total term grade)

EXAMPLE 2: ASSESSING LEARNING USING PROFICIENCY/COMPETENCY RUBRICS

This approach focuses on a set of proficiencies/competencies that are spelled out at the beginning of the grading cycle or term. Teachers using this system usually include eight to ten proficiencies aligned with content learning standards and habits of learning. Some teachers give students the choice to select some of the proficiencies from among a wider array than is required. A one-to-four grading rubric accompanies each proficiency, where

4 = exceeds proficiency;
3 = meets proficiency;
2 = emerging proficiency;
1 = not yet proficient.

To earn a particular grade, students must achieve a 3 or 4 on a predetermined number of proficiencies/competencies, say eight out of twelve. For example, a student would earn an A by achieving a 4 on at least five proficiencies and at least a 3 on three other proficiencies. A student would earn a C by achieving at least a 3 on at least five proficiencies and at least a 2 on three other proficiencies. Students would earn an "Incomplete" or "Not Yet" (requiring a specific window of time to complete work necessary to achieve proficiency) if most proficiencies were assessed at a 1 or 2 level.

From Developing an Assessment System to Designing a Student Assessment Form

There are three important decisions you need to make before designing a student assessment form:

1. What are the five or six categories of assessment that spell out what you will be assessing and grading? (Remember, you are assessing what you want students to learn and be able to do.)

2. What percentage and specific number of possible points will you assign to each assessment category?

3. What are the individual tasks that you will grade or the individual skills that you will assess within each category? How do these tasks and skills help students learn and meet important academic standards and benchmarks?

The benefits of thinking all of this through before school begins are twofold. First, this creates a way for you to link your expectations to student learning and standards. Right away students and parents will know where you stand; they will know that all kinds of learning tasks and skills count in your classroom, not just paper and pencil tests, quizzes, and homework.

Second, a well thought out assessment system becomes a compelling document that, in effect, puts on paper your philosophy about student learning, achievement, and assessment. It's a handy way to articulate what you think good teaching and good learning are all about. Given the pressures teachers feel about high stakes testing, it becomes your defense for teaching to the skill and the standard, not to the test. If you work in a high school where the debate over testing is raging, sharing and discussing assessment documents can be a good starting point for thoughtful conversation around testing and evaluation.

Here's one way to assign percentages and points:

Major assessments: 40% (400 possible points)

These include tests, projects, essays, products, experiments, and presentations that require extensive study, planning, and/or preparation. These assessments are the ones you want to link to specific learning standards and benchmarks that shape your teaching units. Think about not having more than four or five major assessments in any nine-week grading period, 50 to 100 points for each one. Some of these assessments will probably require step-by-step check-ins, editing, revision, and self-correction, so you want to give yourself enough time to check-in regularly with the group and individual students along the way. You want to give your students enough learning time to complete an assessment satisfactorily or perform at a level of proficiency.

In-class tasks: 20% (200 possible points)

These tasks include graded practices, notes, and demonstrations associated with newly intro-duced topics and skills, quizzes and "quick writes" used to check for understanding, specific individual and group learning activities, graded discussions, and written reflections and self-assessments. You might have 10 to 15 of these tasks over the course of nine weeks, each worth between 10 and 20 points, e.g. five quizzes, four reflections and self-assessments, and six learning activities.

Homework: 20% (200 possible points)

Homework assignments are the concrete evidence that a student has been reading, think-ing, reflecting, experimenting, practicing, collecting data, or problem solving. Homework often includes the following kinds of activities: practices that develop skill competency; logs, graphic organizers, or journals in which students communicate their observations, understanding, and questions about what they are learning and reading; evidence of study, research, investigations, and interviews; creation of questions and problems; and smaller tasks that are part of a major assessment.

The remaining 20% of a student's grade can be distributed among the three L's:

Learning How to Learn Skills	5%	50 possible points
Literacy Skills	5%	50 possible points
Life Skills	10%	100 possible points
TOTAL	**100%**	**100 possible points**

Using round numbers like 1000 points makes it easy for you and your students to calculate grades by adding up the total points and dividing by ten to get an accurate percentage. (873 points = 87% = B+) By assigning every graded item a letter and a specific number of points, you can easily use a computerized grading system to record and print out students' grades. Students should keep a copy of their Student Assessment Form in their portfolio. The form serves several purposes:

- Students can record their grades when they receive them.

- Students can continuously review how they're doing—they can see visually how their efforts make a big difference.

- Students can attach relevant notes and comments to their form.

- Students can review this with you and their parent/guardian.

Look at the sample Student Assessment Form (p. 151). This sample includes six categories of assess-ment and sample items in each category. When you design your own template, you probably will also want to include some blank spaces for individualized assessment tasks, make-up or extra work, and specific assignments you introduce later in the quarter as you learn more about your students and their learning needs. The sample also includes spaces for post-it note feedback, comments, and contracts as part of your ongoing dialogue with each student. When you make copies for students you might want to make them on bright yellow or lime paper so that they are easy for them to find.

Student Assessment Form

Name _____

Course _____ Period _____ Quarter _____

Major Asessments: % of Total Grade = 40% and Total Possible Points = 400

Letter Key/Points	Points Recieved	Letter Grade	Description	Key Academic Standards
A/50			(Am.Lit.) Choice of essay on "The Crucible"	
B/50			(Algebra 2) Test on functions	
C/50			(U.S. History) Project on immigration	
D/50			(Biology) Community toxic waste inquiry	
E/50			(Health) Self-analysis of risk and protective factors that influence your health	
F/100			(Humanities) Exhibition that compares/contrasts arts and letters from two distinct historical periods	
G/50				
TOTAL				

In-Class Tasks: % of Total Grade = 20% and Total Possible Points = 200

Letter Key/Points	Points Recieved	Letter Grade	Description	Key Academic Standards
H/10			(English 2) Performance of scene from "Raisin in the Sun"	
I/10			(Economics) Global economy simulation	
J/20			(Chemistry) Lab #4	
K/20			Notebook Check #2	
L/20			(Geometry) Problem-solving stations	
M/20			(US History) Discussion and small group analysis – 1900 and 2000 – connections, differences, and commonalities	
N/10			(AP English) Editing and wordsmithing thesis statements for final position papers	
O/10			Reflection and self-assessment #1	
P/20			(Art) Small group critique and feedback	
Q/20			(Science) Quiz on demonstration	
R/10				
S/10				
T/20				
TOTAL				

Student Assessment Form CONTINUED

Homework: % of Total Grade = 20% and Total Possible Points = 200

Letter Key/Points	Points Recieved	Letter Grade	Description	Key Academic Standards
U/30			Journal Check #3	
V/10			Study card for unit test	
W/10			Analysis of population	
X/20			Creation of algebraic word problems and their solutions	
Y/20			Reading log check #2	
Z/10			Outline/graphic organizer for essay	
aa/10			Test corrections	
bb/20			Preparation for speech	
cc/20			Role preparation for mock trial	
dd/10			Choice of three vocabulary tasks	
ee/20			Choice of two investigations on motion	
ff/10				
gg/10				
TOTAL				

Learning How to Learn Skills: % of Total Grade = 5% and Total Possible Points = 50

Letter Points	Student Assessment	Teacher Assessment	Final Assessment	Skills
hh/10				Following directions and routines
ii/10				Bringing necessary materials to class
jj/10				Asking questions for understanding
kk/10				Persevering until completion of task
ll/10				Ability to adapt and change strategies for learning
TOTAL				

Literacy Skills: % of Total Grade = 5% and Total Possible Points = 50

Letter Points	Student Assessment	Teacher Assessment	Final Assessment	Skills
mm/10				Uses multiple reading strategies for comprehension
nn/10				Listens effectively in various classroom contexts
oo/10				Verbalizes thoughts and opinions effectively
pp/10				Uses speech and writing for different audiences and purposes effectively
qq/10				Makes connections between text and personal experience
TOTAL				

Student Assessment Form CONTINUED

Life Skills: % of Total Grade = 10% and Total Possible Points = 100

Letter Points	Student Assessment	Teacher Assessment	Final Assessment	Skills
rr/10				Effective use of intra- and interpersonal problem-solving skills
ss/10				Effective expression and management of feelings
tt/10				Capacity to settle in, focus, and attend
uu/10				Seeks help when needed and communicates needs and feelings appropriately
vv/10				Capacity to tolerate failure, self-correct, and learn from mistakes
ww/10				Exercises initiative, leadership, and persuasion in a group
xx/10				Effective use of active listening skills
yy/10				Encourages others to work productively, appreciates individual and cultural differences and contributions of group members
zz/10				Exhibits cooperation skills with a group
AA/10				Exhibits kindness, consideration, and helpfulness toward others
TOTAL				

	% of Total Grade	Total Possible Points	Total Points Received
Major Assessments	40%	400 Points	_____
In-Class Tasks	20%	200 Points	_____
Homework	20%	200 Points	_____
Learning to Learn Skills	5%	50 Points	_____
Literacy Skills	5%	50 Points	_____
Life Skills	10%	100 Points	_____
		Total Points	_____
		Final Grade	_____

Teacher's Feedback, Reminders, Comments:

Student's Goals, Comments, Contracts:

A Final Word about Equity and Assessment and a Caution about Changing What and How You Grade

Changing the way things are always done is never easy in high schools. So be prepared for the questions that will come your way. The students (and their parents) who may grumble when presented with a more holistic and balanced approach to assessment are most likely to be students who are already school smart and socially adept, self-motivated, and self-aware. Indeed, traditional grading and grade reports in high school favor the sons and daughters of highly educated, highly successful baby boomers, and a lot of other kids are left in the dust. The fact is, low grades that measure a narrow range of subject matter knowledge and skills do not serve as a motivator for average and low-performing students.[4] They have already figured out they can't win the grade game, especially when competing against what an Atlantic Monthly cover story describes as "the organization kid."[5]

So why doesn't a system of assessment that seems to disadvantage so many change? For better or worse, the group of parents who are generally satisfied with a standard curriculum and traditional grading are the same parents who are active on school boards and PTOs and exercise political clout in the larger community. If a content, test, and grade driven system works for their kids, why shouldn't it work for everyone else? The undiscussible fear behind the desire to keep things as they are is the fear that their children will somehow be disadvantaged by changes in curriculum and assessment that are likely to benefit other students.

Your job is to make the case—to your students, parents, your department chair, and your principal—that a wider, more participatory, more multidimensional framework for learning and assessment benefits all students, supporting academic success and healthy development for everyone. Students who participate in assessing what and how they're learning take more responsibility for their learning. When students know what helps them learn, they are more motivated to persevere and make the effort to excel. The more students are exposed to a variety of learning tasks and assessment tools, the sooner students start getting a sense of what really interests them, what throws them, what requires more deliberate planning and complex thinking, and what makes them feel competent and confident.

Moreover, businesses and employers continue to call on high schools to better prepare young people for the world of work in the twenty-first century. Integrating learning how to learn skills, literacy skills, and life skills into your assessment system brings students a lot closer to the kinds of skills associated with on-the-job evaluation. As you experiment with changing your system of assessment, think about what you are doing as trading up from a gold standard to a diamond standard. Gold is good—it's rock solid, but it's one dimensional. Diamonds, on the other hand, are multi-faceted, and every single facet contributes to their total sparkle and brilliance.

Stock Up on Basic Learning Tools and Supplies

Having the right materials handy can make a good learning experience an even better one. As you think about stocking your room ask, "What materials will increase student participation? What materials will help me and my students be better organized? And what materials celebrate what we do together?"

1. **Newsprint, Markers, and Masking Tape**—It's good to have large sheets of paper and marking pens available for group work, brainstorming, instructions, etc., so you can record and post important information for as long as you need it. But chart paper is expensive. Instead, order a ream (500 sheets) of 24" × 36" newsprint. This will probably last for the whole year. (www.uline.com)

2. **Digital Timer**—Timing activities can help improve students' capacity to focus, whether you are taking five minutes to do a quick brainstorm, providing 10 minutes for a small group task, or giving a 15-minute minilecture that students know has an ending time.

3. **Note Cards**—Keep note cards (various sizes, lined, blank, and colored) on hand for giving and getting quick feedback, recording small-group responses, study and review, signs, games, etc.

4. **Calendars**—Have yearly and monthly erasable calendars on hand to identify important deadlines, events, etc. Use different colored markers for each class you teach.

5. **Camera and Film**—Use these to document what students are doing throughout the year.

6. **Radio/Tape Recorder**—Listening to music can help students focus. You might also want to record small-group discussions that you evaluate.

7. **Sticky Notes and Sticky Dots**—Use sticky notes for writing comments about individual students to put in your gradebook, for posting written responses from individuals and groups to specific questions, for posting reminder memos to specific classes. Use colored sticky dots to color code papers and materials for each class you teach.

8. **Folders, Boxes, and Baskets**—Keep work folders, extra copies of handouts, and materials in different boxes or baskets for each class you teach.

9. **Poster Board**—Keep heavier card stock and poster board on hand for information that you want to display permanently.

10. **Steel Clips**—Use clips to organize and separate papers and newsprint for each class.

7

Have on Hand Examples of the Supplies You Want Students to Buy for Class

If you are picky about what supplies students buy for class, gather a collection of the items that work for you and the items that don't. For example, if the ragged edges of spiral bound notebook paper make you nuts, "just say no" to spiral notebooks. If you want students to have a journal, bring in examples. The same goes for math tools or any other kind of special materials.

Arrange Desks and Chairs in a Way That Makes It Easy to See Everyone and Learn Their Names

You will probably want to assign seats for the first couple of weeks so it's easier to learn everyone's name. In the beginning of the year, think about a seating arrangement that will enable you to to see everyone, see the door, and move easily from student to student. Assign seats alphabetically by first name or last name. You might also want to reverse tradition and start with Z instead of A.

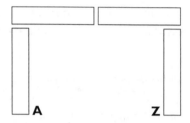

If you have space, arrange tables so everyone can see each other.

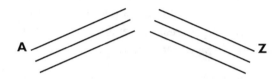

You might want to create a **V** shape with desks or tables, though it's less desireable since students can't all see each other, and it's hard to work with students in the middle rows.

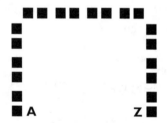

Place desks around three sides of the room so that everyone can see each other. This also gives you a space to do activities in the middle.

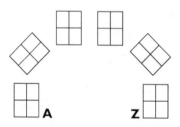

Create working groups of four desks each, so students can turn their chairs around to see each other.

Group chairs in pairs around the room. Everyone can see each other and students can easily work in pairs.

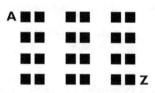

If you need to place students in rows, try placing desks in pairs.

Make the Classroom "Ours"

Turn Walls into Teaching and Organizing Tools

- Keep notes and work in progress for each class on newsprint. String clothesline across the length of a wall for hanging newsprint from large steel clips. I call this one "Power Newsprint."

- Post important goals, routines, and procedures around the room. Identify big goals and the basics that every student needs to know.

- Keep a place for questions that students want to discuss related to an assignment, prepping for a test, etc. Remember, "There's never a stupid question."

- Post the class agenda every day, including what you expect students to do as soon as they arrive for class.

- Whatever your discipline, find provocative articles, quotations, and news clips that make connections between the world students live in and the course you're teaching.

- Create a space to keep extra homework assignments, study guides, and other important papers in one place.

Make a Wall Space for Students

Organize a wall space that includes a place to post important information about class, and that also provides space for you and students to post other things of interest. Take photographs of students doing activities in class. Kids love to see pictures of each other and pictures are a way to affirm community.

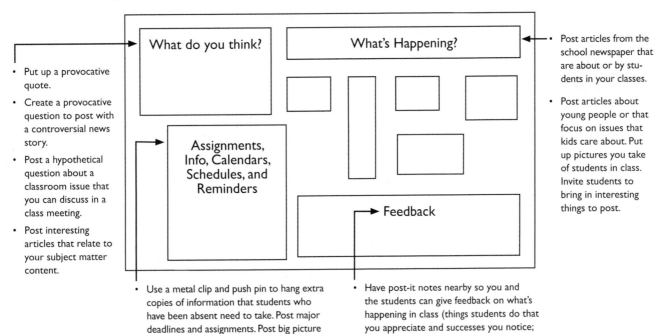

- Put up a provocative quote.
- Create a provocative question to post with a controversial news story.
- Post a hypothetical question about a classroom issue that you can discuss in a class meeting.
- Post interesting articles that relate to your subject matter content.

What do you think?

What's Happening?

Assignments, Info, Calendars, Schedules, and Reminders

Feedback

- Post articles from the school newspaper that are about or by students in your classes.
- Post articles about young people or that focus on issues that kids care about. Put up pictures you take of students in class. Invite students to bring in interesting things to post.

7

- Use a metal clip and push pin to hang extra copies of information that students who have been absent need to take. Post major deadlines and assignments. Post big picture questions and learning goals that help focus attention on what you are currently learning.

- Have post-it notes nearby so you and the students can give feedback on what's happening in class (things students do that you appreciate and successes you notice; student comments; and questions/topics from students about what to review.)

CHAPTER 8

The First Day of Class

The first day of class is the one day in the entire year when students will come home and actually share their impressions of classes and teachers with their families. Your heartfelt hope, no matter how many years you have been teaching, is that more kids leave your class saying, "This is okay. I can handle this," than muttering, "This really sucks. This is going to be bad!"

You get a lot of mileage out of the first day. Think about the start of a school year like the start of a cross-country trip in a brand new car. Everything feels new and fresh, even your favorite old traveling clothes. You're packed and organized with the right maps at your fingertips. There is nothing quite like the sense of anticipation before you take off. You're excited about the journey ahead, but still worried about what you might have forgotten to shut down, cancel, or put in the car. So you're careful and a little low-key on the first day out. You're not hell-bent on zooming from 0 to 70 mph in the first ten seconds of your trip. Instead, you're checking out how the car hugs the road, you're testing out the brakes. There's plenty of time later to cruise flat out on the interstate.

Long road trips are a lot like the school year. Both have a beginning, middle, and end, and both benefit from good planning and preparation. But what makes both of these experiences fun and scary, deeply rewarding and demanding, is that you really don't know the shape the trip will ultimately take when you start out.

Some First-Day Goals

Nevertheless, there is a lot you can predict and prepare for during that first class period, a period that is always over sooner than you would like. This is not the time for lively prosocial bonding, intense conversation, or a high-powered learning activity. Students will spend what little time there is fully occupied in four activities: checking out who's in the room; checking you out; getting a quick impression of what it feels like to sit there for 50 minutes; and most important, hoping that, armored with a lot of vigilance and a little cool, they will get through this class and six others without self-destructing or being embarrassed in front of their peers.

Having said this, the goals for your first day with students are more or less the same as the goals that guide your preparation before the school year begins:

- Do something that makes each student feel welcomed and invited but not exposed.

- Do something that makes students feel respected as young people, but not at the expense of your own authority and presence as the adult in the room. Kids want to feel respected and they want to know you're in charge.

- Do something that sets the tone for what matters in your classroom, but don't overwhelm them with a huge laundry list of rules and expectations.

- Do something that lets students know they have entered a learning environment— not their living rooms, not a basketball court, not the local mall, and surely not a police station.

- Engage students in some practices and procedures that will become daily or weekly routines.

- Do something that communicates organization, purpose, and focus, without being fussy or complicated.

- Do something that encourages high student participation, but with a minimum of noise and physical movement.

- Do something that encourages student voice, but does not sanction silliness or cynicism.

- Do something that is unexpected; the element of surprise goes a long way toward grabbing students' attention.

- And finally, do at least one thing that shows your humor and your heart.

Your first day of class is your first chance to invoke the state of mind you would like learners to inhabit every day. Call it unanxious anticipation, relaxed alertness, or hopeful expectation; whatever you name it, you want to do things on the first day that will bring that feeling into the room.

What Is Your Most Effective Teaching Stance for the First Day of Class?

Your teaching stance is the combination of attitudes, outlook, and demeanor that you wear most often and most visibly. Your stance communicates "first principles"—the things that matter to you the most. It is about how you present yourself to your students, about what you prize and what you want to protect. Some aspects of your teaching stance are like a second skin. Others are harder to come by, requiring time and practice before you can express that aspect of your teaching persona with authenticity and confidence. If you were to ask your students at the end of the year to write down five words or phrases that they think describe what you stand for, their responses would give you a pretty good sense of whether they took in what you tried to convey in the last nine months.

There isn't one right teaching stance, but there are some wrong ones, especially on the first day of class. The question you need to ask is this: What is the most effective teaching stance that will help you put your best foot forward with a group of young people whom you may never have met?

The dilemma is choosing what to play up and what to tone down on the first day. You do want to respond to students' first day anxieties about what to expect. But you don't want your teaching persona to overwhelm students before they've had a chance to watch, listen, and settle in. Some qualities that you prize most about yourself as a teacher and a learner may need to take a backseat that first week.

Most adolescents are justifiably cautious and a little subdued when they encounter new adults in their lives. They don't want to be caught in a position of giving away too much or appearing too vulnerable, and they are rightly suspicious of adults who want to be "up close and personal" during a first encounter. (What you'll need to be ready for is the one kid who walks in as if he's known everyone, including you, for his entire lifetime.) A handy rule of thumb for meeting a group of adolescents for the first time is to avoid extremes. This is the one time when going all out for the middle ground is a good thing. Your first day is about creating the foundation for building the learning community that you and your students will become in the next month or so. Your teaching stance should reflect the attitudes, outlook, and demeanor that will help get you there.

A First-Day Teaching Stance Might Look Like This

Respectful: You can do four things on Day One that let students know you want to be thought of as an adult who is respectful to young people: your preparation of materials and the readiness and attractiveness of the classroom space will tell students they are worthy of your time and effort; your interest in learning all of their names as quickly as you can; your attentiveness to their questions and concerns; and your interest in getting to know them as individuals.

Serious, But with a Touch of Humor: Students will shut down if you present yourself as a stern taskmaster, but don't try to be an MC on Comedy Central, either. Balance and timing are everything.

Friendly: Forget about that "Don't smile until Christmas" baloney. Nobody turns down a smile and a little warmth as a way of saying, "Welcome back." On the other hand, being over-familiar and too personal are about as effective as being cold and detached.

Invitational: You can't demand much of anything from adolescents without risking passive resistance. You can, however, invite students to cooperate and work with you. Use phrases like, "I'd like us to...," "I have a request to make...," "For today, it would be helpful if everyone...," "For the next five minutes, I'd like you to...," "Because we need to... I'm asking if everyone will...," and of course, "Please" and "Thank you."

Knowledgeable: Have something in the room (a curious object, a stack of books, an interesting piece of equipment, a compelling photograph, a provocative quotation, a list of puzzling terms that are specific to your content area, a poster or article linked to your discipline or to people who practice your discipline in the work world) that indicates your passion, curiosity, and knowledge of the course content.

8

Organized: Feeling flustered when you can't find what you need is the day-time version of your worst nightmare. Label, color code, and box everything for different classes; make more than enough copies; make a special tray for all the tools you need for the day; and don't use any electrical equipment if there's even a minute chance that it might go haywire.

Sequential: This is not the day to skip around randomly from one thing to another and hope that "all will be revealed" in the last five minutes. Students should be able to see the connections among the activities you do the first day.

Clear and Succinct: No long-winded speeches, no confusing instructions, no complex tasks—keep it simple.

Calm and Low-Key: If quiet, uneventful, and smooth are words that come to mind at the end of your first day, you're good to go.

A Few Words about Developing a Culture of Caring

A culture of caring develops over time through the sharing of critical events and experiences. Sending the message that you care about your students on the first day sounds and feels phony to adolescents. Your actions during the first month will speak louder and more effectively than words.

A Sampling of Activities and Procedures for the First Day of Class

If your teaching schedule entails fifty-minute periods, it's an even greater challenge to choose what to do and what to leave out on the first day. The fifty-minute agenda that follows is a sample, and only a sample, plan. It includes, however, some essential procedures and activities that can help you get off to a good start. As you read this and develop your own first day plan, think about capturing the spirit of this agenda, rather than implementing it verbatim. Keep asking, "What are the words and ways of expressing myself that will work best for me?"

Procedure 1:

I'm in the right place—are you? Post a sign on your door or next to it that gives the basics—your name, the course, the class period, and the room number. A little humor, a picture, or a bit of bold graphics never hurt a sign!

Procedure 2:

Post the agenda for the day in the place where you will post it everyday. Agendas may vary according to what you are doing and what you want to emphasize each day. Here is a First Day example:

First Day Agenda

Goals:

- To introduce ourselves
- To become familiar with classroom procedures and course basics
- Getting to Work: Complete your student profile forms
- Introductions
- Classroom and course basics
- Preview of next month
- Homework
- Closing

Other Examples:

Agenda
- Academic Goals
- Group Goals
- Personal Goals
- Skills for the Day
- Getting to Work
- Gathering
- Main Activity
- Quick Feedback and Assessment
- Homework

Agenda
- Big Goal for the Day
- Getting to Work
- Summary of Activities
- Checking Out
- Homework

Agenda
- Aims
- Skills for the Day
- Getting to Work
- Checking In
- Learning Task #1
- Learning Task #2
- Learning Task #3

Agenda

This is not a regular day!
- Here's the Plan
- Why?
- Get Ready by...

Procedure 3:

Where to sit? You may want to prepare a seating chart ahead of time if you have accurate class lists. I recommend distributing the chart to the entire class. Though teachers receive class rosters, students rarely do. But it is actually a considerate gesture to give students a chart with everyone's name, especially if you expect them to learn each other's names as soon as possible.

If your class list is still incomplete, or if you prefer not to use a seating chart in the beginning of the year, ask students to take any seat and have markers and card stock available so everyone can make a name card to set on their desks. (See Learning Students' Names page 215)

Procedure 4:

Prepare to pass out a First Day packet as students walk in. Your packet might include the following:

- A seating chart for the class or instructions for where students are to sit

- A "First Things First" page of procedures for students to read after they sit down

- A Student Profile form for students to complete for their "Getting to Work" activity

- The course syllabus

8

- A very brief description of your assessment and grading system

- A list of materials and supplies that you expect students to bring to class on Day Two

- Two copies of a letter to parents/guardians (one to sign and return and one to keep) that introduces you and the course to them

- A page describing the first week's homework assignments

Procedure 5:

Meet and greet: Welcome every student at the door. Say hello, say your name, ask their names, and invite them to take a seat and follow directions on the first page of their First Day Packet.

Procedure 6:

First things first! The first page of your First Day Packet might be entitled "First Things First." See the following page for a sample of what it might look like.

HANDOUT I
First Things First

Please read over these procedures after you take a seat.

| Read This Now!

This classroom is a learning environment and a public place, not your living room (what you do and say there is between you and your family), not the cafeteria (hanging out is not your reason for being here), not the bathroom (this is not the place for personal hygiene care from nails to hair), not the "Fight Club" (no public brawling, cursing, or yelling), not a playing field (no contact sports), and this is not the backseat of a car (please keep your hands and feet to yourself). Thank you.

---

1. **Walking into the room:** Timely, quietly, carefully, and mindfully are the ways to walk into the room.

    TIMELY – because it's a sign of respect for me to start on time and for you to be here on time. If you have NOT arrived ON TIME, you've earned yourself a tardy.

    QUIETLY – because everyone needs a minute or two to catch their breath, put aside what went on last hour, and settle in. If you have NOT walked in QUIETLY, I will ask you to re-enter the room.

    CAREFULLY – because there are a lot of bodies and a lot of stuff in this room. Please be respectful of other people's space and other people's stuff. If you have NOT walked in CAREFULLY, I will ask you to re-enter the room.

    MINDFULLY – because when we begin I'd like you to have your materials organized and in front of you and your mind and spirit fully present so we can focus on the task at hand. If it looks like walking in MINDLESSLY is becoming a habit, I will talk with you privately to check out what's going on.

2. **Taking a Seat:** (Please sit_____.)

3. **Getting to Work:** When you walk in the door, there will always be a question, a check-in, or "Getting Started" activity on the board. It will always be posted _____. Please start now. You will have about five minutes.

4. **Gathering as a Group:** After about five minutes, I will call time. I will be ready to have us gather as a whole group. I expect you to show that you're ready by having completed the "Getting to Work" activity, having appropriate materials on your desk, and directing your attention to the front of the room.

5. **Ending Class:** I will make a real commitment to end on time. However, if anyone, either student or teacher, is in the middle of a sentence and the bell rings, I expect all of us to listen until the person finishes their thought. Then I will say, "Time to go. 'Bye for now." That's when you may get up out of your chairs and leave.

ACTIVITY 1: ⏰ **(5 minutes)**

"Getting to Work" Activity: In your First Day packet think about including a student profile form that every student can fill in quickly, comfortably, and easily. This might include contact information, some basic family data, brief bio facts, and school history. You can always solicit more personal information using an interest questionnaire a bit later. (See pages 208–215)

ACTIVITY 2: ⏰ **(5 minutes)**

Introductions:

1. **Acknowledge the "Rep" That Precedes You:** In high schools, most faculty come with some history to the next group of students they teach—some of it is probably positive and some negative, some accurate and some that's more myth than truth. Asking students what they think they know about you is a great way to show students that you have a sense of humor, that you can depersonalize hearsay, and that you want them to hear from you who you are and what you expect.

   So take a few minutes to invite students to say what they've heard or what they think they know about you and this class. Tell them you don't take this personally, and explain that it's usually a good idea to check out what students assume or imagine so that you can clear up any misconceptions or misinformation. Use any of these approaches:

   - Give them a few minutes to say their assumptions. Don't interrupt or respond to specific things that you hear.

   - Ask students to write their assumptions on note cards and you read some aloud to the class.

   - If you're uncomfortable asking students to do this or you think students will be uncomfortable sharing with you, say something like, "These are some of the things you might have heard about me." Make what you say light and humorous.

2. **Introducing Yourself:** Afterwards, you might say, "So I'd like you to hear from me a little about who I am." Again, keep it light rather than dramatic or ultra serious. Leave students a little curious—don't tell them your life history! Share three or four things about yourself—why you decided to teach; where you're from; something about your family; something you love to do outside of school; or maybe something they would be surprised to know about you. Here are some other ideas:

   - Pronounce your name and say something about your name if it's unusual or hard to pronounce.

   - "You may have heard that I _____. What you probably don't know about me is _____."

   - "No matter what you've heard, I have never _____."

   - Something you like most about teaching and something you don't like about schools or the teaching profession.

- "You'll probably get tired of hearing me say, '_____ ', so I'm giving you a heads up that you'll hear this a lot because it's really important to me."

- Something about the course you're teaching that keeps you fascinated.

- "I could have been a _____ or a _____ , but I chose to become a teacher because _____."

- Close by sharing something about your hopes and expectations: "At the end of the year/semester I hope that many of you will be able to say three things: _____, _____, and _____."

3. **Student Introductions:** Usually, you'll want to take roll while students are doing their "Getting to Work" activity. However, on the first day you'll want to take roll by asking students to say their names. Everyone needs an opportunity to start matching names and faces, and you need to hear how students say their names before you mispronounce them.

   Tell students that you want to learn their names as soon as possible and learn to pronounce them correctly. Say something like, "If you mispronounce my name, I'd probably say, 'Here's how it's pronounced,' and I'd say it again for you. So I'd appreciate it if you will correct me in a way that's respectful and helps me say it right. Please, be patient—I'll probably be asking you to say your name more than a few times over the next week or so."

ACTIVITY 3: ⏰ (5 minutes)

What Do You Want to Know? Tell students that you know they have lots of questions and that you won't be able to respond to all of them today. Explain that you would like to take five minutes to answer questions about things that students want to know right away. Be sure to ask students if there is anything they want to ask about First Things First procedures.

ACTIVITY 4: ⏰ (8 minutes)

What Do You Think This Course Is About? What Do You Think We're Going to Be Doing? Do a quick brainstorm of what students think is going to happen in this class. This is your first opportunity to clarify for students what is and is not part of this course.

Take about five minutes to do the brainstorm and about three minutes to clarify students' responses or fill in some information gaps.

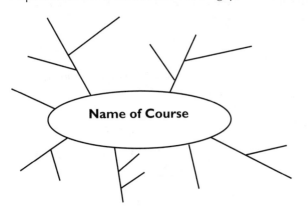

Name of Course	
What's it about?	Skills you'll be learning?

8

ACTIVITY 5: ⏰ **(5 minutes)**

Big Goals for the Year: Have a few of your big goals and/or expectations posted on a large chart or transparency. Or you might choose not to discuss any detailed goals and/or expectations today. Instead, you might want to share a more global belief or hope that speaks to what you value most about teaching young people.

It could be something like this:

"You can count on me not to confuse who you are as a person with the grade you earn on a report card. I know you have a life outside of this course. There are 168 hours in a week. You give this class 5% of your time and effort during the week, and I'll give you 100% of my effort and my support."

OR

"All of you can learn to be successful in this class. I don't start out the year assuming some of you will "get it" and get As and some of you will just "get over" or "get by" with Cs and Ds. I have confidence that each of you has what it takes to do well over the long haul."

ACTIVITY 6: ⏰ **(3 minutes)**

Materials: If you expect students to purchase specific materials and supplies, include them on a page in the First Day packet. Show students examples of required supplies and materials that meet your criteria. Be sure to include examples of what not to buy.

ACTIVITY 7: ⏰ **(5 minutes)**

A Preview of the Next Month: On the board, post the learning goals that you will emphasize during the next month:

- Learning Goal 1: Learn Important Policies and Expectations and Practice Important Classroom Procedures

- Learning Goal 2: Become a Community of Learners

- Learning Goal 3: Learn Course Work

Explain that students will experience activities related to each learning goal every day over the next month. Explain why each goal is important by saying something like this:

For #1, *"It's much easier to remember what to do if you hear it and discuss it in small doses over time. One of my jobs in the first few weeks is to make sure you know what I expect. One of your jobs is to learn what you need to do to be successful in this class."*

For #2, *"Here in the classroom, you work as individual learners and as members of a group. During the first month you will have a chance to learn more about yourselves as learners and*

I hope to learn more about what each of you needs to do your best. I also expect all of us to develop good group skills and form positive relationships so we can work well as a team."

For #3, *"The last goal is about learning* _____*."*

(Preview the first course unit and highlight a few skills and learning activities that are included in the first unit.)

ACTIVITY 8: ⏰ (5 minutes)

Course Work: Have students read the syllabus and circle two topics that, on first glance, seem most interesting to them. Then have them write down at least one question they have about what we're going to study and learn in this class.

Letter Home: If you are planning to send a welcome and introduction letter home to parents/guardians, this is the day to do it. You might want to put two letters in every First Day packet, one for families to keep, and the other for them to send back to you signed.

Getting Started: List the required materials and supplies for tomorrow's class.

Procedure 7:

Ending Class: Wait for the bell. Then say some version of, "Bye for now. I look forward to seeing you tomorrow. You may go."

8

CHAPTER 9

The First Month, Day by Day

As you plan your first month, consider integrating a balanced combination of learning activities, strategies, and practices that help students accomplish these three learning goals:

Learning Goal 1: Learn Important Policies and Expectations and Practice Important Classroom Procedures
Learning Goal 2: Become a Community of Learners
Learning Goal 3: Learn Course Work

Why These Three Learning Goals?

Although few secondary staff would disagree about the importance of the learning goals suggested here, few teachers get around to implementing a set of intentional activities and practices that will help students achieve them. The time-honored excuse is always the same – these efforts take too much time and involve too much off-task behavior. Since rethinking teaching and learning is this book's raison d'être, here are a few talking points that tackle the "yes, but" excuses and summarize the benefits of integrating activities that support these goals during the first month.

1. **These activities and practices involve on-task learning behaviors at the most fundamental level.**
   Learning how to learn skills are metacognitive skills that involve students in reflecting on these types of questions: What will it take for me to learn this? How do I go about planning, predicting, and strategizing? How do I learn with others? How do I assess my performance? How do I motivate myself? What did I learn? What do I think about what I learned? How did I learn it? How can I use what I've learned? What gets in the way of learning effectively? What do I do when I'm stuck? What do I need to change to learn more effectively? A student's capacity and inclination to think metacognitively is one of the most influential determinants of student success or failure.

2. **Front-loading these activities and practices in the beginning of the year gives students what they need so they can do what you want them to do.**
   These activities incorporate basic tools necessary to become successful as independent learners and as members of a group. Contrary to popular wish, most high school students are not as "school-smart," self-motivated, and cooperative as we wish they were. Thus,

9

taking the time to establish classroom procedures and routines, discuss the reasons for them, and monitor students' practice of them goes a long way toward providing the kind of support that will help students meet your academic and behavioral expectations.

You are likely to find more effective training regimens and rigorous practice and feedback in the army, in industry, or at the local firehouse than you will in most high schools. Teaching is not telling. For a vast majority of students and workers (over 70%) effective learning needs to involve the following steps:

– a clear, understandable reason for learning something

– modeling by someone who shares their expertise and experience

– a direct experience involving the skill to be learned and mastered

– good coaching and supervision as the skill is being practiced and regular assessment of performance (This includes self-reflection and self-assessment.)

– opportunities to make personal meaning of what is learned, so it will stick

– positive recognition and appreciation when the skill is being used effectively and regularly

This process holds true for learning any academic or behavioral skill. In the beginning of the year you want students to learn and use procedures that help create a smooth running classroom. Incorporating these learning steps may take a little more time, but the benefits are worth it. The big pay off is gaining more time "on-task" in the long run, because you will spend less time repeating, reminding, and reviewing what you want students to do. Right from the first day, notice and appreciate students when you see them doing the right thing.

3. **Students' perceptions of classroom climate and their feelings toward you personally strongly influence their motivation and capacity to learn.**
    There is a direct relationship between the quality of the classroom climate (Do I feel safe? Can I belong here? Will I be respected and accepted for who I am as a person? Will people make fun of me? Will I be listened to? Will I be treated fairly? Will I look stupid in here? Will I get help when I need it? Will my efforts and talents be recognized?) and a student's receptivity to learning. The degree and measure of a student's positive attitude and good will depend on the relationships you develop with the whole group and with each individual. Consequently, it makes good sense to engage students in learning strategies and activities that help forge positive relationships and establish a positive learning climate.

4. **Pacing the introduction of procedures, reducing the quantity of content, and balancing academic and behavioral goals provide a more equitable start for everyone.**
    By pacing and regulating the sheer quantity of what's introduced day by day, all students, not just the deluxe model of adolescent learners, have a real chance to get on board and get on track with your academic program. Too many kids experience information and procedural overload from day one and never really recover. Furthermore, by stressing the importance of academic and behavioral goals, every student gets the message right away

that their effort and their classroom behavior count. This is as important for students who "ace" exams and essays, but disparage everything else about the class and classmates, as it is for students who walk in with knowledge and skill deficits, and need immediate assurance that they won't be left out or left behind.

Making Time for "Both-and" Instead of Choosing "Either-or"

Teachers tend to approach new class start-up in one of two ways. Many rush headlong into a whirlwind of academic tasks and testing while a few forgo academic course work altogether in favor of an onslaught of teambuilding exercises and group processing. Providing only an "either-or" choice is not a good way to go.

Instead, consider a "both-and" approach that incorporates "Getting Started" activities and "Course Work" into every class period. This is not as easy as it sounds. For starters, it means shifting your own expectations of what you want to accomplish and what you want students to experience in the beginning few weeks. The biggest challenge may be letting go of school and self-induced pressures to elevate content coverage and content learning above all other learning goals and experiences in the beginning of the year.

It would be a lie to say that you can help students accomplish these three goals (1: Learn Policies, Expectations, and Procedures, 2: Become a Community of Learners, and 3: Learn Course Work) and still be at the same place you were in your curriculum last year on September 15. It's not going to happen. But no one is going to die either if you teach one less unit during the year. On the other hand, the "slow is fast" approach is likely to result in fewer students giving up and acting out, more students remaining engaged and motivated, and, most notably, less frustration and greater satisfaction for you and the students you're teaching.

Teachers maintain that the biggest obstacle to changing old habits is the challenge of imagining what class would really look like, day by day, if they took a different approach. I hear comments like, "I did one or two things that encouraged students to get to know each other, but I never thought about changing my whole teaching plan during the first month. For that to happen, I'd need a much clearer idea of how it all fits together."

Preparing Yourself to Shift Your Teaching Focus during the First Month

The sample four-week agenda that follows fills in the details of what it would look and sound like to shift your teaching focus during the first month. Each class period includes "Getting Started" activities and "Course Work." This is not intended to serve as a prescription, but to serve as a model of how you might integrate and sequence activities that focus on each goal: 1. Learn Policies, Expectations, and Procedures; 2. Become a Community of Learners; and 3. Learn Course Work.

All change is accompanied by doubts, risks, and uncertainty. It is useful, then, to spell out some of the trade-offs you'll need to live with as you try out a "both-and" approach during the first

9

month. You may wince a little as you read these cautions and caveats. It's that hard to let go of doing things the way they have always been done.

- During most class periods, you're not likely to have more than twenty to thirty minutes for "Course Work" if your classes are scheduled in fifty-minute time segments. This means "chunking" your first learning unit somewhat differently and implementing it over a longer period of time. This is the most dramatic change you'll make. You've got to make peace with this or "content coverage creep" will kick in by the third day of class.

- You are likely to allocate a couple of entire class periods to "Getting Started" activities — there are some experiences that just aren't very effective if you short change the amount of time to do them and reflect on what you've done. This model includes four whole-period experiences that are spread out over the month.

- Plan for the uncomfortable reality that you will be asking yourself, "So why am I doing this? Is this really worth all the time and planning?" Put into words your most compelling rationale and learn it by heart—to say to yourself, to say to your colleagues, to say to parents, to say to your students. "I'm doing this because…" And then keep saying it to yourself. It might sound like this, "I've made this commitment, and I'm going to see it through because I want every kid to have a real chance."

- You will probably need to defend yourself against attacks of "off-task" guilt. Remind yourself that all learning is "on-task" behavior, not just the narrow definition of learning tasks associated with content coverage. Remember, too, that young people's healthy growth and development depends, in large part, on how adults support the maturity and integration of intellectual, social, and emotional aspects of an adolescent's life. You are modeling just this kind of support by starting out the year in this way.

- You will find yourself spending more time reflecting back and commenting on what you see and hear students doing. Your efforts to do this serve as a model and invitation for students to become more reflective about their own learning and behavior. This reflection/feedback process is a piece of cake for early childhood educators — for high school faculty this particular teaching behavior might feel a little awkward. Try writing yourself a reminder note each day to comment on at least one procedure or skill that you witness the group using well, and privately try giving appreciative feedback to individual students whose behaviors indicate their growing academic and social competence.

- As you move from day to day and week to week, cultivate the habit of PLAN, DO, REVIEW. At the end of the day or at the end of the week, take time to reflect on these questions:

  - How did it go today? What thoughts or questions are in the front of my mind?

  - At what moments were kids most engaged? How do I know that?

  - What do I think worked best? Are there one or two things that happened—that kids said—that I particularly want to remember?

  - Is there anything I'd like to change or do differently next time? Why? What are the benefits?

  - How does today's experience influence my focus and plan for tomorrow? Is there anything I want to shift around or prepare differently for the next class?

  - Finally, don't expect everything to work the way you planned and imagined it. Remember the mantra, "The lesson/discussion/activity wasn't perfect and it was still successful." Nothing you ever do will reach every kid at the same time with equal effectiveness. This "both-and" approach does, however, create a climate and culture that enables you to reach more kids more of the time.

A Day by Day Agenda For the First Month
Each day contains the following format:

DAY 1

GETTING STARTED:

Getting to Work: This is the "walk-in-the-door" activity that is posted in the same place every day. These five-minute start-up activities are usually linked to the previous day's agenda or the current day's agenda.

Become a Community of Learners: These activities help students get to know each other, encourage learner self-awareness and goal-setting, help students identify what they need to be effective members of a group, and introduce students to "Gathering" and team-building activities.

Policies, Procedures, and Expectations: These activities provide opportunities for you to introduce and review policies and expectations, for you and students to discuss and clarify important classroom procedures, and for students to learn some basic problem-solving protocols for individual issues (the problem-solving process) and whole-group issues (class meeting and group negotiation).

9

COURSE WORK:

For each day, this section is left blank for each teacher to sequence in the way that works best for their students. In this daily model, about thirty minutes out of a fifty-minute period are set aside for "Course Work."

HOMEWORK:

Course Work: Your curriculum will shape these assignments.

Getting Started: Scattered throughout the first month are some ten-minute assignments linked to other "Getting Started" activities.

As you read through this model plan, keep in mind:

- The first two weeks include more "Getting Started" activities than the last two weeks.

- By the third week, most "Getting to Work" activities and Homework assignments should probably be linked to "Course Work."

- This plan assumes that students keep some kind of journal/reflections notebook that you can read and respond to about once a month.

- Issues around cultural diversity and harassment are presented and discussed later in the month, when students have a better sense of classroom procedures and guidelines and know each other better.

- Think about what you'd keep, change, or rearrange and be thinking about the wording and language you would craft for openings, instructions, reflections, transitions, and closings.

DAY 2

GETTING STARTED:

Getting to Work: Interview Questions

- ❑ Have students create five questions they would ask another person in class that would help them introduce her/him to the group.

Become a Community of Learners: Partner Interviews

- ❑ Partner Interviews: Have students pair up, interview each other using their questions, and then introduce each other to the class, saying their partner's name and two or three things about her or him.

❑ Let students know that you expect everyone to learn everyone else's name by Day Five. Tell them why this is important to you. Let them know you might stop in the middle of the class to check if there is anyone who wants to try naming everyone. You might want to have some pencils, tokens, etc. to pass out to anyone who can do this during the first week.

Policies, Procedures, and Expectations: Classroom Boundaries

❑ Explain your boundaries, why you have them, what behaviors are boundary violations, and what will happen when boundaries are violated (See *Getting Classroom Management RIGHT: Guided Discipline and Personalized Support in Secondary Schools*).

COURSE WORK:

❑ Discuss course syllabus and answer questions.

❑ Begin teaching your first learning unit.

HOMEWORK:

❑ **Course Work:** Give assignment to students.

❑ **Getting Started:** Choose to write about three questions from Creating a Classroom Vision (See pages 297–299). Write your responses in your journal.

DAY 3

GETTING STARTED:

Getting to Work: Creating a Classroom Vision

❑ Have students choose to write about three more questions from Creating a Classroom Vision. Ask students to share responses to one or two questions with a partner.

Become a Community of Learners: Classroom Vision Learning Carousel

❑ Choose eight to ten questions from the Creating a Classroom Vision to post on chart paper around the room. Divide students into threes using playing cards, and assign each group to the chart paper that contains the same number as the one on their playing cards. (The three students who have 2s will be in the same group, the 3s will be in the same group, and so on.) Give each group of three students a marker and ask the group to write one or two responses to the question on their chart paper. Remind groups to get ideas from each group member and to take turns writing.

Use a timer and give groups about a minute and a half at each station. When time is up, ask each group to move clockwise to the next chart and repeat the process, responding to a different question.

9

If you do this activity with several different classes, you may want to collate all responses to each question so you can create one set of responses to hand back to all of your classes.

Let students know that you will type up the newsprint data so that students can review and use it later in the week when the class develops classroom agreements. Or, if you have students who want to type this up for extra credit, a late or free homework pass, or student leadership points, by all means take them up on it. It's never too early to ask for help.

Policies, Procedures, and Expectations: Procedural Check-in

❑ Clarify, teach, and/or review any important procedures that you have not introduced.

COURSE WORK:

HOMEWORK:

❑ **Course Work:** Your curriculum will shape these assignments.

❑ **Getting Started:** Bring in an article, photo, or anything else that highlights young people in the news, youth issues, popular culture, or interesting events coming up. Post on the board entitled "What's Going On?"

DAY 4

GETTING STARTED:

Getting to Work: Youth Culture

❑ Post anything you brought to put on the "What's Going On?" board.

❑ In your journal, write a response to one of the following questions:

– What three youth culture icons (things, names, products, music groups, etc.) should every adult recognize, so they at least know what it is?

– If all adults could see only one movie, and you had to recommend it, what would you choose? Why?

– If all adults could listen to only one music group or performer, and you had to recommend the selection, whom would you pick? Why?

– If you had to make a list of five things no teen should be without, what would those five things be?

Become a Community of Learners: Getting to Know Each Other

❏ Play a name game or ask students to share some of their responses to the journal questions.

❏ Do a spot check to see if anyone can remember everyone's name.

Policies, Procedures, and Expectations: Your Assessment and Grading System

❏ Explain your system of assessment and grading by reviewing your handout on grading in the First Day packet. Reassure students that they don't need to know everything about the grading system right this minute. There will be plenty of time over the next few weeks to become familiar with it. (See pages 162–164)

For overachievers who won't be satisfied until they know how they can attain every point possible, for worriers who are already imagining themselves grounded after the first marking period, and for protestors who are ready to rally about an unfair system—make a compromise. Set aside 15 minutes before school or during lunch in the next day or so when students can come and talk with you about grading and assessment.

Policies, Procedures, and Expectations: Sharing Big Goals and Expectations

❏ Discuss some of your Big Goals for the year. (See pages 360–363) Talk about your expectations and goals, particularly around issues of quality and completion, and share the ways you will provide support for students to meet these goals. If satisfactory completion of certain tasks or a specific portfolio of work is a big deal for you (and I hope it is!), the "cruisers" who get by with Ds and the "slackers" who may have NEVER completed a thing will be in for a big shock. You will need to tell students exactly what they will be expected to do when they hand in unsatisfactory or incomplete work.

COURSE WORK:

HOMEWORK:

❏ **Course Work:** Your curriculum will shape these assignments.

DAY 5

GETTING STARTED:

Getting to Work: Writing Hopes and Hesitations

❏ Give each person two different color "sticky notes" or two different color note cards to write down at least one hope—something they're looking forward to in class, something that interests them about the course, or something they hope to accomplish in class (orange); and one hesitation—something that concerns them about class, something they don't think they're going to like about class or the course, or something that makes them feel anxious or hesitant about class (yellow).

9

❏ Or ask students to write in their journals using these questions:

What hopes do you bring to this course?
At the end of the year...

- I will know more about _____.

- I will have learned _____.

- I will be able to _____.

- Our class will be able to _____.

What hesitations do you bring?

- I don't know whether _____.

- I'm a little uncertain about _____.

- I don't want to spend a lot of time _____.

- I think my biggest concern will be _____.

Become a Community of Learners: Sharing Hopes and Hesitations

❏ Take two minutes for students to do a Pair-Share with a partner, discussing their hopes and hesitations.

❏ This is the time to reassure students that everyone has some anxieties and dislikes around some aspect of learning or a particular subject. Share a story about yourself and a learning difficulty you've experienced. Then you might say something like this:

"I know some of you hate _____ or have had a bad experience with _____. It's okay to name it and say it. I'm not going to tell you not to feel that way. What I am going to ask you to do is dig around a little to think about where those feelings come from and to consider anything you might want to do differently that will make this year better for you. My job is to support your efforts in any way I can. So let me know when you're frustrated or feel stuck, and we'll work on it together."

Then ask students to post their sticky notes or note cards on a bulletin board or poster board that you have identified for this purpose. (Place the orange notes under HOPES and the yellow notes under HESITATIONS).

Here is another way to discuss these issues, thanks to math teacher, Mehran Divanbaigyzand. Ask students to put their hesitation notes in a small box of three or four drawers. Kids who have really negative, anxious feelings about a given issue can put their notes in the top drawer, while kids who bring fewer concerns or less negative feelings can put their notes in the middle or bottom drawers. Students can take their notes out and move them to another drawer if they sense a change in their attitudes and perceptions of class and the course.

And here's one more idea, thanks to a Carnegie Professor of the Year. Post a humorous Course Subject Bill of Rights that declares: You have the right not to like _____; You have the right to ask questions when you don't understand what we're doing; You have the right to make mistakes and learn from them; You have the right not to get it all the first time you hear it or do it; You have the right to re-do assignments or re-take exams until you achieve a satisfactory level of mastery; etc.

❏ Do a spot check to see if anyone can remember everyone's name.

Policies, Procedures, and Expectations: School wide Rules and Policies

❏ Remind students that you will be using the data from the Classroom Vision carousel to develop class agreements. In order to do this responsibly, you need to explain the difference between school wide rules and policies and classroom guidelines and agreements.

This is a good time to see what kids know, don't know, or have questions about regarding school wide rules and disciplinary policies. If students are really confused, see if you can find some additional school handbooks and make a later time to review school wide rules and policy. You might even want to invite the dean or vice principal of discipline to come in and discuss questions and concerns with students. It's not a bad idea to give students a quiz on important school rules and policies sometime in the first few weeks.

❏ Clarify, teach, and/or review any important procedures that you have not introduced.

See *Getting Classroom Management RIGHT*, Chapter 4.

COURSE WORK:

HOMEWORK:

❏ **Course Work:** Your curriculum will shape these assignments.

❏ **Getting Started:** Bring in one object or picture that reflects your strong point as a learner or (alternatively) reminds you of the way you learn best. Share an object and something about yourself as a learner before students leave for the day.

DAY 6

GETTING STARTED:

Getting to Work:

❏ Quick-write: Ask students to write about a time when they messed up in school or at home (academically or behaviorally). Ask them to describe what adults did to help them deal with the problem and get back on track. What happened? What did the adult do that was helpful? Why did it work? Or ask students what they did for themselves to get back on track. How was it helpful? Why did it work?

9

Become a Community of Learners: Your Strong Point as a Learner

❏ Gathering: Ask students to say their names and share the objects they brought in from last night's homework. Be sure to model the activity again using the alternative question in their homework, and then ask for volunteers. Take about five minutes.

Policies, Procedures, and Expectations: Problem-Solving Protocols

❏ Invite students to share their responses to the quick-write and ask for a volunteer to summarize the kinds of adult responses that felt helpful to students.

❏ Pass out the problem-solving protocols and explain how you expect to use these procedures when students get into academic and behavioral difficulties.

See *Getting Classroom Management RIGHT*, Chapter 1.

COURSE WORK:

HOMEWORK:

❏ **Course Work:** Your curriculum will shape these assignments.

DAY 7

GETTING STARTED:

Getting to Work: Reviewing Data from the Community Vision Learning Carousel

❏ Welcome everyone at the door and hand out the collected responses to the Creating a Classroom Vision questions.

❏ Ask students to read the responses and circle the three responses under each question that they think are most essential to making this class a good place for them. Do a pair-share to compare responses with one partner.

Become a Community of Learners: Making Classroom Guidelines and Agreements

❏ Do a spot check to see if anyone can remember everyone's name.

❏ Share your negotiables and non-negotiables, explaining that all policies and agreements have constraints and limitations. These nonnegotiables need to be considered as students help develop classroom guidelines and agreements. (See pages 296–297)

❏ Give instructions for how you are going to develop classroom guidelines and agreements. Ask students to think about the ideas and suggestions they generated earlier. Encourage them to incorporate those ideas into the agreements you make together. Use the process described on pages 302–306. This will probably take the rest of the period.

COURSE WORK:

❏ Course work may have to be just a brief check-in today, because you want to complete the process of making classroom agreements in one class period

HOMEWORK:

❏ **Course Work:** Your curriculum will shape these assignments.

❏ **Getting Started:** Pass out Personal Pathways maps for students to begin working on. Let students know they will have two days to work on this. (See page228)

DAY 8

GETTING STARTED:

Getting to Work: Personal Pathways Map

❏ Getting Started: Keep working on Personal Pathways map.

Become a Community of Learners: Conversation Circles

❏ Gathering: Conversation Circles (See page 311)

Policies, Procedures, and Expectations: Being "School Smart"

❏ Talk about what it means to be "school smart." What are the benefits of being "school smart?" Share some case study situations and ask students what they would consider a "school smart" response or solution. Let students know that if you notice behaviors that appear to get in the way of learning, you will probably ask to meet them privately to brainstorm some strategies that will help them become more successful in class. (See pages 385–390

COURSE WORK:

HOMEWORK:

❏ **Course Work:** Your curriculum will shape these assignments.

❏ **Getting Started:** Complete your Personal Pathways map.

DAY 9

GETTING STARTED:

Getting to Work: Personal Pathways map

❏ Prepare to hand in your Personal Pathways map.

9

Become a Community of Learners: "Learning How You Learn"

❑ Ask students to share their maps with at least two other students. After this, let students know that these maps will become part of their portfolios. Explain that students will continue to refine and review their goals throughout the year.

❑ Do a spot-check to see if anyone can remember everyone's name.

❑ Do the activity Twenty Things on a Tray to explore differences and preferences in how we learn and retain information. (See pages 270–271)

COURSE WORK:

HOMEWORK:

❑ **Course Work:** Your curriculum will shape these assignments.

DAY 10

GETTING STARTED:

Getting to Work:

❑ Do a reflection activity related to the discipline you teach. For example, you might choose from one of the following:

   – Post several quotations that express different perspectives about the discipline you are teaching: the study of mathematics, history, literature, science, language, etc. The task might be to find one idea that they strongly agree or disagree with and share their reasons for their opinions.

   – Ask students to write down three questions that a mathematician, a historian, a linguist, a scientist, or a writer might continually ask as they pursue their professions.

   – Ask students to create similes about your discipline with these starters:

   – Literature, science, etc. is like (any object) because _____.
   ... is like (anything from nature) because _____.
   ... is like (any sport) because _____.
   ... is like (any specific space or place) because_____.

   – Pose the question, "How would your life be different today if no one had ever heard of_____or if _____did not exist. (Think of a common principle, concept, or innovation that is ubiquitous to your discipline. What would life be like without it?)

COURSE WORK:

HOMEWORK:

❏   **Course Work:** Your curriculum will shape these assignments.

DAY 11

GETTING STARTED:

Getting to Work: Reflections about Group Participation

❏   Hand out three different color "sticky notes" or note cards to each student. On the first one pose this question: "For you to be a good group member, what do you need from the group?" They should answer in this format: "I need to be able to count on other group members to _____."

On the second "sticky note" pose this question: "One quality I bring to a group is_____."

On the third one, pose this question: "I support others to be and do their best in a group by_____."

Become a Community of Learners: Teambuilding

❏   Take five minutes to share students' responses to the three questions. (This is in preparation for the team-building activity.) Then ask students to post their "sticky notes" on three pieces of chart paper where the questions are used as headers.

❏   Team-building activity: Do Chocolate River or any other activity where students work in teams to solve a problem, with the condition that no one can win unless everybody wins (i.e., successfully achieving the goal). (See pages 318–320)

❏   Debrief by using questions included in the activity or by asking how the skills, qualities, and attitudes identified on their "sticky notes" were played out in the team-building activity.

COURSE WORK:

❏   Course work may be just a brief check-in today, because of the length of time required to complete and debrief the team-building activity.

HOMEWORK:

❏   **Course Work:** Your curriculum will shape these assignments.

❏   **Getting Started:** Ask students to complete the following journal assignment: Define cooperative learning in the classroom. What do you like about learning this way? What don't you like about it?

9

DAY 12

GETTING STARTED:

Getting to Work: Working in Groups

❏ Have students perform the following quick-write: Think about a learning experience you really liked when you worked with a partner or a small group of students. What were you doing? What did you accomplish? What made it a positive learning experience for you?

OR:

❏ Think about a time you were involved with a sports team, a music or dance group, a theater production, a newspaper staff, or another team project where you felt good about working with others and what you and your team accomplished was something that made you proud. Why did it work? What did you like about this experience?

Policies, Procedures, and Expectations: Cooperative Learning

❏ Invite students to share their responses from last night's journaling and today's quick-write.

❏ Set the stage for effective cooperative learning. (See pages 274–277)

COURSE WORK:

❏ Begin a cooperative learning activity related to your current learning unit. Examples:

– Geometry: Each group receives a different problem. Each group's task is to construct a geometric proof that works, write their proof on chart paper, and be able to explain their proof to the rest of the group.

– English: Using models and criteria that have already been discussed, each group of four students will choose to write opening paragraphs for a newspaper article of their choice: a crime report; an article on yesterday's sports match between two high schools; an editorial piece; an obituary; an analysis of a current crisis; a report of a local town meeting, hearing, or council meeting; a "puff piece" on a current fashion trend; an opinion piece about a controversial issue; a global event that impacts the U.S., etc. Each group of four will divide into two pairs, and each pair will compose an opening paragraph. When they are finished, the pairs will come back together in their group of four to share the goals of their opening paragraph, identify three things that must be included in it, and explain why the writing style in their opening paragraph needs to be different from the style used for other newspaper articles. Each pair will offer feedback to their partner pair before turning in their final opening paragraphs.

– Graphic Design: Each group must design a brochure for a school club with the goals of doubling club membership and reaching a more diverse group of students who might consider participating in the club.

– Physics: Each group of three must rotate through nine stations that include tools and objects that illustrate principles of simple machines. At each station, each group must agree on the type of machine being illustrated, evidence that supports their description of the machine, and the mechanical principles being illustrated. Each student in the group of three is responsible for recording data at three of the nine stations.

- Foreign Language: Each group of four must choose to create a map or diagram of one room within a house and label at least twenty objects in it. Then the group needs to demonstrate four activities or tasks that different family members might do in this room. While one group member demonstrates the activity or task, another group member describes and explains what the person is doing. Each group member is required to write up one of the tasks or activities.

- Economics: Each group receives a scenario that they will use to explore the concept of "opportunity costs" (when we choose to allocate time and resources for one thing, we are choosing not to allocate time and resources to something else). Scenarios include: A) making a corporate decision about offering more family benefits to employees; B) making a school scheduling decision to include more time for advisory purposes; C) making a personal decision to spend the weekend sleeping and hanging out with friends; D) making a family decision to purchase a second car; E) making a Congress-ional decision to allocate more resources and services for young children; F) making a local community decision to recycle all glass and paper; G) making a personal deci-sion to set aside most of your paycheck for college expenses; and H) making a school board decision to build a new high school and tear down the current structure. Each group must identify three potential opportunity costs that emerge from the decision described in their scenario.

- History: As students explore the implications and effects of a major political decision or the introduction of a new technology or invention, each group picks a card that identifies a specific group or constituency. Each cooperative group must discuss in detail their group's status before and after this decision or technological change, and identify three ways that their group or constituency is affected by this event or technology. They will also need to decide on the overall impact on their group (on a scale from –5 to +5, with 0 being little to no impact positively or negatively) and defend the number they choose.

HOMEWORK:

❏ **Course Work:** Your curriculum will shape these assignments.

❏ **Getting Started:** Instruct students that they should be ready to pass in their journals tomorrow.

Ask them to write a reflection about their first two weeks in class. Choose questions from Self-Assessment Tools. Ask students to write about a page. (See pages 235–237)

Let students know that during the next two weeks you will meet personally with three students a day during the "Getting to Work" activity to do a personal check-in and see how things are going and discuss work they have turned in.

9

DAY 13

GETTING STARTED:

Getting to Work:

- ❑ Have students prepare to hand in their journals.

- ❑ Check in with three students during "Getting to Work."

Become a Community of Learners: Form Home Groups

- ❑ Form Home Groups to establish a student support system.

Policies, Procedures, and Expectations: Cooperative Learning

- ❑ Review how you will be monitoring cooperative learning groups. Be sure to give the class feedback about what you are noticing as you walk around and observe. After students have completed the activity, ask them to reflect on a couple of questions that focus on how they worked together as a group.

COURSE WORK:

- ❑ Continue the cooperative learning activity.

CLOSING CLASS:

- ❑ Introduce a closing at the end of class. Try "Seven Words or Less Headlines." (See pages 313–317)

HOMEWORK:

- ❑ **Course Work:** Your curriculum will shape these assignments.

Day 14

GETTING STARTED:

Getting to Work:

- ❑ Do an activity related to your current learning unit.

- ❑ Check in with three students during "Getting to Work."

COURSE WORK:

HOMEWORK:

- ❑ **Course Work:** Your curriculum will shape these assignments.

- ❑ **Getting Started:** Invite students to make Family Banners (page 403). They will need to complete this to share on Day 16. Have your example to show students.

DAY 15

GETTING STARTED:

Getting to Work:

- ❏ Do an activity related to your current learning unit.

- ❏ Check in with three students during "Getting to Work."

Become a Community of Learners: Cultural Sharing

- ❏ Introduce listening labs using questions that focus on students' family backgrounds and cultural experiences. (See pages 352–353, 402–403)

COURSE WORK:

HOMEWORK:

- ❏ **Course Work:** Your curriculum will shape these assignments.

- ❏ **Getting Started:** Students should complete their Family Banners.

DAY 16

GETTING STARTED:

Getting to Work:

- ❏ Students should be ready to share their Family Banners.

- ❏ Check in with three students during "Getting to Work."

Become a Community of Learners: Sharing Personal Stories

- ❏ Share students' Family Banners.

COURSE WORK:

HOMEWORK:

- ❏ **Course Work:** Your curriculum will shape these assignments.

DAY 17

GETTING STARTED:

Getting to Work:

- ❏ Do an activity related to your current learning unit.

- ❏ Check in with three students during "Getting to Work."

9

Become a Community of Learners: Countering Harassment by Becoming Allies

❏ Read the story, "The Most Mature Thing I've Ever Seen," from *Chicken Soup for the Teenage Soul* and debrief the story by discussing the roles of aggressor, target, bystander, and ally. Let students know that tomorrow the class will discuss harassment. (See pages 408–412 for more ideas for countering harassment.)

COURSE WORK:

HOMEWORK:

❏ **Course Work:** Your curriculum will shape these assignments.

Day 18

GETTING STARTED:

Getting to Work: Thinking About Harassment

❏ Ask students to think about your school and choose to write about one of these questions:

    – What kinds of behaviors do you see around school that you think fall into the category of harassment or bullying?

    – Are there any particular groups or types of kids whom you see playing the aggressor/ harasser role here at school? Why do you think individual students or groups do this?

    – What groups or types of kids are most likely to be targeted? Why do you think that is?

❏ Check in with three students during "Getting to Work."

Policies, Procedures, and Expectations: Harassment

❏ Define and discuss harassment, (pages 409–410). Clarify school wide and legal policies around these behaviors. Explain what you will do if you witness any of these behaviors.

COURSE WORK:

HOMEWORK:

❏ **Course Work:** Your curriculum will shape these assignments.

DAY 19

GETTING STARTED:

Getting to Work: Thinking About Harassment

❏ Ask students to write about one of these questions in their journals:

    – Think about a time when you were targeted or harassed by an individual or group. What was going on? How did it feel? Did anyone intervene as your ally? If not, what would you have wanted an ally to do?

    – Think about a time when you witnessed someone else being targeted or harassed. What was going on? What did you do? If you witnessed a similar situation again, what would you say or do differently?

    – If you were targeted or harassed what would you want a teacher to do? What would you want a friend to do?

❏ Check in with three students during "Getting to Work."

Become a Community of Learners: Responding to Harassment

❏ Ask students to form groups of three or four to share their responses to questions about harassment.

❏ Explore ways that students can respond to harassment using role plays or guided discussion.

COURSE WORK:

❏ Course work may be just a brief check-in today, because of the length of time required to complete and debrief the team-building activity.

HOMEWORK:

❏ **Course Work:** Your curriculum will shape these assignments.

DAY 20

GETTING STARTED:

Getting to Work: Class Meeting Topics

❏ Pass out note cards and ask students to write down classroom or school wide issues that they would like to discuss or any particular problems that they think require a group solution. Collect cards.

❏ Check in with three students during "Getting to Work."

9

Become a Community of Learners: Introduce the language of WIN-WIN and Class Meeting

❑ Learn Win-Win negotiation and consensus.

❑ Introduce the Class Meeting format using a classroom or school wide issue or problem that you would like students to discuss and solve as a group. Let students know that you will use this format for other issues that come up and that your hope is that students will facilitate this process. Read aloud some of the topics that students suggested. Ask for a volunteer to type up the suggestions and later students can prioritize class meeting topics that they want to discuss. (See pages 339–343)

COURSE WORK:

HOMEWORK:

❑ **Course Work:** Your curriculum will shape these assignments.

❑ **Getting Started:** One-month check-in. Have students choose two questions from Self-Assessment Tools to write about.

CHAPTER 10

The Challenges of Changing Classroom Practices

We tend to teach the way we were taught and the way we learn. Our personal experience of schooling shapes what we do in the classroom. If we succeeded and felt affirmed, noticed, and rewarded in a tracked high school where faculty taught a traditional curriculum using a teacher-centered approach, what's not to like about that? But the majority of us who teach high school excelled in a system that works very poorly for so many others. It takes courage, distance, and an open heart to reexamine and critique prevailing practices in the very place that inspired many of us to become teachers.

What we are learning about adolescents, and about how to teach more of them more effectively, is counterintuitive to the norms and assumptions that drive secondary education in the United States. The myths that we sometimes carry around about adolescents and learning are so embedded in high school culture that letting them go is tantamount to experiencing culture shock. Although high school educators might not verbalize their assumptions, we act on these "unexamined shared mental models or 'theories-in-use'" as if they were true.[1] Current research and thinking in the behavioral and learning sciences do much to explode many deeply held assumptions about kids and learning in high school. It is worth exploring some of these assumptions for the purpose of thinking about how we arrived at them in the first place and why we hold onto them.

Assumptions about students and learning in high school

Assumption #1: My job is to teach it to you and your job is to learn it.

Teachers often assume that just because they *taught* a lesson, students actually *learned* it. Facilitating and supporting learning is not the same as teaching the content material. Teacher-centered instruction often looks like this:

- I present the information in the unit.

- Students listen, take notes, read, and answer the questions.

- We review the material at the end of the unit.

- Students take the test and sink or swim.

Learner-centered instruction, on the other hand, involves a continuous feedback and assessment loop that looks like this:

- I frame the learning unit using essential questions, and assess what prior knowledge and understanding students bring to the unit.

- As new skills and knowledge are introduced, I use informal and formal quick-checks, reflections, assessments, and practice to determine what students have learned and what they do and don't understand.

- I observe what students are doing and provide continuous coaching and feedback; then I reteach skills and concepts when necessary.

- Students work on end-of-unit product or performance assessments until they reach an acceptable level of proficiency. For more about assessment for learning see pages 378–384.

Here are two questions that help distinguish teacher-centered from learner-centered instruction:

1. Are students spending more time listening to you and watching you, or are you spending more time observing, coaching, and listening to them.

2. Are students doing your work or their work?

Assumption #2: Some kids are smart and some kids are dumb. I don't believe that all kids can really learn what I teach or pass my class.

The emphasis on ability and final performance reinforces the deficit model of learning—"one of my primary jobs is to show you what you don't know and can't do." This "ability orientation" to learning favors kids who come to school already "school smart" and devalues the role that effort plays in the learning process. The result of this assumption is that many students, early on in school, see themselves as "not smart," give up, and shut down. However, we know that when effort and the process of learning are valued and supported, more kids learn more.[2]

This warning comes from *Your Adolescent*, a guide for parents and teachers from the American Academy of Child and Adolescent Psychiatry. Adolescents who believe that intelligence is fixed tend to see achievement in terms of ability—"I'm smart in this class or dumb in this class and there's nothing I can do to change that." Kids with these beliefs tend to avoid tasks that may appear difficult to avoid being perceived as dumb; they also tend to see errors as failure.

By contrast, kids who see effort as making a difference are more likely to recognize errors and other academic difficulties as part of the process of learning; they are less afraid of taking risks, and more likely to persist and persevere to gain mastery.[3]

Assumption #3: Taking time in class to establish a community of learners and teach students how to work together effectively wastes valuable learning time.

Building a sense of community and developing students' cooperation, participation, and leadership skills are on-task learning activities that result in more effectively managed classrooms and help students practice life skills associated with high performance in the workplace.[4]

Assumption #4: Learning is an intellectual activity.

Research in the field of cognitive science tells us a much different story, revealing the interdependence between knowing and doing, mind and body. High school curricula reflect a decidedly Western intellectual orientation that prizes verbal/linguistic and logical/mathematical gifts above all other kinds of intelligences.[5] Yet even verbal and mathematical aspects of intelligence are given short shrift in schools when they are presented as abstract exercises of the mind, without concrete experiences or a social/emotional context. For most people, understanding and insight go deeper and last longer when multiple intelligences and a variety of senses are part of a learning experience.

Assumption #5: Academic courses are the place where students do serious work.

In many high schools, elective and career and technical courses are often perceived as desserts rather than the main course of the curriculum. This assumption carries with it some ironic twists. A recent University of Chicago study of thousands of adolescents confirmed once again that students' favorite courses in high school are electives and CTE courses (career and technical education)—but there doesn't seem to be much curiosity about why this might be the case.[6] If one does agree that learning involves intellectual, physical, social, and emotional dimensions, consider what goes on in most elective and CTE classes as compared to traditional academic courses:

- Students *choose* these courses; thus personal interest ratchets up motivation and effort.

- Students make choices about the projects they will work on and how they will go about doing them.

- Students get to spend lots of time working on something intensely and usually have additional time to revise, reassess, and correct. They may even experience failure in their early attempts and have the opportunity to begin again, using the lessons they've learned.

- Students get to experience the satisfaction of personal mastery and competence, often using sophisticated tools and techniques.

- Whether students are designing a house using computer-assisted drafting, rehearsing a dramatic monologue, preparing a meal for eight people, throwing a pot, planning a marine biology trip, practicing with the drill team, or proofing the pages for the next newspaper, they are expressing themselves in a way that has personal meaning for them.

- Electives involve authentic assessment of some sort—whether it's a product, project, performance, or portfolio of work—and students' work is often presented to a real audience.

- Students are learning by doing and solving problems.

- Students practice a range of critical and creative thinking skills. These skills, as described in Bloom's Taxonomy and Art Costa's list of intellectual behaviors, are a natural, logical occurrence in electives and CTE courses.

No wonder lots of kids learn more and like what they're doing more in elective and CTE classes! These courses tend to involve a rhythm, sequence, and integration of tasks that nurtures high quality and results in learning that sticks. High schools would do well to consider how to make "academic" courses look and feel more like electives and CTE courses. Even better would be the elimination of the false dichotomy between "academic" and other kinds of coursework altogether.

Think about the prevailing norms of teaching and learning in your own school. Do any of the assumptions described here feel familiar? Are there other obstacles to changing classroom practice that you would add to the list?

Implementing New Practices in the Classroom

As you try out new practices, change your routines, and toss out some of the old parts of yourself, here are some other thoughts to keep in mind:

- Map out the first week of school, introducing one or two practices each day.

- Make sure you've got a good reason for doing what you want to do. What needs does it meet? How does it benefit you, the group, or individual students? How might it help improve student performance?

- As you introduce more practices over the next month, identify three or four that you would like to incorporate into your weekly routines.

- Note the icons that are associated with each practice so that your choice of activities reflects variety and balance.

- Think about practices and strategies that you want to include as part of your closing activities at the end of each grading period.

- Keep checking in with the whole group and individual students who are your "climate barometers" to get feedback about how specific practices and strategies are working for different kids, whether your pacing and timing is about right, and how comfortable and competent students feel about using new skills and doing things in a new way.

Tracking What You're Trying

The goal here is to devise an easy system to document what you've done, when you did it, how it worked, and how you might do it in the future. You don't want to forget the words or the hook you used that got kids' attention and cooperation. You want to note why a strategy worked well for one group and was a dud for others. Most important, you want to remember how you took ideas in this book and reworked them, given your students, your school, and your personal way of doing things. This guide is just a starting point—it's your creative adaptations that you want to save, so write them down!

Whatever system you create, try to keep all your notes in one place—in a notebook or computer file. This provides a visual record of where you started and how your teaching practices continue to evolve. For the obsessively organized, a file box of note cards can do the trick, too. You can "tab" sections by practice, activity type, or time of the year. You can track different classes by using different-colored cards to record what you did in each class and write additional notes on cards later.

And then there are those of us who never have much time to reflect on what we're doing and even less time to write about it. For the organizationally impaired or time deprived, use this book as your journal. Write in it, attach sticky notes to pages you are using, and clip other stuff to the cover.

As you jot down reflections, you may want to ask yourself these questions:

- Describe what practice, skill, strategy, or activity you did, why you did it, and when you did it.

- How did students experience what you did?

- What benefits did you see from doing this? For yourself? The group? Individual students?

- Any differences in how different classes experienced this?

- Any changes you already made or would make the next time you try this?

- Other opportunities when you would like to use this practice, skill, strategy, or activity again?

Going Solo or Working Together?

When it comes to changing habits and practices or starting something new, everyone needs something different to make it work and make it last. Some folks need a big window of time to chew on the idea for a while and try things out slowly, carefully staging and planning along the way. Others just jump right in, do something once, and it becomes part of their repertoire for life. Some of you may prefer experimenting by yourself first, while others get energized by the collaborative dialogue that emerges from working together.

School situations can also influence how you go about implementing changes in classroom practice. For some of you, "going solo" is the path of least resistance, especially if you are in an environment where many of these practices might be viewed as "fluff and frills." On the other hand, your school or your department may have decided to develop a set of common practices and guiding principles that create a more personalized learning environment. In that case, you've got the green light to work with others to get something going that has enormous potential to institutionalize new practices. However you go about starting up, think about how you can build collegial interest in trying on some different ways to think about what students need to succeed, and trying out new ways to meet those needs in the classroom.

Nine Strategies for Changing Classroom Practices

1. **Find an ally, then have a chat with a school power broker.** If you're "on your own," consider sharing what you are doing with at least one other colleague. Talking through what you are experiencing really helps to clarify your own thinking and sustain your motivation to keep going. Then make a time to talk with the most approachable power broker you know who influences decisions about curriculum and classroom instruction. (It might be the principal, but it could be the head of the professional development committee, a department or division chair, the director of curriculum, or the union president.) Discuss your ideas, invite her to share her thoughts, and look for mutual concerns and shared interests. Then hatch a plan that moves you toward implementing other strategies on this list.

2. **Buddy up.** Share this guide with a friend and work out a way to meet and check in once a month. You might both want to try out different practices so you can swap ideas, or try out the same practice to see how it works for each of you.

3. **Attend a summer institute or take part in a year long staff development program.** Work with others to hold a Making Learning REAL summer institute open to all staff, or create a professional development strand that begins in the summer and continues to meet throughout the school year. These opportunities work best when participants provide evidence that they have transferred what they've learned into concrete practice in the classroom over a specific period of time. For example, in some districts, participants don't receive credit or professional development units until they've shared, documented, and reflected on the practices they are refining or trying out. Mixing new and experienced teachers in these opportunities has many benefits: (1) new teachers gain the collective wisdom of veterans; (2) experienced teachers feel renewed and refreshed; and (3) some teachers will emerge as leaders who build school and district capacity to personalize learning in the classroom. As part of its work in high schools, Educators for Social Responsibility helps schools to develop summer institutes. One of the goals is building internal capacity for lead teachers who become mentors, coaches, and advocates with their own faculties to spread the word and support their colleagues in changing the norms of teaching and learning in their classrooms. Some schools require all new, incoming staff members to participate in a series of workshops and dialogues that center on personalizing classroom practice and reaching and engaging all learners. Over time, lead teachers take full responsibility for facilitating all institutes and workshops.

4. **Focus on personalizing learning by grade level.** At another school, the English department set aside the first two weeks of all 10th grade English sections for the teacher and students to establish a real learning community. Since the literature theme for 10th grade was "People and Communities in Conflict," they also introduced communication skills that they would practice throughout the year. Ninth grade students are often overwhelmed by the transition to high school, making a mess of deadlines for big assignments and preparations for big tests or assessments. So 9th grade teachers at one school decided to hold class meetings with all 9th graders to get their input about the problem and to generate solutions that would improve completion rates and performance. A group of teachers and 9th grade students then met to negotiate a set of guidelines, supports, and consequences that greatly reduced students' academic problems.

5. **Focus on a grade-level or smaller learning community faculty team.** If you and your colleagues work with the same group of students for one or two years in a house, special academy, or grade-level cluster, you have the advantage of developing a set of common practices, procedures, and expectations for students across your classes. You can identify social skills that you want all students to develop and then discuss how each teacher will integrate specific practice of those skills into his or her respective courses. Teams also have the advantage of developing common disciplinary protocols, support structures, and rituals and celebrations that recognize the efforts and accomplishments of groups and individuals.

6. **Team up with other SPED or Title I teachers.** If you are a Special Education or Title I teacher, chances are you are already familiar with both the rationale for these practices and many of the practices themselves. This guide can augment the affective and social skill development you already do with young people, and it may be a stimulus for developing some common practices in all SPED and Title I classrooms.

7. **Establish a study group.** Find some stipend money and some time to establish a study group whose membership crosses staff roles and departments, to explore, in depth, current issues around teaching, learning, and adolescents. (See the References section for selected books.) Study groups choose to read and reflect together, interview teachers and students, and gather and analyze data about current practices in their school with the goal of increasing learning and achievement for all students. When study groups have the administration's blessing, they might also write a case statement that gives the group a platform for presenting and discussing their analysis and recommendations with other groups in the school community.

8. **Personalize learning by department or course.** As a department, you and your colleagues might decide to implement three or four practices across all courses in your department. For example, a math department might establish new instructional guidelines that include weekly collaborative problem solving and oral or written reflections about the course and how it's going; they might also be brave enough to dump final exams in favor of developing a set of final, but fabulous and fun, math challenges from which each student can choose three. Or your department might determine that some courses are particularly suited to a specific set of practices. I know a group of physics teachers who designed a whole series of individual and group assessment tools that focused on the quality of collaboration on labs and projects. And you can usually find a fair amount of zaniness in chemistry departments. The chemistry teachers at one school decided to brainstorm all kinds of crazy ways to meet and greet their students when they walked into class. On a more serious note, they also decided to encourage students to express themselves more openly and discuss issues around self-management to lower the levels of anxiety and hostility when kids were experiencing frustration.

9. **Personalize learning in lower-track courses, in "de-tracked" courses, and in honors-track courses where struggling students need extra support.** Universal tracking (where kids stay in the same "ability track" for the duration of their academic course work) is unjust and debilitating. But it's not going away anytime soon. I think we're morally obligated, therefore, to make lower-track classes less dehumanizing and hurtful, and more engaging and

purposeful for the kids who are stuck in them. It's all too obvious that most high schools run into serious trouble trying to teach kids well who are already labeled low ability. The practices in this guide can be particularly helpful in bringing demoralized teachers and kids back to the "land of the living and learning" in lower-track classes.

There is, at least, some good news on the tracking front. There are some passionate parents and teachers who are pushing the boundaries of traditional tracking by demanding that some courses be "de-tracked." For example, at many schools, some whole grade levels or required courses in social studies and English are now grouped heterogeneously, or special sections are open to any student in the school. These "de-tracked" classes are often intentionally designed to be more learner-centered, student-friendly, and community-minded without sacrificing rigorous academic work and high expectations.

In one school teachers agreed that every student in every American studies course would complete and present an action research project linking a historical issue they studied to a current issue in their community or the nation at large. Because teachers made the decision that no one could fail, the entire approach to teaching and learning changed. Practices that offered a wider array of learning strategies, more assignment choices, a stronger sense of connectedness, and more support for individual students were crucial to helping every student get to the finish line successfully.

Some schools also offer special classes for struggling, but hungry, students who want to keep up and succeed in their college prep or AP classes. These teachers have introduced practices that encourage students to support and teach each other. They also make a habit of beginning Monday's class with a gathering where students identify their goals and challenges for the week, and ending Friday's class with a closing assessment of their efforts and accomplishments.

Other ways to use *Making Learning REAL:*

- Preservice students enrolled in undergraduate and graduate secondary teacher education programs use *Making Learning REAL* as a primary text during the semester when they are engaged in their practice teaching.

- Career changers who are new to the profession (and make up 40% of new teachers) enroll in week long *Making Learning REAL* institutes before they begin teaching.

- Design teams involved in new school startup or major restructuring initiatives at the middle and high school levels use *Making Learning REAL* as a guide for developing a shared set of norms and expectations that will shape teaching and learning in their new schools.

- Aspiring principals and administrators who have adopted personalization as a major strategy for improving achievement and a measure of teacher quality use *Making Learning REAL* as a resource in their teacher evaluation tool kit.

- Professional development facilitators and instructional coaches use
  Making Learning REAL as a component of new teacher induction
  programs and protocols for working with struggling teachers.

Become an Advocate for the School Students Deserve

Unfortunately, changing norms that define quality teaching and learning will never happen one teacher at a time. Too often the teachers I meet who are the most gifted at reaching and teaching a diversity of students are the ones who feel the most isolated. Even though their classrooms reveal exemplary efforts to balance intellectual rigor, relevance, and relationships, these teachers worry about provoking sneers and jeers from "old school" faculty and administrators. The self-contained nature of classroom life (one teacher and a group of students behind a closed door) often leads to exceptionalizing teaching excellence. It's commonplace to hear teachers brush off innovative practices by saying, "Well, she can teach that way, but that's just her. I could never do what she does."

Therefore, good practice often goes underground and unrecognized, while teaching norms that have outlived their usefulness go unchallenged among the whole faculty or school leadership team. Teachers are more likely to continue experimenting and pushing the boundaries of their practice when there is time to reflect on their work with like-minded colleagues.

In addition, it is easier to feel committed and hopeful when your efforts in the classroom are supported by systemic reforms within the larger school culture. You can go it alone and close your classroom door, or you can join like-minded colleagues in becoming advocates for changes that will make your high school a better place to learn and teach.

Being prepared to defend your teaching practices is a big deal. Know why you believe what you believe and do what you do. Think about how to frame your arguments in ways that support the goals of more traditional teachers. Share personal stories that show how changes you made helped you to turn around a class or student.

When I hear about school change initiatives that bomb, I ask around to get a sense of what happened. One dynamic that contributes to the defeat of good ideas is almost always the same. The teachers who are the most committed to implementing changes are likely to be either too quiet or too zealous in faculty association meetings where new initiatives need to be discussed and approved.

Great ideas aren't enough when large faculties hesitate to vote yes on anything that shakes up the status quo. Silence or fuzzy explanations don't make converts out of fence-sitters. Knowing in your gut what should be done is one thing, but making a convincing case to skeptics and fence-sitters is something else. (It's important to separate the "negaholics" from the skeptics and fence-sitters. "Negaholics" say no to virtually any new idea. This stance shouldn't be confused with a skeptic's interest in critical inquiry.)

High school faculty are often uncomfortable taking on an advocacy position. Most secondary school teachers pride themselves on playing the role of the informed skeptic, a role honed by training in the liberal arts and sciences that encourages sorting for differences, looking for what's missing or wrong, and doubting any idea that promises too much. After all, these are the same higher-order thinking skills we want our students to use. So letting go of our practiced ambivalence is hard. But if we don't let go, we risk being unable to act. Serious change will never happen if schools insist on resolving every last "yes, but" before taking the first step.

William Perry, an ethical theorist, gives us a way out of paralysis without sacrificing the roles of critical friend and friendly critic. He suggests that, given the available evidence and an awareness of one's own values, people can choose to make a commitment that emerges from a new understanding of the many sides of truth. "I will be whole-hearted while tentative, fight for my values yet respect others, believe my deepest values are right yet be ready to learn."[7] One would be hard pressed to find better advice for negotiating the change process in schools.

Mustering up the courage to claim your public voice is hard to do by yourself. Form a group with people who share your vision. Savvy teachers make use of tried and true democratic practices—dialogue, collaboration, compromise, and "back-door politicking"—to get what they want. Time spent rehearsing and preparing presentations, listening carefully to concerns and responding to them honestly, finding key allies who will speak up (especially AP teachers, coaches, pushy parents, and board members), and shmoozing one-on-one with the undecided—all of these activities will help to galvanize the support, trust, and good will necessary to implement changes that really stick.

So talk to other teachers and parents. Write a grant that supports you and your colleagues in efforts to tackle issues you care about. Ask students what they think, and involve them in the process. The good news is that a cadre of powerful teachers can make things happen, particularly in pilot programs that only involve volunteers in beginning phases. In time, these kinds of efforts can set the stage for more ambitious systemic reform.

Final Suggestions

As you think about getting started, I'd like to pass on a couple of last suggestions. When you are trying something new, try taking on the perspectives of observer and learner. Forgive your imperfections before you even start, and while you're at it, forgive your students, too. Nobody has it all together the first time. Instead, love the moment when everything clicks, because it won't last nearly long enough. Love your capacity to take in what is happening, so you can stop to check things out before bulldozing your way to silence or anarchy. Love that you really can learn from your mistakes, and love that you've got two more sections to try it out again and see if it works any better. Love the safe climate you've created so kids will be straight with you and show you who they really are. And the next time you try something that works for nineteen kids but bombs out for six, say to yourself, "The lesson wasn't perfect and it was still successful!" Good luck.

SECTION THREE
THE CORE PRACTICES

CHAPTER 11

Practice 1: Develop Positive Relationships Among and Between Students and Staff

Meet and Greet Students

Gather Data and Key Information about Your Students

Learn Students' Names

Create Opportunities for Students to Get to Know Each Other and Work Together

Make Connections through 10-Second "Hits"

Create Opportunities When You Only Listen

Make Time for Meaningful Closing Activities

Key Strategy	Meet and Greet Students
	• Develop personal connections among and between students and teachers
Life Skill Connection (See page 112–114)	• Engage in conscious acts of respect, caring, helpfulness, kindness, courtesy, and consideration (36)
Sample Activities, Strategies, and Routines	• 12 Ways to Meet and Greet

The "meet and greet" that teachers do before class seems to be a critical benchmark for lots of students. Many students tell me how much it means when teachers hang out by the door saying "Hello" and greeting them by name. Furthermore, kids say that teachers who "meet and greet" are the ones who also care about them personally, and this personal interest motivates them to do better in class. It's easy to assume that this is a common practice; yet, my informal polling with students indicates that this is the exception and not the rule. "Meet and greet" doesn't need to happen every day—two or three times a week is fine—and varying what you do keeps students guessing about what's going to happen in your class that day.

12 Ways to Meet and Greet

1. In the beginning of the year, when you are trying to match names to faces, ask each student to say her or his name as she or he walks into class so that you can hear it and repeat it.

2. Shake hands and say students' names as they walk in the door.

3. Say "Hello" to students in lots of different languages. If you have students who speak other languages, ask them to write and pronounce "hello" in that language so you can make different "hellos" part of your greeting repertoire.

4. Give everyone a review question as they enter the room. Ask students to record their responses and remind them to discuss their responses with at least one other person to check for agreement. You might use this strategy as a way to begin review for a test or exam.

5. If you are reviewing concepts, sequential steps, or terms, pass out cards to each student as they come in. For example, one student's term matches another student's example, one student's concept matches another student's illustration, or one student has a step that forms a sequence with three other students. This is a way to get kids into small groups or a way to help students focus on the agenda for the day.

6. Cut up a set of about 40 two-inch squares and write the numbers from 1 to 10 on different squares. As students enter the room, say "Hello" and ask them to pick a number from 1 to 10 from your basket that indicates how they're feeling right now—10 (I'm ready, focused, feeling

good) to 1 (I'm tired, grumpy, and would rather be any place else). When everyone is seated, ask students to hold up their numbers to get a read on how people feel. Based on where they are on the scale, you might want to do a quiet energizer that helps everyone to focus.

7. Post a sign on your door that asks, "Are you ready? Name one thing you're ready and willing to do in class today." Ask students to share their "one thing" as you greet them at the door. Or post a sign that asks, "What's one personal goal you're bringing with you to class today?"

8. Once a quarter give each student a personal written greeting that mentions something you appreciate about their presence in your class. Alternate weeks for different classes so you create a cycle that you can repeat every quarter (1st period–Oct.____, 2nd Period–Oct.____, 4th period–Nov.____, 5th period–Nov.____, and 7th period–Nov.____). One way to make this less daunting is to put a list of 30 or 40 appreciation responses on your computer. You can write in the students' names, print out your messages, and cut them into strips. For example:

> *Dear Cho, I know that talking in class is not your favorite thing, so I have really appreciated your participation in small-group work.*

> *Dear Alicia, I've noticed that you've been on time for the last two weeks. I really appreciate the effort you've made to do this.*

> *Dear Manuel, Thanks for participating in the discussions we've been having. Your questions have challenged all of us to be really clear about what we mean.*

> *Dear Mia, I have really appreciated your efforts to pick up and organize stuff at the end of class. It makes it so much easier to do projects when people are ready to pitch in. Thanks.*

> *Dear Greg, I know this is not an easy class for you, so every day you're here shows that you're willing to stick with it and keep trying. I appreciate your tenacity.*

9. Make a sign that says, "Do not pass until you answer a question." Then ask a question to each student walking in. If you use content questions, ask a variety of questions that students can answer easily. You can also do a wacky version of this by asking everyone silly or personal questions that everyone can answer. For example, "What color are your shoes?" or "When did you get up this morning?" When students look at you as if you've lost it, you might say something like, "Just checking to see if everyone is alert and ready."

10. Pass out interesting quotations that students can write about in their journals, linking something about themselves to the quotation. If you type them up on cards and copy them, students can pick one at random.

11. As students come in, ask them to share something that they've learned in the last week in any class they're taking.

12. Use your computer to create a "Thought for the Day." Use a label template to repeat the same thought on the page 20 times. Print out several copies on card stock, cut them apart, and pass them out to students.

Key Strategy	Gather Data and Key Information about Your Students
	• Develop personal connections among and between students and teachers

Life Skill Connection (See page 112–114)	• Activate hope, optimism, and positive motivation (15) • Work for high personal performance and cultivate your strengths and positive qualities (16) • Develop, manage, and maintain healthy relationships with adults (26)

Sample Activities, Strategies, and Routines	• First-Day Student Profile • Write or Map Your Personal Story • Personal Inventory • I Feel Survey

It is unlikely that you will be in a situation where you can personally interview each student in the beginning of the year. So gathering data and key information about your students the first day and the first few weeks can help you develop a more complete picture of each student. This kind of information comes in handy for several reasons:

- It helps you make connections between individual students and what is being learned in your curriculum.

- It provides a starting point for personal conversations.

- It gives you a "heads-up" about issues that might affect a student's progress and learning.

- It provides a bridge for parental/guardian contacts.

Keep the data and information you collect in a special folder for each class, so it's easy to review and retrieve it.

First-Day Student Profile

On the first day, you don't want to put students in a position of disclosing all sorts of personal stuff about themselves. You do want to collect information that will give you the basics that you would like to know about each student from the beginning. The following handout provides you with a sample student profile.

First-Day Student Profile

Last Name: _____ First Name: _____ Middle Name: _____

Birth date: _____

Three words that best describe me are _____ , _____ , and _____ .

My first language is ❑ English or ❑ _____ .

Home Address:

Street _____ Apartment _____

City/Town _____ Zip Code _____

How long have you lived at your current address? _____ years or _____ months

How long have you lived in this community/town/city? _____ years or _____ months

Home Phone Number (_____)_____ E-mail _____

Family Information:

Full name of parent/guardian

_____

Full name of parent/guardian

_____

First Language:

❑ English ❑ Other _____

Contact Phone Number (_____)_____

Email _____

First Language:

❑ English ❑ Other _____

Contact Phone Number (_____)_____

Email _____

First-Day Student Profile CONTINUED

Names and ages of brothers and sisters:

Name _____ Age _____   Name _____ Age _____

Name _____ Age _____   Name _____ Age _____

Name _____ Age _____   Name _____ Age _____

Educational Information:

This is my ❑ first ❑ second ❑ third ❑ fourth year at this school.

The last school I attended was _____.

Are there any health issues that might affect your attendance, on-time arrival to class, or class participation?

❑ No or ❑ Yes _____

During the school year, I work at _____ about _____ hours per week.

After high school graduation, I am currently planning to:
❑ get a full time job
❑ work part-time and go to college part-time
❑ attend 4-year college
❑ attend technical school ❑ community college
❑ get an apprenticeship
❑ join military service

Course Schedule: (to be filled out later in the week)

Class Period	Name of Course	Class Period	Name of Course
1st		5th	
2nd		6th	
3rd		7th	
4th		8th	

Write or Map Your Personal Story

Do this activity at the beginning of the year and keep it in the student's folder for reference and future conversations:

Who are you? Describe yourself in as many ways as possible. What words describe you? What do you like? Dislike? What are your favorite activities? What are your strengths? Gifts? Talents?

History: What important things have happened in your life? Highlight people, places, events, successes, challenges, and achievements.

Dreams: What hopes do you have for the future? How do you imagine your life 10 years from now? What are your dreams concerning school, work, life experiences, friendship, and fun?

Fears: What do you not want to happen in your life? What barriers or challenges might make your dreams hard to achieve?

Needs: Looking at your history, personal qualities, dreams, and fears, what do you need to make your dreams come true? What will make your high school experience move you toward your hopes? What experiences do you want to have during your high school years? What questions do you want to answer? What passions might you develop?

Personal Inventory

Develop a personal inventory to find out more about your students, including what they care about, what interests them, and what they are concerned about. Students often assume that most teachers only care about their academic performance. Surveys or questionnaires can be a first step in making personal connections with each student. While you are developing this survey, think about what might be fun, interesting, and helpful to know about students that you think they would be willing to share. Depending on your students, before they fill out the inventory, you might want to humor them by acknowledging that sex is a possible response to many of the questions. You could say something like, "Since I already know that, I'd prefer that you not get that personal. So stretch your thinking a bit." Here are some starters:

1. Something I think about all the time is

2. Something I do outside of school that is very important in my life is

3. One thing I can teach others to do is

4. Three things I love to do with my friends are

5. Favorite music group / TV show / movie / website / athlete / radio station

6. Something I like/enjoy doing that would surprise people is

7. Something I worry about is

8. Two people I really admire and respect are

9. The most boring thing in my life is

10. The most exciting thing in my life right now is

11. I make my family proud when I

12. One thing my family expects of me is

13. One thing that makes my family special/different/fun is

14. Three jobs I expect to have sometime are

15. The job I want most in my life is

16. Three things I will need to do to get this job are

17. Things I participate in at school: sports/community service/clubs/special groups/other

18. What do you like most about being a student? What is your "best thing" as a student?

19. What do you like least about being a student? What is your "worst thing" as a student?

20. As your teacher, what should I know about you that will help you learn and do your best in this class?

21. What makes you happy?

22. What do you love to do?

23. What do you really want to learn about or become an expert at doing?

24. What personal talents do you want to develop and strengthen?

25. What three things in life matter most to you?

26. What do you want to accomplish in your life?

27. What people in life do you most admire?

28. What words would your friends, family, and teachers use to describe you?

29. What makes you different from every other person on earth?

30. What do you want people to remember about you?

31. What inspires you?

32. What motivates you?

33. What have you learned from your family about living a good life?

34. What will you need to do to live the life you want to live?

35. What keeps you going when you feel down and discouraged?

36. What messages or self-talk guide you through the day?

37. What are your hopes for your own future?

38. What are your hopes for the world you live in?

39.   What do you imagine yourself doing 10 years from now?

40.   What will it take to make your dreams a reality?

I Feel Survey

If you use any of these questions for journaling you might want to give students the Feelings Vocabulary words to help broaden their personal repertoire of feelings words.

- When I enter a new group, I usually feel... because...

- When I meet new people, I usually feel... because...

- When I enter a new space, I usually feel... because...

- When I'm in a sports crowd, I usually feel... because...

- When a stranger speaks to me, I usually feel... because...

- When a teacher calls on me, I usually feel... because...

- When I stand up in front of a large group, I usually feel... because...

- When I'm with my friends, I usually feel... because...

- When I'm involved in a conflict with someone, I usually feel... because...

- When I'm alone, I usually feel... because...

Feelings Vocabulary

afraid	affectionate	agitated	aggressive	aggravated
alert	accepted	amazed	ambivalent	amused
angry	annoyed	anxious	apologetic	argumentative
ashamed	awkward	bad	belligerent	bored
brave	calm	cared for	cautious	challenged
cheerful	clear	clumsy	cold	concerned
confused	contemptuous	contented	cranky	curious
defeated	delighted	depressed	despairing	desperate
determined	disconcerted	disappointed	disgusted	disrespected
down	ecstatic	elated	embarassed	empty
energized	enraged	enthusiastic	envious	exasperated
excited	exhausted	fearful	focused	foolish
friendly	frightened	frustrated	funny	furious
good	grateful	greedy	grief-stricken	guilty
happy	hateful	heartbroken	helpless	hopeful
horrified	hot	humiliated	hurt	hysterical
impatient	independent	indifferent	inferior	intimidated
irritated	jazzed	jealous	jolly	joyful
jumpy	kindly	left out	let down	lonely
loved	loving	mad	malicious	mellow
mischievous	miserable	mixed up	negative	nervous
nice	sorrowful	obstinate	optimistic	pained
paranoid	peaceful	peeved	perplexed	playful
persecuted	pleasant	powerful	powerless	prepared
proud	puzzled	ready	regretful	relieved
remorseful	respected	righteous	sad	safe
satisfied	secure	sedate	smart	supported
self-conscious	self-pitying	shocked	shy	skeptical
silly	spiteful	strange	stuck	surprised
suspicious	sympathetic	tenacious	tense	terrific
ticked off	threatened	thrilled	timid	tired
trusted	uncertain	uncomfortable	uneasy	unsafe
unworthy	up	upset	vengeful	victimized
victorious	vindictive	wary	wonderful	weird
worried				

Key Strategy	Learn Students' Names

	• Develop personal connections among and between students and teachers
Life Skill Connection (See page 112–114)	• Engage in conscious acts of respect, caring, helpfulness, kindness, courtesy, and consideration (30)
Sample Activities, Strategies, and Routines	• Seven Ways to Learn Student Names Quickly

11

If people don't know each other's names, it's hard to call a group a community. Learning and remembering everyone's name is a sign of respect. Taking time to discover who we are in a group always pays off. The more we know about each other, the more comfortable we feel working together.

Seven Ways to Learn Student Names Quickly

If you've got four to six classes of students, learning students' names is no easy task. Yet, like "meet and greet," this is one of those practices that makes a tremendous difference to students. Too often, students tell me about teachers who still don't know their names by the end of first semester. How you learn names may depend on your room set-up and the memory devices that work for you. The following suggestions come from teachers who have learned everyone's name within two weeks. It's also important to give yourself permission to get names wrong the first few times. Simply apologize when it happens and correct yourself.

1. At the start of the school year, have students say their first names every time they speak.

2. Have students create triangular name plates out of 8 1/2" × 11" card stock. Ask students to fold the sheet into three strips. Then ask them to write their first names in large letters on the middle strip. Then fold the sheet into a triangle that will stand on its own in front of the table or desk where each student is sitting. Have a box for each set of name plates and ask students to pick them up and return them to the box each period.

3. When students are writing, reading quietly, or working in pairs or small groups, spend this time saying each person's name silently three times as your eye roams from one end of the room to the other. Keep the same order of saying names a couple of times, and then try to connect names with faces randomly in no particular pattern.

4. Link a word that begins with the same letter as the student's first name to each student—any word that describes something positive about that student.

5. Tell students they can't enter your classroom until you say their names correctly. Give students bonus points if you can't remember.

6. Take a "head shot" picture of each student. Ask volunteers from each of your classes to create a photo collage, either assembling them in a framed space on a bulletin board or gluing photos and names on a large cardboard "pizza round" to hang from the ceiling.

7. Play a name game or introduction game:

   • Silent Names A to Z: Have students line up silently by first or last name alphabetically and then have them say their names.

   • Name Toss: On a 5" × 8" note card, ask everyone to write one word that begins with the first letter of their first name that reflects something about them (e.g., Carol=creative). In a circle, ask everyone to say their name, the word, and the connection they have to the word. Place the cards in the center of the circle. Using a timer, ask for three volunteers to see how long it will take them to return the correct card to the person who wrote it. Do this a number of times to see if successive groups can beat the previous time.

   • Name Game with Motion: Have the group form a circle. Ask students to say their names and make a gesture or movement that reflects something they like to do. After each person says his or her name and makes a gesture, everyone in the group repeats the name and the gesture. Model the activity first, then go around the circle.

   • Group Juggling: Get eight to ten soft fabric balls that are three to five inches in diameter. Ask students to form a circle. If you have more than 15 people, you might want to split the group in half and have one facilitator for each group. Say to the group, "We're going to establish a pattern of tossing and catching the balls. I will say a student's name and then toss the ball underhand to her. That student will then say another student's name and toss the ball to him. You need to remember who tossed the ball to you and who you tossed the ball to. You will always catch the ball from the same person and always throw to the same person. We will do this a couple of times, using one ball to get the pattern." After you've practiced with one ball, tell students that you are going to steadily add more balls and remind students to say the name of the person to whom they are tossing their balls. The goal is to see how many balls the group can juggle. Stop the activity and start over when too many balls are dropped.

When your selected activity is over, take a few minutes to discuss it. What did you like about the activity? What didn't you like? What kinds of skills did you need to be successful? Was there anything we could have done as a group to be more successful? What made this activity challenging? Can you make any connections between being successful at this activity and being successful in class?

Key Strategy	Create Opportunities for Students To Get To Know Each Other and Work Together
	• Develop personal connections among and between students and teachers
Life Skill Connection (See page 112–114)	• Exercise assertiveness; communicate your thoughts, feelings, and needs effectively to others (18) • Develop, manage, and maintain healthy peer relationships (25) • Develop, manage, and maintain healthy relationships with adults (26) • Respect everyone's right to learn, to speak, and to be heard (28) • Encourage and appreciate the contributions of others (29)
Sample Activities, Strategies, and Routines	• What Do We Have in Common? • Find Someone Who • Finding Out about Who We Are • "You Like, I Like…" • Mix It Up When Students Work Togeher

Take five to ten minutes several times during the first two weeks to engage students in activities that help them get to know each other. These activities also provide ways to practice active listening, expressing feelings, and cooperation.

What Do We Have in Common?

Give each student a sheet that has three columns and a place for three students' names. Then ask students to pair up with someone they don't know well or use grouping cards to place people in pairs. Give each pair two minutes to write down all the similarities they can think of (physical characteristics, family stuff, things they both do, possessions they both own, etc.). Then ask students to pair up two more times, repeating the process. At the end of the activity, ask: "What surprised you about what you discovered you had in common with someone else?" "How many similarities did you find the first time?" "The last time?" "Did it get easier for anyone?" "Why?" Point out that when we are having a disagreement or having trouble working together, it's especially important to remember what we have in common.

Find Someone Who

Create a bingo sheet using the information you collected from the Personal Inventory Survey so that each box asks for information that only matches one person. For example, *"Find someone whose birthday is on _____; find someone who was born in _____; find someone who knows how to _____; find someone who has visited _____; find someone who speaks _____; find someone who has _____."*

Finding Out about Who We Are

Create an interview sheet with the following questions. Have students find a partner and choose a question that interests both of them. Have them interview each other and jot down their partner's name and something they want to remember that their partner said. Give them a few minutes and then have them find a new partner. You could end this activity by asking students what they learned about each other.

- Describe your family. What is something funny, weird, unusual, or special about one person in your family?

- What's one place you would like to visit in your lifetime? Why do you want to go there?

- What's your favorite TV show and why do you like to watch this show?

- If you had to eat the same meal everyday for a month, what would it be?

- What's one thing you would like to change about your neighborhood that would make it a better place to live?

- What worries you the most about the world you live in today?

- Name one thing you could teach someone else how to make or how to do.

- What's your favorite holiday of the year? What makes this holiday your favorite?

- What's one thing that you would like to change about your school that would make it a better place for you?

"You Like, I Like..."

This is a terrific activity that meets two goals: you get to hear everyone's names repeatedly and you find out something interesting about each person. Call out a question that invites students to name something they like or like to do. Going around the circle, each person must repeat the names of the five previous students and what they like. For example, if the question is, *"What are your two favorite things to wear?"* and the first person who speaks says, *"I like to wear jeans and hoop earrings,"* the next person would say, *"Marisa likes to wear jeans and hoop earrings, and I like to wear patched overalls and leather jackets."* Continue around the circle until everyone has had a turn to speak.

Mix It Up When Students Work Together

If one of your expectations is that every student works with every other student by the end of the first quarter, here are some suggestions for making this happen.

- Give every student a class roster so they can check off with whom they've worked.

- If your first activity involves partners, give every student someone's name as they walk in the door and invite students to find a place in the room to stand and discuss the question with their partner.

- Use any of the random grouping strategies on pages 278–279.

- Whenever students are working with someone new, ask them to say their names and ask them to each respond to a light hearted "Question of the Day."

- When you've got a few minutes at the close of the period or need to shift the energy, invite students to name five students and one thing they know about each of them.

Key Strategy	Make Connections through 10 Second "Hits"
	• Develop personal connections among and between students and teachers
Life Skill *Connection* (See page 112–114)	• Develop, manage, and maintain healthy relationships with adults (26)
Sample Activities, Strategies, and Routines	• Sample 10-Second "Hits"

Imagine for a minute that every student is a website, generating "hits" everyday. Some students get deluged with positive social and academic hits all day long from peers and adults. Others may get more negative than positive hits, but a hit is a hit nonetheless—someone is paying attention. Now think about some of your students who belong to the "invisible middle"—these are the kids who might go through a whole day with no hits at all from peers or adults. Everyone wants to feel noticed, important, and respected. When teachers take the time to direct specific comments to individual students, kids feel that someone cares about them personally.

Sample 10 Second "Hits"

These "10 second hits" help build rapport and strengthen the connections between students and teachers. For some kids, these "10 second hits" can make all the difference in motivation to learn and succeed in your classroom. Before class, during class, or after class, make comments to individual students that let them know that you notice who they are:

- Say something about their appearance—a new hairdo, a cool T-shirt, unusual earrings, a different color fingernail polish, a jacket you like, etc.

- Ask or comment about things that kids are doing outside of your class— sports events, extra curricular activities, other events and projects that students participate in, inside and outside of school.

- Give students positive feedback about something they've done well in class recently. Check in with kids who look tired, upset, worried, or rambunctious by reflecting back to them what you see. The suggested responses below give you a way to acknowledge and learn more about what you see, and give students a way to name what they're feeling and get ready to refocus for class. For example:

    - "You look kind of tired; it's been a long day, huh?"

    - "Wow, you look like you've got energy to spare. We can sure use your energy in the activity we're doing today."

    - "So _____, you look like this has not been your best day; need a minute to get it together?"

- When you are summarizing a discussion or linking ideas, mention students' names and comments they made earlier that contributed to a better understanding of the topic.

Key Strategy	## Create Opportunities When You Only Listen
	• Develop personal connections among and between students and teachers
Life Skill **Connection** (See page 112–114)	• Listen actively to demonstrate to others that they have been understood (17)
Sample Activities, *Strategies, and* *Routines*	• Listening to Students

Sometimes teachers are first-rate talkers and second-rate listeners. It's easy for us to interrupt, overexplain, finish a student's ideas, give advice, correct someone too quickly, or make sure we have the last word, especially if it's clever or funny. It takes a conscious effort to only listen without responding. This simple gesture surprises students when we do it.

Listening to Students

Here are a few ways to try it out:

- Check yourself during discussions. When you really want to listen to what students have to say, use a timer, set it for five or ten minutes, and invite students to respond to an open-ended question that might generate lots of different viewpoints.

- When you have made a choice to conference with students one-on-one (especially when you've discovered that there's a concern or a problem), use your favorite opener to invite someone to talk. For example, "So what's going on?" or "How's it going?" or "You don't seem your usual self. Anything going on that's getting in the way?" Then stop. Don't fill the space with conversation. Sit with the silence and listen.

- Here are some questions you might ask students when you take time out to only listen. Let them know that you'll set the timer for five to ten minutes and invite students to speak to any of these questions. Remind students that this is an opportunity to hear different perspectives—it is not the time to begin a debate, but to really listen to each person's take on the question.

  - What do you like best about going to school here?

  - What do you like least about going to school here?

  - On a scale of 1 to 10 how respectful do you see the staff being to students? How about students being respectful to staff? Students to students? Staff to staff? Say a little about the number you chose.

  - On a scale of 1 to 10 how safe do you think students feel here at school? What kinds of things make a school feel safe for students? What kinds of things make school feel unsafe to students?

  - Are there some groups of students here who seem to get more attention, more resources, more privileges than other groups? Why do you think that is?

  - Are there some groups of students you think feel left out at school? Who gets less attention? Who gets targeted or harassed more? Who can't seem to find a place where they belong? Why do you think that is?

  - If you could make changes in scheduling or the curriculum what would you recommend? How would these changes benefit students?

  - Are there any ways that you feel some students are treated unfairly?

  - When you talk to your friends, what do they complain about the most? What worries them the most about going to this school?

Key Strategy	Make Time for Meaningful Closing Activities
	• Develop personal connections among and between students and teachers
Life Skill Connection (See page 112–114)	• Encourage and appreciate the contribution of others (29)
Sample Activities, Strategies, and Routines	• Closing Rituals • Invite Students to Write Letters to Students Who Will Be Taking This Course Next Year

In high school, the concepts of closure and celebration are part of big events like graduation and awards assemblies, but not usually daily classroom life. We get so caught up in the testing and grading cycle that it takes incredible discipline to invite students to stop and reflect on their classroom experience. Develop rituals that give you an opportunity to acknowledge what the class has accomplished and give students a chance to reflect on what they've learned, appreciated, and experienced throughout the course.

Closing Rituals

- Give every student someone's name in the class—their task is to write an appreciation note to that person. That might include something they appreciated about this person as a classmate; something about this person that is interesting; something this person did in class that was cool, funny, smart, impressive, or unexpected; something they will remember about this person from the year. Collect the cards and pass them out on the last day.

- Create a memories bulletin board where students can write their responses to any of these sentence starters:

  - One thing I won't forget about this class is...

  - At the end of this class, I'm more aware of...

  - At the end of this class, I'm no longer nervous about...

  - For me, the best thing about this class was...

  - The funniest thing that happened in this class was...

  - Before this class I thought that... Now, I think...

  - This class got me thinking more about...

  - The biggest challenge for me in this class was...

11

    – One thing I would change about this course is...

    – I surprised myself this year by...

    – The one thing I never want to do again is...

    – Goodbye _____. Hello _____.

- At the close of the course, ask each student to share a response to one of the sentence starters above.

- If students keep a journal, ask them to write about any of the sentence starters above or any of the questions suggested in the letter writing activity below, or incorporate a reflection essay into your final exam. Students turn in their essay on the day they take their exam.

- For each class you teach, share a few memorable stories that stand out for you.

- Review the "big goals" and expectations you set for the year. Discuss whether and how successfully the class met them.

- Create a congratulations banner or poster that acknowledges what students have accomplished during the year.

Invite Students to Write Letters to Students Who Will Be Taking This Course Next Year

Here are some ideas for what students might include in their letters:

- What's the one piece of advice that you would give a student who is taking this course next year?

- What are two things you liked best about class and two things you disliked?

- What did you find to be most challenging about the course?

- What did you find to be kind of fun?

- What did you find to be the most interesting and least interesting things that you studied or learned how to do?

- What was the biggest surprise for you during the year?

- If students want to "learn the ropes" to be successful in class, what should they know?

- What's something they will need to learn how to do well during the year?

CHAPTER 12

Practice 2: Emphasize Personalized, Student-Centered Learning

Offer Choices from Day One

Make Personal Goal-Setting and Reflection Regular Practices

Use Self-Assessment Tools throughout the Course

Invite Students' Worlds Into the Classroom

Increase Engagement through Well Paced, Student-Centered Learning and Instruction

Make Project- and Problem-Based Learning Part of Every Unit

Encourage Independent Learning

12

Key Strategy	Offer Choices from Day One
	• Emphasize personalized, student-centered learning
Life Skill Connection (See page 112–114)	• Work for high personal performance and cultivate your strengths and positive qualities (16)
Sample Activities, Strategies, and Routines	• Examples of Everyday Choices and Options

One of the ironies of adolescence is how little choice students experience in the classroom. My colleagues and I have often observed that kindergartners have more choices of what to do in a day than a sophomore might have in a week's worth of classes. The power of choice confers ownership and makes almost any task feel more doable and more satisfying.

Providing more choices is a win-win solution for teachers and students. First, choices convey that there isn't just one way to meet a goal or complete a task, thus acknowledging that every class exhibits a wide range of learning preferences, styles, and motivators. Second, choices encourage self-efficacy and self-expression. Students get to say to themselves, "I chose to do it this way and here's why." Third, providing more opportunities for choice comes with the expectation of being more personally responsible and accountable. And finally, offering academic and behavioral choices invites cooperation, reduces student resistance to learning, and minimizes adversarial relationships between students and teachers.

Examples of Everyday Choices and Options

1. Develop a list of options for how students can demonstrate what they know and what they've learned that includes nontraditional assessments like the eight Ps:

    - Participation

    - Performance

    - Portfolios

    - Presentations

    - Problem posing and analysis

    - Products

    - Proficiencies

    - Projects

    Then let students choose several assessments to do for a particular unit of study.

2. Give five homework options a week. Students choose three they want to complete.

3. Give some assignments at the beginning of the week that are due at the beginning of the next week. For those who complete their assignments by Friday there is no weekend homework. Others have the weekend to finish.

4. Give students one free homework pass each quarter.

5. Choose different ways that you and students present information on a particular topic. During the year, ensure that each student has an opportunity to teach something to the class.

6. Create 120-point tests in which students need to complete items that total 100 points, including some required items.

7. If students keep a portfolio of their work, ask them to choose pieces that they polish and correct until the results are a "perfect" paper. These will then be included in a folder sent home to parents at grading period. Or choose a set of papers that reflect a continuum of progress during a semester to discuss in an assessment conference or to send home to parents at grading period.

8. Create at least one opportunity every quarter or semester where students engage in some form of independent learning where they choose what they want to learn more about or what they want to learn how to do.

9. When you offer a menu of choices for assignments, leave room for students who want to develop their own ideas as long as they meet the assignment criteria.

10. Give students the option of creating one 3" × 5" study card that they can use while taking a test. You would be surprised how creative students are in organizing information on one little card. By creating the card they have gone a long way toward learning the content.

11. Give students several options for how they want to be tested on specific content.

12. Review and grade tests in class (have special pens or colored pencils so students aren't tempted to rewrite original answers rather than correcting or adding new information). Encourage students to make notes and ask questions. Then offer opportunities for students to take the test again.

13. Invite students to create questions and problems for tests and performance demonstrations.

14. Have students choose "study buddies" who help each other review and study before a test.

12

	Make Personal Goal-Setting
Key Strategy	**and Reflection Regular Practices**

• Emphasize personalized, student-centered learning

Life Skill Connection
(See page 112–114)

• Make big and litttle goals and make plans (13)
• Prioritize and "chunk" tasks, predict task completion time, and manage time effectively (14)
• Work for high personal performance and cultivate your strengths and positive qualities (16)
• Assess your skills, competencies, effort, and quality of work accurately (17)

Sample Activities, Strategies, and Routines

• Personal Pathways
• Thinking about Personal Goal-Setting and Planning
• Reflection Prompts
• See, Feel, Think, Do
• General Debriefing Questions for Experiential Leraning Activities
• Two Glows and a Grow

These "learning to learn" skills increase students' self-awareness and self-efficacy. Try integrating these practices into gatherings, closings, journal writing, and debriefing after an activity has been completed.

Personal Pathways

The following activity was developed by Rachel Poliner. It works well at the beginning of the school year as a way for students to reflect on their past and set goals for the current year.

Personal Pathway

Personal Pathway for _____

Think about your life experiences, people who are important to you, and goals. Fill in the areas along your path with drawings or writing representing where you have been, people and events along the way, and where you might be headed.

Where I started —
family, neighborhood,
state, country

Someone or something that
influenced me along the way

Where I've been,
what I've done
(schools, sports,
groups, interests)

A turning point in my life —
I used to..., but now I...

Where
I am
headed

Where and when
I sometimes
stray
off course

One goal I have
for school this
year and one
goal in my per-
sonal life

One thing that makes
me a little nervous
about the start of the
school year

Three things I liked learning
or learning how to do in the past

Thinking About Personal Goal-Setting and Planning

Offer different ways that students can develop and review course goals and plan major tasks to be completed:

1. During this week I expect to complete _____
    to ask for help with _____
    to take time to _____
    to earn a _____ on _____

2. Develop quarterly course goals and review your goals during the quarter.

    Name of Course _____

By the end of this quarter I will...	
Why does this goal matter to me?	
Three steps I will take to achieve this goal	
Two obstacles and what I can do to overcome them	
Three indicators that I'm on my way to reaching my goal	
Who will I talk with about my goal? What support do I need?	
Comments during the quarter:	
Results at the end of the quarter:	
What worked? What didn't? What will I do differently next quarter?	
What did I learn about myself?	

3. Ask students to review last week's course notes and assignments from their agenda book. Ask them to give themselves a grade for last week. For the current week...

   – **Prioritize** tasks, beginning with what's most essential.

   – **Predict** how much time the most important tasks will take.

   – **Plan** ahead and write down important To Dos that you know will need to schedule time for during the week after next.

4. If students don't have agenda books, create a weekly assignment and planning sheet:

Weekly Assignments and Responsibilities

Name _____

Course _____

Description of Work to Be Completed	Due	Done

5. Expect students to create product and project maps to keep on track:

   • What exactly are you promising to do?

   • What steps will it take to complete your product or paper?

   • How long will it take to complete each step?

   • How will you know when you are halfway there?

   • What resources will you need to complete your product or project?

   • What help from others will you need to complete your product or project?

12

Reflection Prompts

You might want to post these sentence stems in your classroom and invite students to choose one to respond to either in writing or verbally when you debrief learning activities.

- As I began this activity, I felt...
- At the end of this activity, I felt...
- One thing that surprised me was...
- As we worked together, I kept thinking about...
- Now I'm more aware of how important it is to...
- I liked this activity because...
- I would have changed this activity by...
- One thing that was fun, challenging, or eye-opening was...
- After participating in the activity I realized...
- In thinking about our classroom, it would be great if we could...
- I found it really difficult to...
- I found it easy to...
- This helped me to learn more about...
- I can take what I learned from this and apply it to...
- I want to remember this experience the next time I...

See, Feel, Think, Do

Use the following questions to help your students reflect on their experience after an activity:

See: What did you observe? What did you notice about what you were doing and what others were doing?

Feel: What feelings did you experience during this activity? In the beginning? In the end? What were your reactions? Did your feelings change?

Think: (the so-what question) How did this work for you? What insights did you gain about yourself, or others? What did you learn about _____? Given your insights from this exercise, what are the implications for _____? Why does this matter?

Do: (the now-what question) Now that you are aware, what will you differently? How can you use these insights and information? What might you want to change? What actions might you want to take?

General Debriefing Questions for Experiential Learning Activities

At the close of an activity, a project, or a learning unit, use reflection questions to debrief what students have experienced.

- What tools, skills, and attitudes helped you to be successful? Helped you complete the task? Helped you meet or achieve the goal?

- How did this activity work for you? What made this experience (interesting, hard, frustrating, comfortable, uncomfortable, strange, different, surprising, challenging)?

- Was there anything you didn't like or would have changed?

- What's one thing you want to remember from today?

- What's one thing you can take from today and apply to your life?

Two Glows and a Grow

Use the following handout to have students reflect on their day.

12

HANDOUT 2
Two Glows and a Grow

Something you did today that felt productive and satisfying for you

One way you felt you put forth your best effort as a learner

Something you experienced today that was a growing edge for you – a skill or competency you want to continue to strengthen and improve

Key Strategy	**Use Self-Assessment Tools throughout the Course**
	• Emphasize personalized, student-centered learning

Life Skill Connection (See page 112–114)	• Make big and little goals and make plans (13)
	• Prioritize and "chunk" tasks, predict task completion time, and manage time effectively (14)
	• Work for high personal performance and cultivate your strengths and positive qualities (16)
	• Assess your skills, competencies, effort, and quality of work accurately (17)

Sample Activities, Strategies, and Routines	• Use Assessment Questions throughout the Year
	• Making the Grade

On any given month try not to overuse one assessment tool. Incorporate a mix of what you assess (specific activities, the week, a unit, mastery of a learning standard, quarterly progress, the end of the year) and how students are assessed (verbally in whole-group sharing, pairs, or in a quick conference with you; journaling; or entrance and exit slips). Below are a number of tools to use at different times during the year.

Use Assessment Questions throughout the Year

There are several ways that you can use assessment questions with students:

- Choose some of these questions for a written assessment.

- Give students the whole series of questions and invite students to select a few that they choose to answer.

- Select some questions for discussion in small and large groups (you might want to tape record responses) and select some questions for written reflection.

Assessing the Day's Class or a Specific Learning Activity

- What worked best for you today?

- Any new insights or ideas?

- Are there any questions or issues you want to make sure get addressed tomorrow?

- Any other comments or suggestions?

A Weekly Assessment

Take time every week in your classes to do a quick informal assessment using any of these suggestions:

- What is something important that you learned?

- What is something that you want to remember?

- What is something you learned that you want to know more about?

- What is something you learned about yourself as a learner that surprised you or made you think about yourself differently?

Looking Ahead Questions for Before a Test, Performance, or Demonstration

- What topics do you feel confident about?

- What topics are you unsure about?

- How are you going to clear up the concepts that you have yet to master?

Looking Back Questions for After a Test, Performance, or Demonstration

- What strategies did you use to prepare for the test?

- Which strategies were the most helpful in preparing for the test?

- Did you do as well as you felt you should have, based on your preparation?

- Why did you get the grade you did?

- What will you do next time?

- If your friend were taking this test tomorrow, how would you tell him or her to prepare?

Assessing a Learning Unit

Pick one unit of study and post a list of every activity and task that has been part of that unit. Ask students to review the list and respond to these questions:

- What three activities helped you most to understand _____. Why?

- What two activities helped you most to demonstrate what you learned? Why?

- What activity would you have left out of the unit or added to this unit? Why?

- What activity did you like best? Why?

- What activity did you like least? Why?

At the End of the Quarter, Semester, or Course

Give students the whole series of questions and select a few that you want all students to answer. Invite students to select a few additional questions that they would like to answer.

- What are three things you want to remember most from this course?

- What are two of the most important things you've learned in this course?

- What's a skill you've learned and used that you're sure you will use again?

- Give one example of how you know yourself better as a learner at the end of this course.

- Think of specific situations in this course (inside or outside the classroom) that show how you managed yourself successfully in the following ways:

  - An experience when I felt really self-disciplined (I did what I needed to do without being nagged or getting it together at the last minute.)

  - An experience when I overcame my frustration, upsetness, or anger successfully

  - An experience when I felt self-motivated

  - An experience when I did whatever it took to complete a project/assignment successfully

- Describe one thing you've learned about yourself that surprised you.

- What questions do you have at the end of the course that you'd like to think more about?

- In what ways was this course taught differently from other courses? Describe two or three activities you liked best and two or three activities you liked least. Why?

- What two or three issues and/or activities do you wish all students in your school could experience? Why would you recommend these issues or activities?

- In thinking back on this course, what images and experiences stand out most for you? Why?

- Did this course make it easier for you to get to know other students? Explain.

- Did you feel safe enough in this course to take the risks of being open and honest and sharing your stories with others? Why or why not?

- If you were to summarize what this course was about to another student, what would you say? Use two or three sentences.

- Do you think this course will change the rest of your time in high school? How?

- What might you be more aware of or do differently because you took this course?

- What's one attitude or skill you hope students will take from this class when they leave?

Making the Grade

You might also ask students to predict their grades several times a quarter—naming what grade they would give themselves and identifying one or two reasons why they feel this grade is an accurate reflection of their effort in class. You might also invite students to predict what it would take to improve their grade over the next few weeks.

Key Strategy	Invite Students' Worlds into the Classroom
(S)	• Emphasize personalized, student-centered learning
Life Skill Connection (See page 112–114)	• Empathize; understand and accept another person's feelings, perspectives, and point of view (22) • Recognize and appreciate similarities and differences in others (31)
Sample Activities, Strategies, and Routines	• Connecting to Students' Worlds • Acknowledge Students' Preoccupations • Check It Out • Create a Teen Trading Bin

Acting like a kid ("Let me show you how cool I am" or "You'll like me as a teacher because I'm just like you") turns students off. On the other hand, letting students know that you're curious about their world, that you're paying attention to their reality gets you lots of points. Connected teaching is all about how you meet students where they are (acknowledging what they are thinking and feeling here and now) and how you link their lived experiences to what they are doing and learning in the classroom.

Connecting to Students' Worlds

Use examples, metaphors, and analogies from their world to make learning real. One of the best pieces of advice I ever got about teaching was to collect examples, metaphors, and analogies from students' everyday experiences so that I could use them to reinforce and illustrate what we were learning in the classroom. Think about how young people spend their time outside of school, what kinds of big ideas or issues grab their attention, or what they know a lot about—then begin making connections:

- When you're teaching a particular skill, in what ways might it connect to the skills one needs to play a particular sport, drive a car, work on a food service line, play in a band, or complete a job or college application?

- Link the everyday conflicts students experience with friends, parents, siblings, supervisors, police, customers, or teammates to conflicts they encounter in literature and social studies classes.

- Adolescents gravitate toward any conversation about money and power, sex and violence. Use their perceptions and experiences around these big ideas as a connector to key concepts in politics, economics, biology, chemistry, etc.

- Ask students to do a five-minute brainstorm around this question: What's going on in your world right now that's cool/uncool, fascinating, unfair, outrageous, or worrisome? Once you've got a list, keep your eyes and ears peeled for examples from their world that can help explain and illustrate your world in the classroom.

Use learning strategies that get students talking to each other. Make time in any curriculum unit for students in pairs and threes to share…

- What they know about a particular topic

- Their opinions and perceptions of an issue being discussed

- The thinking processes they use to solve problems

- How they might respond given a particular situation—what they think would be a good or bad decision, and why

Acknowledge Students' Preoccupations

Acknowledge where your students are and then get started. When they are anticipating a big school event or rite of passage that's happening the same day or week, take a few minutes to acknowledge it by saying, "I have a hunch (some, most) of you are thinking about _____." Invite them to share a few comments about what's going on, what they're thinking or feeling about this, or why they're dreading or looking forward to this event. If it's SATs, report card day, college acceptance letter day, or the like, reassure your students, using your own brand of humor, that no one will die, that they will get through this, and that you will see them all the next day. Then say, "So here we are in _____. What's one thing you can do that will help you focus for the next _____ minutes?" Get a couple of comments and close with your version of "Okay, let's do it."

Check It Out

Check out what young people are reading, viewing, and listening to. One way to check into their world is to ask them occasionally what's going on out there. Sometimes when you have a minute or two of a class period remaining before end time, ask your students one of these questions or bring in something to share that piqued your curiosity.

- "So it's the weekend. Got any suggestions for a video I should rent?"

- "I'm actually going home today right after school's out. If I wanted to take a look, is there anything good to watch on TV?"

- "In the last week, I've heard people say _____ a bunch of times. What does that mean to you and your friends?"

- Hold up the school newspaper or local paper and share an article that has a youth connection. Ask students what they think about the topic or issue.

- Sometimes when there's a new fad, fashion, or music group that grabs kids' attention and leaves you scratching your head, just ask kids. "I noticed/heard/saw _____. What's that all about?" A lot of kids are more than happy to tell you something they know that you don't.

- "If I had two hours this week just to hang out, what three websites should I check out? What TV shows should I check out? What radio station should I listen to?"

Create A Teen Trading Bin

Place a box somewhere in your classroom where kids can drop magazines, paperback books, computer games, tapes, etc. that they don't want anymore and are willing to trade for something else. As long as they've put something in the box, they can take something out.

Key Strategy	Increase Engagement through Well Paced, Student-Centered Learning and Instruction
	• Emphasize personalized, student-centered learning
Life Skill Connection (See page 112–114)	• Focus and pay attention (12) • Prioritize and "chunk" tasks, predict task completion time, and manage time effectively (14) • Work for high personal performance and cultivate your strengths and positive qualities (16) • Assess your skills, competencies, effort, and quality of work accurately • Cooperate, share, and work toward high performance within a group to achieve group goals (27)
Sample Activities, Strategies, and Routines	• Five Elements of Well-Paced, Student-Centered Lessons • Sample 90 Minute Block Lessons • Expand Your Teaching Tool Box for Engaging All Learners • Beyond Instruction: Unpacking Other Key Teacher Roles

Activity management (the choice of activity, sequence, staging, pacing, and transitioning of activities within a lesson, a week, or a unit of study) is a critical skill set in any teacher's tool box.[1] Boredom and monotony are major contributors to inattentiveness and low-level disruptive behaviors. Well-paced lessons that incorporate high interest, student-centered learning strategies and challenging work will keep most students focused, on task, and engaged most of the time.

Five Elements of Well-Paced Lessons

Although pacing is one the most obvious elements of good instruction, it's not so easy to do in practice. We tend to talk too much and drag things out beyond the point of interest or attention span. The chart on page 242, illustrates five elements that should vary continuously throughout a lesson: Time chunks, learning strategies, grouping structures, noise levels, and instructional supports.

Think back to the lessons you taught to one group of students in one course during the last week.

- How did you alternate short and long chunks of time and incorporate a wide array of learning strategies, grouping structures, noise levels, and instructional supports throughout each instructional period?

- Over the course of each lesson, did students spend more time listening to and watching you OR did you spend more time observing, coaching, conferencing, and listening to students as they worked on their own? This question asks you to think about the ratio of passive vs. active learning time during any instructional period.

- Consider the benefits of increasing the amount of time students are directing their own learning and reducing the amount of passive, teacher-directed time when you're the "sage on the stage." The sample 75 minute "workshop" on the right shows a three part lesson model with a 1:3:1 ratio: **A:** teacher-directed mini-lesson; **B:** student-centered work time, and **C:** oral and written reflection and feedback. When students are working on their own in groups or independently, you get to spend more time monitoring and assessing what students are actually learning; you reduce the incidents of students goofing off during whole group instruction; and you get more time to do personal check-ins and conferencing with individual students.

SAMPLE WORKSHOP LESSON MODEL:

	(7)	**Do NOW or Gathering**
A	(10)	**Mini-Lesson** Connections / Teaching point / Directions 3 ways
	(15)	**Guided Practice** Try It out /Active engagement in learning task
	(3)	**Check for Understanding** / Link to follow-up tasks
B	(20)	**Independent Practice or Small Group Tasks** (Students are working and you are teaching by "walking around", coaching, conferencing, and working with small groups)
		Activities for Early Completers
		Assessment for Learning
C	(15)	**Reflection, Discussion, and Feedback** informed by high level questions
	(5)	**Homework / Preview / Personal Check-ins**

FIVE ELEMENTS OF WELL-PACED, STUDENT-CENTERED LESSONS

Time Chunks	Learning Strategies	Grouping Structures	Noise Level
③ MIN	Reading, Research, Text-Based Protocols	Whole Group	Silence
⑤ MIN	Writing, Recording, and Representing to Learn	Small Group	Quiet Conversation
⑦ MIN	Viewing/Observing Listening and Lecture **MINI-LESSON**	Pairs	Team Work
⑩ MIN		Independent Work	
⑮ MIN	Thinking and Reflecting	Individual Conferencing, Coaching, and Check-ins	
⑳ MIN	Gatherings, Closings, and Brain-Body Energizers		
㉚ MIN	Seminar and Structured Discussions	Small Group Tutorials and Reteaching	
	Presenting and Performing		
	Labs, Projects, and Studios		
	Games and Team Challenges		
	Drawing and Charting		
	Guided Practice and Problem Solving		
	"Hands On" and Experiential Learning		

✔ INSTRUCTIONAL SUPPORTS

Class keeping and planning

Helping students settle in and get ready to learn

Clear expectations and instructions

Physical, visual, and verbal prompts

Modeling and effective group facilitation

Signals for silence and getting students' attention

Smooth transitions from one activity to another

Reminders, clues, tips, and suggestions

Examples and explanations

"Real time" positive, corrective, and appreciative feedback and formative assessment for learning

Personal and group encouragement

Individual and group check-ins

Celebrations, recognitions, and incentives

Sample 90 Minute Block Periods

More and more high schools are moving to a block schedule of longer periods that support the workshop model and more sustained student-centered learning opportunities. Pages 242–246 illustrate extended learning periods designed for four different purposes: 1. Quiet Independent Work Day and Conferencing; 2. End-of-Unit Catch-up/Study Day; 3. Seminar or Cooperative Learning Day; and 4. Hands-on Project/Experiential Learning Day.

I. Quiet Independent Work Day and Conferencing

7 MIN	DO NOW/Entry Ticket Materials Preparation Evidence of Homework (Random Check)	
3 MIN	Agenda Check Academic Goals and Skills (WHAT we will be learning) Life Skills/Habits of Learning (HOW we will be learning)	
5 MIN	Connections (Yesterday-DO NOW-Today's Focus) Think-Pair-Share about topic	
10 MIN	Mini-Lesson (Teaching Point, Product Rubric, Directions 3 Ways)	
20 MIN 10 MIN 15 MIN	**Text Reading** / "While You Read" Protocols Walk-Talk-Decide Text Reading/Cornell Notes (double entry notes) Personal Check-ins, Conferences, Coaching	
	— OR —	
20 MIN 10 MIN 15 MIN	**Lab, Studio, Independent Projects** Pairs – Back and Forth Cards Lab, Studio, Project (con't) Personal Check-ins, Conferences, Coaching	
	— OR —	
20 MIN 10 MIN 15 MIN	**Representing to Learn Product** Product Rubric Check-in Representing to Learn Product (con't) Personal Check-ins, Conferences, Coaching	
	— OR —	
20 MIN 10 MIN 15 MIN	**Guided Practice** Pairs – White Board Check-in Independent Problem Solving Personal Check-ins, Conferences, Coaching	
7 MIN	Team Challenge Assessment (Jeopardy; Game/Set/Match; 3-2-1 Summarizer; One Minute Problems; Stick-It-Up; or Relay Review)	
7 MIN	Closing Questions linked to homework/Next class preview	

2. End-of-Unit Catch-Up / Study Day

(7) MIN		Gathering (Grouping Card Sort) Materials Preparation Evidence of Study Cards		
(3) MIN		Agenda Check Academic Goals and Skills (WHAT we will be learning) Life Skills/Habits of Learning (HOW we will be learning)		
(5) MIN		Connections (Yesterday-Gathering-Today's Focus) Post "Need to Knows" & Questions		
(10) MIN		Q & A / Final Thoughts		
(20) MIN		**Team Challenge Assessment** Your group can only use your study cards and Q & A notes!! (Jeopardy; Problem Relay; Game/Set/Match; WordConnect; Four Corner Multiple Choice; Pictionary; or Tableaus)		
(40) MIN		**End-of-Unit Catch-Up** • Study Buddies or Home Group Study Teams • End-of-Unit Products • "Climbers' Club" Check-ins (studens who are trying to climb out of the hole) • Work on End-of-Unit Self-Assessment • Study Cards • Personal Check-ins/Conferencing • Independent Projects		
(5) MIN		Exit Ticket and Shout-Out: 1) I feel more confident about _____. 2) I still need to review/study_____.		

3. Seminar or Cooperative Learning Day

7 MIN — DO NOW (Problem of the Day)
Materials Preparation
Evidence of Homework (Random Check)

3 MIN — Agenda Check
Academic Goals and Skills (WHAT we will be learning)
Life Skills/Habits of Learning (HOW we will be learning)

5 MIN — Connections (Yesterday-DO NOW-Today's Focus)
Think-Pair-Share about topic

5 MIN — Mini-Lesson (Teaching Point, Seminar Rubric, Directions 3 Ways)

15 MIN — Seminar Prep using DBQ's and other posted questions

40 MIN — **Seminar or Structured Discussion**

- - - - - - - - - - - - OR - - - - - - - - - - - -

5 MIN — Mini-Lesson (Teaching Point, Product Rubric, Directions 3 Ways)

40 MIN — **Group Work Time** / Walk Around Check-ins

10 MIN — Silent Gallery Walk (Post products with high level guiding questions)

5 MIN — Debriefing/ Discussion

10 MIN — Group and Self-Assessment Feedback / Teacher Feedback

5 MIN — Follow-up Homework
Next Session Preview
Assignment Notebook Check

4. Hands On Project / Experiential Learning Day

7 MIN	Gathering: (Thinking like a _____, what's one thing...) Materials Preparation
3 MIN	Agenda Check Academic Goals and Skills (WHAT we will be learning) Life Skills/Habits of Learning (HOW we will be learning)
5 MIN	Connections (Yesterday-Gathering-Today's Focus) Essential Question for the Day
15 MIN	Directions, Text Reading, and Protocol to prepare for experiential activity
5 MIN	Mini-Lesson (Teaching Point, Participation or Project Rubric, Directions 3 Ways)
35 MIN	**Simulation OR Small Group Projects OR The BIG Problem**

------------------------------ OR ------------------------------

5 MIN	Mini-Lesson (Teaching Point, Presentation and Feedback Rubric, Directions 3 Ways)
15 MIN	**Preparation and Rehearsal**
35 MIN	**Group Performances / Presentations**

| 10 MIN | Debriefing and Feedback |
| 10 MIN | Exit Ticket Follow-up Homework Next Session Preview Personal Check-ins |

Expand Your Teaching Tool Box for Engaging All Learners

Most current curriculum specialists and instructional coaches would argue that effective instruction rests on your capacity to deliver lessons that:

- begin with explicit aims and learning outcomes aligned to content standards;

- help students navigate through an anticipatory set, a mini-lesson, and guided practice;

- emphasize formative assessment to monitor student learning;

- and wrap up the lesson with review, closure, and homework.

What could possibly be objectionable about a lesson plan recipe that is used in almost every school in America? Yet, relying on just one lesson type assumes that your job is to teach expert lessons, rather than becoming an expert at engaging students authentically and rigorously in the subject you love. With adolescents, (many of whom do not particularly like school to begin with), lesson planning which includes a more eclectic array of group processes and learning strategies will grab students' attention, build a sense of group-ness, heighten their interest and curiosity, and engage their emotions as well as their intellect. Engagement increases when student interest goes up.

Researchers have differentiated between two types of student interest: personal and situational.[2] Personal interest is a "function of individual preferences and characteristics" and the value that students place on the course content or the goal that they associate with the topic or task; it is most often connected to WHAT students are learning. Situational interest is more about HOW students are learning. It refers to "catch" and "hold" processes and strategies that emphasize group work, the use of technology, puzzles and games, learning activities that are perceived as "fun", and opportunities where students get to "learn the material ourselves" or "do something" involving hands-on activities.[3] Other strategies that increase student engagement include personalizing learning and involving students in planning and decision making related to the content and delivery of the course.

The learning and social needs of the group should shape the structure and pacing of your lessons, not the other way around. Discovering and capitalizing on each group's personality, preferences, and rhythm is what authentic teaching is all about. The next page, "Expand Your Teaching Tool Box for Engaging All Learners" presents a snapshot of group processes and learning strategies that align with the qualities and characteristics of adolescent learners and help prepare students to be college, career, and life ready in the 21st century. As you design instructional units and develop weekly plans and individual lessons, think about how you might incorporate some of these suggestions to boost student engagement.

Expand Your Teaching Tool Box for Engaging All Learners

Student Voice and Civil Dialogue

- Pair/shares & small group listening labs
- Class meetings and negotiated learning
- One minute rants, raves, reviews, opinions
- Student-led activities
- Student surveys and feedback (what students like and what they don't)
- Opinion continuums, four corners, walk-abouts, learning carousels, and concentric circles that get kids moving and talking

Self-perpetuating Routines

- Group gatherings
- Group closings
- Goal-setting, self-assessment, student directed record keeping of academic progress
- Assignment notebook review and check-ins
- Journaling
- End of week/unit/quarter learning reflections
- Progress report check-in's (mid-term and end-of-term)

Making Learning Personally Relevant

- Give students options and choices
- Link learning to students' interests and real world problems/issues/applications
- Utilize experiential learning through field work, labs, interviews, simulations, role plays, mock trials, etc.)
- Learn from a practitioner's perspective (Think like a _____ or imagine yourself as…)
- Make the most of your personal relationship with the student (I'll learn and work for you because you care about me)
- Emphasize authentic assessments for real audiences

Group Building Tools

- Explicit expectations
- Group guidelines and agreements
- Sit in a circle/oval/square so everyone can see each other
- Know everyone's names
- Class keeping and group check-in's (How's it going?)
- Cooperative learning and collaborative problem solving
- Assessment of habits of learning and life skills
- Celebrations and recognition

Game It Up!!!!

Games are organized structures for learning that involve:

- A common goal or task
- A challenge or problem to solve
- Obstacles to overcome
- Playfulness
- Positive energy
- Rules
- Roles
- Cooperation and/or competition
- Strategic thinking strategies
- Social navigation and negotiation
- Interpersonal and group efficacy
- Emotional investment
- Group norming
- Reflection about what you experienced
- Links to real life

Grabbing Students' Attention and Interest

- If you were in this situation, what would you do? How would you feel?
- Problematize anything and everything (Here's the problem. Here are the rules, constraints, resources. Your job is to solve it/Construct the best solution. Go!!!)
- You decide…You be the judge…
- Your group needs to agree on/choose/design…
- Here's the situation… YES/NO?; RIGHT/WRONG?; FAIR/UNFAIR?; GOOD/BAD CHOICE?

Beyond Instruction: Unpacking Other Key Teacher Roles

Teacher preparation, mentoring, and supervision focus almost exclusively on the teacher's role as instructor, often at the expense of understanding the importance of other teacher roles. Implementing engaging, well-paced, student-centered learning and instruction requires that you juggle two tasks simultaneously: supervising and supporting THE GROUP and meeting the learning needs of INDIVIDUAL STUDENTS. Take a look at the rules below. Which of these roles (group facilitator, advocate, listener, coach, and interventionist) are more familiar and comfortable for you? Is there any role that represents a "growing edge" that you want to improve? Are there any skill sets described that you want use more intentionally or more often?

WITH THE GROUP

You're a Facilitator who assists, guides, and enables the group to do its work effectively by…

- Modeling the spirit, presence, behaviors, and skills you expect of participants
- Reading the group and what it needs in the moment
- Spending more time observing, coaching, and listening to the group than group spends watching and listening to you
- Making purpose transparent: Why are we doing what we're doing?
- Making observations transparent: Here's what I'm seeing/hearing.
- Asking questions that enable the group to focus, probe, reflect, and assess; encourage curiosity and insight; deepen understanding; and help the group apply what they have learned
- Redirecting and helping the group to get back on track
- Insisting on group accountability for working effectively together/achieving the goal/completing the task
- Insisting on individual responsibility for learning
- Debriefing the group experience

WITH INDIVIDUAL STUDENTS…

"I'm on Your Side and on Your Case!"

You're an Advocate

"I believe in you."

- Words of encouragement
- Confidence in your capacity to meet learning expectations
- Support when you need it
- Mirroring your assets

You're a Listener

"Tell me more about _____."

- Discovering who you are, what you need, what you know, and what you can do
- Learning about your strengths, assets, talents, aspirations, and plans for the future
- Learning about your challenges and frustrations

You're a Coach

"I will help you get it right."

- Explicit academic and behavior expectations
- Giving immediate and concrete feedback to help students correct mistakes and get it right
- Guided instruction, re-teaching, tutorials, individual conferencing
- Providing practice and rehearsal
- Sharing experiences and reflecting on lessons learned
- Pushing for quality and excellence
- Transparent assessment and record keeping

You're an Interventionist

"So let's take a look at what's happened and what you need to do."

- Straight talk and personalized academic and behavioral conferencing
- "Workouts" with students during lunch or after school
- Probing, planning, and problem solving
- Behavioral and learning contracts
- Student referrals for additional support services and interventions

Make Project- and Problem-Based Learning Part of Every Unit

Key Strategy

• Emphasize personalized, student-centered learning

Life Skill Connection
(See page 112–114)

• Work for high personal performance and cultivate your strengths and positive qualities (16)
• Assess your skills, competencies, effort, and quality of work accurately (17)
• Cooperate, share, and work toward high performance within a group; achieve group goals (27)

Sample Activities, Strategies, and Routines

• Linking the Classroom to the Real World
• The Six As of Instructional Design for Project-Based Learning
• Design Variables for Projects, Problems, and Inquiries
• Guidelines for Collaborative Problem Solving
• Resources for Problem Solving and Project-Based Learning

Consider making project-based and problem-based learning an important feature of every semester's work. Independent or small-group projects meet a number of learning goals, including the following:

• Students have the opportunity to make many choices within a framework of clear expectations and project criteria.

• Projects offer the opportunity to link academic class work to real-world problems and investigations.

• Projects enable students to experience a full range of learning tasks, from development of an idea to the final presentation or product.

• Projects enable students to capitalize on their personal interests and learning strengths while developing new skills.

• Teachers have the opportunity to provide more personalized guidance, coaching, and support to individual students.

• Goal-setting, reflection, assessment, and revision are embedded in the project process from start to finish.

Project- and problem-based learning are "authentic experiential forms of learning centered on the collaborative investigation and resolution of messy real world problems." A problem/ project-based learning curriculum provides students with the critical thinking abilities to address problems that impact their lives, their community, and their world; they discover and learn new knowledge as they attempt to solve the complexities of real world problems. Research projects, case studies, critical investigations, and collaborative learning are the conduits that enable students to solve issues that have multiple solutions.

"Projects are complex tasks, based on challenging questions or problems, that involve students in design, problem-solving, decision making, or investigative activities; give students the opportunity to work relatively autonomously over extended periods of time; and culminate in realistic products or presentations."[4]

Problem-based learning is minds-on, hands-on learning organized around the investigation of "ill-structured" problems that are carefully crafted to maximize students' engagement as problem solvers. Students identify the root problem and the conditions needed for a good solution, pursue meaning and understanding, and become self-directed learners. Teachers are problem-solving colleagues who model interest and enthusiasm for learning and are also cognitive coaches who nurture an environment that supports open inquiry.[5]

Project-based learning and problem-based learning fit well with technology-rich learning environments where the focus is not on the hardware and software, but on the learning experience. Technology is used to facilitate learning; it may be a tool to organize ideas, search for current information, or present ideas. However the focus of learning is the student's excitement about solving a problem or exploring a topic or issue they find meaningful.

Linking the Classroom to the Real World

Invite people who practice your discipline in the world outside of school to listen, discuss, and assess your students' work around a specific problem or project that places students in role of writer, historian, scientist, mathematician, artist, media consultant, investigator, chronicler, etc. Ask practitioners to be part of a discussion about ways students can expand and complicate their thinking about their work.

When presenting a project or problem that you expect every student to complete, work along with students, completing your own project or solving your own problem during the same timeline.

The Six A's of Instructional Design for Project-Based Learning

Project-based learning is at the heart of Schooling for the Real World, a wonderful how-to guide to student-centered real-world learning in schools and classrooms. Adria Steinberg has developed a framework called "The Six A's of Instructional Design" as a guide for creating rigorous and relevant projects across the disciplines.[6] Use them to connect your projects to life outside of school walls.

1. **Authenticity**

    - Where in the "real world" might an adult tackle the problem or question addressed by the project?

    - How do you know the problem or question has meaning to the students?

    - Who might be an appropriate audience for students' work?

2. **Academic Rigor**

   - What is the central problem or question addressed by the project?

   - What knowledge area and central concepts will it address?

   - What habits of mind will students develop (for example, concern for evidence, viewpoint, and cause and effect; precision of language and thought; persistence)?

   - What learning standards are you addressing through this project (for example, those of the district or state)?

3. **Applied Learning**

   - What will the students do to apply the knowledge they are learning to a complex problem? (Are they designing a product, improving a system, organizing an event?)

   - Which of the competencies expected in high-performance work organizations (for example, teamwork, appropriate use of technology, ability to communicate ideas, and ability to collect, organize, and analyze information) does the project provide opportunities to develop?

   - Which self-management skills (for example, developing a work plan, prioritizing pieces of the work, meeting deadlines, identifying and allocating resources) does the project require students to use?

4. **Active Exploration**

   - What field-based activities does the project require students to conduct (for example, interviewing experts, participating in a work site exploration)?

   - Which methods and sources of information are students expected to use in their investigations (for example, interviewing and observing, gathering and reviewing information, collecting data, model-building, using online services)?

5. **Adult Connections**

   - Do students have access to at least one outside adult with expertise and experience relevant to their project who can ask questions, provide feedback, and offer advice? Does the project offer students the opportunity to observe and work alongside adults during at least one visit to a work site with relevance to the project?

   - Does at least one adult from outside the classroom help students develop a sense of the real-world standards for this type of work?

6. **Assessment Practices**

   - What are the criteria for measuring desired student outcomes (for example, disciplinary knowledge, habits of mind, and applied learning goals)?

   - Are students involved in reviewing or helping to establish the project criteria?

- Which methods of structured self-assessment are students expected to use (for example, journals, peer conferences, teacher or mentor conferences, rubrics, periodic review of progress vis-a-vis the work plan)?

- Do students receive timely feedback on their works-in-progress from teachers, mentors, and peers?

- What work requirements are students expected to complete during the life of the project (for example, proposals, work plans, reflection papers, minipresentations, models, illustrations)?

- Do students prepare a culminating exhibition or presentation at the completion of the project that demonstrates their ability to apply the knowledge they have gained?

Design Variables for Inquiries, Projects, and Problems

Here are some guidelines for crafting projects and problems. Think about students' prior experiences with project-based learning. Different groups of students may need more direction and coaching than others.

What do you provide? What do groups or individuals decide?

❏ You ❏ Student   Essential framing question or problem (See "Asking good questions" on page 355–356)

❏ You ❏ Student   Given information

❏ You ❏ Student   Missing information

❏ You ❏ Student   New, "add-on" information

❏ You ❏ Student   Student's role in approaching the inquiry/problem/project (You are _____ / You are serving as a(n) _____)

❏ You ❏ Student   Real-world context and connections

❏ You ❏ Student   Type of product or presentation

❏ You ❏ Student   Audience for final product or presentation

❏ You ❏ Student   Use of media tools

❏ You ❏ Student   Time frame for project

❏ You ❏ Student   Level and kinds of research and investigation necessary

❏ You ❏ Student   Constraints and limitations (what resources you have or don't have; what people impacted by the problem want and need; what you determine and what others determine; what already exists, what's possible and what's probable; what you can do, what you must do, what you can't do)

❏ You	❏ Student	Rubric of required steps, resources, tasks, components / Who evaluates? How is it evaluated?
❏ You	❏ Student	Levels of collaboration and "legwork"
❏ You	❏ Student	Levels of autonomy, intellectual risk, skill sets, initiative, supervision

We tend to forget that project- and problem-based learning doesn't have to begin with the "big one." Start out with inquiries and problems that take a few minutes to a few periods to complete so that students can develop the tools and skills to work more independently for more extended periods of time later in the year.

Short-Term Inquiries and Problems

- Student or group generates the questions for inquiry/research/investigation.

- Student or group chooses the question to investigate from multiple options presented to them.

- Student or group chooses HOW to investigate the question.

- Student or group generates the problem constructing a "What if..." question.

- Student or group chooses a problem from multiple options.

- Student or group solves a problem presented to them.

Unit Projects and Problems

- Student or group designs project given fairly broad guidelines and specific competencies and learning standards.

- Student or group generates project specifics after they are given the framing questions, criteria, and constraints.

- Student or group chooses project from multiple options.

Long-Term Projects and Problems

- Student or group designs a long-term project that will ensure that students demonstrate comprehensive knowledge and concepts learned during the semester.

- Group is presented with a problem and students take on different roles and tasks in their efforts to solve it.

- Group receives information, then frames the problem and the question.

Guidelines for Collaborative Problem Solving

Collaborative problem solving engages small groups of students in a process of

- Defining a problem

- Gathering information and assessing the steps necessary to solve the problem

- Generating alternative solutions

- Selecting the means and resources to solve the problem in a way that factors in constraints and meets some interests of everyone in the group

- Implementing the plan or solution

Steps:

1. Describe the problem in detail.

2. Set the challenge and goal. Let students know there are many ways to solve the problem.

3. Ensure that students have enough information to tackle the problem comfortably. Brainstorm possibilities and review the challenge to make sure that students know what they are doing.

4. Set constraints on what you can and cannot do.

5. Limit resources and materials.

6. Set criteria for assessment.

7. Limit the number of students in a group. Group students in a way that ensures a balance of skill abilities, expertise, and learning strengths.

8. Give everyone a role and responsibility.

9. Divide time between planning and doing.

10. Give instructions in several ways and use examples, illustrations, and models to show what to do or how to do it.

Resources for Problem Solving and Project-Based Learning

***Get It Together: Math Problems for Groups, Grades 4–12*, by Tim Erikson**
(Berkeley, CA: Univ. of California, Lawrence Hall of Science, 1989)

***United We Solve: 116 Math Problems for Groups, Grades 5–10*, by Tim Erikson**
(Oakland, CA: eeps media, 1996)
Don't let the word MATH in these titles scare you off! Both books by Tim Erikson contain fabulous jigsaw collaborative learning problems for groups of four to six students that emphasize logic, number theory, strategic planning and organizing, geometry, algebra, measurement and functions, pattern blocks, and global data and statistics. Each problem helps students strengthen their metacognitive and learning-to-learn skills and uses content that crosses all disciplines. The simple format asks each group to define the problem, solve the problem, and, finally, check for accuracy. Since many problems do not have one right answer or solution, groups can share solutions, engage in thoughtful inquiry, and appreciate the efforts of other groups.

***Problems as Possibilities: Problem-Based Learning for K–16 Education* (2nd edition), by Linda Torp and Sara Sage**
(Alexandria, VA: Association for Supervision and Curriculum Development, 2002))

***Real-Life Problem Solving: A Collaborative Approach to Interdisciplinary Learning*, by Beau Fly Jones, Claudette M. Rasmussen, and Mary C. Moffitt, eds**
(Washington, DC: American Psychological Association, 1997)

Odyssey of the Mind *(www.odysseyofthemind.com)*
Odyssey of the mind is an international educational program that provides creative problem–solving opportunities for students from kindergarten through college. Kids use their creativity to solve problems that range from building mechanical devices to presenting their own interpretations of literary classics. They then bring their solutions to competition at the local, state, and international level. The website describes the annual problems and includes directions for over 50 problems for classroom use.

Edutopia *(www.edutopia.org)*
This website's section on project-based learning includes hundreds of links to "how-to" articles, sample problems and PBL learning unites, and snapshots of schools and classrooms that emphasize project-based learning.

Buck Institute for Education *(www.bie.org/pbl)*
The project-based learning section of this website includes downloadable problem-based learning handbooks, planning tools, and rubrics.

Oracle Foundation *(www.thinkquest.com, www.think.com)*
The Oracle Foundation sponsors an annual international website competition for students. The websites include all the tools for researching and creating websites and a ThinkQuest library of over 5,000 websites created by students for students.

Rubistar Rubric Maker *(www.rubistar.4teachers.org)*
This U.S. Department of Education-sponsored website enables teachers to create their own customized project rubrics.

IMSA Center for Problem–Based Learning *(www.imsa.edu/team/cpbl/whatis/whatis/slide6.html)*
At this site you can find a tutorial introduction to problem-based learning, sample problems, downloadable articles, and a list of resources.

Problem–Based Learning: How to Gain the Most from PBL
(www.chemeng.mcmaster.ca/pbl/pbl.html)
This is a book by Donald Woods that can be downloaded in its entirety in PDF format.

The Problem Log *(www.imsa.edu/team/cpbl/pbin/log.html)*
Back issues of The Problem Log, the Problem-Based Learning Network's newsletter, are available in PDF format online.

Key Strategy	Encourage Independent Learning
	• Emphasize personalized, student-centered learning
Life Skill Connection (See page 112–114)	• Make big and little goals and make plans (13) • Prioritize and "chunk" tasks, predict task completion time, and manage time effectively (14) • Work for high personal performance and cultivate your strengths and positive qualities (16) • Assess your skills, competencies, effort, and quality of work (17)
Sample Activities, Strategies, and Routines	• Prepare Students to Learn Independently • Use "Sponge" Activities that Encourage Independent Learning • Embed Independent Learning Activities into Every Learning Unit • Design Independent Learning Projects and Contracts

In the article "Rigor Redefined" and in the book, *The Global Achievement Gap*, author Tony Wagner cites seven "survival skills" critical to succeeding in college, work, and public life in the 21st century.[7] They are:

1. Critical Thinking and Problem Solving

2. Collaboration and Leadership

3. Agility and Adaptability

4. Initiative and Entrepreneurialism

5.   Effective Oral and Written Communication

6.   Accessing and Analyzing Information

7.   Curiosity and Imagination

Independent learning as well as project-based learning (described in the last section on pages 250–257) generate powerful opportunities where students can learn and strengthen these skills and make them their own.

Prescriptive curricula, pacing guides, and standardized exit exams can severely limit opportunities for students to learn independently and choose what they want to learn. Making matters worse, content coverage pressures leave little time for students to develop and practice the skills necessary to become independent, resourceful learners. Too often we expect students to engage in independent learning (IL) in class or at home without the requisite competencies to succeed. Think about how you might scaffold learning experiences (in class and at home) to help students develop and strengthen these critical competencies. The following suggestions might serve as a springboard.

- During the first couple of months of the school year, create scavenger hunts, learning centers, rotation stations, or a problem of the week where students participate in "low-risk" activities that help them generate questions, search out information using various media and search tools, and record, map, and represent what they've observed, heard, viewed, or read.

- As part of your assessment systems, expect students to develop competency in a minimum number of independent learning skills. For example, students might choose three competencies and you might require three competencies using a comprehensive list of independent learning skills. (See pages 259–260)

- Create a system in which students can trade in their IL competencies (see the activity that follows) for library time to work on independent learning projects or contracts in lieu of participating in a regular classroom learning unit.

- Set aside time each semester when students can complete a learning unit on their own (with coaching as needed). Give students the option of crafting their own independent learning projects or choosing among teacher-designed projects.

Prepare Students to Learn Independently

Taking the initiative to learn what you don't know, learning more to become more efficient or effective, and learning more to make original contributions are prized assets in the work world. Post a set of competencies associated with becoming an independent learner and integrate opportunities for multiple practices assocated with these competencies.

A Partial List of Independent Learning Competencies

- Complete at least three significant tasks on time.

- Demonstrate your capacity to stay on task without being distracted during an entire class period on a regular basis.

- Provide evidence of setting and achieving an academic goal.

- Provide evidence of a planning map that documents the tasks and timeline you used to complete a required course project.

- Provide evidence of revising and editing your work after self-assessment and/or feedback from others.

- Indicate how a piece of your work meets a specific learning standard or objective.

- Identify samples of your work that range from shoddy or mediocre to "exceeds proficiency" and be able to explain what contributed to the difference in quality.

- Complete at least three learning journals/reflections using "Habits of Mind" questions from page 147 or any of the reflection/self-assessment questions on pages 232–237.

- Read an article on your own, provide evidence that you understood what you read, and cite the source correctly.

- Read a book on your own, provide evidence that you understood what you read, and cite the source correctly.

- Write a one-page paper in which you make an argument/take a stand or position and use and cite quotations that support your case.

- Identify and explain at least three perspectives or possible solutions using a controversial topic or problem of your choice.

- Write a synopsis or précis of a text reading of your choice.

- Create an outline/double-entry notes/or a graphic organizer that represents what you learned from a text reading.

- Transcribe an interview with an expert on the topic of your choice.

- Develop a range of questions (from factual to interpretive to speculative to evaluative to essential/framing) about a topic that interests you (See "Asking Good Questions" on pages 355–356).

- Provide evidence that you can generate a thesis statement or hypothesis from the questions that emerge from your topic or issue.

- Draw a diagram or chart that depicts relationships among different facts and concepts or causes and effects.

- Generate at least five "headers" for an internet search using a topic of your choice.

- Identify the human, material, and experimental resources needed to accomplish a task or meet a learning objective.

- Generate at least two samples of relevant, reliable, and substantive data or information on the net and two samples of irrelevant, unreliable, and insubstantial data or information on the net using a topic and framing question of your choice.

- Provide evidence of effective information searches for the following sources, using a topic and framing question of your choice: phone book; internet; periodicals; atlas/map; library texts; newspapers; film/visual media; statistical data.

- Provide evidence that you have organized, analyzed, and evaluated data that enable you to generate valid answers to your questions.

- Compile a set of readings, documents, data, artifacts, print and visual materials from at least three sources using a topic of your choice.

- Create an attractive quality product that demonstrates a wide range of computer-formatting skills.

Use Sponge Activities that Encourage Independent Learning

Sponge activities take three to ten minutes, relate to the immediate lesson or learning unit, and require students to complete the activity on their own without your help. Do them:

- before the bell rings

- when all students are expected to complete a common task and you anticipate that some students will finish before others

- during transitions from one mode of learning to another

- when you need to attend to administrative tasks for a few moments

- as a wrap-up at the end of class

Because of their brevity, sponge activities provide excellent opportunities for students to practice working silently and independently on a regular basis. Sponge activities are different from other types of "gatherings," "do nows," "bell-ringers," and "closings" that may require whole-group conversation, physical movement, cooperative work with other students, complicated directions and explanations, informal coaching, or student monitoring during the activity. Effective sponge activities meet these criteria:

- The directions are clear and simple and posted on the board, overhead or PowerPoint.

- Students complete the activity in silence.

- Students complete the activity independently.

- The activity requires either no materials or just pencil and paper.

- The content is such that every student has a shot at completing the activity successfully.

Typical types of sponge activities include:

- Quickwrites

- Review (name one, give two examples that illustrate, list three)

- Choosing the right word/vocabulary

- In two minutes write everything you know about _____.

- Puzzles and logic problems

- Find the errors

- What ifs

- If you were _____, what would you do or say? Or: If you were _____, how would you respond to _____?

- Analogies and metaphors

- Mental math/Estimation

- Question generating and problem posing

And the award for "Best Sponge Activity Ever" goes to...

PULSE High School: In preparation for the New York State English Regents Exam, at least twice a week teachers across disciplines composed and posted an original paragraph, memo, or letter on the overhead that incorporated content from the previous day's lesson. The written statements always contained a total of seven errors of four types that students needed to identify and correct: errors in syntax, punctuation, spelling, and content accuracy. This elegantly simple exercise was one of the contributing factors that enabled students to achieve an 86% pass rate on this exam!!!

Embed Independent Learning Activities (ILAs) into Every Learning Unit

Independent learning activities (ILAs) are activities that students can work on while:

- You provide remedial instruction to individuals and small groups

- You engage in personal conferencing with individual students

- You coach individuals who require more feedback and supervision to complete a task

- Other students complete assignments or tests

- Other students correct, revise, and redo their work

The content for ILAs should relate to the unit that all students are studying or will be studying; however, projects should allow enough latitude for students to extend their learning in ways that interest them. Teacher responsibilities include reviewing project options, standards of quality, and assessment rubrics; approving student-designed project plans; monitoring progress and providing feedback. The number of students involved in a single activity will vary depending on the scope and time available. Here are four independent learning activity types:

On Your Own Unit Project that individual students work on by themselves at any time when they have completed assignment work:

Examples:

- Create a PowerPoint presentation

- Design a web page

- Select images, create drawings, and write text about a topic for students in a lower grade level.

- Create a bilingual story

- Design a map that serves a specific purpose

- Choose a country and follow events and issues for one semester

- Create a trip brochure to a country whose home and language is the language you're learning

- Create a FAQ (frequently asked questions) fact sheet about a unit top

- Design a "how-to" manual for a specific process or technique

- Compose a taped narrative that captures the story of discovery in your discipline

- Create a map and guide for a place and/or organization that supports work related to your course discipline

- Prepare a data research report using a question that emerges from the current unit of study

- Create an annotated filmography highlighting a topic or issue related to your course content

- Create an art piece inspired by the current unit of study

- Prepare a storyboard for a documentary about _____

- Read a book of your choice on a topic or issue related to the learning unit

Class Unit Project to which ALL students contribute:

Examples:

- Ilustrated alphabet book that focuses on the current learning unit

- Classroom newspaper where students write a variety of articles using typical newspaper formats, styles, and themes

- Stained-glass window project where groups of students research a cathedral town and replicate a major window by gluing tissue paper on acetate

- Make place names in the foreign language you're studying to post around school

- Create a composite book of the _____'s work (historian, writer, artist, etc). Students research or interview someone who works in a field or discipline related to the course and create a collection of portraits of people on the job

- Investigate various jobs and careers at different entry levels that illustrate the range of opportunities within a career pathway related to your course content

Buddy Unit Project that a pair or small group of students can work on:

Examples:

- Bulletin board

- Create an exploration station that invites students to learn about a related topic or issue

- Word wall for current learning unit

- Create a game or crossword puzzle

- Design, administer, analyze, and present results from a survey

- Create a math problem book using real-world situations and scenarios

- Design an experiment or problem or choose to do an experiment or problem from a range of options

- Organize a panel discussion involving people in the community that highlights the work associated with your course discipline.

Required Unit Project that ALL STUDENTS must complete during a specific learning unit.

Design Independent Learning Projects and Contracts

The guidelines in this section can be used for planning teacher-facilitated group projects or supporting student-designed independent learning contracts. They are adapted from the I-Search model developed by the Education Development Center (www.edc.org) and *Personalized Learning: Preparing High School Students to Create Their Futures* (Scarecrow Education, 2004). The sample project (a trip to South America) referred to throughout the guidelines illustrates an individual student's planning process; however, this project outline could just as easily be used for developing variations on the same project for an entire class of students.

Independent Learning Project Guidelines

Phase 1: Topic immersion and question generation

1. Choose a topic, issue, or problem that interests you.

2. Reflect on why you're curious/hooked/intrigued by this topic.

3. Jot down what you already know about the topic and what you don't.

4. Use many sources to browse for essential information about the topic.

5. Begin generating questions that might drive your project.

6. Students draft a project statement, select a few questions that are personally relevant and meaningful, and identify possible products.

Course: World History

My topic is the merging of cultures in South American countries.

I chose this topic because my parents are from mixed hertiage from South American countries.

Three of my best questions for review and feedback:
- How do native and European cultures blend and clash in South American countries?
- What are the important native and European traditions and landmarks that make South America different from any other continents?
- If I had a chance to go to South America, where would I want to go?

Possible Products: How will I communicate/represent what I learned? A multi-media presentation, a trip itinerary; a travel show.

---

7. Student gets feedback from teacher and/or peers and crafts an essential question that will drive the project. What would a three-week trip look like that captures the ancient and modern spirit and different cultures of South America?

Phase 2: Developing Your Plan

Students need to include the following in their independent learning project plan:

- **Purpose:** What do you expect to be able to do as a result of your project or presentation? *Communicate ideas/Plan a trip/Share my heritage with others*

- **Culminating Product, Exhibition, or Presentation** that will organize and represent what you have learned: *Design a complete three-week itinerary for Bill and Ted, who expect to have an excellent adventure. They want to discover how modern South American culture grew from its native and European roots. They also want to hike in the Andes and raft on the Amazon River. They want to travel in the spring or fall and want to visit at least four of the following countries: Argentina, Brazil, Peru, Chile, Bolivia, Colombia, and Ecuador. Between them they don't want to spend more than $5,000 for the entire trip.*

- **Specific Product Components:** *(1) A written introduction to South American culture, past and present; (2) a triptych that includes an appropriate map, illustrations, and itinerary for each day of the trip; (3) expense budget; (4) an annotated list of books, readings, and websites for the travelers, etc.*

- **Tasks Along the Way:** All the tasks that will enable you to acquire the skills and knowledge to complete the final product, exhibition, or performance. *(1) Interview a travel agent; (2) map travel routes and estimate air fare and ground transportation costs; (3) learn about pre-Colombian history and landmarks; (4) learn about European settlement in countries on the trip; (5) identify significant regional and national celebrations and cultural events; (6) find illustrations of places clients will visit; (7) design triptych, travel brochure, etc.*

- **Learning Standards Aligned to Tasks:** Be sure to review disciplinary content standards, applied learning standards, and career and life skills standards.

  - **Solving Problems:** *Recognize and investigate problems; formulate and propose solutions supported by reason and evidence.*

  - **Technology:** *Routinely and efficiently use online information resources to meet needs for collaboration; select and apply technology tools for research, information analysis, problem solving, and decision making in content learning.*

  - **Social Studies:** *Describe how tensions in the modern world are affected by different political ideologies; describe how trade patterns developed between the Americas; describe the immediate and long-term social impact of slavery; describe how cultural encounters among peoples of the world affected the environment.*

- **English:** *Use standard English to compose and edit documents; produce documents of publication quality; produce multimedia works for a specific audience. Design and present a project using various formats and multiple sources.*

- **Math:** *Apply formulas in a wide variety of real-world measurement applications. Convert within and between measurements and monetary systems; estimate distances.*

- **Assessment Criteria and Rubric:** For each product or presentation, what qualities of student work will be assessed? What are the rubric categories for the Triptych Travel Brochure: writing/organization; grammar, spelling, and proofreading; content accuracy; visual attractiveness; sources and citations; graphics/pictures; links to learning standards

- **People, Material, and Electronic Resources**

- **Timeline for tasks and conference check-ins and feedback**

Phase 3: Gathering and Integrating Information

1. Follow your research plans, revising them as necessary.

2. Gather information from all of your sources, keeping a running list of citations.

3. Record the information, using paper and pencil, drawing, tape recorders, video, and other electronic tools.

4. Integrate information from various sources, using notes and visual organizers that help you sort, prioritize, categorize, create charts and figures, draft summaries, etc., in order to make sense of information and construct meaning.

5. Write in your project journals, reflecting on your research process.

6. Start drafting paragraphs for the written parts of your final products.

Phase 4: Representing Knowledge

1. Design, Draft, Revise, Edit, and Produce/Publish your final products or presentation.

2. Compose a cover page for your project that includes:

   - Final project statement (topic, rationale, questions, description of final products, exhibit, or presentation).

   - A log of readings, websites, and other print material that helped you learn about your topic with appropriate citations.

- Steps you used to complete your project.

- Description of tools, technology, and materials you used.

- Description of skills and knowledge you gained.

- Reflections of your learning.

3. Prepare your physical or electronic project portfolio, including cover page, all product components, project journals, project plans and timelines, and artifacts.

4. Present and share your work with a specific audience.

5. Debrief the project process.

12

CHAPTER 13

Practice 3: Integrate Multiple Ways of Knowing and Learning

13

| Key Strategy | Explore Ways You Learn and Remember |

⌘

• Integrate multiple ways of knowing and learning

| *Life Skill Connection* (See page 112–114) | • Work for high personal performance and cultivate your strengths and positive qualities (16) |

| *Sample Activities, Strategies, and Routines* | • 20 Things on a Tray • Reflections on the Ways You Learn |

The activities in this section help students to explore how they categorize and retain data and to reflect on the kinds of intelligences and learning tasks that they prefer. These activities also provide an opportunity to introduce and discuss three important ideas: 1) There isn't one right way to learn; 2) Everyone learns a little differently because each of us brings a different set of perceptions, interests, and experiences to any learning situation; and 3) No one is equally proficient at all learning tasks.

20 Things on a Tray

1. Introduce the activity by saying that you are going to explore differences and similarities in learning styles. Place 20 things you have collected on a tray or cloth on a table where everyone can gather around and look at them.

2. Explain to the group: "You will have two minutes to look at the 20 objects I have placed on the table. Your goal is to use any strategies you can to remember all 20 objects. Then you will have two minutes to write down as many objects as you can remember when you go back to your chairs. This is not a contest. No one will know how many objects you remembered or not. When you come up to the table, imagine you are in a state of relaxed alertness so that you can focus your attention. When everyone has found a place where you can see, I will uncover the objects and ask everyone to be silent for two minutes as you look. Ready?"

3. Set the timer for two minutes and uncover the objects.

4. Call time and give students two minutes to write down the objects that they remember.

5. Discuss what strategies people used to remember the objects. The sharing will be rich. It is amazing to hear the different ways people organize data (i.e. numbering; alphabetizing; categorizing by color, shape, size, kinds of objects, male/female; making up a story using all of the objects; repeating the names of objects over and over; creating a picture to walk through, touching the objects; studying their placement; dividing objects in rows). Write all of the strategies.

6. Here are more discussion points:

– What objects were easy to remember? Why was that? What objects were hard to remember? Why was that? (The easy to remember objects are usually linked to a personal experience. The hard to remember objects are usually ones that students are unfamiliar with or don't have a name for.) This is an opportunity to explore how we link new learning to prior experiences.

– Look at the strategies you posted and discuss how students use these strategies in different subject areas to study and retain information. Add other strategies to the list that students use.

– Invite students to think about why people used different strategies to meet the same goal. Point out opportunities in class where they have choices for how to reach a common goal.

Thanks to Rachel Kessler for this activity.

Reflections on the Ways You Learn

The following guide to Howard Gardner's seven different intelligences can be used in various ways.

• Students can identify strengths, preferences, and "growing edges"—ways of learning that are outside their comfort zone.

• For some independent or cooperative learning projects, you might require students to use at least three intelligences in developing a presentation or creating a product.

• Students might set goals for building new competencies in one intelligence in depth every quarter.

HANDOUT I
How do you like to learn? What do you like to do?

Are there one or two intelligences where you are a match for almost every statement in the list?
What statements most closely reflect learning tasks that you find particularly appealing or feel like a natural fit for your? What statements reflect learning tasks that are difficult or boring for you?

Logical/Mathematical
- I like solving logic puzzles.
- I like working with numbers and solving problems with numbers.
- I like to do experiments.
- I like to estimate things and make predictions.
- I like to use tools and equipment.
- I like to reason things out and look for solutions to problems.
- I like to label, order, and categorize information.
- I like working with theories and models.
- I like to design programs on the computer.
- I like things to be logical and orderly.
- I like sorting out and analyzing data.
- I like statistics.
- I like having structures and formulas that will help me get the right answer.
- I like playing games that require strategy.
- I like finding evidence and proving that something is correct.
- I like making lists.
- I like to know how things work.

Kinesthetic
- I like doing things with my hands.
- I like testing my physical strengths and skills.

- I like working with tools and equipment to make and fix things.
- I feel more myself when I'm active, moving, playing, or exercising.
- I like to dance.
- I like to play sports.
- I take care of my body and I'm interested in doing things that keep me healthy.
- I like to perform in plays and skits.
- I like to try out and test things by physically doing something.
- I like to create movements or gestures as a way to remember or give something meaning.
- I like expressing myself physically.
- I prefer doing something rather than reading about it or listening to an explanation of it.

Interpersonal
- I like hanging out with my friends.
- I like to work with others to learn something.
- I'm good at working out conflicts and differences with others.
- I like parties and gatherings with friends or family.
- I like to organize and plan activities and events.
- I'm good at communicating my needs and feelings to others.
- I like helping others.
- I like being a leader.

- I like to figure out what makes people do what they do.
- I like being part of a team or group that has a purpose.
- I'm sensitive to the moods and feelings of others.
- I make friends pretty easily and get along with most people.
- I like to talk to others before making a decision.
- I'm a good participant in a group.
- I like meeting new people in different settings.
- I like learning about different people and cultures.

Naturalist
- I feel more myself when I'm outside in nature.
- I like learning about the natural world.
- I like animals and I like to take care of them.
- I like plants and gardening.
- I'm tuned in to the sensory world outside (water, sky, outdoor sounds and smells, weather, the earth).
- I like to camp, walk, hike, climb, canoe, sail, etc.
- I like to spend time outdoors by myself.
- I like to observe the natural world in different settings in all its detail.

How do you like to learn? What do you like to do? CONTINUED

- I connect other things to natural images and analogies.
- I like exploring new places.
- I like returning to the same place over and over to see what's changed.
- I like to see the connections between living things.
- I like doing field studies in the natural environment.

Visual/Spatial

- I like to draw, paint, or create three dimensional forms.
- I like to look at art, architecture, and the built environment.
- I like to work with color, pattern, space, and form.
- I like to present things visually, using pictures, charts, graphs.
- I like to do lettering and calligraphy.
- I like to design things.
- I remember things by creating mental pictures and images.
- I like to spend time imagining things.
- I like to transform objects and spaces into something new.
- I can find my way around different spaces and environments easily.
- I notice details about the spaces I'm in.
- I like solving spatial and pattern puzzles.
- I like making maps and diagrams.

Musical/Rhythmic

- I like listening to music.
- I play a musical instrument.

- It's easy for me to remember musical lyrics.
- I find myself looking for a beat, trying to discover the rhythm of things.
- I like to sing.
- I can recognize different kinds of music and different composers.
- I like participating in musical performances.
- I like attending musical performances.
- I remember things by making up a song.
- I like to hum or whistle or have music playing when I'm working.
- I like creating rhymes and sayings that have a beat.
- I like practicing a musical piece until I get it right.

Verbal/Linguistic

- I like the experience of reading.
- I like writing things as a way of remembering.
- I like learning new words and exploring their meanings.
- I like playing with words and making up words.
- I like explaining things to others.
- I like discussing issues with others.
- I like telling stories and making up stories.
- I like poetry.
- I like to write poetry.
- I like creative writing where I can express myself in words.
- I like to write reports and essays.

- I like learning languages.
- I prefer listening or reading about something, rather than watching something or actually doing something physical.
- I like making a good argument.
- I like word games.
- I like listening to stories.
- I like crafting a good sentence.
- I like to analyze and discuss literature.

Intrapersonal

- I like to spend time thinking by myself.
- I am very aware of my own moods and feelings.
- I like being alone.
- I like working independently.
- It's easy for me to make goals for myself and accomplish them.
- I usually know what's the right decision for me without asking others.
- I trust my own judgment.
- I feel comfortable "in my own skin."
- I know who I am and like who I am.
- I have a good sense of what works for me and what doesn't.
- I like sitting back and watching and observing others.
- I like reflecting about what I've done and experienced.
- I like to write my thoughts in a journal.
- I like school work that has a personal meaning for me.

Key Strategy	Set the Stage for Effective Cooperative Learning
⌘	• Integrate multiple ways of knowing and learning
Life Skill Connection (See page 112–114)	• Cooperate, share, and work toward high performance within a group to achieve group goals (27)
Sample Activities, Strategies, and Routines	• Guidelines for Cooperative Learning

Although cooperation and collaboration are hallmarks of the new business style, working cooperatively still runs counter to traditional individualistic and competitive school settings where students might even question the value of cooperation. Particularly in high schools, teaching practices and student assessment can often pit students against each other for favored status in the "winner's circle."

In his book, *Nobody Left to Hate*, written after the Columbine shootings, Eliot Aronson makes a compelling case for building collaboration and empathy in the classroom through the use of cooperative learning strategies. He urges us to think about the learning climate we create, noting that how we engage students in learning will influence whether they learn and what they learn. Do we encourage excessive competition where winners and losers are predetermined? Or do we create a learning environment where everyone is expected to work together, look out for each other, and acknowledge the collective talents and insights that each person brings to the task at hand?

Cooperative learning is an intentional restructuring of the learning process where students share a common purpose to complete tasks in ways that include every group member. Especially when activities are structured for "positive interdependence"[1], one student's success is linked to the success of others. A cornerstone of effective group work is the use of the "jigsaw" process, where each student brings information, research, or resources to the group that is necessary for full understanding of the problem and successful completion of the task or final product.

Students who work together are learning how to get along together. When students engage in cooperative activities they are developing life-long social skills by learning how to:

- Communicate in ways that encourage listening and understanding;

- Deal effectively with people's differences in work styles, skills, interests, and points of view;

- Acknowledge the contributions of others as they help each other and ensure that everyone is included;

- Share leadership, roles and responsibilities, and accountability;

- Practice the kind of "give and take" necessary to make decisions and plans that everyone agrees to implement.

In classrooms, we often assume that students know what collaboration is and we assume that they know how to cooperate. Neither of these assumptions is necessarily valid. Cooperative learning provides the opportunity for teaching and practicing these skills intentionally.

Furthermore, the structure of cooperative learning helps support effective classroom management and discipline. Teaching students to work effectively in small groups helps them improve their self-management skills. Secondly, cooperative groups enable you to observe students learning, provide immediate feedback from your observations, and engage in one-to-one coaching while students are working. Finally, when you do have to intervene with a student and handle a disciplinary problem on the spot, you can do it more privately, without an audience and without interrupting the learning activity.

Guidelines for Cooperative Learning

These guidelines go a long way to ensure successful cooperative learning activities. When teachers complain about ineffective, unproductive group work, I ask them to take a look at this list and identify the guidelines they used for preparing and implementing the group activity. The most common response is, "Maybe I used one or two. I gave the assignment and students got into groups and started to work." Effective cooperative learning requires more deliberate setup and monitoring, but it also produces a more satisfying learning experience and better quality work.

- Divide students into groups of two to five, depending upon the task, students' prior experiences, and levels of skillfulness.

- Identify specific goals for each group. "During this activity, your group is expected to _____."

- Identify specific academic skills and social skills that you expect students to practice. Let students know exactly what you are looking for and listening for when you observe them working. (See Assessing Cooperation, Group Participation, and Leadership Skills in Chapter 15, pages 320–326.)

- Insist that students discuss and make a plan before they dive into the activity. Ask each group to check in with you and share their plan before they start.

- Either assign roles and responsibilities to every group member or invite students to choose roles (facilitators, time keepers, checkers, recorders, reporters, readers, summarizers, encouragers, supply organizers, etc.) and divide up tasks among group members.

- If it's appropriate, frame the activity as a problem to solve. (See collaborative problem solving on page 255.)

- For complicated projects, develop proficiency criteria and describe procedures for completing each task so that students can monitor what they've accomplished and identify what remains to be done. You might also suggest general time frames for completing each task or stop groups at midpoint to review progress.

- Incorporate positive interdependence and group accountability by designing a sequence of tasks where the work of one group member can only be carried out when another group member has completed a previous task. Or "jigsaw" resources where each student receives different information that she or he must share or explain to others in the group in order to complete the task. Or distribute limited resources that students need to share, such as one response sheet for per group. Or assess students on their collaboration skills, taking points off if some students didn't contribute. Give each group a grade for their final product or presentation.

Step-by-Step Jigsaw	
Sequence of Steps	**Purpose**
1. Clarify goals and tasks for all groups.	Focusing
2. Divide tasks into sections and divide students into teams.	Structuring
3. Assign each member of the team one part of the total task. Individuals work on their learning tasks.	Independent work
4. Members who are assigned the same part of the task meet together to review, check for understanding, decide what's essential for the rest of their group to learn, and share ways to teach it.	Expert groups
5. Members return to their teams and take turns teaching their parts.	Peer teaching
6. Individual and/or group assessment/demonstration of what students learned.	Assessment
7. Identify effective teaching strategies.	Debriefing

- Incorporate individual accountability by expecting all students to be able to explain a solution or present what was learned to the rest of the class. You might identify who's selected to represent the group's work by "cosmic chance," pulling student's names from a basket. Or motivate students to help everyone learn all the material by giving a group quiz where each group member receives different questions or problems. Assess students' individual contributions. You might want to consider assigning more individual points than group points in your grading scheme.

- Make time for reflection of the group process itself. As students become more aware of the skills they are using to accomplish a task, they can begin to ask questions about how they learn and work in a group. Individual and group reflection can take the form of an "exit slip" that the group fills inat the end of the activity; a journal response; a paired "quick write"; or a whole-group discussion. Here are a few reflection questions. You might also want to look at the section Assessing Cooperation, Group Participation, and Leadership Skills.

  - How did your group work together? What was easy? What was hard? Were there obstacles you didn't count on that made it more difficult to complete your task?

  - Could you have completed this task by yourself?

  - What would you do differently next time?

  - Was everyone listened to? How do you know?

  - How did you make decisions?

  - What did you do that helped your group accomplish its goal?

  - What did you learn that can be applied to other situations?

Teachers serve as coaches and observers as well as instructors in cooperative learning environments. When teachers observe groups working, they have opportunities to monitor, assess, and reinforce behaviors that enable students to interact positively with each other. Conversely, teachers can intervene at times to help students identify and practice a social skill that will help a group to function better.

For students who have an unusually difficult time working in a group, try one of these strategies:

- Assign an individual task that in some way connects to the larger learning experience.

- If you have two or three squirrelly group members, make a time to meet with them outside of class and coach them side-by-side through a cooperative activity, stopping throughout so students can describe what they're doing and name the skills they're using at every point.

- Assign a student to be the "feedbacker" for the period, observing groups and writing comments related to particular skills students are expected to use in the activity.

- Give the student a piece of information that every group needs to complete the task. The student's job is to share/explain the information to every group. This strategy allows a potentially disruptive student to participate, but contains the boundaries of a narrowly defined task and limited group interaction.

Key Strategy	Think About How You Want to Group Students
⌘	• Integrate multiple ways of knowing and learning
Life Skill Connection (See page 112–114)	• Cooperate, share, and work toward high performance within a group to achieve group goals (27)
Sample Activities, Strategies, and Routines	• Ways to Group Students • Role Cards • Other Grouping Ideas

Ways to Group Students

Home Groups

You may want to consider forming home groups of four students each who work together throughout the year. (See "Form Home Groups" on pages 327–329.)

Random or "Cosmic Chance" Groups

Create random groups of twos, threes, and fours when the "luck of the draw" is least likely to have a negative effect on the quality of group participation. Forming random groups can help change the pace and energy; this also offers the bonus of getting students out of their seats for a few minutes. The potential dread of being grouped with "the kid I can't stand" is less of an issue when students know that random grouping will be used primarily for shorter and less intense activities.

- Count off. If you have a group of 30, create groups of six by counting off 1–5. For groups of five, count off 1–6; for groups of four, count off 1–8; for groups of three, count off 1–10.

- To create pairs, ask students to find a partner who is wearing at least one color that is the same or one piece of clothing that is the same.

- Have students create composite groups where each group has to meet all the criteria that you have identified. For example: "Create a group of five people that includes at least one male, one female, two people of different racial origins, one person with a younger sibling, one person born between January and June, one wearing glasses, one person wearing athletic shoes, and one person who owns a pet." Remind students that one person can fit more than one category. This is a good choice when you need to change the energy and get students to focus. Ask students to make up some composite groupings.

- Create laminated puzzles from calendar pictures and photographs. For 30 students, cut 10 puzzles into three pieces each, eight puzzles into four pieces each, and six puzzles into five pieces each.

- Use playing cards to divide students into four groups, having them group according to the face cards.

- To create pairs, find two identical sets of trading cards or art card decks so that matching pairs of the same design can work together.

- Find interesting wrapping papers that depict multiple variations of the same object (shoes, hats, plants, animals, tools, stars, kids' faces, etc.) for groups of three, four, or five; cut out and laminate the objects from identical sheets of wrapping paper.

- Use different-flavored wrapped candies to divide students into groups.

- To create pairs, ask students to find a partner who has at least one initial that is the same as theirs.

- For any size groups, keep a basket of students' names that can be pulled out to create groups.

Teacher-Selected Groups

Sometimes you may want to group students in ways that ensure that students in each group have a balance of specific academic and social skills for a particular task.

Student-Selected Groups

There are times when it's good to invite students to select their own partners or groups. This might be the best strategy when students are selecting "study buddies" or when students may be working on a long-term project together. When problems arise in self-selected groups, use the "teachable moment" to encourage students to reflect on what's not working, and share what they need to make it work and try to problem solve.

Rotation Groups

If one of your commitments is to ensure that everyone works with everyone else and that students have a stake in supporting each other to do their best, you might want to think about creating different table groups each week. Have four students work together for the whole week, and then have students move to different groups the next week.

Role Cards

Use colored paper to make multiple sets of 12 role cards. Make at least 10 sets so that you can make groups with three, four, or five roles, choosing the size of the group and specific roles for group members that are best suited for the activity that students are going to do.

Facilitator Gets group started, initiates group discussion, and monitors work process, ensuring that everyone listens and speaks respectfully	**Summarizer and Decision Checker** Summarizes key information and discussion points at each step of the process; checks for agreement on key decisions
Writer/Recorder Records group's responses and/or edits what group has written	**Gatekeeper** Makes sure that group stays focused on goal (tracks time, checks to see if criteria for task are covered, monitors noise level)
Encourager/Cheerleader Encourages individuals to participate and makes supportive comments as people say and do things that help group meet its goal	**Feedbacker** Watches and listens instead of doing; jots notes about how group is working together and how group meets its goals

Reader Reads the problem, story, information, or instructions to the group	**Question Asker** Asks questions to seek clarity, more information, greater understanding, and alternative solutions and possibilities
Resource Monitor Picks up, distributes, collects, and puts away materials	**Investigator/Researcher** Seeks out additional information and resources to complete the task
Reporter Presents ideas, solutions, decisions, and/or insights to the larger group	**Clarifier** Checks with teacher or facilitator to clarify rules, guidelines, instructions when the group has questions

Other Grouping Ideas

Academic Grouping Cards

For any academic subject, pair students by

- writing key words or terms on cards and cutting cards in half;
- writing key words or terms and their definitions on two sets of cards that create matching pairs.

For Math

- 2s — two equations that have a common unknown
- 3s — drawn geometric figure, word description of figure, and the degree of angle associated with figure
- 3s — fraction, decimal, and percentage equivalents
- 3s — three equations that equal the same number

For English and Foreign Language

- 2s — antonyms and synonyms
- 3s — words associated with same part of speech (nouns, verbs, adjectives, prepositions, etc)
- 3s — clusters of words that have a similar meaning
- 4s — sets of four characters associated with each book, play, or story
- 4s — attributes, behaviors, and quotes associated with a specific character

For Social Studies

- 2s — match cities/states; landmarks/countries; famous people/cultures; leaders/countries, etc.
- 3s, 4s, 5s — groups of cities that are located on different continents; groups of famous people who lived in same time period; objects and art associations with different cultures, geographical features (names of mountains, river systems, deserts, lakes, seas, etc)

For Science

- 2s — names of chemical elements and their symbols
- 3s, 4s, 5s — groups of animals and plants that are associated with the same classification
- 3s, 4s, 5s — groups of animals and plants that live within a specific ecosystem or belong to a specific ecological niche
- 3s — features of various systems of the body
- 3s — objects that create different sounds (rice, paper clips, ball bearings, pop corn, tacks, etc.) contained in plastic film canisters.

Key Strategy	Use Collaborative Learning Strategies
⌘	• Integrate multiple ways of knowing and learning

Life Skill Connection (See page 112–114)	• Cooperate, share, and work toward high performance within a group to achieve group goals (27) • Respect everyone's right to learn, to speak, and to be heard (28) • Encourage and appreciate the contributions of others (29) • Engage in conscious acts of respect, caring, helpfulness, kindness, courtesy, and consideration (30) • Recognize and appreciate similarities and differences in others (31) • Exercise effective leadership skills within a group (33) • "Read" dynamics in a group; assess group skills accurately; identify problems; generate, evaluate, and implement informed solutions that meet the needs of the group (34)
Sample Activities, Strategies, and Routines	• Brainstorming • Card Sorts • Carousel • Concept Synectics/Making Metaphors • Demonstration • Drawing/Mapping/Charting • Interview Rotation Stations • Object, Postcard, or Picture Check-Ins • Pick Three/Pick Five • Popcorn-Style Sharing • Walkabouts • Webbing

13

The activities in this section engage students in collaborative learning tasks in pairs, small groups, and large groups. Other learning strategies are located in Practice 5: Making Group Talk Good Talk on pages 344–358 and in Appendix A: Learning Protocols for Professional Development.

Brainstorming

Brainstorming is a process for generating ideas that foster creative thinking. The teacher proposes a topic or question and lists student responses on the board or on chart paper. The idea is to generate the maximum number of solutions for consideration. Here are some guidelines for brainstorming:

- All ideas are accepted and written down.

- There should be no comments, either positive or negative, on any of the ideas.

- Say anything that comes to mind, even if it is silly.

- Think about what others have suggested and use those ideas to get your brain moving along new lines.

- Push for quantity.

Card Sorts

To help students organize and clarify content information, you can have them sort and rank cards with information related to the topic you are teaching. Here are a couple of examples:

- Make up sets of cards listing a series of possible titles for a book, story, or play that the group is studying. Each card in the set lists a different title for the same work. Divide students into groups and give each group a set of cards. Ask each group to choose the best title and the worst title. Have them defend their choices to the class. You can also do this type of sorting activity with any problem or controversy in which multiple factors influence the situation. Students can rank order factors from least to most important and then defend their choices.

- Make up sets of cards listing a series of historical events—for instance, events leading up to the Civil War—and ask groups to arrange the cards in chronological sequence. Or create cards that describe key experiences and milestones in someone's life, for example the life of Frederick Douglass, and rank these experiences from most to least influential.

Carousel

Carousel gets kids moving and thinking at a quick pace in small groups. The strategy can be used to:

- Solicit ideas and solutions to questions and problems related to a specific topic, issue, or problem.

- Provide practice by making suggestions and corrections using anonymous samples of student work (i.e., thesis statements, opening paragraphs, math and science problems, etc.).

- Give feedback and pose further questions about work generated by small groups.

1. Divide students into groups of two to four and give each group two to three minutes at each piece of chart paper.

2. Students in the small groups take turns soliciting ideas, feedback, suggestions, or corrections from their small group and then posting their comments on the chart paper.

3. When time is up, students rotate to the next piece of chart paper and repeat the process.

4. Repeat the process three or four more times.

Here are some prompts that can be used at the beginning of the year:

- One positive thing I bring to a group

- A personal strength or skill that I bring to working out problems

- A contribution I've made to class during the last week

- An attitude that helps me get through difficult situations

- Something I've learned how to do that has made it easier to participate in group activities

- One way I've helped someone this week

Concept Synectics/Making Similes

Word version: Connect concepts to objects or pictures (saying "concept X is like picture Y because...")

Physical version: Teachers and selected students act out or physically represent a particular concept for the class, using only their bodies or simple props that can be made from poster board, tape, string, and markers. You might want to select volunteers and practice the demonstration with them ahead of time, or divide the class into groups of four or five and give each a concept to present to the rest of the class. This can be fun and even silly, and it can help students grasp the essence of a concept, particularly those covered in algebra, geometry, physics, chemistry, ecology, and economics.

Demonstration

Don't forget to use demonstrations when giving directions. Many students need to see how to do it before they can do it for themselves. Demonstrations also offer the opportunity for everyone to see and hear the same information at the same time so that questions and reactions from all students are emerging from the same shared experience.

Drawing/Mapping/Charting

Drawing a concept, charting or mapping a process or problem, and using words, symbols, and pictures to express an idea offer ways for students to translate their ideas from one medium to another. By personally expressing their ideas on paper, students create their own ways of making meaning, understanding relationships, and organizing information.

Interview Rotation Stations

Rather than presenting a panel discussion (where kids often glaze over after a few minutes), you can use this process for investigating multiple perspectives for any current or historical topic or controversial issue.

What do you think you know?	**What do you think you know but you're not sure of?**
What do you want to find out? Know more about? Understand more clearly?	**What are your sources of information for what you could know? What other sources could you use to find out more?**

1. After you have chosen a topic or issue, use a four-question frame or another "door opener" to discover what interests students the most and determine the direction of your investigation. Students can respond to these questions as a whole group or you can divide the class into four groups, having each group respond to one question frame.

2. Prioritize the questions and issues that are most compelling to students.

3. Brainstorm a list of speakers and organizations that might help you better understand your topic or issues. Select three individuals who will offer different perspectives on your chosen issue or topic.

4. Go back to your four-question frame and agree on the three or four questions that you want all speakers to address.

5. Ask for student volunteers to arrange for speakers to come to your class at the same time. Make sure students prepare the speakers by providing them with the questions all speakers will address.

6. Time and space logistics—you will need to reserve a large enough space where you can have one group of students meeting with each of three speakers at the same time. You also need to arrange for at least an hour and 15 minutes time.

7. Given the questions you have agreed to use, develop an organizing grid that students can use to compare and contrast what each speaker says. The frame could look like this:

Topic or Issue	Question 1	Question 2	Question 3
Speaker 1:			
Speaker 2:			
Speaker 3:			

Before the speakers arrive:

1. Have students prepare the question grid.

2. Divide students into three groups and identify the speaker who will talk to each group first.

3. Make sure you have students who will introduce the speakers.

4. Let everyone know what the format will be: Each speaker will spend 20 minutes with each group of students. They will spend about ten minutes speaking to the predetermined questions and about ten minutes addressing other questions from students. Then each speaker will move to the next group.

5. Introduce the three speakers to the whole class and give them each about two minutes to say a little more about themselves and/or their organizations. Then have each speaker move to the assigned group and begin.

6. Follow up:
   Have groups summarize areas of agreement and disagreement among the speakers.

   • Go back to the four-question frame and assess what you have learned that you didn't know before.

   • Gandhi said, "Everyone has a piece of the truth." What piece of the truth did each speaker contribute to a more complicated, but deeper understanding of the issues?

   • What did people say that surprised you? "Before, I thought, felt, assumed... Now, I think, feel, know, am aware of..."

   • What new questions do you have now? Are there any areas of confusion that need further clarification?

Now that you have a better understanding of the issue, what do you want to do with your information? How do you want to act on what you learned? How can you share your understanding with others?

Object, Postcard, or Picture Check-Ins

Collect a bag of toys or small objects OR a set of photographs or postcards with interesting images of people, animals, elements of nature OR create a set of object cards using clip art. Spread your objects, pictures, or cards on the floor or a large table and ask students to select one that reflects something about themselves or something related to subject matter content.

Personal Reflections

Pick a _____ that reflects:

- One positive thing you bring to a group.

- Something you've learned how to do that has made it easier to be successful in this class.

- One way you've helped someone in class this week.

- A skill you want to improve this quarter.

- Something you've done that is helping you achieve your goals.

- Something that's been keeping you from achieving your goals.

- Something you need to complete your project on time.

Subject Matter Reflections

Pick a _____ that reflects:

- The most influential quality/attribute of your favorite character in _____.

- A critical element of the _____ cycle/process/model.

- An opportunity or obstacle for _____.

- A quality of leadership exhibited by _____.

- A condition necessary for _____.

Pick Three/Pick Five

This strategy helps students working in small groups to focus attention quickly on the task at hand. When small groups are expected to generate a list of ideas, examples, evidence, reasons, solutions, etc., first give students a few minutes to brainstorm. Then ask them to discuss and evaluate their ideas in the group with the goal of agreeing on the three or five most important, most unusual, most illustrative, most descriptive, most representative, most interesting ideas that they have generated. For example, using a novel or text, students could pick three phrases that best describe a particular character or three pieces of evidence that support a group's rationale for making a specific decision.

Popcorn-Style Sharing

In this technique, a set amount of time, usually about four minutes, is allotted for the whole group to share ideas on a topic. Free expression of ideas should be encouraged in a nonjudgemental atmosphere. The sharing is "popcorn" style, meaning that rather than going around in a circle one by one, students are welcome to voice their opinions in random order. There is no pressure for students to share if they don't wish to.

Walk-Abouts

Post lots of questions, problems, pictures, or any other material related to a specific topic all around the room. Give students 3" × 5" cards and ask them to pair up and choose three or five items to respond to. Pairs discuss the item, agree on their response, write it on their card, sign their card, and tape it next to the item they discussed.

Webbing

This strategy gives students the opportunity to visually connect various aspects and levels of a particular topic. It can also be used at the beginning of a unit to help the teacher gauge students' level of familiarity with and understanding of a topic. The key word or concept is placed in the center of the diagram. Students then suggest words, images, phrases, feelings, and ideas that they associate with that word or concept. These associated words are added to the diagram, branched off from the center. Related ideas are clustered together.

Key Strategy	A Quick Tour of Differentiated Learning and Instruction
⌘	• Integrate multiple ways of knowing and learning
Life Skill Connection (See page 112–114)	• Work for high personal performance and cultivate your strengths and positive qualities (16) • Assess your skills, competencies, effort, and quality of work accurately (17)
Sample Activities, Strategies, and Routines	• 8 Elements of Differentiated Learning

The following guide to differentiated learning and instruction is by no means an attempt to replace the wealth of resources available to teachers. However, in a book that emphasizes personalized learning, we felt that a quick tour of differentiation in the classroom would be a helpful reminder.

8 Elements of Differentiated Learning

Personalization

1. **Learn About Each Student and Size Up the Group**
How do you make connections with each individual student? What do you do to become familiar with each student's interests and developmental needs, level of academic readiness, and learning profile? How do you size up the range of developmental needs and academic readiness within the group? Are there any dominant characteristics or extremes within the group that will influence your approach todifferentiation?

Content

2. **Flexible, Differentiated Content, Skills, and Delivery**
What do you expect ALL students to know, understand, apply, and be able to do? What's essential? What's negotiable? In what ways can students make choices about what content they learn? Do students have a choice among proficiencies they have to meet in order to pass the course? How are content and skills connected to students' personal choices and interests, their identity and adolescent culture, and direct applications in the community and world of work? Are three different and equally compelling whys that meet the "relevance test" for different groups of students? Who gets what, when, how, for how long, and how much? (variations in pacing and content of curriculum; texts and materials; independent study/learning contracts; topic, skill, or task by choice; pull-out skill clinics, group tutorials and study groups; academic competitions and submissions; activities for individuals, small groups, and whole class.)

  • Print materials about the same subject that reflect a range of reading difficulty.

  • Optional units of study/optional books from which students can choose.

  • Ways that students can earn alternative learning options for homework, a specific set of lessons, or an entire learning unit.

  • Condensed vs. more scaffolded, skill-saturated versions of same learning unit, depending on students' prior knowledge and current competency levels.

Learning Strategies

3. **Differentiation of a Single Learning Strategy**
What accommodations, variations, and alterations of a specifc learning strategy will meet each student's academic readiness/level of proficiency, personal choices and interests, and learning profile (degree of challenge, complexity, difficulty, and risk; degree of independence or collaboration; degree of explicit direction, supervision, chunking, and scripting of the task)?

  • A range of graphic organizers from simple to complex

  • A range of strategies for engaging with text during reading, from which students can choose or teacher suggests for different students

Learning Strategies

- A range of project options from teacher-designed projects with explicit steps and directions, to completely student-designed projects carried out independently

- A range of math practice problems from one problem type to a variety of problem types, from problems with models to problems without models

- A range of study guides from more teacher scripted to more student annotated

- Several versions of the same lab, from simple step-by-step to more elaborate or extended investigations

- Activity stations working with simple and complex machines with three challenge levels

Learning Strategies

4. **Differentiated Learning Strategies and Tasks**

Are there different learning strategies and tasks that students can use to meet the same learning objective, considering each student's academic readiness/level of proficiency, personal choices and interests, and learning profile?

- A choice of homework tasks that meet the same objective

- Students provide evidence that they used one among many study strategies before they take the exam

- Choices for how students represent their understanding of a concept or principle/text reading/lecture/documentary film

- Students choose to complete a task on their own, in pairs, or in a small group

- Students can choose from among five intelligence-related strategies to demonstrate their interpretation of a scene in a play

Metacognition

5. **Differentiated Practice and Ongoing Reflection and Assessment**

Who needs what and how much and how often?

- Students can earn their way out of study and practice sessions before major written and performance assessments and tests depending on their prior track record in class.

- Teacher provides an array of practices that meet the same learning outcomes and enhance students' mastery and application of a particular skill set. Students either self-select practices based on interest or teacher recommends specific practices based on need.

- Students choose to respond to optional reflection prompts or they can create their own reflection prompts.

- Students choose two editors/critical friends for a term who will give them feedback and suggestions on their writing and final products.

13

Metacognition

6. **Differentiated Adult Support, Monitoring, Supervision, Feedback, Coaching, and Interventions**

Who needs what and how much and how often?

- Students engage in peer or teacher conferencing to review rubrics and stage of project completion, depending on their self-monitoring capacities and coaching needs.

- During project work time some students check in with teacher at the completion of every step or task before they can move to next stage, while others check in less frequently.

- One day a week students are grouped based on level of content or skill mastery in order to provide reteaching, minilessons, catch-up work session, or independent learning activities.

- Teacher works with students who have serious learning gaps or more than three incomplete or uncorrected pieces of work in order to develop learning contracts or a set of academic interventions. Some students are required to meet during out-of-class time for remedial, "catch-up," "re-do" workout sessions.

- All students engage in personal conferencing with the teacher on a rotating basis.

Products and Assessments

7. **Differentiation of a Single Assessment Aligned to Same Standards and Content**

What accommodations, variations, and alterations of a specific assessment will meet each student's academic readiness/level of proficiency, personal choices and interests, and learning profile?

- One product type with a range of challenge levels.

- One test with required, optional, and challenge sections that allow students choices to reach a cumulative score of 100%.

- All students are required to make an oral presentation; however, they can choose from among a variety of formats.

- The type and sophistication of a written assessment for individual students will depend on proficiencies they have already mastered; or press them to expand their "repertoire of expression."

8. **Differentiated Assessments Aligned to Same Standards and Content**

What options do students choose to demonstrate what they've learned, given their academic readiness/level of proficiency, personal interests, learning profile, and course requirements?

Written Assessments
Advice Column
Book
Case Statement
Character Sketch
Critiques and Reviews
Dialogue
Editorial/Opinion
Essay
Feature Story
Guidebook
Instructions
Interview
Itinerary
Legal Argument
Letter
Lists
Magazine Article
Memoir
Memorandum
Monologue
News Story
Outline
Picture Dictionary
Poem
Policy Statement/Position Paper
Reflection
Report
Research Paper
Review of Literature
Rubric
Sales/Marketing Brochure
Scene
Script
Stories and Tales
Study/Tutoring Guides
Summary/Précis
Technical Report
Travelogue or Brochure

Individual and Group Presentations and Performances
Broadcast Interview
Character Portrayal
Competitions
Demonstrations
Exhibit
Facilitate a Discussion
Fair Submissioons
Informative Speech
Job Interview
Marketing Campaign
Meeting of the Minds
Musical Offering
Oral Interpretation Panel
Discussion
Poem
Reflection
Scene or Scrirpt
Travelogue
Persuasive Speech
Political Campaign
Public Service Announcement/Campaign
Reenactment
Role-play
Speech
Teach a Lesson
Theatrical
Tutoring
Workshop

Graphic Organizers
Budget
Chart
Database
Flowchart
Graphs and Tables
List

Map
Plan
Poster
Schematic Drawing
Spreadsheet
Survey or Poll

Artistic Products
Bulletin Board/Display
Cartoon
Collage
Computer Graphics
Diorama
Drawing/Painting
Game
Jewlery/Clothing
Label/Container
Mobile
Mural
Photography
Poster
Sculpture

Technical Products
Actual Products
Design Innovations
Food
Inventions
Math/Scientific Models
Scale/Working Model
Technical Drawings
Tech Manual/Specs

Electronic Productions
Audio- or Video tape
Musical Recording
PowerPoint
Radio or TV Ads/Documentary Feature/News Feature

Products and Assessments

13

CHAPTER 14

Practice 4: Establish Clear Norms, Boundaries, and Procedures

Clarify Classroom Boundaries
Activities pages 296–297

Create a Vision of Your Classroom Community
Activies pages 297–299

Talk About the Issue of Respect
Activies pages 300–302

Make Group Guidelines and Agreements
Activities pages 302–306

14

Key Strategy	Clarify Classroom Boundaries
⟲	• Establish Clear Norms, Boundaries, Procedures, and Consequences
Life Skill Connection (See page 112–114)	• Make responsible choices for yourself by analyzing situations accurately and predicting consequences of different behaviors (7)
Sample Activities, Strategies, and Routines	• Clarify What's Negotiable and Nonnegotiable in the Curriculum

Effective discipline begins with the boundaries and limits you set in the classroom. Rachel Kessler, a colleague who has spent a lifetime exploring what makes a classroom a genuine learning community, has this to say about discipline, "We as teachers must take primary responsibility for creating an environment that is safe. Effective discipline includes clarity of purpose, a positive image of what discipline means, inner strength to be able to risk being disliked, and an understanding of and willingness to use one's whole person in an expression of personal power." Students need to know what you stand for as a teacher and as a human being. Think about how you choose to use your power and authority to create a safe environment where everyone can learn, where everyone feels safe, and where everyone belongs.

Most issues about how students work and learn together in your class can be negotiated. However, every teacher has some nos and bottom lines that are nonnegotiable; these are the issues where you're willing to exercise your authority consistently and fairly with no exceptions. Boundaries and bottom lines are good for everyone. Students learn what your values are through what is absolutely not okay. They also learn important life lessons when they violate boundaries and bottom lines. A useful guideline is "fewer are better."

Clarify What's Negotiable and Nonnegotiable in the Curriculum

As you discuss course expectations and course requirements, students need to know what's negotiable and what's not. There may not be many options and choices about what students need to learn; however, there may be many options and choices for how students can meet a course requirement, complete an assignment, or demonstrate what they have learned. Make a list of five or six boundaries that are nonnegotiable. On the "What's Negotiable?" list, begin with two or three suggestions, and as a group brainstorm possible ideas for what can be negotiated within the course content and what procedures and policies might be negotiable around homework, tests, and in-class tasks, etc. Here is a sample:

What's Non-negotiable?	What Could Be Negotiable?
• Everyone must demonstrate proficiency in... • Everyone will read four required books during the year. • Students who fail a test must retake the test until they pass it. • Everyone will be required to take a final exam.	• Students can choose from several options for how to demonstrate their proficiency in meeting some standards. • The class can negotiate and come to agreement on two books to read as a whole group. • On major exams there will be optional sections and questions that students can choose from to complete the required number of points for an exam.

Key Strategy	## Create a Vision of Your Classroom Community
	• Establish Clear Norms, Boundaries, Procedures, and Consequences
Life Skill Connection (See page 112–114)	• Exercise assertiveness; communicate your thoughts, feelings, and needs effectively to others (18)
Sample Activities, Strategies, and Routines	• Four Ways to Gather Data • Questions for Creating a Classroom Vision • How Can You Use This Student Data?

14

What makes a classroom a safe space to be? What kinds of work are a challenge for different students? As the teacher, what do you hope that every student will learn and experience? When you create a vision together, you engage everyone's imagination in the art of the possible. The result is a road map to help you make it happen. Students are often surprised and pleased to know that their ideas and suggestions are taken seriously. As you develop frameworks for learning together, implement a couple of student suggestions right away in the first week or so. It's your actions that will let students know you're paying attention to their ideas and feelings.

Four Ways to Gather Data

Creating a classroom vision is an opportunity to discover what students have to say about classroom life. It's also a chance to get a sense of who they are as learners and what they look for in a teacher. Using any of the questions that follow this section, try one of these strategies for generating students' ideas:

1. Post several questions, set the timer for 10-15 minutes, and take time to only listen when students are sharing their ideas—no interrupting, summarizing, or sermonizing. This is harder to do than it sounds, but students will appreciate it when you give them uninterrupted air time.

2. Type up a set of your favorite questions to give to students. Invite students to choose three or four questions to write about in their journals.

3. Hand out blank note cards and invite pairs of students to respond to several questions from your list. Have students share their responses out loud, but also collect their response cards so that you can collate all of their data.

4. Post questions on separate pieces of chart paper around the room and invite small groups to write down their ideas for each question using a "rotation station" learning strategy.

Questions for Creating a Classroom Vision

Personal Perspectives:

- What things can I do as a student to be successful in this class?

- What can the teacher do to support my success in class?

- What kinds of support from teachers help me to do my best, especially when I'm struggling?

- What makes a classroom a safe space where I can be honest and open, where I can say what's on my mind?

- What kinds of learning tasks, activities, and homework are easiest for me to do?

- What kinds of learning tasks, activities, and homework are hardest for me to do?

- What do kids do and say that annoys me the most? What happens in class that makes me mad?

- What hopes do I bring with me to this class?

- In what ways do I like to be challenged?

- Are there any hesitations that I have about this class that might get in the way of my success? (I don't know whether... ; I'm unsure about... ; I don't like spending a lot of time... ; I think the biggest potential problem for me will be...)

- When I'm having difficulty or get stuck, what can a teacher do to help me get back on track?

Classroom Perspectives:

- What are three ways that teachers can show respect toward students?

- What are three ways that students can show respect toward each other?

- What are the most important qualities of a good teacher?

- What are the most important qualities of a good student?

- What can you do to support other students to do their best in class?

- What makes learning fun in class?

- What things do you hope a teacher will never say or do?

- What things do you hope students will never say or do?

- What kinds of pressures and obstacles do some students face that make it tough to be a successful student?

How Can You Use This Student Data?

- These conversations and the information generated can become the foundation for making group agreements (See Make Group Guidelines and Agreements later in this chapter).

- Summarize and post suggestions that emerge from student pairs and rotation stations. Use this summary as a way to stay on track and assess how things are going in class.

- You can summarize key points from students' personal journal responses to illustrate how no one strategy or activity works equally well for all students. This information gives you a way to let students know that you will be introducing lots of different strategies and learning activities, knowing that each person will like and learn more from some experiences than from others.

- You might put students' personal journal responses to these vision questions in their assessment folders. This information can be useful as you work with each student and can be especially helpful when students are experiencing difficulties.

14

Key Strategy	**Talk About the Issue of Respect**
⟲	• Establish clear norms, boundaries, procedures, and consequences
Life Skill Connection (See page 112–114)	• Engage in conscious acts of respect, caring, helpfulness, kindness, and consideration (30)
Sample Activities, Strategies, and Routines	• Whom Do You Respect? • On Self-Respect • Learning Carousel on Respect

Everyone needs to talk about respect as a foundation for building positive relationships in the classroom. Versions of "You disrespected me" are the most common sources of conflict between and among students and teachers. Respect is a global word that can mean something different to each person in the room. It is very helpful for you and students to identify specific, observable behaviors that individuals perceive as being respectful and disrespectful. It is also helpful to explore why people are disrespectful, so that the group can counter experiences of disrespect with behaviors that encourage everyone to be more respectful of each other.

One more thing: the "Golden Rule" is not enough in diverse learning communities where students come from many different family experiences and cultural and religious traditions. Yes, it's important to consider treating others as we would like to be treated; but it's just as important to treat others as they tell you they would like to be treated.

Whom Do You Respect?

Ask students to write down (very quickly) three to five names of people (living or dead, young or old, personal acquaintances or people in the larger world) whom they respect a lot, and to identify two or three characteristics/qualities that all the people on their personal lists have in common. Ask students to close their writing by explaining why they associate these qualities of character with people whom they respect.

Invite students to share what they wrote. You might want to record these qualities on newsprint and follow up with a few questions that deepen the dialogue:

- Is the way you show respect toward some individuals or groups different from the way you show respect to other individuals and groups?

- Is respect different from admiration, appreciation, and popularity? How so? Can you respect people and not like them? Why or why not? If you disagree with someone can you still show respect toward them?

- Is everyone entitled to be treated respectfully regardless of what they do? Are there people you are automatically respectful toward? Does everyone have to earn your respect regardless of age, position, and status? Or does everyone start out getting your respect, but earn the privilege of keeping your respect?

On Self-Respect

In groups of two or three, make a list of five Dos and five Don'ts that are indicators of self-respect.

SELF-RESPECT	
The DOs of self-respect	**The DON'Ts of self-respect**
Examples: I do keep my word and my promises. I do take care of myself physically.	Examples: I don't let people walk all over me. I don't take chances that put me in a dangerous situation.

Learning Carousel on Respect

Implement a "learning carousel" where each question is posted on newsprint and every group of four students has two to three minutes to add their responses to each question as they move as a group from one question to the next. These framing questions offer some critical entry points for a dialogue around respect.

Student-to-Student RESPECT	
What do students do and say that shows respect and disrespect toward other students?	
Disrespectful Behaviors	Respectful Behaviors

Teacher-to-Student RESPECT	
What do teachers do and say that shows respect and disrespect toward students?	
Disrespectful Behaviors	Respectful Behaviors

Student-to-Teacher **RESPECT**	
What do students do and say that shows respect and disrespect toward teachers?	
Disrespectful Behaviors	Respectful Behaviors

What are some ways students can disagree with a teacher and show respect at the same time?	**What are some ways teachers can disagree with students and show respect at the same time?**

Think about why people are disrespectful. What have people experienced that may lead to disrespectful behavior toward others?	**What kinds of experiences help people become more respectful?**

Key Strategy   ## Make Group Guidelines and Agreements

⟲   • Establish clear norms, boundaries, procedures, and consequences

Life Skill Connection
(See page 112–114)

• "Read" dynamics in a group; assess group skills accurately; identify problems; generate, evaluate, and implement informed solutions that meet the needs of the group (34)

Sample Activities, Strategies, and Routines

• Suggested Instructions for Making Group Agreements

Shifting the emphasis from "my rules that you follow" to "guidelines we agree to implement together" communicates mutual responsibility for establishing a positive classroom climate where everyone is a stakeholder. When we invoke tons of rules in the classroom, we may unintentionally pit the rule breakers against the rule keepers. Furthermore, rules tend to keep the focus on negative behaviors—catching kids doing the wrong thing becomes the goal.

In contrast, agreements that describe desirable behaviors that are observable, concrete, and positive invite everyone to recognize and encourage the regular use of these behaviors. In addition, group guidelines become a natural assessment and reflection tool. Teachers and students can engage in an ongoing process of reviewing how well agreements are kept and discussing how to modify agreements so they are more effective.

Group guidelines can make any learning process more meaningful. When students know how to approach a learning task and know what skills and behaviors will help them complete the task, more kids will be more successful. In addition to developing general classroom agreements, students can help develop specific guidelines for making an effective oral presentation; working effectively in teams; and discussing controversial issues, when students may bring strong feelings and disparate opinions to the dialogue.

At both levels, students engage in the authentic practice of conflict resolution skills: defining the problem; sharing perspectives and listening to all points of view; exploring what's negotiable and what's not; identifying mutual interests; brainstorming possible solutions; and reaching a mutually satisfactory agreement. Students can use this process later for class meetings and negotiating other classroom issues.

14

Suggested Instructions for Making Group Agreements

1. Say, "The first thing we're going to do today is make some agreements that we can live with as a whole group. I'd like you to help brainstorm some guidelines that reflect how you think we should work together, talk to each other, and treat each other."

2. Say, "Here are a couple of examples of the kinds of agreements we can make." Choose two or three examples from the list below to write on the newsprint.

   Sample List of Group Agreements

   • Let people finish what they have to say before someone else speaks.

   • Share the talk space. Give everyone a chance to speak.

   • Take care of your own needs. If you have a question, ask it. If you need to say something, say it.

   • Start on time.

   • It's okay to make mistakes and self-correct.

   • Use "I Statements." Speak from your own experience.

- Respect yourself and others.

- Listen carefully.

- Be honest and open.

- Be a willing participant.

- Help each other out.

- Check things out before you make assumptions.

- Have fun!

- Confidentiality.

- Don't make fun of what other people say or do.

3. Say, "What agreements would you like to add to the list that will make our time together productive and positive?" Another way to say this is, "What kinds of agreements can we make as a group that will make this class work for you, that will help you be your best?" Brainstorm for about 10 minutes and write down all suggestions on the chart paper.

4. Use any of these questions to review the list: "Now look at the list. Are there any final suggestions? Any suggestions you'd rather leave out? Any that can be combined? Any words or phrases that you're unclear about? Any objections or concerns about any of the suggestions? Any words that you would like to replace?"

    Key Points to Remember:

    - Respect is a word that illustrates the problems with "global language," i.e., language that is abstract and often means different things to different people. It is essential that students name very concrete behaviors that show (through words or actions) how to treat someone with respect. Here are two ways you can encourage students to clarify what they mean when someone says, "We need to respect other people."

        - "What could someone do or say that would show you that you're being treated respectfully?"

        - "If I had a movie camera here in the classroom, what behaviors would I film that show you treating each other with respect?"

    - If this is challenging to students, you might begin by generating specific behaviors that show disrespect and then identify what you would like someone to say or do instead.

    - Take the time to work through the wording of agreements until everyone is fairly comfortable with the list. This process lets your students know that it's okay to discuss areas of difference and that it's valuable to reassess and modify "first thinking."

5. Check the list for "positive framing." This is the time to transform any statements that are negatively framed into statements that are positive and proactive. For example, in the sample agreements list above, #1 has been changed from "Don't interrupt," to "Let people finish what they have to say before someone else speaks."

6. Use a consensus process to reach agreement. Explain that consensus decision making means that everyone participates and has a say before reaching agreement on a decision that everyone can support. Remind students, "You have been using this process already. Now we've reached the final stage of consensus. Each of you needs to decide if you can live with and support this list of agreements for our class. It's important to remember that this list is not forever. We can revisit, discuss, and change these agreements if the group feels the need to do so. So I will ask two last questions."

    –   "Are there any objections to the agreements as they stand right now? If you still have a strong concern or objection, it's important to bring it up now, and we can address it before we move on."

    –   If there are no other objections at this time, move to the final question. "Are these agreements good enough for right now so that you can support them and use them during our time together? I will ask each of you to say, 'Yes' or 'No.'"

7. When everyone has said, "Yes," including you, you may want to suggest that everyone initial the group agreements that you have made.

8. Ask for a volunteer who is willing to rewrite the group agreements in large, clear print so that you can post them in the classroom.

Take a few minutes at the end of every week to revisit your agreements. Here are some questions you might ask:

-   What have you noticed that indicates that we are keeping most of our agreements?

-   Have you noticed anything that indicates that we are not keeping some of our agreements?

-   Which ones are hardest for the group as a whole to keep? What can we do to help everyone get better at keeping this agreement?

-   Is there anything at this time that you want to add, delete, or change?

-   Would anyone like to share how these agreements have made this class a different experience for you?

14

More about Agreements

- Agreements work hand-in-hand with consequences and interventions you apply when students violate classroom boundaries or fail to follow procedures you have taught.

- Agreements in the classroom can't replace school-wide rules that are universally enforced (i.e., If there is a schoolwide rule that no food or drink is allowed in classrooms, you can't make an agreement that supersedes the school rule.)

- The practice of making classroom agreements is carried out on two levels: general guidelines for how students work together, learn together, and treat each other, and more specific guidelines for how to engage in a specific learning experience. General group guidelines involve all students in envisioning the kind of classroom in which students feel safe, respected, cared for, and motivated to learn.

CHAPTER 15

Practice 5: Build a Cohesive Community of Learners

Introduce Gatherings
Activities pages 309–313

Introduce Closings
Activities pages 313–317

Introduce Teambuilding Activities
Activities pages 318–320

Assess Cooperation, Group Participation, and Leadership Skills
Activities pages 320–326

Form Home Groups
Activities pages 327–329

Create Routines and Rituals that Involve Every Student
Activities pages 329–331

Recognize and Celebrate the Group's Efforts and Accomplishments
Activities pages 331–333

Recognize Individual Accomplishments In and Out of the Classroom
Activities pages 333–334

Teach Win-Win Basics
Activities pages 335–337

15

Create Opportunities for Negotiated Learning

Activities pages 337–339

Use Class Meetings to Support and Maintain a High-Functioning Group

Activities pages 339–344

Make Group Talk Good Talk

Activities pages 344–358

Key Strategy	Introduce Gatherings
	• Build a cohesive community of learners

Life Skill Connection (See page 112–114)	• Recognize and name your own feelings (1)
	• Exercise assertiveness; communicate your thoughts, feelings, and needs to others (18)
	• Respect everyone's right to learn, to speak, and be heard (28)

Sample Activities, Strategies, and Routines	• Opening Go-Rounds and Connection Time
	• Conversation Circles
	• Strong Feelings Pair-Share
	• Feelings Connection
	• "I Like My Neighbors Who..."
	• Pick a Color that Reflects _____?
	• Whip

Gathering activities set the stage for learning by inviting everyone to participate in a brief common experience. Gatherings usually take about ten minutes. They are a quick and fun strategy to share personal information and perspectives. Through expressing their own thoughts and hearing from their peers, students strengthen a sense of what I call "group-ness"—a feeling that we are all important and we all have something important to say. Gatherings are a great way to open Monday class and welcome the new week.

Because gatherings elicit a lot of personal information, teachers get a fuller picture of who their kids are. The informal data gleaned from gatherings can provide direction for future interactions and instructional approaches with individual students.

In any of the activities described, allow students the "right to pass" if they are not comfortable responding to a particular question.

Opening Go-Rounds and Connection Time

Opening Go-Rounds give every student a chance to respond to a statement or question.
Ask students to sit in an arrangement where they can all see each other. Introduce the go-round topic in the form of a statement or question. Students then take turns responding, going around the room. A person always has the right to pass when it's his or her turn to speak. After most students have spoken, you can go back to those who passed to see if they want to say something now.

If you don't feel you have enough time for everyone to speak during one class period, introduce variations of Connection Time, where some, but not all, students will get the opportunity to speak.

- Set the timer for five to seven minutes and invite anyone who wants to share to speak to the statement or question; or

- Invite half the group to speak on one day and the other half to speak on the next day; or

- Invite students to speak to the statement or question on the basis of a specific category: everyone who's wearing glasses; everyone who ate breakfast this morning; everyone who's wearing black; girls only or boys only; anyone whose last name ends in F through P, etc.; or

- Limit responses to the first 10 students who volunteer.

However you choose to mix it up, be sure that everyone gets a chance to speak at some point during the week.

Topics should be ones that all students can comment on without feeling embarrassed or defensive. Go-Rounds and Connection Time can be purely personal or they can connect to a subject topic, or classroom, school, or community issue. Here are a few examples of each:

Personal

- What's something new and good in your life right now?

- Five years from now, I'd like to hear people say this about me: _____ is a _____.

- What's a wish or hope you have for a friend or someone in your family?

- Yesterday I felt _____; today I feel _____.

- One thing I hated that now I like is _____.

- What is something you have that you would fight for—even risk your life for—if someone tried to take it away from you? Why is this important to you? (This can be a material possession or something intangible, like a good reputation.)

Community, School, or Classroom Related

- Share a recent story from the news about someone who made a life-altering choice, and ask students: What would you have done in this situation?

- What is one schoolwide rule that you would change that you think would make school a better place for everyone?

- What's something you would like to learn about or learn how to do that's currently not offered here at school?

- What's something you hope we do again in class; we never do again in class; or we might do in class before the course is over?

- If you were a reporter for the news right now, what story would you want to investigate?

Subject Matter Related

- **Literature:** So far this year, who is the character you've read about with whom you identify the most?

- **Math:** What math skill do you think you'll use the most when you graduate from high school? If you were a geometric figure, what figure would you most like to be? Why?

- **Science:** What chemical element would you most like to be? Why? If you were a scientist, what problem would you most like to explore and solve?

- **Social Studies:** What century would you most like to live in if you were not growing up in the twenty-first century?

Conversation Circles

Divide students into two equal size groups. Ask one group to form a circle facing outward. Then ask the other group to form a second circle around that one, facing inward. Each person in the inner circle should be facing a partner in the outer circle. Tell students that they will each have about 45 seconds to share with their partners their responses to a question you will pose. All pairs of partners will speak simultaneously. Identify whether the inside partners or the outside partners will speak first. After the first partner has had a chance to share, signal that the other partner should begin speaking. When both partners have answered the question, ask students to move one, two, or three spaces to the right and pose another question to the group. Have students change partners for each new question.

Sample opening questions:

- Talk about the neighborhood in which you grew up as a kid. Where was it? What did it look like? What was something you liked about growing up there?

- What is the best present you've ever received? Why was it special?

- What do you think makes life hard for kids growing up right now?

- What do you think are the qualities of a good friend?

- What's something special that's been passed down in your family (a story, an object, an event, or tradition)?

- Who is the most interesting adult outside your family that you've ever known? Why do you find this person interesting?

- What is one thing your parents do or say that you don't ever want to do or say?

- If you become a parent, what is one thing you'd want to teach your children?

- What troubles you most about the world we live in today?

- If you could change one thing about your neighborhood or town, what would it be?

15

Strong Feelings Pair-Share

Invite students to pair up and describe a strong feeling they have experienced in the last week and some reasons for that feeling. (See Feelings Vocabulary handout on page 214.)

Feelings Connection

This activity helps students link their feelings and behaviors. Ask students to form a circle. Choose a feeling word for the activity, such as *angry, peaceful, upset, happy,* or *scared.* Begin by completing the sentence, "I feel [feeling word] when..." Use a soft ball or special object to pass to a student who would like to go next and complete the sentence. Ask that student to toss the ball or pass the object to another student. The second student repeats what the first student said, shares their statement, and then tosses the object to another student. You can also use, "Today I want to feel _____ so I am going to..."

"I Like My Neighbors Who..."

This activity is a variation on Musical Chairs. Have students arrange their chairs in a circle and sit down. Stand in the center of the circle and complete the sentence, "I like my neighbors. I especially like my neighbors who..." (insert any descriptor that some students will also identify with, e.g., who like basketball, who are wearing jewelry, who love to sleep late, etc.) All students who identify with the descriptor you've stated should stand up, leave their chairs, and try to move into another empty chair. At the same time you will try to find an empty chair to sit in. Whoever is left standing will complete the sentence, "I like my neighbors. I especially like my neighbors who..." and continue the game.

Pick a Color that Reflects _____

Cut up a large quantity of 4" × 4" construction paper squares in a wide variety of colors. Be sure to include colors that are light and dark, intense and muted. Ask each student to choose a color or group of colors that reflects

- how I'm feeling today;

- how I'm feeling about my progress/current project/upcoming exam in this class;

- my perception of conflict (or any other concept you want students to think about);

- the effort I'm putting into this class right now;

- my feelings about the coming week/the weekend;

- my thoughts/feelings about _____.

Either in the large group or in smaller groups of five or six, have students share the colors they chose and why they chose them. (If you split up into smaller groups, come back together at the end and ask a few volunteers to share which colors they chose and why.)

Whip

A whip is a positive, incomplete statement that is completed in turn by each person in a circle. It goes quickly, with each person answering in a short phrase. Some possible whips are:

- Something I'm good at that ends with "-ing"

- I hate to spend time...

- If you could trade places for one week with anyone currently living, who would it be?

- If you could invite two people to have dinner with you and your best friend, who would you choose?

- One word that describes how I feel today is...

Key Strategy	Introduce Closings
	• Build a Cohesive Community of Learners
Life Skill Connection (See page 112–114)	• Exercise assertiveness; communicate your thoughts, feelings, and needs to others (18) • Respect everyone's right to learn, to speak, and be heard (28)
Sample Activities, Strategies, and Routines	• Closing Go-Rounds • Connections • Encouragement Cards • Goodbye/Hello • Checking It Out • Ticket Out

Closing activities provide a way to wrap up the time the group has spent together and send off the group at the end of class or the end of the week. Like gatherings, closings create opportunities for every student to be heard. While gatherings focus mostly on sharing personal data, closings provide an excellent vehicle for students to give feedback on what they have experienced in class, communicate what they have learned, and assess their progress and personal development. The quick "read" you get from the group can help shape what you do the next day or guide changes you make to your instructional plan.

Closing Go-Rounds

Personal

- What's your favorite music to listen to when you want to relax?

- When you feel discouraged, what do you say to yourself to keep going?

- If you could drop two things from your life right now to ease the pressure, what would they be?

- What's the best thing that happened to you this week?

- What's one thing you're looking forward to this weekend?

- What's one thing you could do this weekend that would make someone in your family happy?

Classroom and Subject Related

- In five words or less, what's the most important thing you learned today about yourself, about the group, and about the topic?

- What's a banner headline of seven words or less that would best summarize what we did/learned/discussed in class?

- When you have a lot of homework, what strategies do you use to refocus and get it all done?

- As you think about tackling the homework problems tonight, what's the one thing you want to remember while you're working?

- As you continue reading tonight, what piece of advice would you give (name of character) in the book _____?

- What's something you've accomplished this week that you're proud of?

Connections

If students have just seen a powerful film or listened to a moving story or speech, you might say: "Let's take five minutes for connections. After watching/listening to_____, what thoughts or feelings do you have right now? Anyone can speak who wants to. The only guideline is to speak about your personal reactions from your perspective, rather than responding to someone else's comments or opinions."

Encouragement Cards

Distribute index cards. Ask students to write anonymously one sentence expressing words of encouragement they might offer to other students in the class. Collect the cards and invite different students to read some of the cards at the end of class period.

Goodbye/Hello

Ask students what old habit they would like to say goodbye to and what new habit they would like to try on. Go around with each student completing the blanks in the statement, "Goodbye..., hello..."

Checking It Out

- Review learning goals (what students are learning and how students go about learning it) you set for class, and ask students to offer evidence that, as individuals or the whole group, they met or did not meet the goals for the day.

- If class did not meet your usual performance expectations, invite individual students to share one thing each person can do to make class run more smoothly tomorrow.

- Get a "group read" regarding students' readiness to move on by asking: "Using 1, 5, or 10 fingers, indicate where you stand right now."

  - How prepared do you feel to _____?

  - How complete is your understanding of _____?

  - One more review of _____ would be helpful before _____.

Getting a quick read of the group can help you decide whether to proceed with the whole group, divide into different task groups, or pair students up to work together.

Ticket Out

Use "Ticket Out" as a closing strategy for students to...

- Summarize important concepts/ideas from the day's lesson

- Check for understanding of a key concept presented in the day's lesson

- Check for proficiency of a key skill presented in the day's lesson

- Provide feedback on the day's lesson

- Reflect on habits of learning used in class today

- Solicit questions that emerged from the day's lesson

- Make connections between lesson content and students' thoughts and experiences

- Link lesson content to real-world application

Collect tickets before students leave your class. You might also invite students to share a few responses out loud or share some of the responses at the beginning of the next class.

TICKET OUT

Name _____

Write down three words or phrases that best describe

_____

_____ .

Explain:

1.

2.

TICKET OUT

Name _____

(Show me the money!)

Here's the problem:

_____

_____ .

Solve it:

TICKET OUT

Name _____

After exploring

_____

in class today, what question would a Scientist/Historian/
Journalist/Lawyer ask to move the investigation forward?

TICKET OUT

Name _____

Give a "real-world" example that illustrates how and
where you might use this formula/model/process:

TICKET OUT

Name _____

Rate your habits of learning today:

3: I did it with no help.   1: I did it with lots of help.
2: I did it with prompting.   0: I didn't do it.

____ I followed task directions on my own.
____ I worked silently during silent start-up.
____ I brought everything I needed to class.
____ I took time to check for accuracy and review, correct, and revise my work.
____ I stayed on task without bothering others or getting distracted by others.
____ I sustained my focus and effort even when work was boring or difficult.

TICKET OUT

Name _____

3 things I can explain/teach to others from this learning unit

2 strategies I will use to study for the unit test

1 question I want answered in our unit review tomorrow

15

Key Strategy	Introduce Teambuilding Activities
	• Build a cohesive community of learners
Life Skill Connection (See page 112–114)	• Cooperate, share, and work toward high performance within a group to achieve group goals (27) • Exercise effective leadership skills within a group (33)
Sample Activities, Strategies, and Routines	• "Chocolate River": A Group Challenge • Resources for Teambuilding Games

Whether they take 15 minutes or an extended time period, teambuilding activities help students strengthen the skills of cooperation, communication, leadership, strategic thinking, and problem solving. A key objective of effective teambuilding activities is that no one wins unless everyone wins.

However much fun these challenges are to do, it is the debriefing and reflection questions afterward that make these activities important learning experiences. The Recommended Resources at the end of this guide include many teambuilding activity resources.

"Chocolate River": A Group Challenge

1. Explain to students that they are going to participate in a group challenge and then discuss it afterwards.

2. Set two ropes parallel to each other about 25 feet apart. Divide the group in half, with each group on opposite sides of the ropes like this:

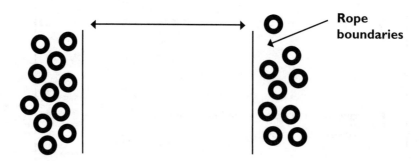

Rope boundaries

3. Give each group cardboard or carpet squares of about 12" × 12", using this ratio:
    20 students on each side = about 10 squares for each group
    15 students on each side = about 7 or 8 squares for each group
    10 students on each side = about 5 or 6 squares for each group

Explain to the group, "The space between the ropes is a chocolate river. The problem is that it's boiling hot, so that falling in it would be a disaster. Your goal here is to get everyone across the river, from one side to the other. The squares you have are marshmallows; they will float on top of the river, so if you use them to step on, you can get across safely. However, there is a problem. If you fall off a marshmallow or touch the river at any point, you have to go back and start over. And there's one more thing. I'm a monster in the river and I love marshmallows. If I see a marshmallow in the river that no one is standing on, I will snatch it up and eat it. You will have about five minutes to strategize with your group and then you will have about 15 minutes or so to solve the problem."

You might want to suggest three guidelines for this kind of physically active experience: PLAY HARD, PLAY FAIR, PLAY SAFE. Discuss with the group how they think each of these guidelines applies to this particular team challenge.

Let students know that you'll answer three questions before they begin. If anyone asks whether they can talk to the other group, you can say that each group can identify one person to negotiate with the other side. It's likely that both groups will figure out that if they share their resources and work together it will be much easier to get everyone across. Give the group about five minutes to strategize and then give them about 15 minutes to solve the problem.

Note: During the activity, if the groups are having a lot of difficulty listening to each other, or working cooperatively, stop, and ask everyone to freeze. Take three comments from each group, saying: "I'm open to hearing three observations from the group that help describe what's not working." Then say, "I'll take three suggestions from the group of strategies that you think will help you achieve the goal of getting everyone across Chocolate River."

4. Use any of these questions for postactivity discussion:

    *   What happened? How did you feel about doing this activity? What did you like or not like?

    *   How did your group decide what strategy to use? Was everyone listened to or included in the decision? How do you know?

    *   What did you observe about how your group worked together? What did your teammates do or say that helped your team be successful? Is there anything you could have done that would have helped your group to be more effective as a team?

    *   How would you describe the role you played? How did it feel to be a leader or a follower? What would you personally do differently next time if you were involved in a similar activity?

    *   What learning can you take from this experience that you can apply to our work as a group in the classroom every day?

5. Close the activity by saying, "We're not born with the skills to work together effectively in a group. We learn these skills by watching other people and practicing them ourselves."

Resources for Teambuilding and Games

***Classroom Rituals for At-Risk Students,* by Gary Phillips**
(Bainbridge Island, WA: The National School Improvement Project, 2004)

This very practical book describes over a hundred rituals and routines. In addition, the author suggests many strategies and tips for creating conditions and relationships that will increase student motivation and engagement.

***Moving Beyond Icebreakers: An Innovative Approach to Group Facilitation, Learning, and Action,* by Stanley Pollack with Mary Fusoni**
(Boston: The Center for Teen Empowerment Inc., 2005)

Moving Beyond Icebreakers is a compendium of new and tried and true icebreakers along with hundreds of strategies, tips, and ideas for building respectful, connected, high-functioning groups. The book thoroughly addresses group process and development and offers an array of tools, skills, agendas, formats, and planning documents for facilitating effective meetings and workshops. The activities are intended for use with all age groups; consequently, many of the examples are presented from adult perspectives. Even so, activities and trouble-shooting strategies are easily adaptable to student groups.

Project Adventure (www.pa.org)

Project Adventure is a not-for-profit organization that offers training, publications, equipment, props and workshops to facilitate experiential, adventure-based, "challenge by choice" educational experiences. They have over 25 years of experience working in schools and with youth. If you have a budget for supplies, this is a great place to buy the props and equipment needed for many well-loved and well-known team building and group-building activities.

Assessing Cooperation, Group Participation, and Leadership Skills

Key Strategy	
	• Build a cohesive community of learners
Life Skill Connection (See page 112–114)	• Assess your skills, competencies, effort, and quality of work accurately (17)
Sample Activities, Strategies, and Routines	• Develop a Participation Assessment Log • Adding or Subtracting – What's My Impact?

To work together effectively in groups, whether they be study groups, classrooms, groups of friends, or sports teams, people in the group need to exercise positive leadership, communication, and conflict resolution skills. We need to analyze the barriers to working together well and learn techniques to surmount them. This section includes a variety of tools and strategies for assessing cooperation, group participation, and leadership skills.

Develop a Participation Assessment Log

Taking cues from agreements, procedures, and expectations that you have already established develop a list of specific behaviors and attitudes that indicate active participation in class. This list might include:

- Raises thoughtful questions that help the class gain a deeper understanding of an issue or topic of discussion.

- Takes a leadership role in carrying out an activity.

- Gives helpful feedback about class activities and experiences.

- Participates in debriefing discussions after an activity is completed.

- Takes on various roles and responsibilities in small-group learning activities.

- Shares personal perspectives with others in small and larger groups.

- Participates in role-plays and demonstrations.

- Helps to set up activities, distribute materials, and clean up.

- Gives words of encouragement to other students.

- Helps create a good-humored climate that invites laughter and enjoyment.

- Shows appreciation for other students' contributions.

- Participates in problem solving when issues and concerns arise that affect the group and the class.

- Volunteers when help is needed.

- Shares responsibility within a group.

- Encourages all students within the group to participate.

- Takes a risk to try things that are new and challenging.

- Shows friendliness toward other class members.

- Provides positive energy when the group needs it.

- Takes turns recording and documenting small-group work.

- Works effectively with different students.

- Listens to others without interrupting.

- Makes transitions from one activity to another easily.

- Respects other people's personal space and comfort zones.

15

- Stops and comes to closure when time is up.

- Speaks openly and honestly to make others aware of a problem or concern.

- Disagrees with others in ways that are respectful.

- Acknowledges and accepts other students' ideas.

The participation assessment log sheet can be used for teacher, student, and small-group assessment. Make enough copies so you have a copy for each student and each student has a copy to keep in their portfolio.

Teachers can use the participation log sheets to:

- document students' participation grades, checking the behaviors you notice and jotting down observations that give you a snapshot of each student's skills.

- give students personal feedback on their participation skills throughout the course.

- set goals and check in with students to assess how they are meeting chosen goals.

Students can use participation log sheets to:

- assess the strengths that they already bring to class.

- identify skills they find challenging.

- set their own goals for skills they want to improve and use more regularly.

- reflect on ways that their participation in class has changed, and how those changes have affected how they think and feel about the class and their peers.

- write about one way that they have participated in class that has made a positive difference, something they have done or said that has helped make the class a better learning community for everyone.

- assess skills small groups have used effectively in cooperative learning activities.

- identify specific skills that individual students have used in large-group activities.

Adding or Subtracting—What's My Impact?

When students have been together two or three months, some of their helpful and not so helpful behaviors will have shown up. Take advantage of this timing to introduce students to language for identifying skills and behaviors that add to or subtract from the effectiveness of a group. The important thing is to introduce the language and reflection before negative behaviors become entrenched.

Use the handout "Adding or Subtracting—What's My Impact?" Have students fill it out individually, encouraging them to take their time and really think about how they interact in group activities, discussions, and tasks. If you have home groups you might want to ask students to assess their home group partners. The positive and negative behaviors apply to small and large groups.

Help students to understand the following concepts:

- It takes many skills for groups to be effective. Organizing is not the only one.

- How we behave in a group helps or hurts the group. We can add ideas, enthusiasm, order, and harmony; or we can subtract ideas, enthusiasm, order, and harmony.

- We can help the groups we're involved in by increasing what we add, and by decreasing what we subtract. So even if we aren't ready to be the main initiator, we could perhaps cut down on distracting behaviors.

- It's OK to admit that we demonstrate negative behaviors at times. Noting that we sometimes use behaviors that have a negative impact on others does not mean we're bad people; it means we're honest with ourselves and can be responsible for changing.

- Depending on the developmental readiness of your students, encourage them to consider how others perceive their behavior, in addition to how they perceive themselves. For example, some students might think they are assertive while others see them as dominating.

The questions below can be used for journaling, pair/shares, or personal conferencing immediately following the handout reflections, and/or later as follow-up.

Questions Related to "The Positives"

- Which of the positive skills do you enjoy using and use well? Describe an experience.

- Which of the positive skills feel difficult or uncomfortable?

- What might you do to add more to the advisory group?

- How do you think other people would score your skills for effective group work? What are they seeing that gives them the impressions they have?

- How does your use of the positive skills vary from small to large groups, from advisory to classes, or from inside to outside school? How do you feel about those variations? What could you do about them?

- Describe the people you identified as good models of the positive skills.

- What actions showed you they were adding to their group's efforts? How do you feel when you're in a group with these people?

15

Questions Related to "The Negatives"

- Describe one of the times when you subtracted from the group. What did you do? How did you feel? What else might you have done or said?

- What can you do to decrease your use of these behaviors?

- What can members of your group or your advisor do that would help you?

- What can you do for others to help them avoid these behaviors?

- Do you think other people perceive you using the negative behaviors more or less than you see yourself using them? What are they seeing that gives them the impressions they have?

- How does your use of the negative behaviors vary from small to large groups, from advisory to classes, or from inside to outside school? How do you feel about those variations? What could you do about them?

Group process questions for individual reflection, journaling, and/or group discussion

- Which of the positive skills do you find come easiest for you? Which do you find the most difficult or uncomfortable? How could you strengthen these abilities?

- What positive skills did you see other group members using? Please tell them you noticed.

- When you found yourself doing things which got in the way of effective group functioning, what were you feeling? How could you express those feelings in more positive ways? When you're feeling this, what could you do to help yourself? What might you want other members of your group to say or do that might help you and the group get back on track? How might you ask for this kind of help?

Group Feedback

Ask each group to record their responses to any of these questions:

1. Name one way each person in your group participated and/or contributed?

2. Name three specific positive behaviors you noticed that helped you meet your goal and complete the task.

3. What situations, actions, or statements made it more difficult for the group to work together effectively and how did the group handle these challenges?

4. How could you have worked together to be more effective? What positive leadership, communication, and conflict resolution skills could you practice to improve the way you work together in the future?

Developed by Rachel Poliner and Sam Diener.

Adding or Subtracting – What's My Impact?

The Positives

There are many different skills and behaviors that add to a group's effectiveness. When everyone knows about these skills and behaviors, and can talk about them, the group can more easily improve how it works together. On the chart below rate yourself on a scale from 1 to 5, where:

    1 is low (you don't like or are not great at this role) and

    5 is high (you like this role and play it well).

Then, think of a person – in or out of school – who uses this skill really well.

Positive group skills and behaviors that encourage collaboration	Rate yourself low—high	Name a role model
Initiating/Problem Solving: proposing ideas, suggesting next steps, experimenting, carefully confronting disruptive behaviors	1 2 3 4 5	
Organizing/Coordinating: keeping the group on track, focusing on goals, suggesting timelines, proposing fair division of labor	1 2 3 4 5	
Seeking: identifying what information and resources are needed, doing research, connecting different ideas, asking related questions	1 2 3 4 5	
Encouraging: encouraging everyone's participation and thinking, praising efforts, staying positive	1 2 3 4 5	
Harmonizing: checking on feelings, sensing when the group needs a break or a heart-to-heart talk, suggesting ways to work better together	1 2 3 4 5	
Clarifying/Summarizing: clearing up confusion, checking to see if everyone understands and if the topic has been discussed enough, offering conclusions	1 2 3 4 5	

Adding or Subtracting – What's My Impact? CONTINUED

The Negatives

Everyone has moments when they make it harder for their group to work, when they subtract ideas and energy. When we use any of the behaviors below, we push the group offtrack, undermine confidence, or damage how people talk and work together. What can you do to get out of this role next time?

Negative group roles and behaviors that discourage collaboration	Your experience In what situations do you fall into each role? What helped you get out of the role?
Dominating: tellings others what to do, insisting my ideas are better than others', hogging the spotlight and the credit	
Distracting: talking about everything except the task at hand, fidgeting, telling jokes, calling attention to myself	
Blocking: being stubborn, rarely offering an idea but always finding flaws in others' ideas, disagreeing without listening carefully, playing the devil's advocate long after it's useful	
Withdrawing: being consistently silent or out of the loop, not sharing ideas, not doing a fair share of the work, drifting along	
Doom and Glooming: expecting the group to fail, claiming projects won't work and ideas are bad, spreading a sour mood	

Key Strategy	Form Home Groups
	• Build a cohesive community of learners

Life Skill Connection (See page 112–114)	• Develop, manage, and maintain healthy peer relationships (25)

Sample Activities, Strategies, and Routines	• Ways to Use Home Groups • Options for Forming Home Groups

You may want to consider forming home groups in your classes. Home groups are usually composed of four students and last throughout the year. They provide a structure and safe place for students to support and work with each other during "the long haul." Wait a few weeks to do this, so that you know a little bit about how different students learn and students know a little bit about each other.

Home groups are helpful when students need to discuss problems that arise in class and provide a structured forum for dealing with schoolwide issues or community concerns that affect your students.

Ways to Use Home Groups

- Share learning goals with group members and support each other to meet them.

- Hold weekly check-ins about how things are going with each person in the group.

- Disseminate information and address maintenance and housekeeping issues.

- Share feelings and reactions when a sad event or crisis impacts the school community, before discussing the situation with the whole class.

- Reflect and share what they have learned in a particular activity.

- Apply what you have learned using the group's understanding of a particular topic, problem, or concept.

- Rotate responsibility for explaining assignments to, and reserving sets of assignment materials for, the students in your group who are absent.

- Brainstorm a list of questions and topics that your group wants to address before a major test, exam, or performance assessment.

- Review and study together in order to prepare for a test or exam.

- Support each person in the group to meet a certain level of mastery of a particular skill.

- Correct quizzes, problems, and tests.

15

- Review homework in preparation for a discussion.

- Have students take responsibility for a particular question to discuss, a topic to investigate, or problem to solve, and have them share what they have learned with the rest of the class.

- Give feedback to each other after they have practiced specific communication, cooperation, and problem-solving skills.

- Create home group team competitions using Jeopardy™, Trivial Pursuit™, or other game show formats.

Options for Forming Home Groups

Students Choose Home Groups within the Limits You Set

Assign students to one of four colors that each reflects a different group in your class. Students form groups of four by choosing one person from each color group. For example, red could represent students who are academically able, quiet, reflective; yellow could be students who are academically able, verbal, highly social; green could be students who are more academically challenged, verbal, highly social; blue could be students who are more academically challenged, quiet, reflective. You might also assign equal numbers of boys and girls to each color so students know that they need to form mixed-gender groups. This process ensures that each home group includes students with a diverse range of abilities and attributes. Grouping this way also helps avoid having groups that include two students who really clash with each other. If these clashing students receive squares of the same color they won't be able to be in the same home group.

Directions:

1. Cut up paper squares using the four colors you have selected. For example, if you have 24 students, cut up six squares for each of the four colors. Write each student's name on the assigned color square.

2. The day before students choose their home groups, share some of your hopes and expectations for home groups so that students can consider that information when they make their choices.

3. On the day that students choose their groups, pass out the color squares to every student. Tell them that they need to form groups that include one person from each color group. Give students about ten minutes to choose and then ask each group to fill out their Home Group Information card. Collect sheets and make copies so that each student has a copy of their Home Group information.

You Choose

You assign students to home groups, balancing diverse abilities and personalities in each group. The limitation of this option is that students have no choice in forming their groups.

Students Choose

Students choose their own home groups. The limitation of this option is that students' skills, abilities, strengths, and weaknesses may vary dramatically from home group to home group and each group may have less diversity than you would like.

After the home groups have been formed, have them each fill out a Home Group Information card with the information for the group. Have each group also make a card for you.

Home Group Information

Your Home Group Members

- Name, Color, Phone #, Birthday

- Name, Color, Phone #, Birthday

- Name, Color, Phone #, Birthday

- Name, Color, Phone #, Birthday

Person in charge of assignments and homework (Rotate this role every week.)

Week of _____   Name _____

Week of _____   Name _____

Week of _____   Name _____

Week of _____   Name _____

Key Strategy	Create Routines and Rituals That Involve Every Student
	• Build a cohesive community of learners
Life Skill Connection (See page 112–114)	• Engage in conscious acts of respect, caring, helpfulness, kindness, courtesy, and consideration (30)
Sample Activities, Strategies, and Routines	• Sample Routines and Rituals That Involve Everyone

15

A feeling of belonging emerges in part from shared expectations and experiences. Everybody gives and everybody gets. Sometimes, we start relying on volunteers and giving students the option of opting out too early into their adolescence. Inadvertently, this can create a classroom culture where students take on permanent roles of "doers" or "slackers." Try out some ideas below that communicate to students, "We're all in this together."

Sample Routines and Rituals That Involve Everyone

1. Everybody has a birthday. Announce and congratulate students on their special day.

2. Do three-minute check-ins with every student on a rotating basis. Students can assess how they're doing and ask questions, and you can give feedback and review students' progress. When check-ins with every student are routine, it becomes less intimidating for struggling students to seek you out when they're experiencing difficulty. Think about doing personal check-ins during the first ten minutes of class, when students are involved in independent learning tasks, when students are involved in sustained cooperative learning activities, or when students are starting on their homework.

3. Keep a stock of cards at school that you can use for different occasions. When a student is ill for an extended period of time, when a student has a suffered a death in the family, even when a student is suspended for an extended period, send a card home that every student has signed that says, "We're thinking of you, we're pulling for you, we hope you're okay."

4. If you generate math or science problems, case studies, or "what if" situations as part of your course work, use every student's name in the scenarios you write up. Just remember to keep problems light and neutral—no personal situations that would feel embarrassing to anyone.

5. Every teacher can use extra hands in the classroom—setting up labs, distributing and collecting materials, helping out with special equipment, making sure the room is neat at the end of the period, etc. Make this an expectation by identifying one person who serves in this role each week. Rather than creating an alphabetical rotation, make it truly random by putting everyone's name in a container and asking a student to pick out a name each week.

6. Depending upon what your schoolwide food rules are, when kids eat lunch, and when a class meets, you might want to offer a snack option. If everyone pays a buck, you're willing to keep a snack supply in the classroom, but here's the deal. Everyone contributes a dollar or it doesn't happen. And if students like the idea, let them collect the money and go to the wholesale food store to buy the snacks. When you run out of snacks, students can decide if they want to do it again.

7. Ask each student to contribute a thought or story for the week. If you make this a weekly routine, every student will have a turn before the year is out. Keep books around that students can draw from: *Chicken Soup for the Teenage Soul, Seven Habits for Highly*

Effective Teens, Golden Nuggets, books of quotations and meditations for young people, etc. This kind of activity does triple duty: every student chooses something to share with the whole group; every student plays the roles of both speaker and audience; every week you've created an opportunity for quiet listening and reflection.

	Recognize and Celebrate the Group's Efforts and Accomplishments
Key Strategy	• Build a cohesive community of learners
Life Skill Connection (See page 112–114)	• Encourage and appreciate the contribution of others (29)
Sample Activities, Strategies, and Routines	• Congratulations! • Create a 100% Club

A group starts to become a group when everybody in the group got it, did it, enjoyed it, or endured it! The more you acknowledge what the class has accomplished together, the more students will see themselves as members of a team where everyone belongs.

For the following activities, the word "group" really does mean every student in the class. These activities support high academic and behavioral expectations for all kids, not just some of them.

Congratulations!

When every student has completed a project, performed satisfactorily on an assessment, or worked as a team to accomplish something as a whole group—do something special to acknowledge how much you appreciate their efforts. You might consider:

- Composing a written "Thank you" that you read to the group and post on the class's bulletin board space.

- Posting a giant "Congratulations" sign when every student in the class has endured and successfully completed a particularly challenging learning unit, task, or assignment.

- Naming or eliciting from students the qualities and skills the group used to accomplish a task successfully.

- Passing out colored ballpoint pens that you buy in bulk at most office supply stores.

- Declaring a "no-homework" night.

- Giving everyone "bonus points" toward their quarter grade.

Create a 100% Club

This is a strategy that can be particularly helpful in high schools or classes where students have a tougher time conforming to expected behavioral norms, and where teachers need to be more mindful of creating structures that encourage more cooperative and self-disciplined behaviors by all students in the class. The goal is to identify, recognize, and record occasions when all students in the class have met a specific expectation. This is a sample list that one high school faculty developed:

- Everyone arrived on time to class.

- Everyone settled in and got to work on the activity with no prompting.

- Everyone focused on completing the task for the entire time allotted.

- Everyone completed the homework assignment on time and satisfactorily.

- Everyone brought all necessary materials to class.

- Everyone contributed to tidying up the room so that it was clean and neat at the end of the period.

- Everyone helped, supported, and encouraged their peers to participate positively in a group activity and complete the task successfully.

- Everyone earned at least a (C) (B) on the test, quiz, or assignment.

- Everyone contributed to a productive discussion by sharing ideas, asking related questions, restating and summarizing key ideas, and seeking and offering more information and evidence.

- Everyone exhibited good listening and observation skills during the presentation/lecture/demonstration.

- No one used abusive, profane, or negative language during the class period.

- No one interrupted the person currently speaking at any time during the class period.

Keeping a tally sheet where you record when the whole class "did it" serves a number of purposes:

- From week to week the class can review and assess how they are doing as a group and set goals for the next week.

- Recording the data shows graphically where the group is succeeding and where the group needs to improve. The data also provides the opportunity for students to discuss what is not working and take responsibility for generating ideas that will help them succeed.

- The 100% Club can also serve as a cooperative/competitive activity that involves all of your classes. For example, when every class you teach has earned 100 points, consider doing something fun in class that has nothing whatsoever to do with your course. Or you might create a competition among your classes to see which class earns 100 points first. The class that earns the first 100 points gets to choose something special they want to do in class. Then the slate is wiped clean and all the classes begin accumulating points for the next round.

Recognize Individual Accomplishments
In and Out of the Classroom

Key Strategy	• Build a cohesive community of learners
Life Skill Connection (See page 112–114)	• Encourage and appreciate the contribution of others (29)
Sample Activities, Strategies, and Routines	• Give a Big Hand for... • Wall of Fame • Did You Know? • Appreciations • Stick With It

Recognizing individual accomplishments is as important as recognizing whole-group successes. Our competitive "I win, you lose" culture doesn't always support taking pleasure in the accomplishments of others. Create opportunities that encourage students to appreciate the efforts of their peers.

In addition, we don't often recognize students' talents and competencies if they don't show up in the classroom. When you acknowledge that students do important things in their lives outside of school, you have the power to help students broaden their definitions of success and excellence, as well as break down stereotypical views of their classmates. Every time a student says to herself, "Wow, I didn't know that about _____. That's awesome!" something good has happened in your classroom.

Give a Big Hand for...

Every week or so, invite students to recognize accomplishments of their peers in class. Invite the group to recognize three or four students and then give all of them a big hand. To make this feel less awkward, you may want to ask some of your best "informers"—who know everything about everyone—to start it up the first time you do it. Use a simple formulaic statement at first to make this easy:

_____, _____ showed a lot of _____ when s/he _____.
  (when)   (name of student)   (quality)   (accomplishment)

Wall of Fame

If you have a bulletin board space for each class, or for all of your classes together, encourage students to post articles, pictures, performance programs, announcements, etc. that recognize what students are doing in and out of school. If you find out about interesting activities your students are involved in, make a small certificate on your computer that you can post. Here's a sample:

Did You Know?

I have never met a kid who didn't perk up when you ask them to talk about their unusual experiences or special knowledge. When you have opportunities to link what students are learning to real-world situations and contemporary culture, invite students to share their unique perspectives by saying, "We have a resident expert on _____. What can you tell us about _____?"

Appreciations

Set the timer for three minutes. Tell the students they have the opportunity to say something they appreciated about the class today, about the group, or about an individual's contributions. Model by speaking first, then invite anyone who wishes to speak to do so.

Stick With It

Use "sticky notes" to communicate with individual students when you notice that they did something in class that was particularly skillful, responsible, helpful, considerate, etc. In your note be sure to link the specific intellectual, social, or emotional quality that was reflected in the act or behavior you witnessed.

Key Strategy	Teach Win-Win Basics
	• Build a cohesive community of learners

Life Skill Connection (See page 112–114)	• Use Win-Win problem solving to negotiate satisfactory resolutions to conflicts that meet important goals and interests of people involved. (24)

Sample Activities, Strategies, and Routines	• "Kisses" • Keys to Effective Group Problem Solving

Most of us carry around the myth that conflict is always a contest where one person wins and the other person loses. In fact, many problems can be resolved using a Win-Win process (where both parties are satisfied with the outcome) and nearly all conflicts can be approached from a Win-Win perspective. If believing in the possibility of Win-Win becomes a routine way of thinking, we are more likely to participate in a problem solving process that results in a Win-Win solution.

"Kisses"

1. Begin the activity by explaining to participants:

    "We're going to play a game now. The name of the game is called "Kisses" because the object of the game is to acquire as many chocolate kisses as you can. We need two volunteers to come sit at this table. Each volunteer will represent one half of the larger group."

    Identify two volunteers who are approximately the same size, and share the same hand-edness. Then identify the half of the group that each volunteer is representing. Position volunteers so that they are facing each other across the table, their right or left elbows are on the table, and they are clasping each other's hands. This is an arm wrestling position but DO NOT use the term. If someone says that this looks like arm wrestling, explain that it's similar, but the rules are different.

2. Continue the instructions:

    The object of the game is for each person to get as many chocolate "Kisses" as possible for their team in the time allowed. The rules are as follows:

    *   From now on the two players may not speak to each other.

    *   Every time you get the back of the other person's hand on the table, you will receive a chocolate "Kiss" for your team.

    *   Someone from each team needs to keep track of the number of "Kisses" your team receives.

    *   You will have 30 seconds to get as many "Kisses" as you can.

    Note: You can also call the game, "Points" if you don't have or don't want to use chocolate kisses.

3. Say, "Begin," and say "Stop" after 30 seconds. Participants will probably compete against each other and will probably only get a few "Kisses" or none. Discuss what happened.

"What did you see? How many 'Kisses' did each team receive?" If the players received very few "Kisses," ask, "What was the goal of the game?"

Ask participants if they can think of another way to play the game so teams can get more "Kisses." (Usually groups will suggest ways that the two students can alternate placing the back of the person's hand on the table.)

4. After the group offers suggestions, play one more 30-second round and ask participants to describe what was different when they played the game the second time. You might also want to ask:

"What words describe the approach you used this time?"

"How do these two approaches to the game reflect ways that you handle conflict?"

5. Teach the concept of win-win. Explain that the game illustrates that conflict doesn't always have to be a win-lose contest:

"In a highly competitive society, it's easy to assume that 'For me to get what I want and need, I have to win and you have to lose.' This approach is called Win-Lose." (You might invite students to explore these questions: Think about the society in which you live. Why does win-lose thinking have such a powerful hold on people? In what aspects of your life do you experience the strongest win-lose messages? Does high school reinforce a win-lose approach to problems or life in general?)

Sometimes neither person will get what he or she wants, in which case the result is called Lose-Lose.

AND, like in the game, it's also possible that both people can get what they want or need in the situation. This result is called Win-Win.

The win-win approach to working out problems is the one that we will practice here in the classroom. I'd like our first take on classroom problems to be one where we try and seek a solution that works for everyone involved. A win-win solution is a solution that is nonviolent, meets some important needs of all parties involved, and helps us to maintain positive relationships. We will use this process when we negotiate how and when to do things in class. I also expect students who have a problem with each other to use this process, and we will use it when a student and I are involved in a problem-solving conference around a behavioral or academic situation that needs to be resolved."

Keys for Effective Group Problem Solving

- Encourage students to paraphrase and summarize the ideas of other students.

- Explore different points of view and make sure there is room for respectful disagreement.

- Listen and respond to others empathetically.

- Ask open-ended questions to gain a deeper understanding of various suggestions.

- Share the "air time" and ensure that everyone's voice is heard.

- Develop several desirable solutions to choose from.

- Anticipate and predict different outcomes for proposed solutions (If... then...).

- Evaluate advantages and disadvantages of various solutions: Does this solution work for some people at the expense of others? Does everyone get something they need so it feels like it will work for them?

Key Strategy	## Create Opportunities for Negotiated Learning
	• Build a cohesive community of learners
Life Skill Connection (See page 112–114)	• Use win-win problem solving to negotiate satisfactory resolutions to conflicts that meet important goals and interests of people involved (24)
Sample Activities, Strategies, and Routines	• Guidlines for Negotiated Learning • Ten Ways to Negotiate in the Classroom

Negotiated learning is about the "give and take" of classroom life with adolescents. It doesn't mean that teachers relinquish authority or stop teaching the standard curriculum. It does mean that where and when it is appropriate, teachers and students engage in shared decision making and problem solving in all aspects of classroom life.

We know issues around respect, authority, and arbitrary demands cause the most tension in secondary classrooms. And it's true that a significant percentage of adolescents will go along with the program, accommodating each teacher's style, standards, rules, and curriculum without complaint or confrontation. Yet, for lots of other students, disengagement and resentment begin on the first day of school, when teachers lay out "how it's going to be" for the rest of the year, with little room for student input and even less room for flexibility.

A key aspect of negotiated learning is shifting orientation from My Classroom to Our Classroom and Your or My Problem to Our Problem. When students are involved in decision making they become more accountable for their own behavior. As you provide more opportunities and support for making decisions, both you and the students reap the benefits of a more productive learning environment. Ultimately, a teacher's role is not to decide things for young people, but to help them see that they have lots of possibilities as they develop the capacity to make good choices throughout their lives.

15

Guidelines for Negotiated Learning

1. There is rarely just one way to do things in the classroom. Negotiated classrooms offer lots of choices and opportunities for shared decision making. Teachers who negotiate are willing to let go of preconceived blueprints and are committed to exploring alternatives that meet important goals and common interests.

2. Most classroom conflicts and disagreements can be handled through problem solving rather than punishment. The disciplinary focus is on how to keep agreements and change undesirable behaviors, rather than on who is breaking the rule.

3. Teachers and students seem to feel better about themselves and each other when everyone is clear about boundaries—identifying what's negotiable and what's not, what's on the "not okay" list for teachers and students, and what special needs, constraints, or criteria must be considered as you negotiate together.

4. Shared decision making means sharing the responsibility—students are expected to take a more active role in their own learning and in the day-to-day functioning of class.

5. Negotiated learning works best in a climate where people are reassured that mistakes are part of the process, that nothing will ever be perfect, and where "good enough" is sometimes enough.

6. Student and teacher assessments, informal check-ins, and discussions about how things are working are essential features of the negotiation process.

7. Teach the language of win-win. (page 336)

8. Use the A, B, C, D, E problem-solving procedure (pages 341–343) for group negotiations.

9. Keep these negotiation guidelines in mind:

   - Negotiation is a voluntary process; you can't coerce anyone to negotiate;

   - Create a positive climate;

   - Clarify positions (what someone demands—it's the only way to get what you want) and interests (underlying needs and concerns—the "whys" behind the position);

   - Identify your goals (short-term and long-term) that satisfy mutual interests;

   - Be willing to seek alternative solutions that are different from original positions;

   - Develop criteria for a good solution that will meet some important interests of everyone involved;

   - Be respectful of value differences—you can't change people's values, but you can change people's behavior.

Ten Ways to Negotiate in the Classroom

1. Prioritize and negotiate the topics of study in a particular learning unit, knowing that it's impossible to study every topic you'd like to investigate. Or offer a "my turn, your turn" approach—"I choose one story, novel, topic, or issue and you choose one."

2. When you are required to teach required material that students find exceptionally boring and tedious, negotiate how you will all get through learning it. For example, you could explore how the group wants to attack it—a small dose everyday or an intense marathon.

3. Make class decisions about the sequence of learning units—in many cases, the arbitrary order of curriculum units is just that.

4. Negotiate the number of pages of texts or novels students agree to read per week.

5. Negotiate learning contracts with individual students.

6. Invite students to negotiate a package of review activities before a test or exam.

7. Negotiate test and project deadline days as you and the students consider other events and due dates in the next week or so.

8. Negotiate how to use limited resources and equipment in class.

9. Negotiate procedures for how things are done in class. Develop classroom solutions for the mundane problems of classroom life, such as when students don't have pencils and all the materials needed for class (See *Getting Classroom Management RIGHT*, Chapter 5).

10. After the first quarter, discuss the learning strategies that students found most and least helpful, interesting, and engaging. Negotiate what you will do more of and less of for the next quarter.

15

Use Class Meetings to Support and Maintain a High-Functioning Group

Key Strategy	• Build a cohesive community of learners
Life Skill Connection (See page 112–114)	• "Read" dynamics in a group; assess group skills accurately; identify problems; generate, evaluate, and implement informed solutions that meet the needs of the group (34) • Use a variety of strategies to make decisions democratically (35)
Sample Activities, Strategies, and Routines	• Setting the Stage for Class Meetings • Class Meeting Types • Suggested Procedure for Problem-Solving Meetings • Bringing Issues of Concern to a Larger Audience • Help Students Represent Their Ideas Effectively

The class meeting is the support structure for the learning community that you and your students create. It's the vehicle for dealing with all things that affect how the group functions. Several features set class meetings apart from other learning structures:

- Students take primary responsibility for generating the agenda and facilitating activities for class meeting.

- Students are expected to practice effective communication and problem-solving skills as participants and facilitators.

- Students play a primary role in solving problems and making decisions about issues addressed in class meeting.

Class meeting serves many purposes. One of the most important is creating a special time and space to confront and solve problems that impact the group—whether it's too much noise during work periods, issues around name calling and teasing, or problems with meeting deadlines.

Equally important, however, are class meetings that provide opportunities for students to do things that strengthen their desire and capacity to be a high-functioning group.

Setting the Stage for Class Meetings

- Develop specific, positive guidelines for facilitating and participating in class meeting.

- Meet in a circle or square where everyone can see everyone else.

- Create an agenda that becomes a routine.

- Review the agenda and identify the purpose and specific goals of the meeting.

- Facilitate the meeting (see the seven activity meeting types described below).

- Solicit feedback about the meeting before you close.

- Invite students to take various roles as they become more comfortable: class meeting facilitator, summarizer, note taker, time keeper, feedbacker, activity leader, etc.

Class Meeting Types

1. **Dialogue:** The goal of this meeting is to provide a safe space to raise concerns, share feelings and perspectives, and gain deeper understanding of issues and concerns raised by students or the teacher.

2. **Problem Solving:** The goal of this meeting is to use negotiation and problem-solving strategies to make decisions and resolve issues of concern and interest that affect the group and the learning environment.

3. **Hypothetical Discussions:** The goal of this activity is to discuss hypothetical situations or case studies as a way to anticipate and generate solutions to problems before they happen. ("If this happens, then _____.")

4. **Skill Building:** The goal of this meeting is to learn or revisit essential communication, conflict resolution, and problem-solving skills that are necessary for effective group functioning.

5. **Group Maintenance:** The goal of this meeting is to provide maintenance and support for the group. These meetings usually involve group goal setting, check-ins, assessment, planning, and celebrations.

6. **School Citizenship:** The goals of this meeting are to gather, disseminate, and share information about schoolwide rules, policies, events, and projects; participate in specific tasks related to official school business and stewardship; and participate in specific tasks that promote school spirit and a positive school climate.

7. **Crisis Meetings:** The goal of this meeting is to address situations that require immediate intervention and attention in a serious, sensitive, and supportive way. Crisis meetings are an important vehicle for reducing tension, restoring order, dealing with a critical concern, or providing caring and support for students impacted by a crisis.

Suggested Procedure for Problem-Solving Meetings

Although you want to communicate your expectation that students will become comfortable facilitating class meetings over time, you will probably want to model this procedure two or three times in the beginning of the course. To make good on this commitment to involve students, you may want to invite three or four volunteers who are interested in facilitating meetings to be part of a class meeting planning group. This communicates that you and your students are partners in class meetings from the beginning; it gives a small group the tasks of reviewing, deciding, and planning agendas; and it allows students to be part of a process that will prepare them to facilitate meetings effectively.

An A, B, C, D, E procedure is used here that is similar to other problem-solving protocols in this guide. The teacher, a teacher and student together, or two students can facilitate the problem-solving process.

After you bring the class together, the facilitator reviews the agenda and identifies the purpose of the class meeting.

Assess the Situation and Ask, What's the Problem?

Invite two or three people (teacher and students) to describe how they see the problem and why they think it's a problem. Ask the class if they have other thoughts about the problem—how they feel about the situation, what's not working, why it's important to solve the problem, etc. Remind students that this is not a time to point fingers, scapegoat, or criticize individuals. The task is to stay focused on the problem and problem behaviors—not attack individuals. Form a clear statement of the problem and the goal for solving the problem. Write this on the board.

The problem is _____. A good solution will enable us to _____.

Brainstorm Solutions

Invite the class to brainstorm potential solutions to the problem. Picture what the situation would look like if it were solved. Do this without criticizing or evaluating anything suggested.

Consider Each Choice Carefully

Review the solutions with the class. How does each choice meet the needs and interests of everyone involved? What are the benefits of each choice? What are the negative constraints and limitations? Is the choice respectful, responsible, and reasonable? Cross out the choices that the group feels are the least effective.

Decide on Your Best Choice and Do It

Discuss the remaining choices and come to agreement on the best solution. Be mindful that the best choice might include a combination of several possible solutions. Invite students to share their preferred solutions and the reasons for their choices. Encourage as many students as possible to speak, even if their comments are in agreement with others who have already spoken. This is the way you begin to get a good "read" on the direction the groups seems to want to go.

Summarize the comments and state what the group seems to think are the most important things to incorporate in the best choice. Use any of the following decision-making protocols to reach final agreement. As much as possible during this process, let the students be in charge. The more they feel like the owners of the solution, the more likely it is to work.

- **Reaching Consensus:** Propose the solution that looks like the people's choice. Say, "This looks like the solution that has the most agreement. If there's anyone who has serious objections, this is the time to speak up and tell us what changes would make this work for you." Solicit any other changes or edits until it looks like you have got the agreement of the group. Do a final consensus check by asking students to raise a hand if they fully support it as the best solution; put one thumb up if it's good enough for now; or thumb in the middle if they're not crazy about it but can live with it.

- **Straw Poll:** If the group has narrowed the field to two or three final ideas, ask people to vote for their #1 preference. If there is a clear winner, modify it until the solution works for everyone.

- **Prioritize Ideas:** If the solution involves a set of recommendations, give each student three sticker dots to place on the three ideas they like the best. The ideas with the greatest number of sticker dots become the highest priority to implement.

- **Small-Group Proposal:** If all of the information feels unwieldy—if there are opposi-tional solutions with strong support—ask for a few volunteers to consider all of the data and perspectives and make a proposal to the group.

Have the class or a small group plan precisely how the solution will be implemented. The class should also be able to suggest ways to evaluate how effectively the solution achieves the goal for solving the problem.

Evaluate Your Choice after You Have Implemented It

At a later class meeting, or as a gathering or closing, evaluate the decision the group made. What happened? Did it work? What evidence do you have that it worked effectively? Is there anything that would help the group implement the solution more effectively?

Bringing Issues of Concern to a Larger Audience

Sometimes issues come up that students would like to take to a larger audience. I have worked with hundreds of students who have used the following process successfully to prepare their case and present it to faculty associations, student-faculty forums, school leadership teams, parent groups, and student government.

Presentation Steps

1. Identify the problem and the desired goal or outcome. Share five examples (without naming names) that illustrate the problem so other students and adults will understand your perspective. If the problem is solved, what would be different? Example: Problem: Students are suspended unfairly. Desired Goal/Outcome: Rules for suspension are fair and clear to everyone and apply to all students the same way.

2. Why is this a problem? How does it affect students and staff? How does it make people feel? How does this problem get in the way of learning, being successful at school, or feeling positive about school? Offer time for questions from the audience.

3. Develop four or five detailed suggestions that would help the school solve the problem. Make sure your solutions meet the Five R criteria. Is the solution **Related** to the problem? **Respectful** to all students and adults involved? **Responsible** so that everyone involved agrees to something constructive to make it work? **Reasonable** so that you are not asking anyone to do anything hurtful, illegal, unethical, silly, or offensive? **Realistic** so you have the time, resources, information, and expertise to make it happen? Offer time for ques-tions from the audience.

4. Name three action steps that need to happen in order to implement your suggestions.

15

Help Students Represent Their Ideas Effectively

Use the following questions to help your students begin to consider the factors in writing a persuasive speech and defending their ideas. You can use these as a basis for a handout, or read them aloud for them to consider.

1. Do you have an opener (a compelling story, incident, quote that sets the context and personalizes the problem so that the audience understands how this issue affects real people)?

2. Do you define and describe the problem clearly in ways that illuminate the conflict, identify what's not working, or describe what needs are not being met?

3. Have you given the audience the facts (specific examples, data, statistics, comparisons, illustrations, anecdotes, etc. that connect conditions and situations to real individuals and groups)?

4. Have you told the audience why "doing something" is important? What might happen if nothing is done? How does this problem affect the community, the nation, the world?

5. Have you shared suggestions for solutions? Do you compare this solution to other possible solutions? Why is this a better idea? What needs to be done? What is the plan? Who will make it happen? How much will it cost? Where will the money come from?

6. Have you made an appeal to your audience? What do you want your audience to think about, reconsider, or do after they listen to your speech?

Key Strategy	Make Group Talk Good Talk
	• Build a cohesive community of learners
Life Skill Connection (See page 112–114)	• Exercise assertiveness; communicate your thoughts, feelings, and needs to others (18) • Listen actively to demonstrate to others that they have been understood (19) • Empathize; understand and accept another person's feelings, perspectives, point of view (22)
Sample Activities, Strategies, and Routines	• Guidelines for Group Discussion • Use Dialogue Potocols to Deconstruct Active Listening • Pair-Shares • Listening Lab • Paraphrasing Circles • Opinion Continuum • Fish Bowl • Practicing and Assessing Good Talk

During Discussion

- Sit in a circle
- Use a talking stick
- Paraphrase previous speaker
- Say, "I agree _____ and..."
- Write first, then speak
- Use a speaker's list
- Use wait time
- Check for understanding

Guidelines for Group Discussion

- **Limit the size of the group** involved in a dialogue. Divide the group in half using two facilitators, or provide a different activity for the other half of the group so that each student has more opportunities to participate.

- **Sit in a circle** or horseshoe shape so that everyone can see each other.

- **Identify behaviors that shut down discussion** and make some students afraid to speak; identify behaviors that encourage all students to feel comfortable speaking.

- **Prepare students for oral presentations** by creating guidelines for being a responsive audience before listening to oral presentations or guest speakers.

- **Prepare a set of questions beforehand** that students have helped to generate. You might want to prioritize questions or identify three or four that students are eager to discuss.

- **Use a speakers' list** to avoid constant hand raising and track who wants to speak. Rotate students who manage the speakers' list.

- **Use a talking stick** or small stuffed toys or soft fabric ball when students are involved in a whole-group or small-group discussion—the only person who can speak is the person with the object.

15

- **Use talking chips** (plastic poker chips) to ensure that students share the air time. Each student receives two or three chips; when students speak they set aside their chips in the upper-right corner of their desk.

- **Increase "wait time" before inviting students to speak.** Silence encourages deliberative thinking. Use index cards or create a dialogue response sheet that students can use to compose their thoughts before they speak, jot down follow-up questions, and reflect on the dialogue when it's over.

- **Limit talk time** to less than a minute ("Twenty seconds please."). Or limit the number of times each person can speak ("You've spoken twice already. I want to hear what others have to say.") For students who always have to have the last word or who want to speak ad nauseam, say, "That's an interesting point. Let's see what others have to say."

- **Use constraints for who can speak at any given time** by inviting different subgroups to respond to different questions—boys, girls, certain letters of the alphabet, sides of the room, etc.

- **Listen for and post verbal encouragers** that students use to encourage each other to speak during discussions and cooperative group work.

- **Remind students about agreements/guidelines.** When students are talking out of turn or engaging in sidebar conversations, remind them of the agreements/guidelines you have made about how the group talks and listens during whole-group discussions and presentations.

- **Have a procedure in place for students who talk during whole-group listening activities.** Your procedure might sound like this: "The first time I notice that you're not focused on the speaker and the task, I will give you a nonverbal cue, remind you of our guidelines, or assign you a quick-write task to help you focus. The second time it happens during the same class, I will ask you to sit somewhere else where you will be less distracted."

- **Encourage students to empathize with another person's circumstance** in a current life situation, in a piece of literature, or in a historical conflict. Ask, "How do you imagine this person feels?" or "How would you feel if you were in that situation?" or "Why might someone feel (frustrated, angry, confused, upset, etc.) in that situation?"

- **Help students clarify their thinking** and provide more detail using these questions and openers:

  - Tell us more about that.

  - Can you say more?

  - What other thoughts do you have about _____?

  - Is there anything else you want to say about _____?

  - What do you think that's about?

  - Do you think other people see this the same way?

  - What else should we know about _____?

- **Encourage students to clarify their viewpoints.** Are they speaking from their own experience or making observations about what they have read, heard, or seen?

- **Remind students that listening doesn't equal agreement.** Respectful listening isn't about agreeing or disagreeing with the speaker—it's about taking in what someone says and communicating that you have understood them. Respectful speaking is about communicating your own thoughts and feelings in ways that your audience will hear and understand.

- **Discuss the differences between dialogue and debate.** Many students never talk because they always feel like they are in the middle of somebody else's contest! With the whole class, brainstorm a list of the differences between dialogue and debate. Think about how the goals differ, how people attend and respond differently, and the strengths and limitations of each type of discourse.

- **If the dialogue starts to feel combative** or emotionally intense, stop for a minute and do a feeling/reality check. Ask how people are feeling about what's being said. How do others see this issue? Who else wants to respond before we move on? Is there anyone else who has another opinion? Is there anyone else who agrees?

- **Remind students that changing positions isn't backing down**, but rather involves listeners in reassessing their views after taking in more information and perspectives.

15

- **Loaded, provocative, or negative language heats up tensions** and sucks positive energy from the room. You may want to encourage the group to think about how they want to call attention to negative language. For example, a student might say, "I'm not sure that language helps us better understand _____," and then request that a word or phrase be replaced with less emotionally charged language. Or say, "That crosses the line. Could you use language that's more neutral and less charged?"

Use Dialogue Protocols to Deconstruct Active Listening

Teachers ask all the time, "How do we really practice and assess active listening?" One solution is to use various dialogue protocols that focus on very specific active listening skills. Dialogue protocols help students pay closer attention to the conversation. Structured discussions have the advantage of slowing down thinking, thus improving listening and encouraging participants to choose more carefully what they say and how they say it. Experiment with these process suggestions to determine what structures work best for different groups and different types of discussions.

Here are suggestions that call for students to use specific active listening skills:

Active Listening involves...

- Nonverbal attending—demonstrating your full attention through your body language and facial expression

- Interested silence when you only listen

- Verbal encouragers that invite someone to continue speaking

- Restating what people say so that they know they've been understood

- Checking for accuracy of understanding

- Empathizing by reflecting a speaker's feelings in ways that acknowledge the person's emotional state and the feelings he/she attaches to the issue being discussed

- Asking open-ended questions that give the speaker a chance to clarify his/her thinking, provide more information, or discuss underlying needs and concerns

- Summarizing key ideas, solutions, issues

- **Read aloud every week.**

- **Use paired reading** when students are working with challenging texts. Partners take turns reading the text in small sections and then the other person paraphrases what was just read.

- **Try a "trio read and respond."** Students form trios and take turns reading the text with these two instructions: (1) You can't read more than a page when it's your turn; and (2) You stop reading when you've found something you want to discuss, something you're confused about, something that feels important to underscore, something that triggers a question, something that connects to the rest of the text, or something that connects to your own experience.

- **Time minilectures.** 10 to 15 minutes is about the limit for good retention. Students tend to be far more attentive when they know the lecture will be over soon!

- **Check for understanding** by inviting a volunteer to paraphrase instructions. Or ask students to pair up to clarify their understanding of an assignment, directions, a problem that is posed; then invite a student to restate the problem, assignment, directions in her own words for the whole group.

- **Every 10 to 15 minutes, take 2 to review.** After a minilecture, read-aloud, or video, have students work individually, in pairs, or in home groups to review what they understood, fill in the gaps from their notes independently, or respond to two or three questions.

- **Start discussion with a "go-round"** using an open-ended question where everyone who wants to respond gets to speak before the group before students raise questions or shift to back-and-forth dialogue.

- **Use partner paraphrasing** to practice listening for understanding. One partner explains a problem or process or shares her/his perspective on a topic or question. The other person writes down the explanation as accurately as possible. Then partners switch roles. This strategy is effective when you want students to explain a mathematical solution step by step, summarize a lab experiment, rehearse responses to essay questions, or describe causal relationships linked to a historical event.

15

- **Use conversation movers** that strengthen both connections among the participants and the collaborative quality of the conversation. In their book *Discussion as a Way of Teaching*, Stephen Brookfield and Stephen Preskill suggest distributing a card to each participant that contains one conversation mover. Participants are invited to make an intentional effort to use their conversation mover during the discussion.

  - Ask a question or make a comment that shows you are interested in what another person has said.

  - Ask a question or make a comment that encourages someone else to elaborate on what they said. "Can you say more about _____?"

  - Use positive body language to communicate your interest in what others are saying (leaning forward in the direction of the speaker, focusing your full attention on the speaker, nodding when you agree, furrowing your brow when you're listening to something new or puzzling, etc.).

  - Make a comment that underscores the link between two people's contributions and make the link explicit in your comment.

  - Disagree with someone in a respectful way.

  - Invite others to share their points of view about an issue that's been raised. "Do others agree or have different perspectives on _____?"

  - Make a comment indicating that you found another person's ideas interesting or useful and be specific about why that is the case.

  - Contribute a comment that builds on what someone else said. "I'd like to add something about that..."

  - Paraphrase/restate an important point that someone made before sharing your own thoughts.

  - Pose a different way to think about the issue on the table. "Here's another way to think about..." "I wonder if..."

  - Ask a question that probes the assumptions of a speaker. "What are you assuming about...?" "What else do you believe about...?" "How do you know...?"

  - Make a summary observation that takes into account several people's observations that seem to touch on a common theme in the discussion.

  - Express your appreciation for the insights you gained from the discussion. "I'd never thought about..." "Your comment about _____ helped me look at _____ differently."

- At the end of the discussion invite people to share the conversation movers they used and debrief how and why using these conversation movers affected the discussion and their sense of being a group. You might post conversation movers as a reminder or distribute the list to students so that they can choose one or two to practice using intentionally.

- **Before students rush to argue,** ask them first to identify something they agree with before they share their perspective. Say, "I agree with _____ and I'd like to add/ask _____."

- **Close with summary points** linked to what students just heard or viewed by (1) pairing up and writing down three key points to remember; (2) assigning numbers to students so that there are four 1's, four 2's, four 3's, and so on. At the close of the lecture or discussion ask each group to put their heads together and prepare a summary or a response to their assigned question. Take three minutes for groups to talk it through and then share responses with the whole group; or (3) taking a two-minute time-out to pair/share, write about, or reflect as a group on these questions: "What issues are clearer for you? What's still vague or confusing? What are the two or three things that have been said that have helped to deepen your understanding of _____?"

Pair-Shares

This is a simple technique to get everyone engaged in conversation at the same time. Ideally it is a way to brainstorm, begin discussion on a compelling question, frame a topic or study question, exchange first thoughts, or assess what people know.

Directions:

Students pair up in twos facing each other in order to bring their knowledge, opinions, and experiences to the topic at hand. The facilitator frames the issue and invites one person in each pair to speak for one to two minutes in response to the question. Then the other partner speaks for one to two minutes, thus reversing the roles of listener and speaker.

It is important to remind students that when they are in the role of listener, their goal is to focus their complete attention on the speaker and listen in interested silence.

After the pair-share, invite students to share their own thoughts or paraphrase their partner's thoughts as a way to continue discussion. You might want to use newsprint to record various student responses that reflect a range of ideas and opinions.

15

Listening Lab

A listening lab is a structured small-group experience in which people deepen their understanding of each other's perspectives through speaking and listening. Students who are reticent about speaking in a large group find this format a less intimidating way to share their thoughts with others. In groups of three to five, students take turns responding to the same question. Each person has a specified amount of time (45 to 90 seconds) to respond. When one student speaks, other students are expected to give that student their full attention and interested silence. Listening labs are not a time for back-and-forth conversation, but rather provide all students with an opportunity to share their perspectives and experiences without being interrupted.

Directions:

Divide students into groups of three to five. Have students circle up so they can see each other. Here are some guidelines for participating in a listening lab.

1. Speak from your own experience (your thoughts, feelings, and perspectives).

2. Sit with the silence if one person finishes speaking before time is up.

3. ONLY LISTEN; don't comment on what the speaker says.

4. It's okay to pass if you need more time to think or would rather not respond.

5. Be aware of your own comfort zone. Share what feels comfortable to share.

6. What's said in the group stays in the group. Can we make an agreement that what we share among ourselves in small groups will stay within the group?

Ask for a volunteer from each group who is willing to speak first. Have volunteers raise their hands so that you know when all groups are ready to begin. State the question. Then clarify the question using an example that illustrates various ways students might respond to it. Set your timer for about 45 seconds. Repeat the question and say, "It's time for the first person to speak." When time is up, say, "It's time for the second person to speak." Continue until each student in each group has had a chance to respond to the question. The first time you use a listening lab, you might want to ask students,

- What was this process like for you?

- What did you notice about how you were listening?

- What did it feel like to be listened to in this way?

- What made this easy or challenging for you?

Sample Questions:

- **Literature:** In groups of four, each student takes on the role of a character and responds to a series of questions from the perspective of that character.

- **Science:** Discuss social and ethical consequences of environmental policies.

- **Any subject:** Use listening labs as a way to review essay questions, rehearse and prepare for discussions, share project proposals or project findings.

- **Any subject:** Use a listening lab before exams so students can share perspectives on what makes exam time stressful; what they do to relax and focus; what kinds of "self-talk" and beliefs about themselves will help them feel confident and prepared.

- **Personal Perspectives:** Use any of the gathering and closing questions on pages 310–317 or the reflection questions on pages 232–237.

Paraphrasing Circles

This is a variation of the listening lab format. The goal is to use paraphrasing (accurately restating a person's thoughts in one's own words) to ensure that everyone who speaks is understood. Each group of three or four students sits in a circle facing each other. You might want all groups to discuss the same issue or questions, or you can invite groups to choose which two to three questions they want to discuss from a larger list of questions.

In paraphrasing circles, the first student in the group responds to the chosen question without being interrupted. Then the second student paraphrases what the previous student said and checks for accuracy. The first person can correct or clarify the restatement at this time. Then the second student responds to the same question without being interrupted. The third person paraphrases the second person, checks for accuracy, and shares her/his perspective on the question. This process is repeated until everyone has had a turn.

You might want to add one more part to each round. Invite one student from each small group to summarize students' perspectives by reporting to the larger group. Or you might invite one student to record any questions that arise after everyone in the small group has spoken.

15

Opinion Continuum

Moving opinion polls are a way to get students up and moving as they place themselves along a STRONGLY AGREE to STRONGLY DISAGREE continuum according to their opinions about specific statements. The most powerful aspect of this exercise is the insight, new to many students, that people can disagree without fighting—in fact, that people can listen to various points of view respectfully and even rethink their own opinions upon hearing the views of others. Create a corridor of space in your room, from one end to the other end, that is long enough and wide enough to accommodate your whole class. Make two large signs and post them on opposite sides of the room:

Strongly Agree   **Strongly Disagree**

Explain to students, "You will be participating in a moving opinion poll. Each time you hear a statement, you are to move to the place along the imaginary line between 'strongly agree' and 'strongly disagree' that most closely reflects your opinion. If you strongly disagree, you will move all the way to that side of the room. If you strongly agree, you will move all the way to the other side. You can also place yourself anywhere in the middle, especially if you have mixed feelings about the question."

"After you have placed yourselves along the continuum, I will invite people to share why they are standing where they are. This is not a time to debate or grill each other. Rather, this is a way to hear what people are thinking and get a sense of the different ways people perceive the issue."

When you do this activity, begin with a statement that indicates noncontroversial preferences like, "Chocolate is the best ice cream flavor in the world." Then introduce statements related to a topic you're exploring in your course work. You might want to "muddy the water" by modifying statements slightly, using different qualifiers, conditions, and contexts to see if students' opinions shift. For example, one statement might be, "Local communities should have a general curfew of midnight for all teens under 18." Another statement might be, "Local communities should have a school night curfew of midnight for all teens under 18."

Fish Bowl

A "fish bowl" is one way to engage the entire class in one small-group dialogue. This technique is especially useful when emotions are heated or when students bring vastly different perspectives to a controversial topic. Invite five to seven students to this "fish bowl" conversation. Ask them to make a circle with their chairs in the middle of the room. Try to ensure that this group reflects diverse points of view on the issue being discussed.

Ask everyone else to make a circle of chairs around the fish bowl (you will have a smaller circle within a bigger circle). Only people in the fish bowl can speak, thus the process facilitates a kind of sustained, focused listening that is seldom experienced in secondary classrooms.

Here's one way to facilitate a fish bowl:

1. The facilitator asks a question and invites the students in the fish bowl to speak to the particular topic or question in a "go-around." Each student in the fish bowl speaks to the question without being interrupted.

2. Then the facilitator designates a specific amount of time for clarifying questions and further comments from students in the fish bowl.

3. After 15 minutes or so, invite students from the larger circle who would like to be part of the fish bowl to join the conversation by tapping a fish bowl student on the shoulder and changing places with that student. Make a request that students don't join in all at once, but leave a small space of time between "tap-ins."

4. Continue the fish bowl, introducing other questions when it feels like the right time to move on.

Practicing and Assessing Good Talk

A. **Ask good questions.**

Good open-ended questions spark curiosity, call for a variety of responses, and invite students to defend their opinions and construct their own meanings.

Here are three approaches to crafting good questions with your students:

#1

Factual questions have one correct answer. Answers might be simple and easy to find or they could be deep and complex, requiring intensive research—it all depends on the question. "What is _____?" "How does _____ work?" "What happened to _____?"

Interpretive questions have more than one answer. These questions are often the focus of text-based discussions because they require us to support our thinking with evidence from the text. "Why does _____?" "What is meant by _____?" "How is _____ different from/similar to _____?" "What influenced the decision to _____?" "Why does _____?" "What are his motives for _____?" "Why would _____ say _____?" "Are there other reasons why _____?" "What's the connection between _____ and _____?" "How do you know _____?" "What supports your thinking about this?" "What would be an example of _____?" "Could you explain _____?" "How does this relate to that?" "What prompted you to say that?" "What do we know about _____?" "What don't we know about _____?"

Evaluative questions have no wrong answers. These questions solicit our opinions, beliefs, and personal perspectives. "Is it better to _____ or _____?" "What's your opinion about _____?" "What might be the best solution for _____?" "Is _____ wrong?" "Is it acceptable to _____?" "Who's your favorite _____?" "Should all citizens be required to _____?"

15

#2

Clarifying questions ask for further explanation and information: "What else happened?" "When/where/how?"

Analytic questions require us to judge the information and reasoning processes being presented: "What's missing, misleading, or confusing?" "Why would someone consider this to be the right action to take?" "What's the reasoning behind _____?" "How does the argument hold up?"

Speculative questions are about possibilities: "What might have happened if _____?" "What might be the consequences of _____?" "If _____, then _____?" "Is it possible to _____?" "What options does _____ have?" "What would it look like if _____?"

Reflection and closing questions are about our own thinking and insights: "What does this remind me of?" "How does this connect to my world?" "What did I learn that was new?" "This happened a hundred years ago: why are we studying it today?" "After reading and discussing _____, how has your thinking changed?" "What's the question you want to continue to ponder?"

#3

Essential questions frame a discussion, a unit of study, or an entire course. They often require us to make a decision or develop a plan of action. "Is it acceptable to _____?" "Did _____ make the right decision?" "Should all wetlands in the U.S. be preserved and protected?" "Is U.S. history more about fulfilled promises or broken dreams?" "How does an organism's structure enable it to survive in its environment?"

Foundation questions include all the questions we might ask that help us search out information and possible responses to essential questions.

B. **Use assessment questions to debrief discussions.** Generate criteria for what makes a discussion engaging and productive. Brainstorm questions that will help the group assess the quality and process of small- and large-group discussions:

- Were all points of view heard? Were they all respected? How do you know?

- Are there any points of view that we've left out?

- What new ideas, questions, and facts were introduced into the discussion that complicated your thinking about this issue?

- Were there any new insights or information that shifted your thinking during the discussion?

- Was there any question or comment that really grabbed your attention and made you stop and think, reevaluate, or want to find out more?

- Are there any important questions that haven't been asked yet?

C. **Identify specific kinds of thinking you're looking for in students' responses to a particular topic or issue:**

- Name what you think you know and/or understand;

- Explore what you don't know and/or don't understand;

- Explain your reasoning using specific examples;

- Make connections to your own experience;

- Make connections to other ideas in the text or discussion;

- Identify what you agree with and disagree with and why;

- Compare, contrast, and summarize different perspectives, positions, assumptions, and conflicting viewpoints;

- Identify patterns and trends;

- Categorize information;

- Link generalizations, conclusions, and explanations to specific evidence;

- Pose possibilities or alternative solutions.

Use a simple rubric to assess students' responses:

3 = complete, fully articulated response
2 = adequate response
1 = partial response
0 = inappropriate; not applicable

D. **Use volunteer "feedbackers"** who watch and listen during a discussion, assessing both the substance and the flow of the conversation. Feedbackers can report to the group, naming specific ways in which the group met the goals and criteria for the discussion and offering suggestions for ways to improve the discussion next time.

E. **Develop text-based seminar guidelines.** Text-based seminars are different from more freewheeling dialogues. The primary purpose is to understand and make meaning of the text. Therefore, all comments and questions should emerge from and link to particular passages in the text. In other words, "What comments or questions can help me and others fully understand the text?" Text-based seminars usually begin in one of three ways: (1) students choose passages to read that trigger their thoughts and questions; (2) students generate questions; (3) a teacher generates the framing question.

15

Gene Thompson-Grove, of the National School Reform Faculty suggests some special guidelines to ensure that text-based seminars stay true to their purpose:[1]

- Refer to the text and challenge others to go to the text. Use page numbers, wait until everyone has found the quote before you begin speaking, and read aloud the part of the text to which you are referring.

- Listen actively and, if it helps, take notes.

- Don't step on others' talk. Allow for silences and pauses. If the conversation is moving too quickly, ask people to slow down.

- Build on what others say. If you plan to change the subject with your thought or comment, ask first if anyone else would like to speak to the topic at hand.

- Let the conversation flow as much as possible, without raising hands or using a speaker's list.

- Converse directly with each other, without going through the facilitator.

- Make the assumptions underlying your comments explicit to others. "Here's why I'm thinking this way. The text says _____ and I think _____."

- Emphasize clarification, amplification, and implications of words, phrases, and ideas. Ask each other questions. Say what you don't understand in the text. "Is the text saying _____ or _____?"

- Watch your own air time, in terms of how often you speak, when you speak, and how much you say.

F.   **Use a rubric to assess the quality of talk in text-based or Socratic seminars:**

Humanities teacher John Trampesh's assessment rubric in Socratic seminar makes it easy to notice and record the quality and frequency of students' responses. John creates a template that can be used for each seminar. This template includes a place to name the topic and text, a list of all students in the seminar, and boxes to record all student responses during the seminar, using these symbols:

C = comment (+ = very deep, = adequate, – = nonsequitur)

Q = question (+ = very deep, = adequate, – = nonsequitur)

T = text-based citation (+ = very deep, = adequate, – = nonsequitur)

I = interrupted speaker

E = energy drain

R = efforts to redirect or refocus discussion

S = summary statement

CHAPTER 16

Practice 6: Provide High Expectations and High Personalized Support

16

Key Strategy	Identify Your Big Goals, Expectations, and Daily Learning Objectives
HH	• Provide high expectations and high personalized support
Life Skill Connection (See page 112–114)	• Set big and little goals and make plans (13)
Sample Activities, Strategies, and Routines	• Lay Out Your Big Goals for the Year • Communicate Daily Learning Goals and Objectives • Use "Doing" Verbs to Frame Classwork and Homework

Students bring fresh hope and old hesitations to every new learning situation. Teachers often bring a short list of critical skills, experiences, and understandings that they want every student to leave with by the end of the class. This is the time to give students an idea of the big picture, the big questions, and the significant experiences that will mark the year. It's also a way to communicate your confidence that everyone can achieve these goals.

In addition, think about the different ways you want to communicate learning goals and objectives every day.

Lay Out Your Big Goals for the Year

Right from the beginning, kids need to know what really matters to you, and they need to know the standards and basic requirements that they are expected to meet in your course. Put this information on posters, so that it's easy to refer to at any time. You might want to insert metal rings through the posters, so that you can hang them from a dowel or wall hooks. This way your posters are accessible and easy to flip over and review. Here are some examples:

Poster Title	Goal	Example
Skills for Learning and Working Together	Identify five or six social skills that you expect everyone to learn and practice in the classroom.	Active listening; expressing and managing feelings; negotiation; using "I-Speak"; and group cooperation skills
Requirements Everyone Needs to Meet	Identify the five most important requirements, exhibitions, or demonstrations that you expect every student to meet in this course. Let students know that you expect them to help each other meet these essential course requirements.	First semester requirements in English: 1) revise and polish three of your best writing pieces 2) correct all spelling, errors, run-ons and fragments on all of your writing 3) explore an issue of your choice using fiction, nonfiction, interviews, art, music, drama, or dance 4) synthesize your findings in a written document 5) prepare a seven-minute presentation for class
When You Leave This Class You Will Be Able to...	Give students a "heads-up" about what matters most to you by asking yourself this question: Before students leave, what are the things that you are determined that everyone will be able to do successfully?	English: You will be able to write paragraphs and papers without using run-ons or fragments. Chemistry: You and a partner will conduct and explain a lab experiment for the class. History: You will be able to defend and illustrate how one individual changed the course of history. History: You will be able to defend why it's important to learn history, using your own stories. Math: You will be able to create your own _____ problems and explain your solutions. Any Course: Each one of you will work with every student in class. Any Course: You will be able to meet important deadlines on time.

16

Poster Title	Goal	Example
How Will You Earn Your Grade?	Give students a clear explanation of how they earn their grades by identifying percentage values of grade components.	____%Practice Work, Editing, Revisions, Corrections ____%Discussion, Demos, Presentations ____%Journals, Reflections, Notes, Evidence of Reading/Study ____%In-Class Labs, Activities, and Group Work ____%Major Written Tests, Projects, Products ____%Habits of Learning
Big Picture Questions	Every course has a few key questions that you probably want students to think about throughout the year: Questions that connect one learning unit to another Questions that reflect the big ideas that are at the heart of your course or investigation Questions that inform major students projects and exams	Use these questions informed by "The Habits of Mind" developed by the faculty of Central Park East School: (Perspective) From whose viewpoint are we reading, seeing, hearing? (Evidence) How do we know what we know? What is the evidence and how reliable is it? (Connections) How are things, people, events connected to each other? How do they fit together? (Speculation) What's old, what's new? Have we run across this before? How else might we look at this? What if...? (Significance) What does it mean? So what? Why does it matter? What difference does it make?

Communicate Daily Learning Goals and Objectives

Consider which questions are important to answer given your goals and objectives for the day:

- What do you expect students to learn, practice, demonstrate in a particular learning activity?

- What do you expect students to do as a result of a specific learning experience?

- What will students do that provides evidence of what they have learned, accomplished, or practiced?

- How do you expect students to learn in a particular activity?

- What academic skills do you expect students to use?

- What habits of learning and self-discipline skills do you expect students to use?

- What communication and problem-solving skills do you expect students to use?

- What group skills do you expect students to use?

- How do you expect students to connect what they do today with what they did yesterday and what they do tomorrow?

Use "Doing" Verbs to Frame Classwork and Homework

An important way to link effort to achievement and performance is to use concrete "doing" verbs to frame all work that students do. Communicate to students the specific learning processes they are expected to use to complete a task. You might want to refer to Anderson and Krathwohl's *A Taxonomy for Learning, Teaching, and Assessing: A Revision of Bloom's Taxonomy of Educational Objectives*; Marzono's *Dimensions of Learning*; and Baron and Sternberg's *Teaching Thinking Skills*.

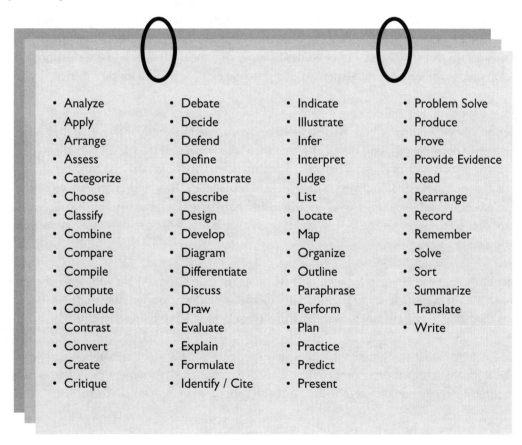

- Analyze
- Apply
- Arrange
- Assess
- Categorize
- Choose
- Classify
- Combine
- Compare
- Compile
- Compute
- Conclude
- Contrast
- Convert
- Create
- Critique
- Debate
- Decide
- Defend
- Define
- Demonstrate
- Describe
- Design
- Develop
- Diagram
- Differentiate
- Discuss
- Draw
- Evaluate
- Explain
- Formulate
- Identify / Cite
- Indicate
- Illustrate
- Infer
- Interpret
- Judge
- List
- Locate
- Map
- Organize
- Outline
- Paraphrase
- Perform
- Plan
- Practice
- Predict
- Present
- Problem Solve
- Produce
- Prove
- Provide Evidence
- Read
- Rearrange
- Record
- Remember
- Solve
- Sort
- Summarize
- Translate
- Write

16

	Create a Culture of Quality and Completion
Key Strategy	Where Every Student Is Expected To Succeed
HH	• Provide high expectations and high personalized support

Life Skill Connection (See page 112–114)	• Prioritize and "chunk" tasks, predict task completion time, and manage time effectively (14) • Work for high personal performance and cultivate your strengths and positive qualities (16) • Assess your skills, competencies, effort, and quality of work accurately (17)

Sample Activities, Strategies, and Routines	• Explore How Effort Produces Success • Monitor Use of Assignment Notebooks • Record and Reflect on Progress Every Week • Show Me the Evidence • Require All Students to Achieve Proficiency on Important Assignments • Expect, Insist on, and Support Completion and Quality

Creating a culture of excellence is not an easy sell to most teenagers, who are immersed in a world where fast gets more play than well done. Even defining academic excellence, proficiency, and mastery can be an elusive proposition for students. It's worth exploring examples of excellence that young people experience in their own lives and solicit from them the criteria that make a sports team, a piece of clothing, a movie, or a meal excellent. In the classroom, develop rubrics for important assignments that describe explicit criteria for proficiency.

For many students, recognizing the differences between excellent and mediocre end products or performances is blurry at best. Ask students to share something in their lives that they have mastered successfully or a skill or talent where they have increased their level of competence. Explore the differences between a personal performance they would describe as lousy and a personal performance that indicates a high level of proficiency. This kind of critique requires lots of practice and the patience to observe and compare different results systematically, with an eye for detail. Students need to look at and discuss a variety of work samples that run the gamut from shoddy to superior quality.

Students also need to develop an accurate assessment of their efforts. What will it take for them to reach a level of proficiency or high performance? Ask students to spell out what specific efforts they think are necessary to earn an A and what kind of effort earns a D.

The point here is that many students will never experience the personal satisfaction and pride that accompany a high level of proficiency unless we create an environment that expects excellence from everyone and we provide the push and support to help them get there.

Explore How Effort Produces Success

The Number Search exercise below takes students through a series of practices and reflections that enable them to increase their scores in successive attempts. Debriefing questions follow the directions.

1. We're going to do an exercise that we'll talk about after we do it.

2. This exercise is a silent one. You see a lot of numbers on the page. You will have one minute to see how many consecutive numbers you can touch on the page, beginning with the number 1.

3. Here's the rule: You need to use your forefinger (show to class) to physically touch the numbers in sequence, beginning with the number 1 (have everyone find number 1 on the page), and touch it with your finger. Then you need to find the number 2 and touch it with your finger, then 3, and so on. When I say STOP, you need to write down how many numbers you touched consecutively.

4. Any questions? GO! (Practice One)

5. Ask everyone to STOP after one minute and write down how many numbers they touched.

6. (Practice Two) Repeat the exercise for one minute and then say STOP.

7. Ask students to turn their papers over so they can't see the numbers.

8. Put this question to the group: "If I give you a minute to experiment and try out strategies that would help you touch more numbers the next time, what strategies would you try? I'll take five suggestions from the group." (You may need to say, "If you had a pencil or marker, what could you do on your paper that might help?")

9. You might also want to ask, "Is there anything you noticed about the placement of the numbers on the page?" There are patterns that can help some people scan for numbers. (For example, left side-odd numbers and right side-even numbers.)

10. Now give everyone a minute to use their strategies to practice (Practice Three). This time don't record the numbers you touch. This practice lets you experiment and try out your strategies.

11. (Practice Four) Now do it one more time. GO. .

12. Now write down the total numbers you touched this time. Now subtract your first total from your last total.

13. Ask students how many more numbers they touched the last time. For students who did not touch more numbers, ask them if they have any thoughts about what happened and what they might do differently next time.

16

Debriefing Questions:

- What did you like about this activity?

- What did you notice about yourself and how you approached this task?

- Let's review WHAT we did together in this exercise (many practices, had time to discuss, share ideas, experiment with strategies to improve, we recorded data so we could assess what we did).

- What choices did you have in HOW you accomplished the task? (We could use any strategy we wanted. If we heard another student's idea in the discussion that might work, we could try that. We were competing against ourselves, not others. We focused on our own progress.)

- What aspects of the exercise helped you to be successful? (I got to practice, choose from many strategies, etc.) **All the things you mentioned describe EFFORT—the things you do that will help you successfully complete a task or achieve a goal.**

- How did you feel BEFORE you completed the first round? After you completed the fourth round?

- In what ways did this exercise help you understand your learning style or how you approach a task? What are one or two aha's that helped you improve?

- What strategy did you use? How did you increase your ABILITY to do this task? (Through effort and practice.)

- What's something you're proud of doing well that required a lot of practice?

- Which strategy do you think was best?

- How can you apply this process to other tasks?

- What, if anything, would you do differently if you were to do this again?

- Think about how EFFORT and ABILITY affect achievement.

Touch the numbers

1st time _____ 2nd time _____ 4th time _____

1   53   39   16   54

28

27   15   40   6

2

13   51   5   26   52

17

41   14   50   30

3

29   38

25

37   49   18   4   42

55

7   23   36   34

46

31   12

35   43   22   44   24

19   57

11   8   32   58

47   45   20   56

33   60

21   9   59   48   10

Monitor Use of Assignment Notebooks

Many schools require middle and high school students to use planning calendars or assignment notebooks. Some organizationally savvy students already use calendars or task lists. However, those who are organizationally challenged (this includes many adults and most adolescents) can benefit from exercises and writing prompts that help make this practice a tool for success. Try any of the following ideas for making assignment notebooks a meaningful tool for goal setting, planning, reflection, and assessment.

- Provide time for writing and reflecting on weekly or quarterly goals, making task lists, and creating timelines for long projects. Coach students so their lists and goals are clear, specific, and realistic.

- Have students create symbols, color coding, or graphics that help them plan ahead and look back on individual tasks or their weekly calendar. The following descriptors can help students become more aware of themselves as learners.

____ Easy to do

____ Hard to do

____ Fun to do

____ Done!

____ Not finished yet

____ A major accomplishment in my life—hooray for me!

____ Do first

____ Do last—if I don't have time, save it for later

____ Don't do this late at night

____ Don't do this early in the morning

____ I'm stuck and need help

____ Work with a study buddy

____ STOP! I'm in big trouble here

____ Big effort with big pay off

____ Shoddy effort and the poor results to prove it

____ If I get this done, I will feel loads of relief

____ If I don't get this done, I'm going to feel guilty, stressed, or mad at myself

____ This requires serious planning, lots of time, and my undivided attention

____ I need to check in with someone who will hold me accountable (supervise or nag me), or this will never get done

____ An overload week—get ready to buckle down!

____ A stellar week—I kept on track every day!

- After a week of using assignment notebooks, ask students to share how this effort has helped them.

- Take time during class for students to review, edit, and supplement the notes and reminders they have recorded in their assignment notebooks.

- Ask students to predict how long it will take them to complete various assignments. The next day, ask students to report whether their predictions were accurate or off the mark.

- Give each student a sticky note to stick next to an important assignment or project that they have not yet started or completed. Ask students to write down a deadline date for completion and three specific steps that will help them complete the task.

- Encourage parents to sign assignment notebooks on a weekly basis and write little notes that congratulate and encourage their children.

- If you are in the habit of checking all or some of your students' assignment notebooks, jot down your own comments, kudos, and questions in their notebooks. Simple statements can be very supportive. "Tell me how this project turned out when you've completed it." "Wow, this looks like a heavy-duty week for you. Let me know how it's going." "Is it getting any easier to keep up with your reading in AP History?"

- At the beginning of a week, ask students to pair up and assess how they did the previous week and share their goals for the week ahead.

- At the end of the week, ask students to review the week and share the one thing they were most proud of accomplishing.

- During personal check-ins and individual academic conferencing, invite students to refer to their assignment notebooks as they assess what's going well and what needs improvement.

- Offer an incentive when everyone has noted all of their assignments sufficiently for the entire week.

Record and Reflect on Progress Every Week

Use any of the suggested formats in Procedure 31 in *Getting Classroom Management RIGHT: Guided Discipline and Personalized Support in Secondary Schools* Chapter 4.

16

Show Me the Evidence

Discuss the kinds of evidence that are indicators of students' efforts to...

- Study for a test

- Comprehend and make meaning of a text reading

- Review notes

- Prepare for a discussion

- Prepare for a presentation

It may take a while for students to truly understand that you mean it when you say, "Show me the evidence." So you might have to be a little dramatic (not draconian) and not allow students to participate in the activity or take the test when everyone else does if they come without evidence of preparation. However, this doesn't mean students are off the hook—it just means they will need to participate in a work session on their time during your lunch, your prep period, or before or after school. If your follow-through is consistent during the first few weeks of school, students will get the message.

Require All Students to Achieve Proficiency on Important Assignments

Choose at least one project, problem, performance, or product each quarter that every student must complete at a high level of quality. Think about the hill you're willing to die on, because you'll probably have to help push some kids up the hill. Develop criteria for completion; ask students what they will need in the way of support; block out time to meet with students individually; create a way for students to indicate the status of their work; develop ways for students to share and critique their work with other students; choose how the class will celebrate everyone's successful completion.

The chart on the following page shows the kind of support that will enable all students to reach a standard of proficiency.

Expect, Insist on, and Support Completion and Quality

Many teachers share the opinion that students who choose not to complete work must accept the consequences of their choice—a lot of zeros in the grade book. Unfortunately, this policy makes it difficult to help students acquire the tools that make completion a consistent habit.

Failing or marginal students often attribute their turnaround to teachers who "dog" them, who won't allow them to do nothing. Develop a set of strategies that back up your expectation of completion and your ZAP mantra (zeros aren't permitted). Think about creating common practices across your team or grade level. Everybody wins when adults have consistent expectations. Consider the following strategies:

Establish a required conference hour (one day before school and one day after school) for students who have more than three assignments missing.

Marcus: Motivated and Proficient	Randy: Resistant and Unmotivated	Alicia: Academically Struggling
Expectation to complete a project with proficiency	Expectation to complete a project with proficiency	Expectation to complete a project with proficiency
Marcus accepts the challenge of doing a project that involves more complicated research and a more elaborate product.	Teacher conferences with Randy to sift through ideas to find one that connects with a personal interest. Randy has a checklist of aspects of the project that he thinks will be fairly easy to do and hard to do.	Alicia needs a visual step-by-step project guide and a simplified topic and product that will make completion possible. During project time she meets with the teacher and a few other students who have poor reading and research skills.
With the challenge comes the freedom to work in the library during project time and the responsibility to write brief status reports on what he's accomplished.	Randy loves his idea but has no work to show at first-round check-in. Randy calls up Mom with the teacher by his side and tells her that he will need to stay after school tomorrow to complete Round I tasks if they're not finished.	The librarian has also agreed to work with students on their topic searches so that they can move beyond the first click for information.
Marcus checks in with his teacher at lunch to talk about his progress.	Randy was a "no-show" for two days and is behind again. Teacher checks in with Randy to see what's up and reignite the fire.	Alicia tracks her progress and the teacher does a quick check-in to reflect what she's seen Alicia accomplish. Alicia's never been in a place where she can actually explain her topic and refer to reading material that supports her ideas.
Every student does peer review/ feedback with another student, using the project rubric.	Every student does peer review/ feedback with another student using the project rubric.	Every student does peer review/feedback with another student, using the project rubric.
There is a 3-day window for turning in projeects. Early completers get bonus points.	There is a 3-day window for turning in projects. Early completers get bonus points.	There is a 3-day window for turning in projects. Early completers get bonus points.
Teacher encourages Marcus to explore opportunities for shadow days and internships connected to the big issue in his project.	Even with the special project cleanup day during deadline week, Randy's not done. Another phone call and Randy knows he's required to attend the "After-School Special" from 3 to 6 p.m. next week with other non-completers.	The completed project is awful and Alicia is devastated. Teacher talks to Alicia and explains what she has to redo in order to meet profciency. She also attends the "After-School Special," where the teacher has enlisted a couple of peer tutors to work with students who need to rewrite.
One week later ALL students have completed their projects at a proficiency level. Everyone shares their work and celebrates. The principal stops by to congratulate the class.		

16

- Implement a system of partial credit for completing work late and retaking tests.

- Establish a required "homework" hall with other teachers so that a group of you can rotate monitoring after-school sessions.

- Develop learning contracts that you, the student, and a parent/guardian sign that state what each person will do to support student's completion of schoolwork.

- Set up a required "homework hall" and/or Saturday School for students who turn in shoddy or incomplete work or who need to revise or correct classroom assignments. Rotate supervision with other teachers on your team or who teach the same grade level.

- Meet weekly with grade-level or looped team members to discuss specific academic and behavioral interventions for specific students. Consult with student support staff to develop effective strategies.

- Monitor and track academic progress and achievement in all courses every three to five weeks. Implement midterm adjustments in students' personal learning plans if student is not making expected progress and achievement.

- Implement required Guided Study (special study halls with fewer than 15 students) that may provide targeted academic support for specific courses.

- Spell out purpose, timelines, and work plans for products and assessments at the beginning of each curriculum unit.

- Begin a study group with interested faculty who have the charge of rethinking grading systems, progress reports, homework, and assessment in general. What would it take to eliminate zeros? What would it take to create a culture where all faculty insist that major student work is redone or completed at a proficiency level? What scheduling structures and reallocation of responsibilities would be needed to support more reteaching and more immediate academic interventions?

If you haven't achieved proficiency or completed 3 assignments, you will be required to...

▸ Attend Homework Hall

▸ Attend work sessions during my conference hours

▸ Attend Saturday School

▸ Conference with me during lunch or conference hours

▸ Develop a learning contract

▸ Attend guided study or clinics

To pass this quarter, you will need to demonstrate proficiency in...

▸ 5 out of 8 core competencies as reflected on tests, projects, products, and presentations

▸ 3 out of 5 habits (work, mind, participation, discipline, literacy)

and complete...

▸ At least 5 journals and reflections

▸ 5 pieces that show evidence of correction and editing

Key Strategy	## Provide Steady Doses of Encouragement
HH	• Provide high expectations and high personalized support
Life Skill Connection (See page 112–114)	• Give and receive feedback and encouragement (20)
Sample Activities, Strategies, and Routines	• Daily Check-ins • Encourage Students to Tell You What They Need • Saying It Out Loud So You Believe It • You Change – I Change • Develop an Informal Mentoring System

Small doses of encouragement take very little time, but pack a big payoff when they become part of your daily classroom routine. What counts for kids is your honesty. Encouragement rings false when it flatters or overstates.

Daily Check-ins

Quietly seek out hard-to-reach students personally on a daily basis, saying something that says to them "I notice you," offering words of encouragement, checking out how they're doing, or asking them a question about something that interests them.

Encourage Students to Tell You What They Need

For many students, one of the best ways to be supportive is to ask them directly to tell you the kind of support that will help them to do their best or get back on track when they've experiencing difficulties. You might want to ask students to give you their ideas in a journal entry.

Saying It Out Loud So You Believe It

When students have completed a task or mastered a skill, ask them to tell you what internal qualities helped them to be successful.

You Change—I Change

Let students know that when you ask them to make a change in their behavior that they can count on you to do what it takes to support that change. Sometimes this may mean changing something you do in class or saying things in a different way. It can often mean deciding together on the best ways to check in, call attention to inappropriate behaviors, or give students feedback on how they're doing.

Develop an Informal Mentoring System

Meet with teachers who work at the same grade level and make a list of students whom you feel would benefit the most from having an adult mentor who is on their side as an advocate, someone who checks in with them on a weekly basis, provides an extra dose of support and encouragement, listens, does little things that show they notice and care. Each teacher chooses to be a mentor to one or two students. Check in with your teacher group to share information, successes, etc.

Key Strategy	Use Student and Teacher Feedback to Increase Learning
HH	• Provide high expectations and high personalized support
Life Skill *Connection* (See page 112–114)	• Activate hope, optimism, and positive motivation (15) • Work for high personal performance and cultivate your strengths and positive qualities (16) • Assess your skills, competencies, effort, and quality of work accurately (17) • Give and receive feedback and encouragement
Sample Activities, *Strategies, and* *Routines*	• Praise and Criticism vs. Feedback • Guidelines for Giving Feedback • Personal Assets and Qualities of Character • Link Personal Qualities to Specific Behaviors • Formative Assessment = Feedback for Learning

Praise and Criticism vs. Feedback

Here are some thoughts about shifting your emphasis from using praise and criticism to using concrete feedback.

Criticism shuts us down. Criticism usually makes us feel too hurt and defensive to listen, evaulate, and assess what we're hearing. Criticism makes us feel judged as people. Empty praise is praise that is ultimately a judgment of the doer, not the deed, and is too general. Examples of empty praise are, "You're doing great," "Excellent," and "You're terrific." Empty praise often makes us feel uncomfortable and anxious because although the comment is positive, we still feel that we are being judged as people.

Try to give feedback on the deed, not the doer. Effective feedback allows you to give your information and opinion to someone while keeping the lines of communication open. Feedback about the deed puts the focus on what a person did or said and how he or she did it, rather than on whether the person is good or bad. Think of feedback as playing back a videotape of what just happened. Feedback also lets the other person know that you're paying attention.

Guidelines for Giving Feedback

Feedback is an essential tool for creating and sustaining successful classrooms. Feedback gives us a process to share what we've experienced, positively or negatively, without being punitive or judgmental. More than anything else, feedback allows teachers and students to let go of perfection and makes it okay to discuss feelings and reactions honestly and openly without fear of reprisal or recrimination. By sharing observations about concrete, specific behaviors, constructive feedback separates the person from the problem, providing information and insight that people can use to change what's said and done the next time. Here are some guidelines for giving feedback.

Before giving feedback to individual students:

- Make a request and ask for permission.

- Consider issues of timing (now, later, much later).

- Find a private place to talk.

- You might say, "I'd like to give you some feedback about _____. Is now a good time or would you feel more comfortable if we talked at _____?

Good feedback begins with a positive response to the event, task, activity, or behavior under discussion. The person giving feedback can then move on to make constructive suggestions.

Give feedback using concrete, specific language that indicates what you saw, heard, felt, or experienced. If you use general words like okay, great, interesting, not good enough, the receiver won't get the specific informaiton that he or she needs. Feedback statements can begin different ways:

- Naming what you witnessed a person say or do. Examples: "You made everyone in the group feel welcome by inviting them all to say something in the beginning."

16

"You spoke loudly enough so that we could all hear you." "You found three different solutions to the problem."

- Giving reactions from your perspective. When someone gives us feedback, he or she is letting us know how our words and behavior affect them. For example, "I liked it when you..." "I noticed that..." "I observed that you..." "I appreciate it when you..." "It would have helped me understand better if you had..."

When feedback is given, the receiver is in control of the data. The receiver of the feedback can assess what aspects of the feedback ring true for him or her. The receiver also decides what to do with the feedback, how to use it, and what to do next time.

Think about feedback as a package you receive in the mail. You can choose to 1) Return it to the sender because it came to the wrong address, 2) Keep the package, open it, and use what's in it right away, 3) Keep it on the shelf for now and think about using it in the future.

When you are giving feedback:

- Encourage the person to do some self-assessment and reflection first.

- Describe your experience, your observations, and your reactions.

- Give feedback that provides specific information that might be helpful to the other person.

- Be sure to provide positive comments about what's working as well as constructive suggestions.

- Link students' positive behaviors or efforts to the personal qualities that enabled them to do what they did, or invite students to identify the personal qualities that enabled them to do what they did (see list on the next page).

If the feedback is about incomplete or unsatisfactory work or negative behaviors:

- Express your feelings and spell out the specific problems: For example, you might say, "I'm concerned about the three missing assignments on _____." Or "I'm disappointed when I noticed you made several starts on this project and haven't yet turned in your outline." Or "I felt upset when I heard you tease Mia about her clothes." Or "I was surprised when I read your paper and I noticed that you didn't defend your arguments citing examples from the text."

- Pause and invite students to comment and provide more information.

- State your hopes and expectations and invite student to generate suggestions for what they can do to make amends, self-correct, or change course. For example: "My hope is that you can complete the outline by Thursday. Tell me how you can make that happen."

- Sometimes you might want to review what happened and discuss what a student could do differently so the problem doesn't occur again.

Link Personal Qualities to Specific Behaviors

Link students' personal qualities to specific behaviors and academic efforts that you notice and appreciate. Here are some examples: "I noticed how you completed your last three labs. You tackled every part of each lab. That showed real perseverance." "I saw how you encouraged other students in your group to come up with more ideas. I appreciate your leadership." "Before you started on your project today, I noticed that you took the time to check the machinery and get all of your tools out before jumping in. That shows me you've got great self-discipline. You know what to do without being told."

Personal Assets and Qualities of Character

Accurate / Accuracy
Adaptable / Adaptability
Analytical / Analysis
Appreciative / Appreciation
Assertive / Assertion
Attentive / Attentiveness
Brave / Bravery
Careful / Carefulness
Caring / Care
Cautious / Caution
Collaborative / Collaboration
Committed / Commitment
Communicative / Communicativeness
Compassionate / Compassion
Competent / Competency
Concerned / Concern
Confident / Confidence
Considerate / Consideration
Consistent / Consistency
Cooperative / Cooperation
Courageous / Courage
Creative / Creativity
Curious / Curiosity
Decisive / Decisiveness
Dependable / Dependability
Oriented to detail
Determined / Determination
Effective / Efficacy
Efficient / Efficiency
Empathetic / Empathy
Energetic / Energy
Encouraging / Encouragement
Enthusiastic / Enthusiasm

Ethical / Ethics
Even-temperedness
Fair / Fairness
Flexible / Flexibility
Focused / Focus
Forgiving / Forgiveness
Friendly / Friendliness
Generous / Generosity
Gentle / Gentleness
Goal-oriented
Helpful / Helpfulness
Honest / Honesty
Humorous / Humor
Idealistic / Idealism
Imaginative / Imagination
Inclusive / Inclusiveness
Independent / Independence
Industrious / Industriousness
Initiating / Initiative
Insightful / Insight
Intuitive / Intuition
Kind / Kindness
Leader / Leadership
Logical / Logic
Loving
Loyal / Loyalty
Observant / Open-minded
Optimistic / Optimism
Organized / Organization
Patient / Patience
Perceptive / Perceptiveness
Persevering / Perseverence
Persistent / Persistence
Polite / Civility

Powerful / Power
Precise / Precision
Prepared / Preparedness
Problem-solver
Principled
Prudent / Prudence
Purposeful / Purpose
Reasonable
Resilient / Resiliency
Responsible / Responsibility
Reflective / Reflection
Reliable / Reliability
Resourceful / Resourcefulness
Respectful / Respectfulness
Responsive / Responsiveness
Self-aware / Self-awareness
Self-disciplined / Self-discipline
Self-motived / Self-motivation
Self-regulating / Self-regulation
Sensitive / Sensitivity
Skeptical / Skepticism
Skillful / Skill
Spirited / Spirit
Steady / Steadiness
Strong / Strength
Studious / Studiousness
Supportive / Supportiveness
Tactful / Tact
Thorough / Thoroughness
Thoughtful / Thoughtfulness
Tolerant / Tolerance
Trustworthiness
Understanding
Warm / Warmth

16

Formative Assessment and Feedback for Learning

Assessment for learning tells us what students know and don't know and what they can and cannot do at the start of a course, before instruction begins on a particular topic or skill, during "real time" instruction, at key mid-points of a learning unit, or before and after summative exams, products, and performances. <u>Student</u> feedback can help teachers assess students' "in the moment" skill acquisition and understanding and then adjust and differentiate instruction and learning opportunities according to students' learning needs. Especially for students who are confused, don't yet "have it" or know it, or can't yet do it, <u>teacher</u> feedback helps learners become aware of any gaps that exist between achieving the target learning goal and students' current knowledge, understanding, or skills. Formative assessment helps guide students through the actions necessary to achieve the target learning goal.[1, 2]

The most helpful type of feedback for class work, homework, practices, performances, products, and tests provides specific comments about errors, includes specific suggestions for improvement, and encourages students to focus their attention on completing a task with quality vs. doing only what's needed to get a right answer.[3] Assessment for learning helps students answer three questions during the learning process:[4]

1. ***Where am I going?*** (Are the learning targets clearly communicated? What kinds of samples, demonstrations, and examples illustrate quality vs. shoddy work? Are the steps or components of the task clear to me? Can I state the purpose and goals for this work? Do I know what to do?)

2. ***Where am I now?*** (What have I learned? What can I do now that I couldn't do before? Can I accurately assess my progress? Do I know my strengths and areas that need improvement? Do I know where I'm confused? What's getting easier? What's still hard? How am I thinking about myself as a learner?)

3. ***How can I close the gap?*** (Do I know what to do to improve my performance? What kind of effort will it take to improve my performance? What help and resources do I need? How will I know that I've met the target learning goal?)

Feedback for learning can be particularly helpful for lower achieving students.[5] It's non-threatening—it's not about a grade. Instead, it focuses a student's attention on improving the level and quality of understanding or performance. "Formative assessment supports the expectation that all children can learn at high levels and counteracts the cycle in which students attribute poor performance to lack of ability and therefore become permanently discouraged or unwilling to invest in further learning."[6] Formative assessment communicates to students that they can improve as a result of effort.

Teachers control the variety, frequency, and timing of feedback. In other words, the process of soliciting and then giving feedback won't happen without a teacher's intentional commitment to make it part of daily classroom practice. The charts on pages 379–380 illustrate different types of formative assessment and feedback for learning. Examples range from analysis and diagnosis of an individual student's work and thinking to group assessment that gives you a quick "read" of a group's needs and preferences, invites student voice into classroom decision making, and provides opportunities for the group to assess how it's functioning. Although all of the examples in the chart optimize learning and foster a learning culture, regular use of Assessments for Learning (1S) and Corrective and Complimentary Feedback (1Ta. and 1Tb.), offer the greatest potential for students to make dramatic achievement gains. (See shaded areas in chart.) Twenty-three quick tools for formative assessment are described on pages 381–384.

Types of Formative Assessment and Feedback for Learning

<u>Student</u> to Teacher Feedback (S)	<u>Teacher</u> to Student Feedback (T)
1S. Assessment for Learning (What student knows, understands, and can do AND what student doesn't know, understand, or can't do related to the target learning goal or the specific learning task.) *Focus on Learner's Achievement of Target Learning Goal/Completion of Task* *"As I walk around, I'm going to ask you to point to the step where you are right now in solving the problem and then tell me what you think you need to do next. If you're stuck, show me the place where you got confused."* *"Your exit ticket for today contains a sample of the problem type we just practiced. Solve it and let's see what stuck."* *"Okay, groups, post your 3-2-1 summary: 3 characteristics of a salt marsh; 2 benefits of salt marshes within the eco-system; and 1 way the environment would be affected if salt marshes disappeared"* *"Here's the rubric for project completion. Check off what you've completed and circle what's left to be done. Post it on the top right corner of your desk, so I can get a quick read of where you are."* *"As I walk around, I'm going to ask you to explain your arrangement of stickies on your concept maps."* *"When I collect your notebooks on Friday, I will be looking for edits and adds to your double-entry notes, your original questions that reflect your understanding of the material, and your map or organizer that captures essential information about _____ ."*	**1Ta. Corrective Feedback** (What teacher observed, viewed, heard, noticed, or read that indicated errors, confusion, or misunderstandings AND concrete suggestions or re-teaching that will enable student to reach the target goal or complete the task.) *Focus on Learner's Achievement of Target Learning Goal/Completion of Task* *"You'll notice on your essays that I circled all run-on's and fragments. You have about 30 minutes to edit and correct your sentence attempts. Look at the samples on the board that we just corrected. And those of you who are "run-on" and "fragment" free, please work as edit coaches around the room. Make sure that at least two students sign off on your corrections."* *"Your feedback indicates that the concepts in this chapter were very confusing for most of you. Let me talk through what I was thinking as I read this."* *"Now we're dividing up into two groups: Some of you need and have requested a tutorial on _____ . Others can work on independent projects."* **1Tb. Complimentary Feedback** (What student did well; what attributes student used to do it; what student might do to push to a new level of mastery or excellence.) *Focus on Learner's Achievement of Target Learning Goal/Completion of Task* *"Leon, during the last two weeks, you stuck it out and completed every part of the study guide. That's the first time. You really showed perseverance and persistence. What will it take for you to sustain this effort?"*

16

Student to Teacher Feedback (S)	**Teacher to Student Feedback (T)**
2S. Self-Assessment (How student perceives and assesses herself as a learner in this course or in relation to this particular task; what gets in the way of student's learning; what student needs to improve; what student thinks she can do to become more successful) *Focus on Learner* "At the end of the test, remember to complete the last section where you assess: 1) your study efforts and preparation; 2) your confidence level in taking the exam; 3) your grade prediction for this exam; and 4) by the end of the unit, what got easier and what's still hard to do" See self-assessment questions in Chapter 12.	**2T. Supportive Feedback** (How teacher acknowledges and reflects back student's perceptions and assessments of herself as a learner; AND how teacher supports student to think differently about herself ; AND what student might consider doing to become a more successful and high performing learner in this class. *Focus on Learner* "I can see that you've had a tough time this quarter and you're telling me you just don't understand the reading. Let's do some practice with this one reading. Look at these three strategies. Which one do you want to try first?"
3S. Appreciative Feedback (How students support, acknowledge, and recognize the efforts, accomplishments, and contributions of individuals and the group; appreciate progress and improvement within the group and among group members. *Focus on Individuals and the Group* "Okay, it's the Friday round-up. Write your post-it notes about someone or something you appreciated this week in class." See appreciative feedback ideas in Chapter 15.	**3T. Appreciative Feedback** (What teacher does and says to support, acknowledge and recognize the efforts, accomplishments, and contributions of individuals and the group; appreciate progress and improvement within the group and among group members) *Focus on Individuals and the Group* A large sign is posted on the door: "Congratulations, 3rd period CHEM class. 90% of you completed all three essential assignments this week. Great job!!"
4S. Group Assessment (How students are doing as a group; what's working/not working; what students like and don't like; what helps or doesn't help students learn; what students need to do better; changes and choices the group can make about what and how to learn.) *Focus on the Group and the Learning Environment* "Okay, it's time to assess how you are functioning in your home groups. Discuss each question and agree on a group response." See group assessment ideas in Chapter 15.	**4T. Group Feedback** (What teacher says and does in response to class feedback; how students and teacher problem solve to reach desired goals and outcomes in class.) *Focus on the Group and the Learning Environment* "On the end-of-quarter surveys, most of you wanted "study-buddy" time before each test and more independent project time during each week. You'll need to decide what goes in the 'homework bin', so we can set aside more time for these activities in class."

Tools for Formative Assessment:

1. **3-2-1 Summarizer:** A tool for summarizing and connecting ideas from a lesson or unit

   3   Facts about _____

   2   Interpretations, judgments, or conclusions

   1   Connection, application, or speculation

2. **Back and Forth:** "Back and Forth" is a pairs protocol where students take turns writing what the other person says. Student #1 explains a problem, process, procedure, cycle, causal relationship, etc. Student #2 writes the explanation down on a large 5"X8" note card and then checks for accuracy. Then pairs reverse roles and use the same protocol again with another problem, process, procedure, cycle, causal relationship to explain.

3. **Background Knowledge Probe:** For the current topic, invite students to work in groups to complete a four part assessment: 1) What do you know about _____? 2) What do you think you know about _____, but are not sure of? 3) What do you want to know about _____? 4) What are your sources of information?

4. **Concept Maps:** Students in small groups either receive a set of cards or create a set of sticky notes that groups must arrange in ways that show important relationships and connections to a stated main idea or concept.

5. **Entry Tickets:** Students are given entry tickets as they arrive at the door, follow the instructions, and complete the task immediately. Entry tickets are used to:

   - Introduce a new unit by linking a major concept to student's own lives.

   - Bridge the transition from yesterday's lesson to today's lesson to check what students remember; what students can apply; or what questions emerged.

   - Check for understanding if a homework assignment involved reading.

   - Review key content, terms, concepts, skills presented or practiced during the week.

   Example: Here's the term: _____. What is it associated with in this unit? Why does it matter?

6. **Exit Tickets:** (See "Ticket Out" ideas in Chapter 15.)

7. **Four Corners:** Get a "read" on what students are thinking about a particular topic or review what students know and understand about a particular topic. Label each corner of the room, A, B, C, and D. Students choose one of four possible responses to a complex multiple choice question related to the current topic. Post questions and possible responses on an overhead. Students move to the corner that matches their response to the question. Students in the same corner discuss why they think their choice is the correct response. Poll each group. Share the correct answer and invite the whole group to identify errors contained in the other answers.

16

8. **Game, Set, Match!:** Teams of three to five students receive a set of cards that have to be sorted and matched, clustered, or sequenced the following ways:

    1. Headlines with matching summaries of facts or events

    2. Terms with matching definitions/descriptions

    3. Problem models with sample problems associated with each model.

    4. Venn diagram: Distinguishing how two terms, concepts, historical eras, etc. are similar and different.

    5. Clustering distinguishing features of different items within the same category (attributes of different characters in a play; features of different categories of flora or fauna; responsibilities of different branches of federal government

    6. Multiple steps of a process or series of events that must be sequenced correctly

    7. Parts or components of two similar, but different concepts

    This is a useful protocol to use for review at the end of a learning unit or immediately after a reading, mini-lecture or demonstration.

9. **Imagine You Are A _____:** Link what students are learning to working professionals who would utilize the skill set or to people who are impacted by the topic, issue, policy or event.. Post four options for your question prompt. (Examples: *"If you worked in print or broadcast journalism which position would you apply for?* or *As you think about world health, which disease would be your #1 priority for research dollars?* or *If you had lived in the ____th century, who would you rather be?"*) Ask students to select their response to the question, move to that part of the room, and discuss their reasons for choosing their preferred response with a partner in the same group or a partner from another group. Share out a few responses in the whole group.

10. **One Minute Note Cards:** Students write down key points that they remember and find significant after 10 to 15 minutes of lecture, demonstration, oral reading, silent reading, etc. After students complete their cards, take two to five minutes to solicit responses from the class and correct misunderstandings and confusions.

11. **One Minute Sentence:** Students can craft only one sentence that captures the issue, the big idea, the problem model, a causal relationship, etc. that was the focus of the lesson.

12. **One Minute Problems:** Give pairs or trios a problem prompt. Groups must agree on a response, write it in large print on a large sticky, and post it on the board. Then look for thinking errors and misunderstandings and correct.

13. **People Equations, Proofs, and Formulae:** Every student receives a large card with a different number, symbol, or operational sign, etc. necessary to create equations, proofs, or formulae related to the unit of study. You give the problem prompt and the group must physically construct a correct response to solve the problem in less than two minutes.

14. **Pictionary:** Teams of pairs create a "picture" of a key concept, definition, relationship, term, or principle using no more than three words plus drawings and symbols. Pictures can be posted and then pairs can walk around and post their guesses OR pairs can present their picture to the class and the class gets no more than three guesses to name the correct answer.

15. **Problem Relay Review or Quiz**: Divide students into groups of four and give each foursome 10 index cards. Assign each group a different letter and make a place holder spot on the chalk or white board tray for each group to put their cards.

Give each group a quiz or review sheet with 10 questions on it. The group writes the number 1 and the answer to #1 on the first index card. One student walks to the board and puts the index card on the place with their group's letter. The student goes back to their group, and the group answers question #2 and the second person takes card #2 to their place on the tray. Each group keeps rotating students who take the answer cards to the tray until all questions are completed or time is up.

16. **Red, Yellow, Green:** Each student receives a red, yellow, and green card. Students are asked to hold up one card at various points during a lesson that indicate their understanding. (RED=I'm lost-Help!; YELLOW=I've sort of got it, but I need more examples and review; GREEN=I'm good to go. I can explain it /describe it/ show how to do it to someone else.) "Then, what do you REDs and YELLOWs need to become GREEN?"

17. **Stick It Up!:** Students receive large post-it notes or sentence strips on which they write their responses to a question prompt and post them on the board.

18. **Stop and Jot:** Students do a quick write (one or two sentences) at a critical point in the lesson. For example:

   • During discussion: "What's your thinking about _____. Do you agree or disagree with the statement, "_____." Explain your response."

   • At the end of a discussion or text reading: Create your own example; identify key issues or details related to _____.

16

- At a point of transition: "What issue comes next?" "Identify the next stage of the process." "How might the topic _____ that we just discussed connect to _____?" "What still feels 'muddy'?"

19. **Study Cards:** Give students (in pairs) 15 minutes to create study cards (4 × 6 index cards) that they can use when they take an end-of-unit test. Collect cards so you can analyze how students cull and distill what's really important. Give back the cards and provide corrective feedback before the test.

20. **Tableaus:** Teams of seven or eight students use only their bodies, up to four chairs, and up to three hand-made signs to communicate a key term or concept. Even better, ask each team to create two tableaus that communicate contrasting meanings of two related terms or concepts. Examples: from global conflict and security—differentiating between the terms "peacekeeping" and "peace building" OR from economics—differentiating between Asian or European and US market economies OR in any public policy discussion—communicating the costs in one tableau and the benefits in another tableau of _____.

21. **Walk, Talk, Decide**: Students have two minutes to pair up, walk around the room with their partner, and come to agreement about a response to a question prompt. Use this protocol when you want students to 1) talk through their thinking with another person to reach a conclusive response; 2) engage in "mental" problem solving and estimation without the use of calculators and tables; 3) share what they learned immediately after a silent text reading or lecture-discussion. After two minutes, ask students to FREEZE where they are and do a quick whip around the room to hear the group's responses, tease out what might have contributed to errors in thinking, and share short-cuts and tips that pairs used to arrive at a correct answer.

22. **White Board Problems and Check-ins:** Individual students, pairs, or small groups use small white boards and white board markers to post their responses to questions and problem prompts. (Get twelve 9" × 12" WHITE boards for $24.00 from ReallyGoodStuff.com)

23. **Word Connect:** This activity pushes high level thinking. Divide students into trios, and give each trio three seemingly unconnected words. The team's job is to post their three words on chart paper and draw connections and relationships among the three words in a way that communicates an essential concept, principle, event, or term from the current unit of study.

Key Strategy	Help Students Become School Smart
HH	• Provide high expectations and high personalized support

Life Skill Connection (See page 112–114)	• Make responsible choices for yourself by analyzing situations accurately and predicting consequences of different behaviors (7)

Sample Activities, Strategies, and Routines	• Have a Conversation about School Smart Strategies • Share Strategies and Habits that Help Students Do School

Most of us would like to think that high schools provide the opportunity for all kids to learn and achieve a modicum of success. Sadly, the gap between achieving and nonachieving students actually increases between 9th and 12th grades, with already privileged students becoming more so and less privileged students forming an even larger pool of the unsuccessful. High schools tend to reward students who already know how to be smart in school. These kids come to 9th grade with norms, habits, resources, and values that mirror what teachers prize and expect from "good students."

Although all teachers are pretty good at spelling out what will get students in trouble, fewer recognize the importance of discussing and teaching specific behaviors and strategies that will help kids become "school smart." Instead, young people who don't fit the ideal student norm are likely to hear a litany of frustrations and complaints about what they should have learned or known before they arrived. This "sink or swim" attitude is not a big motivator for kids who come to school feeling different, alienated, or discouraged.

Have a Conversation about School Smart Strategies

One step is making time to discuss this topic in class. Acknowledging that high school is not exactly a "student friendly" environment for lots of kids goes a long way toward building trust with students who can't imagine that any adult knows what school is like for them. Equally important is explaining to students that people aren't born with "school smarts." Anyone can learn what it takes to be smart. We do need to be mindful, however, that students who grow up in middle class, educated families, get a lot more practice at this before they ever enter 9th grade. Less privileged students should be able to count on some adults in their lives who will help them decode what high school is all about.

Reassure students that high school primarily rewards one kind of academic success, giving less attention and recognition to other ways of being successful in the world. Even though students have countless occasions outside of school to show how they are capable, competent, and responsible, it's the satisfactory completion of high school and state exit tests that remain the gatekeepers to a young person's future.

16

So helping students learn how to "do high school" is a good thing. Being "school smart" doesn't have to remain a mystery, and it doesn't mean students have to give up who they are. The composition of students in each class will influence whether your conversations occur with the whole group, in small groups, or one-on-one.

If most of your students need to become more "school smart," talking about this openly in class can be positive and supportive. On the other hand, if most kids are already savvy about how to "do school," you may want to share some information with the whole group and discuss other issues privately with students.

How might you begin a conversation about "school smarts"?

1. You might begin by discussing different kinds of "smarts" that students need to survive and succeed. For example, exploring what students need to know to be "street smart" or "work smart" can help them appreciate the need for behaving differently and holding different attitudes in different settings.

2. Brainstorm the benefits of moving successfully from one setting to another, pointing out that people who can do this well usually have more choices and more opportunities in life. How does this ability to move from setting to setting give students more power?

3. Give students information and teach them strategies that help them become more "school smart."

Share Strategies and Habits That Help Students Do School

The following section describes some specific school smart strategies with suggestions for how you might help students develop these strategies and use them more often.

I know how to "read" what really matters from teacher to teacher. For example, I can figure out the bottom line rules I need to pay attention to in each class and I know what to avoid to stay out of trouble.

A Way to Help: Give students a quiz on schoolwide rules and consequences and classroom boundaries, nonnegotiables, and consequences in your class. And be sure they know that it counts toward their grade

I know what to do and say that will get a teacher's positive attention without "brownnosing" or "sucking up."

A Way to Help: Let students know five things they can do to get your positive attention. To lighten things up, have a bag of mini-candy bars or funky prizes to toss out intermittently when you catch students doing the right thing.

I can adjust to different norms from class to class. For example, I know for one teacher tardy means "not in your seat when the bell rings" and for another teacher tardy means "you've got a minute or two before you will be marked late."

A Way to Help: This is a good thing to discuss with students for all kinds of reasons. Are norms consistent or inconsistent from one class to another? Ask students how they navigate this. You might want to explore what's good and what's bad about having different norms.

I know how to become invisible when I'm not prepared or when I'm distracted by something else going on outside of class.

A Way to Help: This is probably a private conversation. The idea that there are things you can do to disappear or avoid drawing attention to yourself is big news for some kids. In the same vein the idea of pretending to pay attention actually helps some kids to focus.

I know how to talk with teachers privately when I've got a problem learning something, completing an assignment, or meeting a deadline. I also know that if I do this sooner rather than later, it will probably be easier to deal with it.

A Way to Help: This is so important that it deserves to be addressed with the whole class. A good way to introduce this skill is to ask students to present two different role–plays, showing ineffective and effective ways to get the help and understanding a student needs. Be sure to do the ineffective role–play first so students can discuss what made it ineffective and what they might do and say differently to make it a more effective request. Keep in mind that students who don't have the words might not have the confidence to do this, so rehearsal is extremely helpful.

I can "buddy up" with other students when I think it will help me study or complete an assignment.

A Way to Help: This may merit a discussion about the difference between cheating, copying, and working collaboratively. You might want to establish "home groups" so students automatically have some study buddies they can work with throughout the year. Or you might explore with a student who they would imagine to be a good partner to work with.

I can identify the students in class who can help explain or show me how to do something when I don't understand.

A Way to Help: Students ultimately feel more personally powerful when they have strategies they can use that don't always involve going to the teacher for help. One idea is to have students identify two others they feel comfortable asking for help. Have students write the names down for you and for themselves. This way you have the information to suggest when it's timely.

16

HANDOUT 2
Habits and Strategies Checklists

You might use the following checklists as starting points when you conference privately with students. Together you can identify habits and strategies a student is already using effectively and disucss others that a student might want to try out or use more frequently.

Habits and Strategies That Help You Do School – What works for you?	I do this a lot and it works	It would help if I did this more often	I'd like to try this out	This would never work for me
Sometimes I let my parents know what I need to do so they can help me keep my commitments by checking in with me or helping me stick to a schedule that keeps me on track.				
I know how to use my parents as a shield to protect my time and avoid doing things that might get me in trouble. For example, I can say, "Look, my parents won't let me go out after eight on school nights," or "You know, if my parents find out, I'll be grounded for a month. I think I'll pass this time."				
I know how to check myself before I say something out loud- I've got a handle on what's okay to say publicly, what's better to say privately, and what's best left unsaid.				
I know when it's not a good idea to "free-style"—I know the times when I need to do things exactly "by the book."				
When I've got a problem at school I've got friends or family I can talk with who can help me sort things through to come up with a solution.				
When I'm upset or angry I know how to "chill out" and not make a major production out of it in class. I can postpone dealing with it until later.				
I can walk away from ignorant comments directed at me, especially when I think there's not much I can do that will change this person's behavior. I have learned, "It's just not worth my time and energy."				
Around school, I know the teachers and administrators who will cut me some slack and those who won't.				

Habits and Strategies Checklist CONTINUED

Habits and Strategies That Help You Do School —What works for you?	I do this all the time	I do this sometimes —I need to do more often	I do once in a while— this is hard to do	I never do this—I need some help on this
I can tell the difference between quality work and work that is shoddy. I know what I do differently when I make an effort and when I don't.				
I manage my time to meet school obligations week in and week out.				
I prioritize tasks and responsibilities.				
I map out plans for completing a complex task. I identify the steps and materials needed to complete it. I "chunk" a big task into smaller parts so it is easier to check what I have accomplished and what I have left to do.				
I make good choices about when and where to do what homework. (For example, I know what is easier to do when I'm tired and what kind of work requires me to be totally focused and alert with no distractions.)				
I accurately predict how long it will take to do various kinds of school tasks and assignments.				
I know that there will be some peak times during the year when I need to gear up and crank out school work at the exclusion of most other activities.				
I know when it's important to use standard English and when it's okay to use different dialects and slang.				
I ask questions that will help me get ready and organized to do work.				
When I'm distracted I use strategies that will help me refocus and pay attention.				

Habits and Strategies Checklist CONTINUED

Habits and Strategies That Help You Do School – What works for you?	I do this and it's pretty easy	I do this, but it's hard	I'd like to learn how to do this	This won't work for me
I use graphic organizers.				
I use sticky notes for summarizing information, for reminders, for markers of things I need to read over or review.				
I number chunks of information that I need to remember in a specific order.				
I highlight or circle words and concepts that might be hard to remember.				
I create a picture in my mind that includes all the things that are related to the same concept or category.				
I draw pictures and symbols to make connections between concepts and ideas.				
I rewrite information on note cards that will help me review and study.				
When I take notes I leave space to correct things, add new information, and write summary points.				

Key Strategy	Help Students Develop a Sense of Optimism
HH	• Set high expectations and provide high personalized support

| *Life Skill Connection* (See page 112–114) | • Make responsible choices for yourself by analyzing situations accurately and predicting consequences of different behaviors (7)
• Activate hope, optimism, and positive motivation (15)
• Work for high personal performance and cultivate your strengths and positive qualities (16)
• Assess your skills, competencies, effort, and quality of work accurately (17) |
| *Sample Activities, Strategies, and Routines* | • Name Your Positive Qualities and Personal Assets
• Talk to Students about Their Future |

The capacities to name one's assets, have ambitions, and imagine oneself in the future help foster resilience and sustain motivation and perseverance. Equally important, this kind of self-awareness is a necessary step before students can realistically match their talents and aspirations to college and career goals that are the right fit for them.

Included here is a sampling of activities that encourage students to develop an optimistic image of themselves.

Name Your Positive Qualities and Personal Assets

1. Once a quarter or semester, write students' names on brightly colored note cards. On one side, write a quality that demonstrates a student's capacity as a learner and what they did that exemplified that quality. Pass out the cards and on the other side ask students to write another quality and what they did that demonstrates that quality. These cards can become part of students' portfolios. (See page 377 for list of qualities and assets.)

2. During one round of regular check-ins with individual students, ask students to prepare for their check-in by writing down the following: "Write down something you're good at that has nothing to do with school and then write down the personal skills and qualities that help you to do this well." During your personal check-in with the student, invite him or her to share what she or he wrote and then explore one way the student might use those skills and attitudes at school to get more interested in something, get better at something, do something new or differently in class, or take a different approach to something that's not working.

Talk to Students about Their Future

We are learning more and more about which students experience success after high school and which students lose their way. Even more than a four-year college degree, it appears that passion related to a career goal and persistence to achieve that goal are critical factors in workplace

16

success. This is true whether that career requires zero, one, two, four, or eight years of postsecondary education. We also know that students benefit from having conversations about future expectations early and often with as many adults as possible.

Use these prompts for quick-writes, pair-shares, gatherings, or informal conversations.

- One/five/ten/fifteen years from now...

  I will no longer _____. Instead, I'll probably _____.

  I won't see myself as _____. Instead, I'll probably see myeslf as _____.

  I won't view my current situation as Instead, I'll probably view the past as

  _____. _____.

- Describe a career that interests you and one quality you have that would help you be good at this job.

- Link a career that interests you with something you have learned or learned how to do in this course or any other course you are currently taking.

- Imagine what your life would be like if you traveled in a time machine 10 years into the future. If you're happy where you landed, what did you do to get there? If you're unhappy where you landed, what can you do now to change course?

- Do you want to go to college? Why or why not?

- Do you expect to go to college? (Are you confident that you have the skills, grades, abilities, and resources to go to college?)

- Are you planning to go to college? (Are you already making personal and academic decisions that will ensure that college is in your future? Have you and your family started to make a financial plan so you will have the resources to go to college?)

- What kinds of postsecondary options match your interests, skills, and responsibilities? What's right for you? How do you know?

- What do you love to do? What interests you? What would you explore, create, investigate, do more often even if you didn't get a grade for it?

- What are you really good at? How do you know?

- What kind of work would you do even if you didn't get paid?

- What kinds of programs and experiences in and out of school will help you be prepared for life after high school?

- What kinds of programs and experiences in and out of school will help you make the right choice about careers and college?

Key Strategy	## Help Students Take Responsibility for Their Learning through Conferencing and Problem Solving
HH	Students engagement, effort, and motivation increase when students take responsiblility for their own learning. Student-Teacher conferencing and group discussions about learning problems strengthen students' metacognitive development by engaging them in reflection, self-assessment, problem solving, planning, and time and task management.
Life Skill Connection (See page 112–114)	• Deal with stress and frustration effectively (8) • Activate hope, optimism, and positive motivation (15) • Work for high personal performance and cultivate your strengths and positive qualities (16) • Assess your skills, competencies, effort, and quality of work accurately (17)
Sample Activities, Strategies, and Routines	• Student-Teacher Conferencing • Problems and Solutions

Student-Teacher Conferencing

Regularly scheduled and "as needed" student-teacher conferencing is a critical classroom practice for six reasons. First, it encourages students to take responsibility for their learning. Second, it enables teachers to personalize learning to meet the needs of individual students. Third, it's the most effective and efficient way to assess and address academic learning gaps. Fourth, it strengthens positive relationships between students and teachers. Fifth, it establishes the use of formative assessment as an on-going regular classroom practice. And finally, it ensures that every student in the class is noticed and heard.

Appendix A, *A Personal Conferencing Primer,* offers a set of tips and tools that can help make student-teacher conferencing an on-going practice in your classroom.

Problems and Solutions

Kids who get in academic trouble are often the same kids who don't know what to do when they're stuck and don't know how to ask for help. Ask students to think about these issues through written reflections and through small-group and large-group discussion. The goal here is to give students both the words and the concrete steps that can help them get what they need by relying on their own resources first, and checking in with peers or the teacher second.

You might want to start with a common problem that many students experience. Solicit ideas to put together a set of sequenced suggestions that you can post. For example:

Problem: If you don't understand an assignment:	**Suggestions:** • 1st, read it over one more time and name what you think you're supposed to do. • 2nd, name what is still unclear or confusing. • 3rd, ask someone in class to share their sense of the assignment. • 4th, if you're still unclear, ask me.

You might use the following chart to brainstorm solutions:

Problems that Make You Feel Stuck...	What Can You Do?	Are There Ways Another Student Can Help?	What Can the Teacher Do?
If you don't think you can complete an assignment on time			
If you failed or received a "D" on a test or exam			
If you're behind in completing assignments and don't know where to begin			

Problems that Make You Feel Stuck...	What Can You Do?	Are There Ways Another Student Can Help?	What Can the Teacher Do?
If you forget your book or materials			
If you've lost an important paper for class			

Key Strategy	Explore How to Give and Get Support
HH	• Set high expectations and provide high personalized support
Life Skill Connection (See page 112–114)	• Seek help when you need it (11)
Sample Activities, Strategies, and Routines	• Reflection Tools for Giving and Getting Support

Resilient adolescents are able to reach out to an array of people in situations when another person's wisdom, opinion, or support helps reduce feelings of anxiety, confusion, frustration, or loneliness. They also know how to access resources that will help them get what they need. Equally important, students who know ways to help themselves through rough periods are more likely to face challenging situations with a measure of confidence and optimism.

Reflection Tools for Giving and Getting Support

The two surveys presented here (Giving and Getting Support and 20 Ways to Support Yourself) can be used in a number of ways. When you're conferencing with students who are having a tough time, some of the questions might provide useful entry points to explore what's going on in a student's life. In some situations, you might ask a student if she or he feels comfortable filling out the survey and meeting later to talk about her or his responses. Finally, some of the strategies suggested may be appropriate to explore with the whole class during particular times of the year (i.e. holidays, exams) when the general level of anxiety goes up a notch or when a violent incident or national crisis makes everyone feel more vulnerable.

16

Giving and Getting Support

Everybody needs support. Think about the people in your life right now who can support you to do and be your best, listen to you, have a good time with you, and be there for you when you need them. Then think about how you play a support role with others.

1. I have friends my own age who really care about me, who can talk with me about my problems, and who can help me out when I'm having a hard time.

    Name _____ Name _____

    If there isn't someone like this in your life right now, who would you like to be there for you in this role?

    _____

    What are two things you could do to make this relationship happen?

    _____

    Are there any friends your own age, or brothers or sisters, for whom you play this role in their lives?

    Name _____ Name _____

    What is one thing I can do to be more supportive to them? _____

2. I have friends my own age who I can study or do homework with, who I can talk to when I'm having a problem in a class, and who are happy for me when I do well in school.

    Name _____ Name _____

    If there isn't someone like this in your life right now, who would you like to be there for you in this role?

    _____

    What are two things you could do to make this relationship happen?

    _____

    Are there any friends your own age, or brothers or sisters, for whom you play this role in their lives?

    Name _____ Name _____

    What is one thing I can do to be more supportive to them? _____

3. I have a parent or other adult close to me who expects me to follow rules, and who helps keep me on track when things get a little confusing, a little crazy, or just plain difficult.

    Name _____ Name _____

    If there isn't someone like this in your life right now, who would you like to be there for you in this role?

    _____

    What are two things you could do to make this relationship happen?

    _____

Adapted with permission from Healthy Kids Survey developed by WestEd for the California Department of Education (www.wested.org/hks)

Giving and Getting Support CONTINUED

4. I have a parent or other adult close to me who is interested in my school work, who believes I will be successful, who always wants me to do my best.

    Name _____ Name _____

    If there isn't someone like this in your life right now, who would you like to be there for you in this role?

    _____

    What are two things you could do to make this relationship happen?

    _____

5. I have a parent or other adult close to me who listens to me when I have something to say and who talks with me about my problems.

    Name _____ Name _____

    If there isn't someone like this in your life right now, who would you like to be there for you in this role?

    _____

    What are two things you could do to make this relationship happen?

    _____

6. I have a parent or other adult close to me who counts on me to listen and be supportive to them when they are having a hard time.

    Name _____ Name _____

    What's one thing you can do to show them that you care about them?

    _____

7. At my school, there is a teacher or some other adult who really cares about me, who listens to me when I have something to say, who works with me when I need help.

    Name _____ Name _____

    If there isn't someone like this in your life right now, who would you like to be there for you in this role?

    _____

    What are two things you could do to make this relationship happen?

    _____

8. At my school, I have several teachers who notice when I do a good job, who believe I will be a success, who always want me to do my best.

    Name _____ Name _____

    If there isn't someone like this in your life right now, who would you like to be there for you in this role?

    _____

    What are two things you could do to make this relationship happen?

    _____

20 Ways to Support Yourself

There are good reasons to get good at doing the things for ourselves that can help us keep on track and moving in a positive direction. Often there is no one around to give us the support we would like. At other times we get satisfaction from working things out by ourselves or doing things that build our inner resources and self-confidence. Take a look at these statements and see what you already do in the way of self-support and what you might like to try out.

20 Ways to Support Yourself	I already do this a lot	I'd like to do this more	I'd like to try this	This doesn't work for me
1. I can work out my own problems if I need to.				
2. I'm willing to try new things that can help me achieve my goals.				
3. I stand up for myself without putting others down.				
4. When I'm feeling down, I can imagine myself in a special place that feels safe and calming.				
5. When something is particularly hard for me I try to picture myself doing that thing.				
6. When I feel overloaded, I can make a realistic plan that will help me get out of the hole.				
7. When friends are pressuring me to do something that's not a good choice for me, I go someplace private and quiet where I can think things through.				
8. I try to understand what other people go through when they are having a bad time. It helps me know that I'm not the only one who has bad days and bad times.				
9. I have some favoite music I listen to that helps me feel calm when I'm upset.				
10. When I've made a good choice for myself that was really hard to make, I go over what I did in my mind so I can use this experience in the future.				
11. Sometimes I write down my thoughts to help me get a clearer sense of what I'm thinking or feeling.				

20 Ways to Support Yourself CONTINUED

20 Ways to Support Yourself	I already do this a lot	I'd like to do this more	I'd like to try this	This doesn't work for me
12. When I'm feeling pressured, I don't try to please everyone or try to do everything at once. I can feel good about just accomplishing one thing.				
13. Sometimes helping other people or doing something special for someone will lift up my own spirits.				
14. When I can't solve a problem by myself, I know where to go for help.				
15. When I've made a bad choice, it doesn't mean that all my choices are bad ones. I have confidence that I can make a better choice next time.				
16. When things are bothering me or I don't feel quite myself, I feel okay about letting someone else know.				
17. After I've done something well, I like going over it again in my mind.				
18. I try to understand my own moods and feelings before I jump to conclusions or do something impulsive.				
19. I'm willing to share my opinions about things even when they may be different from others.				
20. I'm willing to change what I'm doing when things are not working out.				
Is there anything else that you do to give yourself support when you need it?				

CHAPTER 17

Practice 7: Affirm Diversity in Your Classroom

Welcome Diversity into the Classroom
Activities pages 402–404

Become More Culturally Aware of the Students You Teach
Activities page 404

Observe What Students Do
Activities page 405

Teach Students to Match Their Behaviors to the Setting
Activities page 405

Consider Students' Cultures and Language Skills in Developing Lessons
Activities page 405

Make Lessons Explicit
Activities page 406

Promote Student On-Task Behavior
Activities page 407

Countering Harassment and Becoming Allies
Activities pages 408–412

17

Key Strategy	Welcome Diversity into the Classroom
	• Affirm diversity in your classroom
Life Skill Connection (See page 112–114)	• Empathize; understand and accept another person's feelings, perspectives, point of view (22) • Develop, manage, and maintain healthy relationships with adults (26)
Sample Activities, Strategies, and Routines	• Cultural Sharing • Share Personal Stories • Make Family Banners • Make Differences Normal • Make Personal Connections • Identity Cards

Appreciation for differences begins with experiences where students can share their own perspectives and enter into the perspectives of others. By taking the time to share personal stories and experiences, young people can begin to sort out and sift through the real and imagined differences they attach to their peers. While they may learn more about how different they are from some students, they also discover that they have much more in common with others. It is these personal connections that can help a group bond together and feel more comfortable talking openly and sensitively about differences when they become a source of conflict in the classroom. When students identify how they can each help make the group a more caring and effective community, they are more likely to appreciate the benefits that diversity brings with it.

Cultural Sharing

Use any of these questions for journaling, pair-shares, and listening labs of three or four students.

- Where was your family born? Where did people in your family grow up?

- Share something that's a tradition or important event in your family.

- Share two values or beliefs that are really important in your family.

- Describe one way you have felt different from everyone else in the past or in the present.

- Choose to focus on gender, race/ethnicity, class/socioeconomic status, sexual orientation, or religious affiliation for this question. Think about things you like about belonging to this group and things you don't like about belonging to this group.

- Talk about three groups you belong to by birth.

- Talk about three groups that reflect your cultural identity (ethnicity, family history and status, geographic region and neighborhood, religious beliefs, social and economic background, work experience).

- Talk about three groups that you belong to by choice.

Share Personal Stories

Be mindful of opportunities when you can invite students to connect their personal stories to what you're studying or to issues that come up in the classroom. Sharing your own stories invites students to share theirs.

Make Family Banners

The day before doing this activity, give each student a large piece of paper and say, "We're going to create 'family banners.' Write your full name on your paper and add words, symbols, and drawings that symbolize something about yourself, your family heritage, your cultural background, or something important in your life. We will be sharing them tomorrow." At the next class, divide the students into groups of four and give people at least four minutes each to share their family banners.

Make Differences Normal

One way to normalize diversity is to point out people from the past or present who reflect all kinds of differences. During one summer, I worked with a group of teachers from various disciplines who put together lists of people they wanted their students to know about—not only for their accomplishments in their fields and careers, but also for their personal stories that reflected a wide range of cultural backgrounds and experiences; gender and sexual orientation differences; and physical, intellectual, emotional, and social challenges that shaped who they became and their life's work.

Make Personal Connections

Build trust through your personal relationships with individual students. Know each student's correct pronunciation of his or her name. Let students know the ways they can depend on you and the different ways that you will recognize and appreciate each student's contributions in class. Students often reveal that they want their teachers to discover what their lives are like outside of school. Developing a more accurate picture and more sensitive understanding of students' lives also enables the teacher to increase the relevance of lessons and make examples more meaningful.

17

Personal ID Cards

Every kid wants their identity affirmed and appreciated. Invite students to create a personal ID card in which they can self-identify using various descriptors: country of origin, race and ethnicity, gender, groups, organizations, pop culture icons, products, music, media-sports stars with whom they identify. Think about how you can bring connections to these groups into your classroom (stories, real people, case studies, Did You Know?, pictures, cross-cultural exploration around one theme); use different youth culture media, topics, and issues as vehicles for problem posing and skill practice.

Key Strategy	**Become More Culturally Aware of the Students You Teach**
	• Affirm diversity in your classroom
Life Skill Connection (See page 112–114)	• Recognize and appreciate similarities and differences in others (31)
Sample Activities, Strategies, and Routines	• Connecting to Your Students' Families and Cultures

It is important to begin by recognizing and appreciating that everyone has a specific cultural identity. Becoming more culturally aware about the students you teach will help you find more ways to communicate and make connections between the curriculum content and their experiences.

Connecting to Your Students' Families and Cultures

- Learn more about their cultures, their neighborhoods, the people who are revered in their communities, and local resources that can be brought into the classroom.

- Establish positive home-school relationships with your students' families. Create ways to help parents know what's happening in your classroom and what their children are learning. Send notes and announcements of upcoming activities to parents. Make a "sunshine call" just to let a parent know the good things you see in their child. Invite parents to bring their experiences and expertise in the classroom.

- Appreciate and accommodate the similarities and differences among students' cultures. Effective teachers of culturally diverse students acknowledge both individual and cultural differences with enthusiasm. They identify cultural differences in a positive manner and are conscious of offering positive examples, stories, models, and contributions from people and cultures that represent the whole range of human diversity. This positive identification creates a basis for the development of effective communication and positive relationships.

Key Strategy | ## Observe What Students Do

- Affirm diversity in your classroom

Life Skill Connection
(See page 112–114)

- Recognize and Appreciate Similarities and Differences in Others

Focus on the ways different students learn; observe them carefully to identify their task orientations. Once students' orientations are known, teachers can structure tasks to take students' learning preferences into account. For example, before some students can begin a task, they need time to prepare or attend to details. In this case, the teacher can allow time for students to prepare, provide them with advance organizers, and announce how much time will be given for preparation and when the task will begin. This is a positive way to honor their need for preparation and rituals around getting started.

Key Strategy | ## Teach Students to Match Their Behaviors to the Setting

- Affirm diversity in your classroom

Life Skill Connection
(See page 112–114)

- Make responsible choices for yourself by analyzing situations accurately and predicting consequences of different behaviors (7)

We all behave differently in different settings. For example, we behave more formally at official ceremonies. Talk about how people act differently in their home, school, and community settings. Asking students to think in terms of "What's public? What's private?" can help them identify appropriate behaviors for each context. You might discuss differences between conversations students have with friends at home and conversations they have with adults and peers at school or work. How are their behaviors different in each setting? What are the advantages of being able to "code switch"? While some students adjust their behavior automatically, others must be taught and provided with ample opportunities to practice. Involving families and the community can help students recognize the benefits of adapting to different settings.

Consider Students' Cultures and Language Skills in Developing Lessons

Key Strategy

- Affirm diversity in your classroom

Consider students' cultures and language skills when developing learning objectives and instructional activities. Facilitate comparable learning opportunities for students who differ in race, sex, ethnicity, country or region of origin, or family background. For example, students might explore a history of number systems from the perspectives of their countries and continents of origin. Or students might be asked to interview someone of their own gender whose

17

career connects to the content of the course. Or when examining the uses of language, invite students to share examples from their first languages that illustrate how words can change their meaning in different contexts.

Key Strategy	## Make Lessons Explicit
	• Affirm diversity in your classroom

Life Skill Connection (See page 112–114)	• Prioritize and "chunk" tasks, predict task completion time, and manage time effectively (14)

Sample Activities, Strategies, and Routines	• Ideas for Explicit Teaching

Tell students how long a task will take to complete or how long it will take to learn a skill or strategy, and give them specific information about what it will take to complete a task or master a certain skill. It may be necessary to provide extra encouragement and support for students who want to achieve mastery but are struggling to do so. They may need you to assure them that they have the ability to achieve mastery, and they may need to know exactly the kind of effort it will take to demonstrate proficiency

Ideas for Explicit Teaching

- Provide rationales for what you do. Explore and explain the benefits of learning a concept, skill, or task. Ask students to tell you the rationale for learning something and invite them to share how the concept or skill applies to their lives at school, home, and work.

- Use advance- and postorganizers. At the beginning of lessons, give the students an overview and tell them the purpose or goal of the activity. If applicable, tell them the order that the lesson will follow and relate it to previous lessons. At the end of the lesson, invite students to summarize its main points.

- Provide frequent reviews of the content learned and compare and contrast what something is and what it's not, what something does and doesn't do. Take time to briefly review the previous lesson before continuing to a new or related lesson. A good rule of thumb is ten minutes of new material and two minutes of review.

Key Strategy	Promote Student On-Task Behavior

• Affirm diversity in your classroom

Life Skill Connection (See page 112–114)	• Work for high personal performance and cultivate your strengths and positive qualities (16)

Sample Activities, Strategies, and Routines	• Staying On Task

Keeping students on task requires that instruction remain at a level of high intensity. By starting lessons promptly and minimizing transition time between lessons, teachers can help students stay on task. Try to shift smoothly (no halts) and efficiently (no wasted effort) from one aspect of a lesson to another. Provide a purpose and a specific task for students to do at the same time they are listening or reading.

Staying on Task

- Monitor students' academic progress during independent and group work. Do informal checks for understanding with individuals and small groups by asking, "What are you doing right now? Why are you doing it? How are you going about doing it?"

- Check with students during independent reading or work time to see if they need assistance before they have to ask for help. Ask if they have any questions about what they are doing and solicit information that lets you know that they understand what they are doing. Also, forecast when and how various skills or strategies can be used and adapted in other situations.

- Require students to master one task before going on to the next. When students are assigned a learning task, tell them (or generate with them) the criteria that define mastery and the different ways mastery can be achieved. When mastery is achieved on one aspect of the task, give students corrective feedback to let them know what aspects they have mastered and what aspects still need more work. Require students to keep logs of what they have learned and mastered in your course.

17

Key Strategy	Countering Harassment and Becoming Allies
	• Affirm diversity in your classroom

Life Skill Connection (See page 112–114)	• Counter prejudice, harassment, privilege, and exclusion by becoming a good ally and acting on your ethical convictions (32)
Sample Activities, Strategies, and Routines	• Think About Harassment, Bullying, and Bigoted Remarks • Define and Discuss Harassment • Provide Examples of Harassment • Responding to Harassment

A big part of making any classroom a safe place is letting students know the words and behaviors that are outside the boundaries of your classroom. Discussing harassment issues serves five purposes.

1.   First, it lets students know that you will be vigilant about listening and looking for words and behaviors that target others and make people feel uncomfortable, embarrassed, or threatened.

2.   Second, it gives you a chance to spell out the ways that you will intervene in situations that look or sound like harassment.

3.   Third, it gives students an opportunity to discuss their perceptions of harassment and to get clear about the school's harassment policy. Most students do not know this information and have a very narrow view of what harassment is.

4.   Fourth, it gives you a chance to introduce the language of aggressor, target, bystander, and ally. Having a common vocabulary makes it easier to link behaviors to the roles we choose to play in any situation.

5.   Finally, this discussion communicates that you expect students to share the responsibility for making the classroom a safe and respectful place for everyone.

Thinking About Harassment, Bullying, and Bigoted Remarks

Have students think about your school and choose to write about one of these questions:

• What kinds of behaviors do you see around school that you think fall into the category of harassment or bullying?

• Are there any particular groups or types of kids whom you see playing the aggressor/ harasser role here at school? Why do you think individual students or groups do this?

• What groups or types of kids are most likely to be targeted? Why do you think that is?

Thinking about yourself, choose to write about one of these questions in your journal.

- Think about a time when you were targeted or harassed by an individual or group. What was the other person or the group doing or saying? How did that feel? Did anyone intervene as your ally? If not, what would you have wanted an ally to do?

- Think about a time when you felt left out or laughed at? What was the other person or group doing or saying? How did it feel for you in that situation? How did you deal with the situation? Is there anything you wish you had done?

- Think about a time when you witnessed someone else being targeted or harassed? What was going on? What did you do? If you witnessed a similar situation again, what would you say or do differently?

- If you were targeted or harassed what would you want a teacher to do? What would you want a friend to do?

Ask students to form groups of three or four to share their responses to questions about harassment. Invite students to share some of their stories.

Define and Discuss Harassment

You might want to make a web chart with HARASSMENT in the center and ask students, "When you hear the word harassment, what words, phrases, feelings come to mind?" Then chart student responses. Clarify the schoolwide and legal policies around these behaviors. Explain what you will do if you witness any of these behaviors. Here's a sample sequence of interventions:

- If I hear it or see it once, I will stop and name the behavior and speak to you about it privately.

- If I see you do it or say it again, I will call your family and you will be required to come to a conference hour and write up a report form.

- If it continues, I will notify the dean and schoolwide consequences will be enforced. That means...

Provide Examples of Harassment

Use the following to explain harassment to your students:

Harassment (abusive, obscene, or offensive language, gestures, propositions, or behaviors intended to target or harm individual or a group based on race, color, origins, gender, sexual identity, age, religion, class, or disability.) Harassment can make us feel uncomfortable, embarrassed, isolated, and angry. Harassment is an act of discrimination based on prejudice. Harassment is mean, harmful, illegal, and doesn't belong in schools or anywhere else.

17

If someone is doing something to you, or saying something about you, that you are disturbed by or feel uncomfortable about, it's probably harassment. We have the right to be safe. No one has the right to touch us unless we say it's OK. Even if someone is "just joking," if it disturbs the target or spectators of the action, it is still harassment because mean jokes can be harassing, too. If you are disturbed by the cruel way a person is treating someone else, you have the right and responsibility to report the harassment.

Types of Harassment

- Sexual harassment is unwanted, unwelcome sexual comments or actions, including unwanted touching, sexual insults, sexual rumor spreading, staring, unwanted "compliments," and sexual comments or actions with which targets or spectators are uncomfortable.

- Racial harassment includes racist comments and attacks on someone's skin color, native language, or national origin.

- Heterosexist (also called homophobic) harassment includes antigay, antibisexual, antilesbian, and antitransgender attacks. Examples include calling someone a "fag" or "lesbo," or calling something you don't like "gay" or "queer."

- Religious harassment includes attacks on someone's religious beliefs, practices, or group.

- Size-ist harassment means taunting someone because of their height or weight.

- Able-ist harassment means insulting someone based on a real or assumed physical or mental disability. Examples include calling someone "retard," or insulting them because they use crutches, a hearing aid, or a seeing-eye dog.

- Class-ist harassment includes "making fun" of someone based on how much money they or their family might have. Examples include "scrub," "Payless," and describing something you don't like as "welfare."

- Looks-ist harassment means attacks based on someone's looks, including calling someone "ugly," "greaseball," or "dog."

- Bullying is pressuring someone to do something they don't want to do through physical aggression (pushing, tripping, hitting, kicking, etc.), threats, intimidation, and/or insults.

Responding to Harassment

Talk to students about teasing—when it's fun and when it's not fun. What can we say when it starts changing from the fun version to the nasty version? Explore ways that students can respond to harassment using role plays and/or guided discussion. Whether you know the person well, where the incident happens, how often this has occurred, and how disrespected/ violated you feel will determine what you say, how you say it, and when you say it.

If you are the targeted person, you might try this:

1. Say the aggressor's name and show respect. Sometimes this means saying something like, "Steven, I don't mean any disrespect. I just want you to know..."

2. Tell the aggressor what you don't like, and what behavior is bothering you, using any of these suggested responses or rewording a response using language that feels right for you.

    - "I don't like it when you _____."

    - "It doesn't feel respectful when you _____."

    - "That looked and felt like harassment to me. Don't do that again."

    - "Don't go there. That crosses the line."

    - "What you just said felt really uncomfortable. I don't want you to say that to me again."

    - "You know, I would never say that to anyone. No one needs to hear that kind of stuff here at school."

    - "Look, _____, you're my friend. And I've told you before, I don't like it when you say/do _____. It feels like you don't respect my feelings. Please stop using those words. Can you do that?"

    - "I feel disrespected/upset/uncomfortable when I hear you say that to me. I don't deserve hearing that and neither does anyone else."

    - "You know, earlier today, when you said _____, I really felt uncomfortable/disrespected. Please don't say that again."

3. Exit. You don't want to wait for a response or a miraculous conversion. Waiting for an apology or change of attitude risks escalating the situation. Leaving the scene, turning around, walking the other way, or focusing attention elsewhere is what you need to do.

17

If you see someone else being targeted/harassed, you might try this:

1. Say the aggressor's name and show respect.

2. Tell the aggressor to stop, name what you see, and why you don't like it:

    *   "Knock it off with the abusive language, okay. No one deserves to hear that."

    *   "I saw that, and it looked like harassment to me. Lay off."

    *   "If you had said that to me, I would have felt really [uncomfortable/disrespected]. I don't want to hear that kind of stuff when I'm around."

    *   "You know, if Mr. _____ would have heard that he would have labeled that remark as harassment. Clean up the language, okay?"

    *   "That really sounds like a stereotype to me. I don't know _____ well enough to make that judgment."

    *   "Where did that come from? We don't say stuff like that here. That's not what this school is about. Please don't say that here, okay?"

    *   "I heard that. At this school, that's not okay to say to her/him, me, or anyone else."

    *   "Hey, that's an ouch. I wouldn't want anyone to say that to me."

    *   "Watch the language, huh? That's not okay to say to anyone."

    *   "Look, _____, you're my friend. And I've told you before, I don't like it when you say/do _____ around me. It feels like you don't respect my feelings. Please stop using those words. Can you do that?"

    *   "You know, earlier today, I heard you say _____ to _____. If you had said that to me I would have really felt _____. Please don't say that again to her/him or anyone else."

3. Take action:

    *   Help the targeted person to leave the scene.

    *   Go with the targeted person to report the incident.

    *   Report the incident yourself.

APPENDIX

APPENDIX A

A Personal Conferencing Primer

Making the Most of Student-Teacher Conferencing

The guidelines that follow can help make conferencing a powerful tool for learning and thinking. Included in the suggestions are some key tips from Harvey Daniels and Marilyn Bizar, authors of *Teaching the Best Practice Way*, a very practical guide to core instructional methods across the curriculum:[1]

- Explain that conferencing is part of daily classroom life – make it a normal practice that includes every student.[1] In secondary schools, particularly, conferencing can easily be reduced to a strategy that is only used when a student is not learning or when a student's unwanted behaviors have a negative impact on the group and the learning environment. Conferencing, first and foremost is a way for you to know each student personally, learn how each student is actually doing in your class, and witness students' thinking processes in order to adjust your instructional approach for that student. Thus, students' first conference experience should be part of a formal conferencing cycle that includes every student.

- Establish regularly scheduled conferencing at least two days every week for at least thirty minutes while students are engaged in independent work. Conferencing becomes much easier to sustain if you "bookend" your weekly Monday to Friday planning in a way that designates specific learning tasks and routines to different days of the week, week in and week out. Conferencing becomes an expected and natural component of the learning process. Daily informal conferencing goes hand in hand with the use of a workshop instructional model. (See p. 237)

- One caution is worth noting. If the group cannot function on its own, you can never facilitate conferences during class time. Before you set up your conference routine, decide on the habits of learning that students need to practice competently in order for conferencing to become a realistic option. (See pages 146–147.) Students, for example, must learn to work independently or in small groups for extended periods of time without distracting others or requiring your constant attention and monitoring. If this is a huge hurdle in the beginning of the year, introduce conference periods that last only ten to fifteen minutes, aiming for thirty minute conference periods by October.

- Share the goals of conferencing in general (see page 420) and let students know that conferences will usually have a specific academic, behavioral, or personal focus.

- Explain the purpose of informal conferencing and check-ins. This kind of conferencing happens on a daily basis while students are engaged in guided practice, small group work, or independent learning tasks. The purpose is to assess what a student is learning, doing, thinking in the moment, at a particular point in a learning unit, or at particular stage of completion of a product or project. Informal conferencing usually takes place at a student's desk or work space. It can take anywhere from one to three minutes. Nancie Atwell, a writer's workshop pioneer, suggests that "a rolling chair should be standard equipment for a conferencing teacher".[1]

- Explain that formally scheduled conferences have two distinct purposes:

   1. For ALL students, formally scheduled conferences provide a set of bench marks that help students assess their goals, progress, and performance in your course. A formal student conference cycle in which you meet with every student should not extend beyond two to three weeks. A pre-conference writing/reflection task will help students prepare for conferences. (See examples of assessment prompts on pp. 232-233.)

   2. For SOME students, formally scheduled "as needed" conferences provide the opportunity to identify and address specific learning gaps, map out high challenge work for high achieving students, or tackle behavioral problems or personal issues that are getting in the way of a particular student's learning.

      Choose a space for formal conferencing that provides a modicum of privacy for more personal conferences and enables you to can sit side by side with the student.1

      Formally scheduled conferences usually last around five minutes if they occur during class time. "As needed" conferences that focus more on diagnosis and problem solving can take longer, which is why they may need to be scheduled at other times beyond the regular class period.

- Be clear that conferencing provides an opportunity for you to see and hear what individual students are doing and thinking, so the teacher's role is that of a listener and question asker. When you ask a question, give students time to think before you charge ahead.[1]

- Explain that sometimes—when a student is not meeting academic expectations or is having a difficult time becoming a high performing group member—conferencing provides the opportunity for assessing what's not working and making a plan for how to get back on track.

- Explain that sometimes a classroom incident will require urgent, emergency conferencing (immediately after the incident has occurred or before a student leaves at the end of class). If and when an incident warrants immediate action, you want students to know that you will need to step aside with a student momentarily, while the group is expected to continue working.

- Be sure to let students know that they are welcome to request and schedule a conference at any time.

- Although most conferencing will take place during class time, let students know the other times when you will schedule conferences: before or after school, during lunch, or during your prep or conference period.

- For conferences that are prompted by academic or behavioral problems, try to keep some general guidelines in mind:

  ▶ During the conference share some hopeful expectations. *"This conference will give us a chance to clear the air and figure out how to move forward, so you can be successful in this class."*

  ▶ Provide the student with a clear purpose for the conference. Make certain the student understands why the conference was needed and what changes the student needs to make. Ask the student to restate any specific commitments or next steps before the conference is over.

  ▶ Thank the student for his or her willingness to talk and listen and assure the student that you have confidence in his or her ability to make better choices/work harder/ learn to _____, etc.

  ▶ Follow up with several quick check-ins during the next two weeks.

Informal Non-Scheduled Conferences and Check-ins

 Informal Academic Conferences and Check-ins with ALL Students

Process Checks-ins for Understanding[1]

Project, Product, Presentation, and Publication Status Check-ins

Why? The purpose is for students to assess what they are learning, doing, thinking in the moment, at a particular point in a learning unit, or at particular stage of working on a product or project.

Sample Teacher Prompts and Tips:
This is the most frequent type of conferencing you will do while students are engaged in small group work, guided practice, or independent work tasks. Daniels and Bizar note that this "classic" conferences calls for teachers to ask some version of each of these three questions:[1]
- What are you working on? Tell me about _____.
- How is it coming?
- What are you going to do next?

Teachers do very little talking—the goal is for students to strengthen their self-reflection skills and gain confidence in their capacities as independent learners. Process conferences also provide the opportunity to address confusions, deal with misunderstandings, and support corrections of errors. See pages 378–384 for more ideas about using formative assessment on a daily basis.

 Informal Academic Check-ins with ALL Students

Whole Group Learning Task Check-ins

Why? This kind of group check-in is a time for students to make their intentions public when individual students or small groups are working on a range of tasks or projects.

Sample Teacher Prompts and Tips:
Students can share their intentions and post them on the board or chart paper, so you have an good handle on who's doing what.

Clean-up Check-ins

Why? Clean up check-ins are intended to clear up any confusion about what students need to revise, re-do, or complete in order to earn credit (however partial) for the current grading period.

Teacher Prompts and Tips:
Near the end of the quarter, many teachers designate one or two periods for end-of-term clean-up. This is a time to encourage students to take responsibility to check in if they have any questions about what they need to do to earn credit.

Informal Behavior Check-ins with SOME Students

Why? When students are off-task or confused, the informal behavior check-in provides an opportunity for students to self-correct and problem solve.

Sample Teacher Prompts and Tips:
- I see that you are _____. Tell me what you think the task is right now.
- How are you doing with this?
- Show me where you are now.
- Tell me what you're working on right now.
- Tell me what you think is left to do.
- Ask the student to predict how long it will take to do a particular task or a specific part of the task.
- You're welcome to _____ or _____. You decide.
- Tell me two choices you can make for what to do right now. Okay, what's your preference?

For more prompts, see *Getting Classroom Management RIGHT*, Chapter 6.

Informal Personal Check-ins with ALL Students

Why? Although personal check-ins are great for all kids, they are especially important for students who struggle or students who are experiencing a rough patch. Daily personal check-ins that communicate, "I'm on your side and on your case" send a powerful message that you care about how the student is doing in life and about how the student is doing in your class. Although these check-ins don't take more than ten or thirty seconds, the constancy of connection builds trust, dependability, and hopeful expectations.

When? During class when you are teaching and coaching by walking around; during your "meet and greets" as students come into class; as students are leaving class; or while you're on hall, cafeteria, or bus duty

Sample Teacher Prompts and Tips:
- How's it going today?
- How has your week been so far?
- What are you looking forward to this week/weekend?
- What's getting easier to do? What's still hard?
- What's something new and good going on in your life?
- What can do you to have a good day today?
- What's a goal for class that will help you stay on track?

Formally Scheduled Conferences for ALL Students

 Formally Scheduled Academic Conferences with ALL Students

Course Start-Up and Goal Setting Conference

Why? This first conference during the new school year makes students' efforts to set goals feel authentic and important when they discuss their goals with you personally. Try to make this happen between the second and fourth weeks of school.

Sample Teacher Prompts and Tips:
- What are your hopes and goals for this class? Any hesitations?
- Is there any way you want this class to be different from other _____ courses you've taken before?
- What should I know about you, so I can support you to do your best?
- Is there anything particular that you want to know about class or the course?
- What do you think it will take from you to achieve the goals you've set for yourself?
- Tell me something you're interested in or love to do – maybe we can figure out a way to weave that into our course work.

Mid-term or Semester Assessment and Review of Goals

Student-Facilitated Progress Report Conference with Teacher or Teacher and Parent

Why? These conferences provide opportunities for students to review their goals; assess what's going well; reflect on their work and their attributes as learners; identify learning gaps and challenges; and a road map for future academic support and follow-up.

End-of-Course Conference

Why? This is a celebration and assessment of a year's worth of work and effort.

Sample Teacher Prompts and Tips:
Ask students to prepare for this kind of conference using any of the following questions:
- Predict the grade you think you will earn in each course.
- Next to your grade prediction, share a couple of things that support your reasons for assigning yourself this grade.
- Choose two work samples that illustrate high quality products and at least one work sample that illustrates a weak, shoddy, or incomplete product. Be prepared to talk about the differences between the work samples. Were there differences in your effort, the type of task, the skills required, or your attitude about the task?
- Record where you stand regarding the goals you set for yourself at the beginning of the grading period.
- Jot down any skill gaps you want discuss specifically.
- Share something you learned or experienced this term that felt particularly important?
- What have you learned how to do that will help you prepare for college?
- Think about a skill you've practiced that you will probably continue to use outside of class.
- What's something you are proud of accomplishing or improving?
For more self-assessment and reflection prompts, see pages 369–372.

Formally Scheduled Academic Conferences with ALL Students

Portfolio, Capstone Project, of Exhibition Sign-off

Why? When students are near the completion phase of a major piece of work, this kind of conference is the final sign-off and review of what's good to go and what needs to be revised, redone, or completed before it's submitted or presented as a final product. Peer editing and self-editing should be part of the review process before students turn in their work to you for final review and sign-off.

Sample Teacher Prompts and Tips:
- Project rubrics make it easier for students to assess where they are and what they need to do.
- Ask students to review where they think they've met learning goals for the project and where they may have come up short.
- Invite students to ask for specific feedback about one aspect of their project that generates particular concerns about quality or completeness.
- Provide feedback that enables students to polish their work for final submission.
- See page 371, for an illustration of the project process as it is carried out by three students who reflect a wide range of skills and different degrees of perseverance.

Formally Scheduled Behavior Conferences Students with ALL Students

Assessment of Life Skills and Habits of Learning

Why? To discuss and assess improvement and mastery of life skills and habits of learning.

Sample Teacher Prompts and Tips:
- Be prepared to talk about a habit that is getting easier to do regularly and a habit that you're still working on.
- Share one way that you feel you have contributed positively to making the class a good place to be.
- What's one way you're becoming more self-disciplined.
- Share evidence that tells you that you've made a more intentional effort to _____.
- Choose three words that describe your participation in class during the last six weeks.

Formally Scheduled Personal Conferences with All Students

Future Aspirations and Postsecondary Conference

Why? Too few students have multiple opportunities to engage in serious conversations about their future. And thus, many students find it challenging to see the connections between school work and life after high school. In schools that describe themselves as a college-going, career-ready culture, every adult talks to kids about their future aspirations.

Sample Teacher Prompts and Tips:

- What kind of life do you want to live? What will you need to do to live the life you want to live?
- What have you learned from your family about living a good life?
- What are your hopes for your own future? What do you imagine yourself doing ten years from now?
- What do you love to do? What are you really good at? How do you know?
- What kind of work would you do even if you didn't get paid?
- Do you want to go to college? How would your life be different if you completed college?
- Are you already making personal and academic decisions that will ensure college is in your future?
- What kinds of programs and experiences in and out of school will help you be prepared for life after high school?
- What kinds of college options are you thinking about? Four year college, community college, technical school, career preparation through an apprenticeship or the military? What feels like the right match with your future aspirations? What kinds of qualifications are required?

Formally Scheduled "As Needed" Conferences for SOME Students

 Formally Scheduled "As Needed" Academic Conferences with SOME Students

Learning Gap Conferences

Why? When academic learning gaps look like....

- Discrete gaps in understanding and comprehension related to a specific skill set, lesson, learning unit, product, or project –"I just don't get it".
- Readiness issues – students don't have prior experience, knowledge, or skills to do what they are asked to do.
- Honest boredom for students who already understand or have mastered the learning content and need more rigorous, intellectually challenging work (See academic challenge conferences)
- Feelings of inadequacy, lack of confidence, or little belief in one's capacity to complete task successfully.
- Low motivation (Low satisfaction, interest, or value associated with goal or task) or low effort (Specific actions student can take to increase their competencies).
- Mild disabilities or "learning to learn" gaps related to student's metacognitive capacities to pay attention, set goals, follow instructions, manage time, plan and organize, and problem solve and persevere.
- Tensions between the dominant method of instruction and the preferred way a student learns;
- A student's need for more differentiated instruction and learning accommodations. (If you can't learn the way I teach, I can learn to teach the way you learn.)
- Significant skill gaps that impact a student's capacity to complete important tasks proficiently.

Sample Teacher Prompts and Tips:

- What's going on that tells you that things aren't going so well in class?
- How are you feeling about class right now? Where do you feel stuck?
- I'm concerned about _____. What's your thinking about this?
- What's getting in the way of being successful in this class? What would it take to make this class work for you?
- Where are you stuck? What's easy? What's hard?
- What should I know that might help me understand how to help?
- Here's what I see. Does that sound about right to you?
- What are three things you might to do to turn it around in class?
- What can I do to support your efforts to get back on track?

Next steps might include:

- Academic learning contracts
- Guided instruction, re-teaching, re-testing, practice, and rehearsal with you during class or on designated conference hours before, during, or after school
- Required homework hall, Saturday School, owed work time, or before or after-school tutoring or study groups to complete work or improve academic skills
- Verbal and written feedback and coaching
- Personalized encouragement and regular check-in's
- Parental phone call, note, or conference
- Referrals to provide appropriate diagnosis, interventions and services that address serious and/or chronic academic learning gaps

Academic Challenge Conference

Why? For students who communicate intense interest in the course content or who demonstrate sophisticated use of course-related skills, an academic challenge conference provides an opportunity to take stock and explore what kind of challenge project a student might want to pursue.

Sample Teacher Prompts and Tips:

- Is there a particular topic you would like to study in depth?
- Is there any particular career connected to _____ that you'd like to explore or learn more about?
- So you've proven that you can already _____. What might be the next level of work that will provide a real challenge?

Formally Scheduled "As Needed" Academic Conferences with SOME Students

Learning Contract Conference

Why? For students who need close monitoring and feedback, a written learning contract or weekly progress report is a good option.

Sample Teacher Prompts and Tips:
- Here's what I want to work on:
- These are the skills and behaviors I need to learn / practice / do more often.
- I will ask for help when…..
- When I get frustrated, I can….

- During the next _____ weeks, I agree to:
- My teacher agrees to:
- If I don't meet my contract commitments, I agree to…

Learner Profile Conference

Why? This is a good conference choice for students who are the "invisible middles"—they don't give away too much and they haven't shown you enough about who they are as learners to give you many clues.

Sample Teacher Prompts and Tips:
- How would you describe yourself as a learner? What's easy to learn? What's hard to learn? What subject area interests you the most?
- What are you interested in? What's your passion? What do you really want to learn about, become an expert at doing? What personal talents might you want to develop and strengthen?
- What kinds of courses and subjects do you like least? Most?
- In what instances does learning feel real and important to you?
- When you think about this class—what tasks and topics capture your interest? What's boring or difficult?
- What do you imagine yourself doing ten years from now? What are your hopes and dreams?
- How is school helping you get where you want to go?

Climbers' Club Conference

Why? The Climbers' Club conference is with the group of students who are trying to get out of the hole at mid-point in a grading period. These students need close monitoring and check-ins to stay on track.

Sample Teacher Prompts and Tips:
For students in this situation, weekly check-ins are critical, so students can mark their progress.
- What did you do this week that made you proud of yourself? Where do you see yourself improving?
- What was your best effort this week? Talk about why you chose this particular task or experience?
- How was this week better than the last one? What's gotten easier for you to do?
- What's still frustrating? What's your current plan to tackle this?

Side by Side Task Guidance during Academic Workout Sessions

Why? For students who are habitual non-completers or homework shirkers, there is one strategy that seems to help these kids get off the dime: side by side task guidance during lunch or before or after school.

Sample Teacher Prompts and Tips:
- Side by side task guidance can be done one-on-one or with a small group of students. The key to this strategy is closely observing how students approach and complete a task. This is the only way to diagnose where the bottlenecks occur and figure out what kinds of prompts, task chunking, and skill development will help these students find their way to the finish line. It's important to keep your prompts simple and direct.
- How long do you think this will take you to do? What do you need in front of you to complete the task?
- In your own words, tell me the instructions. What's going through your mind as you begin to _____.
- Where are you now? What's the next step? Explain what you just accomplished. What's left to do?
- Walk me through your thinking as you solved this problem.

Formally Scheduled "As Needed" Behavior Conferences with SOME Students

When the same unwanted behavior persists over time…

Why? Nothing will change unless you develop a plan for reducing the unwanted behavior and increasing the use of the desired behavior.

Sample Teacher Prompts and Tips:

- Share what you observed and use non-threatening openers. *"So I've noticed in the last week that _____. What's up?"* OR *"So what's going on this week. You seem out of sorts."* OR *"This hasn't been your best week, huh."*
- Listen and acknowledge student's feelings – let student talk!
- Convey support and understanding of what you heard.
- Probe for sources of the problem and what student needs in order to move forward.
- Identify the specific behavior that needs to **stop** or change and why.
- Spell out desired target behaviors that need to **start**
- Explore at least two or three strategies that will help student get back on track.
- Develop a plan, contract, or conduct card and provide follow-up feedback and coaching.

When a student is persistently angry, frustrated, or upset….

Why? Nothing will change until you talk to the student and try to get at the source of highly charged emotions.

Sample Teacher Prompts and Tips:

- Make an observation or ask an open-ended low threat question. (*"I've noticed lately that _____. Is everything okay?" "Take a deep breath and take a minute to gather your thoughts. I'm here to listen." "So is there anything I should know about what happened today?" "You really sounded (angry, frustrated, upset) earlier. Is that right?" "A lot's been happening. Say a little about what's going on for you." "I'm concerned about _____. Is there something going on that's making this a tough week?"*)
- Your first goal is to defuse the student's emotional intensity. Invite student to talk. *"You sound really upset. You've got my full attention. Tell me what happened."* STOP and only listen. Keep your focus on the student.
- Keep restating what the student says and reflecting back student's feelings until you notice a shift. Wait for the student to respond before you say anything else. (*"I can see you're upset about _____ and now you feel_____. Is that about right?"*)
- Encourage the student to tell his or her story. (*"What happened next? "Tell me more""Can you say more about that?" "How do you feel about that?""Is there anything else bothering you?" "What's stopping you from feeling okay right now?""Is there anything else you can say that would help me understand the situation better?" Help me understand_____.)*
- Sometimes just listening to a student's story is enough. If a student does want to problem solve, you might ask, *"What do you need right now?"* or *"Where would you like to go from here?"* or, *"What would a good solution look like?"* or *"What might be one step you can take toward working this out?"* or *"How would you like things to change?*
- If the student's situation feels particularly worrisome, invite student to consider talking with the right person at school. You are NOT a counselor – you're the person who provides a connection to others who are trained to help students with specific academic, behavioral, or mental health problems or crises that come up. (*"Do you think this is a good time to talk to_____?"* or *"This sounds like something that's important to talk about with _____. Can you do that today? Is there anything I can do to help make that happen?"*)

Formally Scheduled "As Needed" Behavior Conferences with SOME Students

When the student is persistently bored, resistant, and disengaged…

Why? Nothing will change until you talk to the student and try to get at the source of the boredom, resistance, or disengagement. Sometimes resistance emerges when students fear that learning and succeeding in school means losing their identity, betraying friends, or rejecting the world they know. These are conferences that require a light touch and your most curious self. Simply having the conversation is a big, big step.

Sample Teacher Prompts and Tips:
- Try and discover what the student finds really boring and disengaging about school – what's the disconnect? Then probe a bit more to find out more about the student. For example ask, *"Is there anything at school you like doing? What's something you want to spend time getting good at or learning how to do? What words would you use to describe yourself here at school? How would your friends describe you? Would teachers use the same words? What do you imagine other students are thinking when they see you_____?" Tell me what you imagine doing five years from now?"* Try to tease out any personal goal or hopes that can help the student direct his/her focus.
- The first conference is not about getting the student to shape up. It's about showing your interest in who this student really is and what makes her/him tick. You want to close the first conference with an appreciation to the student for being honest. End the conference by saying: "You've given me a lot to think about. Here's what I'd like you to think about – what can I do to make this class an okay place for you to be?"
- The second conference should be about looking for ways to make class bearable by attaching success in class to the student's effort and your encouragement and support. *"What feels like a fair and do-able work expectation for next week?"* Talk it through so the student can say: *"I can do this because it will help me _____. I'll try to make this work because _____. I'll try this out for a week as long as you_____."*
- It's important to note that the quality of the personal relationship with the teacher is the key factor that helps unmotivated kids turn around. Reluctant and resistant learners don't start working because they suddenly find the subject fascinating or develop a five year plan for graduation and college. These kids are likely to come to school with no goals and few hopes, so they work first "for the teacher." Every small success and achievement matters. Students' personal satisfaction from experiencing a "job well done" can lay the ground-work for helping students link their personal goals, hopes, and interests to success in school and success in life.

When nothing you've done so far has worked with a "frequent flier"….

Why? For the student who has been unresponsive to all of your attempts to support her/him, it's time to switch tactics and work on just getting to know more about the student first.

Sample Teacher Prompts and Tips:
- Surprise "frequent fliers" by using a first conference just to listen and find out more. *"What's the day like for you here at school? What's the low point? High point? What words would you use to describe yourself here at school? How would your friends describe you? Would teachers use the same words? What do you imagine other students are thinking when they see you_____?"*
- A first conference is not about a new behavior plan. It's about convincing students that you really want to hear their thoughts and perspectives about school and how they see themselves at school. You want to close the first conference with an appreciation to the student for being honest. End the conference by saying: *"You've given me a lot to think about. Here's what I'd like you to think about – what can I do to help make this class okay for you."*
- The second conference is a time to engage "frequent fliers" in a candid conversation about why everything people have tried doesn't work. *"Here's what we've tried. And here's what keeps happening. Talk about why these strategies aren't working. I really want to know. What am I missing here? What don't I know? What will it take for you to be okay here at school? What's getting in the way? What can I do to help?"*
- The next step is looking for ways that the student can still be himself/herself without being disruptive or distracting in class. It's time to play *"Let's make a deal – here's what I can do for you. What can you do for me? Let's try to work out a way for you to _____ and for me to support that. What feels fair and do-able? Let's agree on one goal for next week."* Talk it through so the student can say: *"I can do this because it will help me _____." "I'll try to make this work because _____. I'll try this out for a week if you_____."*

Formal "As Needed" Personal Conferences with SOME Students

When a student's usual demeanor, attitude, or behavior has changed suddenly or a student is persistently withdrawn or sad....

When you've read, heard, or observed something that might indicate severe emotional distress …

Why? You are not a counselor, therapist, or social worker, but you do see the student every day. Listen to the student to gain more information before you make a referral. You can be the conduit to others who are trained to help students who are seriously troubled or in serious trouble.

Sample Teacher Prompts and Tips:

- Share what you've noticed: *"I've noticed lately that _____. Is everything okay?" "So over the past week I've noticed _____. I'm concerned about _____. Talk a little bit about what's been going on." "This seems like a tough time for you right now."*
- Use responsive listening to encourage the student to tell his/her story.
- Listen and acknowledge student's feelings – let student talk!
- Convey support and understanding of what you heard.
- Probe for sources of the problem and what student wants to do. *"Where do you feel stuck?" "If you had to tell someone else what was feeling awful right now, what would you say?" "What do you need right now to be okay for the rest of the day? "Where would you like to go from here?" "What would a good solution/good plan look like? "What might be a first step to resolving this?" "What could you do or say to work this out?" "Is there any way I can help? Is this a good time to think about a plan that might help you _____?"*
- Support student to get the right help. *"Do you think this is a good time to talk to_____?"* or *"This sounds like something that's important to talk about with _____. Can you do that today? Is there anything I can do to help make that happen?"*
- If you feel you need to report what you've heard and observed immediately, you may want to walk with the student to the appropriate counselor or social worker.

Student Requested Conference

 Student Requested Academic, Behavioral, Personal Conference

Why? Students who take the initiative to ask for a conference usually have a good reason for doing so that could be any of the following: the need to discuss concerns about the class; the need to reaffirm a trusting relationship with an adult; the need to discuss an important personal or school-related issue to get an adult's perspective; the need to disclose a serious incident; the desire to discuss their personal aspirations with someone they trust.

Sample Teacher Prompts and Tips:

- Arrange when you can meet with the student during lunch, your prep or conference period, or before or after school.
- Thank the student for requesting conference time.
- Say, "I'm glad you felt comfortable enough to talk to me. I need to know a little more about how I can help. I can either listen or help you problem solve. What feels most helpful right now?
- Use responsive listening skills described in the PEARS document on page 431.
- Hear what the student is saying without being judgmental or taking sides. Be mindful that some students want to draw a teacher in to their reality.
- If the student needs a referral, offer to accompany the student and make the introduction to the appropriate person.
- Check in with the student within the next few days to see how things are going.

Urgent Emergency Conferences

 Urgent Emergency Behavioral Conferences for a FEW Students

Exit check-in when student's actions warrant immediate removal from the classroom

Why? When a student has committed an egregious act that jeopardizes the safety and well-being of you and the class you need to clarify why student must be removed from class and spell out what will happen next.

Sample Teacher Prompts and Tips:
Immediately after the incident you and the student need to move away from the class, near the door. You may to need to cue another student to seek out a security guard or AP. Depending on the students' volatility, your conference might sound like this.

Option 1 (More conversational)

- I need to see you here at the door right now.
- I am insisting that you leave class for the remainder of the period. Do you know why I'm asking you to leave?
- Okay, so you understand the seriousness of your actions. I will discuss this later with you and the AP and there will be consequences you will need to carry out.
- I'm hoping you will think about how your actions impacted the class and why this was the wrong thing to do.

Option 2 (More directive)

- I need to see you at the door right now.
- I am insisting that you leave class for the remainder of the period because you made a choice to _____. Your words and actions made us/me/_____ feel threatened and unsafe.
- I will discuss this later with you and the AP and there will be consequences you will need to carry out.
- I'm hoping you will think about how your actions impacted the class and why it was the wrong thing to do.

Check-in when student is emotionally upset and needs a moment to recover before re-engaging in class

Why? When a student is experiencing emotional distress and needs a few minutes to recover, a quick check-in gives the students the opportunity to calm down and regain emotional control so that student can re-engage in class without punishment or high drama

Sample Teacher Prompts and Tips:
This is the time when it's best to be direct and brief. Noticing what you see and using calming words of support and encouragement offer the best approach for defusing a student's emotional charge and making a personal connection. Your invitation gives the student the opportunity to collect himself and refocus. Your choice of response will often depend on what the group is doing at the time. If students are involved in small group or independent work, you have a bigger window of time to check in, listen, and assess what might be a good next step.

- You might say, ""Take a minute to get a drink, and when you get back to your seat, we'll start again." OR "I can see you're too upset to focus right now. Take a few minutes to stop, take a few breaths, and relax a bit. Let me know when you think you're ready to rejoin us. Does that work?"
- Name and accept the negative feelings. "I can see you're frustrated with this. It's the last thing you want to be doing right now, isn't it? Take a minute and I'll check back to see where we can go from here." Your quick exit at this point gives students some space. When people are upset they can't solve problems. Come back later to check in.
- For some students, it's better to ask directly what they can do for themselves to cool down. Say, "I see you're upset. What can you do for yourself to feel more relaxed and in control?"
- For students who walk into your classroom already steaming and ready to blow, take the student aside and say, "You look like you're ready to blow. On a 1–10 scale, how upset are you? Take a minute to cool down. Give me a signal when you feel like you're down to a 5."

Urgent Emergency Personal Conferences for a Few Students

Referral check-in when student is too upset to recover during class time

Why? When you witness an incident in which a student's emotional distress is out of control or when you sense that a student's emotional charge is beyond momentary recovery, you need to refer student immediately to counseling or student support services.

Sample Teacher Prompts and Tips:

* Call the student to the most private space in the classroom or near the door and note what you observed and say, "You look too upset to learn right now. I'd like you to go to the counselor's office so you can take some time to get yourself together." OR "Your behavior tells me that you need to leave the classroom now before you say or do something you can't take back. I want you to go to the counselor's office so you can take some time to get yourself together. That sound okay to you? Good."
* Never send an emotionally charged student somewhere else without someone else. Send another student along with a note for the receiving staff person to sign.

Referral check-in when you've read about, heard about, or witnessed any incident of abuse or potential or prior harm to student or someone else

Why? When a student has written or said something that indicates "Double D" behavior (behavior that is dangerous or destructive to self or others), you have a legal obligation to report the incident and the situation calls for an immediate referral to a counselor. At some point in a teaching career, most of us have received at least one suicidal or threatening note, listened to a student's desperate cry for help, or witnessed a kid's sudden meltdown. When these incidents happen, we are in the position of being the "first responder" and need to act.

Teacher Prompts and Tips:

* This is the time to call on your teacher buddy or someone else available who might monitor your classroom for a few minutes while you walk the student to the guidance center. It's important not to be dramatic, and it' equally important to address the situation as soon as possible. Wait until the end of class and let the student know you need to see him or her before s/he leaves. You might say something like, "Ms. _____ wanted to speak with you next period and I promised to walk you there."
* If the student involves is someone you know very well, you might be more candid and say something like, "You know when I read/hear something that sounds harmful or abusive or scary, I need to report it. We can talk about this later if you want, and right now I want to take you to Ms. _____ for a few minutes. Okay?."
* Report the incident to the counselor and follow-through with any other communication and documentation protocols you need to complete according to district policies.

(1) Daniels, Harvey, and Bizar, Marilyn. (2005) Teaching the best practice way: Methods that matter K-12. Portland, ME: Stenhouse Publishers

More Conference Tips for Behavioral and Personal Conferences
Just Remember PEARS!

Paraphrase the facts:

- *"You're saying that _____."*
- *"So you had trouble with _____."*
- *"You want me to know that _____".*
- *"So when_____happened, you _____."*

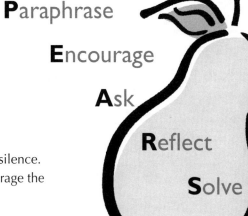

Paraphrase

Encourage

Ask

Reflect

Solve

Encourage the student to speak:

- Focus your whole attention on the student in interested silence.
- Lean in slightly; keep your arms relaxed and still; encourage the speaker by nodding.
- *"Tell me what happened."*
- *"I want to hear your side of the story."*
- *"So tell me more".*
- *"Say that in another way so I can better understand exactly what you need."*

Ask questions that help student clarify the problem and foster self-awareness, self-reflection, and self-assessment:

- *"What exactly happened when _____?"*
- *"How did you feel when_____?"*
- *"What else should I know about _____?"*
- *"What do you think is getting in the way of _____?"*
- *"What do you need so you can _____?"*
- *"Where there any other choices you might have made?"*
- *"What do you think your Mom would say about_____"*

Reflect feelings and defuse highly charged emotions like anger and frustration:

- *"So you're feeling angry about_____."*
- *"I can see you're upset about_____."*
- *"Wow! You sound really excited about_____."*
- *"So you felt _____when _____."*
- *"It must have been difficult for you to _____."*

Invite student to **Solve** the problem if student is ready to take charge and make a plan:

- *"What do you need right now to be okay for the rest of the day?*
- *"Where would you like to go from here?"*
- *"What would a good solution/good plan look like?*
- *"What might be a first step to resolving this?"*
- *"What could you do or say to work this out?"*

APPENDIX B

Learning Protocols for Professional Development

Pre-Reading Protocols

While-You-Read Protocols

Small and Large Group Protocols

Products / Presentations / Report-Outs

Assessment / Feedback / Planning / Closings / Final Thoughts

Making Learning REAL and *Getting Classroom Management RIGHT* have both been designed to be used by:

- Individual teachers who choose to explore these books on their own

- University instructors who teach undergraduate, graduate, and professional development courses in *teaching and learning, adolescent development, assessment, methods and instructional practices, and classroom management*

- Professional development specialists, consultants, principals, and teacher leaders who facilitate district and school-based professional development

- Faculty and administrators who participate in study groups within a district or school

Thus, we have included an appendix of learning protocols that adult groups can use to explore key topics in both publications. We cannot overstate the importance of modeling learning protocols in education courses and professional development sessions that participants can take away and use immediately in their own classrooms. Every protocol cited in the appendix can be used with adolescent learners ("as is" or adapted for use with a particular group or with a specific course of study).

Key to Learning Protocols:

Protocol Description (Left Side of Page)　　　**Topic and Text Connections** (Right Side of Page)

(REAL, (X), p. xx) refers to protocol descriptions located by chapter (X) and page number in ***Making Learning REAL***	**[REAL, [X], p. xx]** refers to topics located by chapter [X] and page number in ***Making Learning REAL***
(RIGHT, (X), p. xx) refers to protocol descriptions located by chapter (X) and page number in ***Getting Classroom Management RIGHT***	**[RIGHT, [X], p. xx]** refers to topics located by chapter [X] and page number in ***Getting Classroom Management RIGHT***

Pre-Reading Protocols	Topic and Text Connections
1. Webbing (REAL, (13) page 289) OR **2. Stick It Up** Give individuals or pairs a large post-it to record and post their first thoughts about a particular topic, issue, or concept. Use either of these exercises to get a quick "read" of the group's thinking about core concepts and principles. "When you hear the word_____, what words, images, or phrases come to mind?"	**[REAL, [1]]**, pages 43-51 Readings 1-7, Personalization; Personalized Learning; Personalized Learning Environment; pages 51-52 Reading 8: Rigorous and Relevant Learning; page 53, Reading 9: Smaller Learning Community; page 54-55 What Does a Personalized Learning Environment Feel Like? **[REAL, [2]]**, pages 57-65, Readings 11-15: Learning Community; Community of Learners; **[REAL, [3]]**, pages 67-74, Readings 16-17: Adolescent Development; pages 75-76, Reading 18: Resilience; pages 77-78, Reading 19: Characteristics of Adolescent Learners; pages 78-83, Reading 20: Developmentally Appropriate Practice; pages 83-84, Reading 21: Expectations/Standards; pages 85-88, Readings 22-24: Personalized Support; pages 89-92, Reading 25: Motivation; pages 92-93 Different Supports for Students, Reading 26 **[REAL, [4]]**, pages 95-96, Reading27: Diversity; pages 96-99, Reading 28: Identify Development; pages 100-101, Reading 29: Dominant Culture; pages 101-107, Readings 30-31: Privilege; pages 108-109, Readings 32-33: Culturally Responsive Teaching **[REAL, [5]]**, pages 111-117, Readings 34-36: Life Skills; **[REAL, [7]]**, pages 139-154 Assessment, Habits of Learning, Grading, and Progress Reports **[REAL, [8]]**, pages 160-162, Teaching Stance
	[RIGHT, [1]], pages 26-27, Unwanted behaviors that get in the way learning OR three unwanted behaviors that you want to reduce in your classroom **[RIGHT, [1]]**, pages 36-41 Frequently Used Terms that are used throughout the book, particularly: Discipline; Self-Discipline; Punishment; Consequences; Responsibility; Accountability
3. Personal Memory Share: With a partner share how you experienced a specific condition of schooling or a specific learning situation that is the focus of the text. What were you feeling? What were you doing? What was the teacher doing? Why does this memory stand out for you? How did this affect your experience of school or your learning? How has this experience been important in your life? Does this experience in any way impact what you do or don't do today?	Think about your own experience in school and share a learning experience.... **[REAL, [1], pages 41-49, Readings 1-7:** that you felt was **personalized** to fit your needs and interests. **[REAL, [1], pages 49-50, Reading 8:** that you considered to be both **rigorous and relevant**. **[REAL, [2], pages 55-63, Reading 11-15:** where you felt you experienced a genuine sense of community with other learners. **[REAL, [3], pages 87, Reading 24:** that was extremely negative for you.
	[RIGHT, [6], pages 200-201, when you were struggling or discouraged and someone helped you turn around and get back on track
4. Entry Tickets and Quick Writes (REAL, (16) pages 381-383)	What do you do when students don't learn? **[REAL, [3], pages 87-93, [16], pages 373-377, [16], pages 385-390** "Thinking about Discipline" question prompts
	[RIGHT, [1], page 19 "Know Your No's, Needs, and Nonnegotiables" question prompts **[RIGHT, [3], page 71**

Pre-Reading Protocols	Topic and Text Connections
5. Where Do You Want Your Kids or School to Be? (REAL, Appendix B, page 437)	*[REAL, [7], pages 139-154,* Grading practices and homework policies *[REAL, [3], pages 80-82, [16], pages 364-373*
	[RIGHT, [5], pages 149-154 Classroom learning supports and interventions for students who are struggling *[RIGHT, [1], pages 209-219,* Student discipline and behavior
6. Quotes Café Select quotes related to a particular theme or issue. Cut typed quotes into separate sentence strips and ask participants to choose a quote that…. • they believe and act on everyday OR • they wish every adult in school believed and acted on every day • Participants then share their selected quotes with three different partners in a "walk-about". • Why did you choose this quote? • How would school be different for students if every adult believed this statement?	*[REAL, [1], page 46, Reading 3,* Personalization *[REAL, [2], pages 60-61, Reading 12,* Teacher Behaviors that Support a Classroom Learning Community *[REAL, [3], pages 67-74, Reading 16,17:* Benchmarks and Facts about Adolescent Development *[REAL, [3], pages 77-78, Reading 19:* How Adolescents Learn
7. Hopes and Hesitations (REAL, (9) pages 179-180) As we think and talk about _____, what are your hopes for this conversation? What are your hesitations (or fears)?	Use before reading and discussing any topics or issues that might be perceived as controversial, emotionally charged, or uncomfortable to confront. For example, discussion around common grading policies, diversity and cultural competency, or disciplinary expectations of teachers are likely to generate an array of opinions and some defensiveness.
8. Prior Knowledge: To get a read of the group's prior experience or familiarity with the topic, issue, or practice, ask the group to 1) pair up and share their prior experience or familiarity with the topic, issue, or practice; AND/OR 2) Ask the group to put up 1 to 5 fingers (a 1 if this is new/unfamiliar, to a 5 if this is something they're very familiar with or use regularly.	Use this whenever you don't know what experience and knowledge the group is bringing to the table about a specific topic and practice in **REAL** and **RIGHT**.
9. K-S-T-W (REAL, Appendix B, pages 437)	Use this with any topics where you think that key concepts and principles may be unfamiliar to some of the group, or some participants may be bringing preconceived ideas or even misunderstandings to the topic that the selected reading may challenge. For example, this would be a useful entry point before examining the characteristics of adolescent learners.

Pre-Reading Protocols	Topic and Text Connections
10. Carousel **(REAL, (13) page 284-285)**	*[REAL, [4], pages 108-109, Readings 32 & 33:* Question prompts about "Culturally Responsive Practice" *[REAL, [7], pages 139-140,* Question prompts about "Assessment and Record Keeping"
	[RIGHT, [6], [7] pages 178-192, 211-212 Post problematic student behaviors and ask pairs or trios to generate teacher responses that invite cooperation or self-correction or defuse, deflect, or de-escalate the provocation.
11. Point of View **(REAL, Appendix B, page 437)** In groups of five, share individually generated definitions and reach consensus on a group definition.	*[REAL] and [RIGHT]* Use with any key term that is likely to generate an array of opinions.
12. By My Side: Create a snapshot of a real student you've taught (think specifically about a student who lives on the margins at school) and take that student with you while you read. After the reading, share with a partner or the group how the ideas and practices in the reading might change this student's experience of school.	*[REAL]* This is especially useful for readings that focus on personalization, high expectations and high support, and culturally responsive teaching. *[Readings 4–7, 10, 22–26, 28–32) and Practices 1, 2, 6, and 7]*
	[RIGHT] This is especially useful for readings in Step 3: Support Individuals and the Group *[5],* Step 4: Invite Student Engagement, Cooperation, and Self-Correction *[6],* and Step 5: Develop Accountable Consequences and Supportive Interventions *[7]*
13. Opinion Continuum: **(REAL, (15) page 353-354)** Create normative statements around faculty practice, student expectations and outcomes, school discipline polices and practices, teacher roles and responsibilities that begin "All faculty should/should not…" OR "All students should/should not…" OR "The school should/should not…" OR "The policy about _____should/should not include…	Use as an entry point with any readings and discussion related to discipline, grading and assessment, creating a academic culture of completion and quality, the role of independent learning, and the first week of school.
14. Why Doesn't It Change? **(REAL, Appendix B, page 437)**	Use when reading about specific practices that have obvious benefits but are rarely implemented widely or consistently. It's helpful to name what gets in the way in order to know what it will take and what faculty need to shift norms and practice.
15. The Wall of Resistance **(REAL, Appendix B, page 437)**	This is a useful exercise when addressing entrenched practices that haven't changed for decades Resistance to… • changing assessment and grading practices; • providing different kinds of time and support when some students don't learn • modeling, teaching, practicing, and assessing habits of learning and life skills • developing accountable consequences • academic and behavioral conferencing • offering great choice and differentiation of tasks and assessments

Prereading Protocols

Point of View

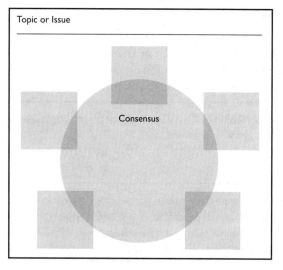

Why Doesn't It Change?

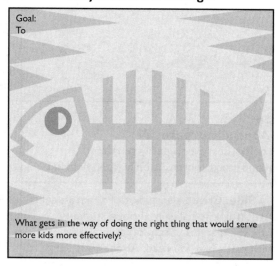

K-S-T-W

1. What do you **know**?	2. What are your **sources** for what you know?
3. What do you **think** you know but you're not sure of?	4. What do you **want** to know more about?

The Wall of Resistance

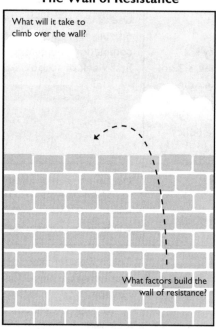

Where Do You Want Your Kids or Your School to BE?

POINT OF VIEW

Topic or Issue

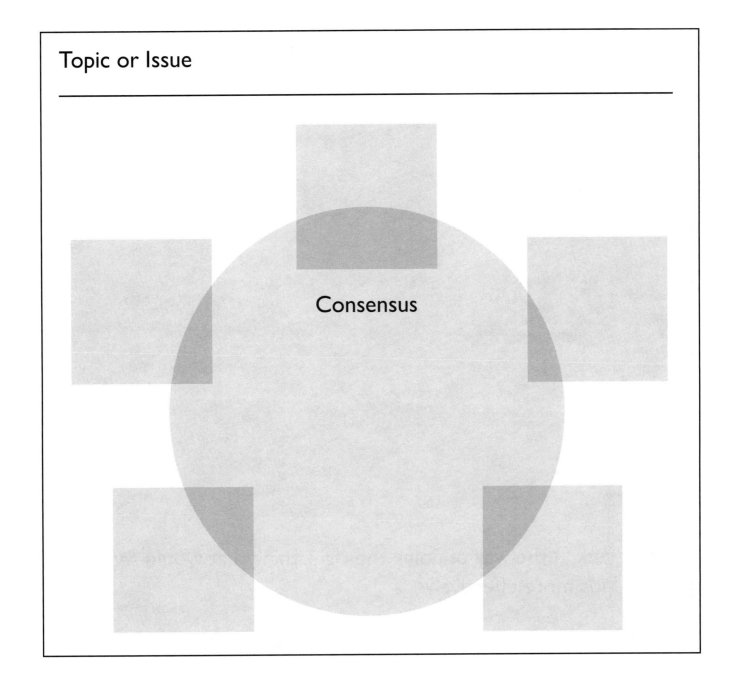

Consensus

WHY DOESN'T IT CHANGE?

Goal:
To

What gets in the way of doing the right thing that would serve more kids more effectively?

K - S - T- W

1. What do you **know**?	2. What are your **sources** for what you know?
3. What do you **think** you know but you're not sure of?	4. What do you **want** to know more about?

THE WALL OF RESISTANCE

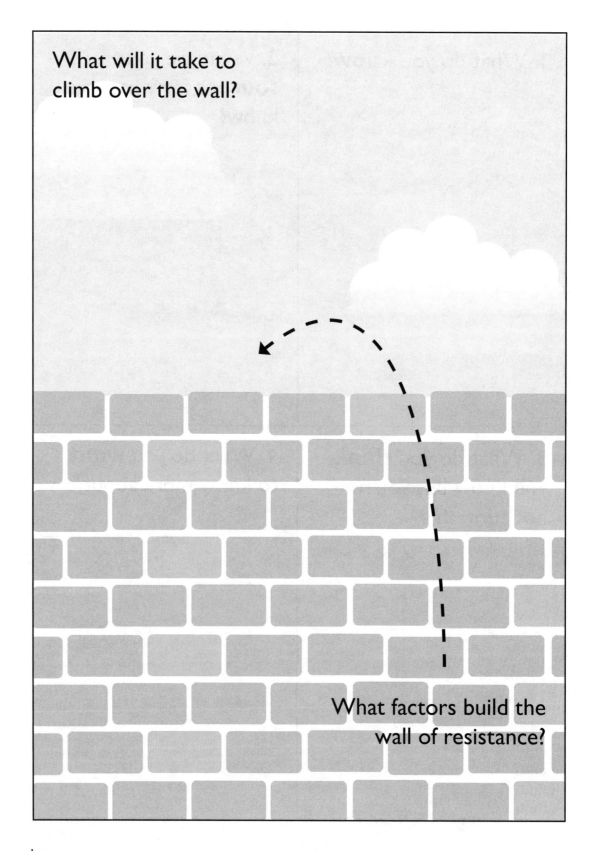

What will it take to climb over the wall?

What factors build the wall of resistance?

WHERE DO YOU WANT YOUR KIDS OR YOUR SCHOOL TO BE?

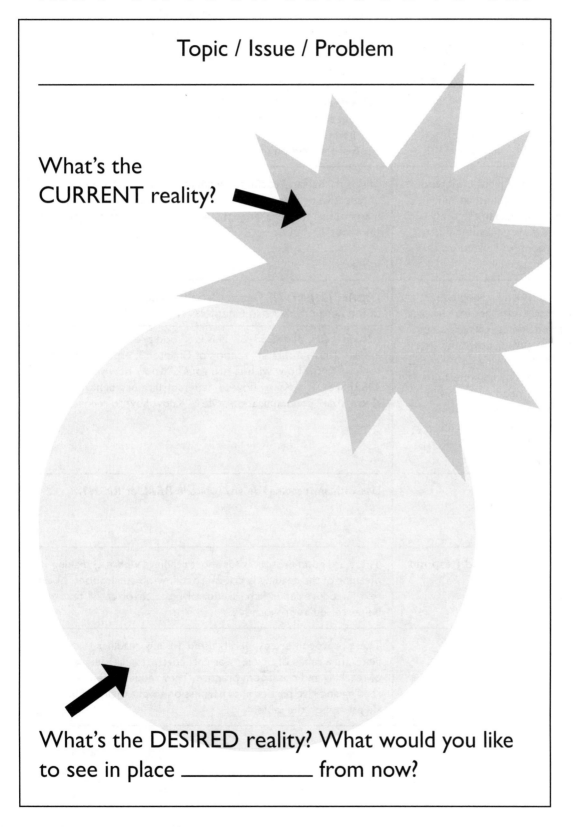

Topic / Issue / Problem

_____

What's the CURRENT reality?

What's the DESIRED reality? What would you like to see in place _____ from now?

While You Read Protocols	Topic and Text Connections
16. Jigsaw Reading (REAL, (13) page 276) Be sure to give each person in a pair, trio, or foursome a focus question for their particular reading or suggest a protocol from this list for capturing what they read so they can bring what they learned back to their group.	**[REAL]** *Introduction, pages 23-25,* Juanita and Benita *[2], pages 57,62, 63,65, Readings 11, 13, 14, 15* *[6], pages 119-129,* A Tale of Two Classrooms **[RIGHT]** *[1], pages 19-23,* Three Approaches to Discipline *[2], pages 43-62,* Case Studies *[4], pages 116-134,* Procedures and Routines *[6], pages 177-186,* Invite Student Engagement, Cooperation, and Self-Correction
17. Double Entry Notes: Fold a piece of notebook paper in half and on the right side jot down and summarize important ideas you read in the text. On the left hand side jot down your comments, reactions, questions, confusions, or reflections that help you make meaning of the text.	This is particularly useful for readings that introduce a new perspective or unfamiliar concept to the group or introduce material that may challenge the prevailing norms and practices of the group.
18. IT SAYS / I SAY / and SO…As people read, invite participants to pick three passages from the text that grab their attention and use this protocol to record and respond. IT SAYS (Write down the text that you've chosen.) / I SAY (Jot down your reactions and comments) / and SO… (Jot down a) questions you have or b) ways you might incorporate this idea or practice or c) what might be the implications or benefits of incorporating this idea into your classroom practice.) (Daniels and Zemelman, 2004, Subjects Matter, Heinemann Press, p. 122)	*[REAL, [11] – [17]]* This is a good protocol to use with any of the core practices in Chapters 11-17 *[RIGHT, [3], pages 63-87* This is a good protocol for readings in the "Know Yourself" section of Chapter 3, especially these topics: "Know how 'with-it' are you?"; "Know how you define DISRESPECT"; "Know how to depersonalize bad behavior"; Know your° communication style"; "Know how to recover"
19. Text Connect (REAL, Appendix B, page 440)	Use with any readings on any topics in **REAL** or **RIGHT.**
20. Paired Reading and **Trio Read and Respond** (REAL, (15) page 349)	These are good protocols for short readings where a) making meaning of the reading is critical to follow-up applications; b) the text introduces an unfamiliar idea or practice; or c) the text may be perceived as provocative.
21. Where Do I Stand (I) **Where Do I Stand (II)** **Where Do I Stand (III)** (REAL, Appendix, page 440)	These protocols are especially useful for any readings that may generate a range of opinions or challenge prevailing norms of teaching and classroom practice. They require attentive reading and give participants permission to put their doubts and skepticism on the table.

While You Read Protocols	**Topic and Text Connections**
22. Question Pairs: Ask participants to read in pairs. The goal of this protocol is to jot down questions while you read. After you and your partner are finished reading, share the questions you crafted. Decide on two questions that you want to refine. Write your questions on newsprint or sentence strips. The questions will be used for later discussion. (Review the section in **REAL, (15), pages 355-356,** "Asking Good Questions" before you use this protocol.	Use with any readings on any topics in **REAL** or **RIGHT.**
23. Text Coding and Underlining: Invite participants to create their own codes and symbols to use as they mark up the text while they read. OR you might develop a group code to try out. (i.e. Underline_____; Circle_____; Put a _____ next to_____; etc.)	
24. Front and Back: On a note card use the front side to summarize important ideas in the text and use the back side for comments and questions you want to raise in the discussion.	
25. 3 Big Ideas: (REAL, Appendix B, page 440)	
26. Bookmarks: Literally create 2-inch × 8-inch paper bookmarks on the computer with the topic or issue printed on the top of the bookmark. Participants write their notes about the reading on the bookmark.	
27. Sticky Notes Posting sticky notes on the text as you read is a great way to make your thinking transparent. You can suggest that participants do "free-range" sticky notes (comments, questions, reactions, connections, or yeah, buts) OR only use stickies for questions that emerge from your reading OR use two colors of stickies and post on text where you agree [first color] or disagree or doubt [second color].	

While-You-Read Protocols

Where Do I Stand (I)

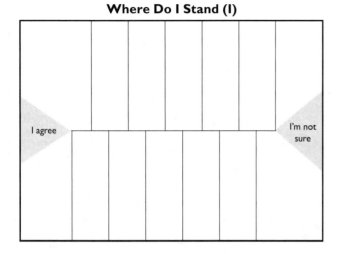

I agree   I'm not sure

Where Do I Stand (II)

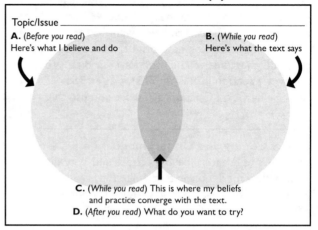

Topic/Issue _____

A. (*Before you read*)
Here's what I believe and do

B. (*While you read*)
Here's what the text says

C. (*While you read*) This is where my beliefs and practice converge with the text.
D. (*After you read*) What do you want to try?

3 Big Ideas

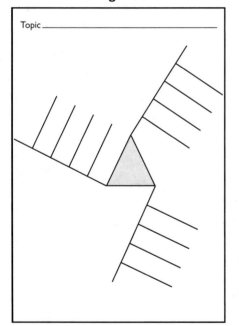

Topic _____

Where Do I Stand? (III)

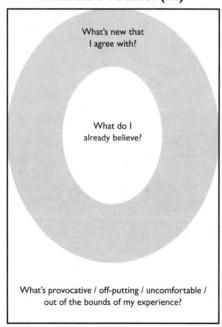

What's new that I agree with?

What do I already believe?

What's provocative / off-putting / uncomfortable / out of the bounds of my experience?

Text Connect

_____

Ideas/Facts that matter	How would teaching and learning change if this informed what we do??

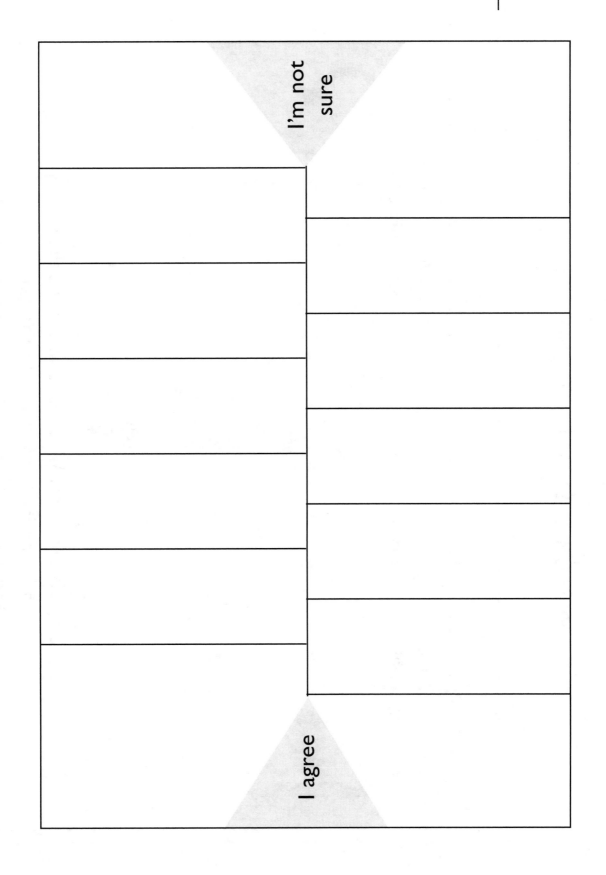

WHERE DO I STAND (I)

I'm not sure

I agree

WHERE DO I STAND (II)

Topic/Issue _____

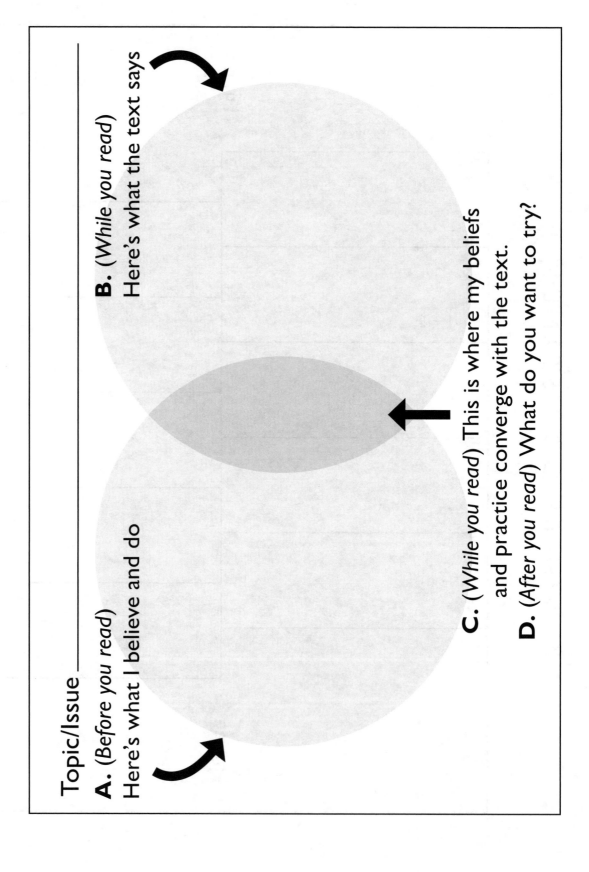

A. (*Before you read*)
Here's what I believe and do

B. (*While you read*)
Here's what the text says

C. (*While you read*) This is where my beliefs
and practice converge with the text.

D. (*After you read*) What do you want to try?

3 BIG IDEAS

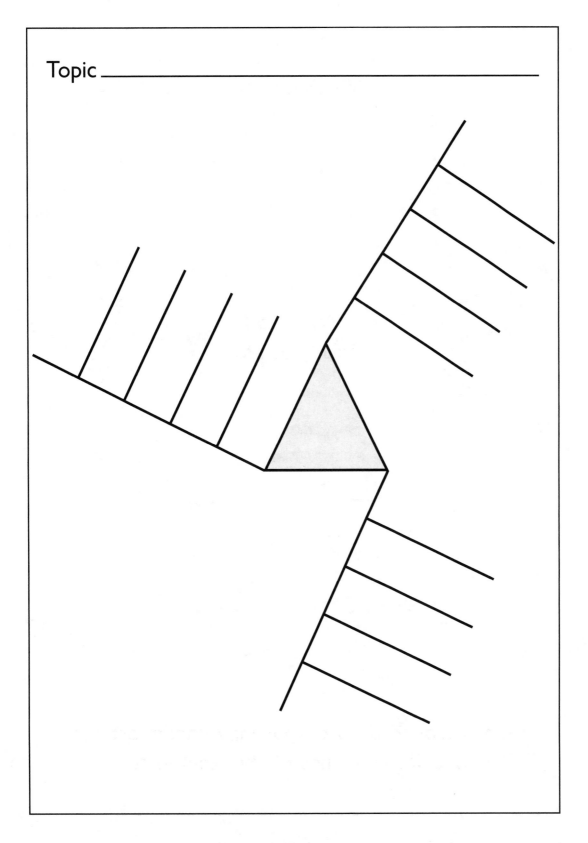

Topic _____

WHERE DO I STAND? (III)

What's new that
I agree with?

What do I
already believe?

What's provocative / off-putting / uncomfortable /
out of the bounds of my experience?

TEXT CONNECT

Ideas/Facts that matter	**How would teaching and learning change if this informed what we do??**

Small and Large Group Dialogue Protocols	Topic and Text Connections
28. Jigsaw Sharing: You have two choices after people finish their readings. OPTION A: Create "expert groups" by having all participants who read the same text meet for a focused discussion to clarify what they read, check for understanding, and raise questions and implications. Then "experts" return to their home groups and share what they learned. Other group members should take notes – every group member is responsible for understanding major ideas in all of the readings. OPTION B: After group members finish their readings they simply continue working in the same group, sharing what they read with each other.	*[REAL]* *Introduction, pages 23-35,* Juanita and Benita *[2], pages 57,62,63,65, Readings 11, 13, 14, 15* *[6], pages 117-127,* A Tale of Two Classrooms *[RIGHT]* *[1], pages 19-24,* Three Approaches to Discipline *[2], pages 43-62,* Case Studies *[4], pages 120-134,* Procedures and Routines *[6], pages 178-187,* Invite Student Engagement, Cooperation, and Self-Correction
29. Case Study Analysis **(RIGHT, (2), pages 43-62)**	*[RIGHT, [2], pages 43-62]* Case Study Scenarios
30. Text-based Seminar **(REAL, (15), pages 355-358)** "Practicing and Assessing Good Talk"	Use with any readings on any topic that need to be read deliberatively with close attention to big ideas and the details.
31. Chalk Talk: Chalk Talk is a silent activity that requires a white board, chalk board, or butcher paper and chalk or markers. Pose a question that's relevant to the reading and write it in the center of the board or paper. Then pass out chalk or markers and invite participants to write down their thoughts and reactions to the question prompt when they are moved to do so. Participants are invited to write comments in response to what others have written; draw connections between their comments and the comments of others; write questions that spring from a comment; circle ideas they find compelling; etc. Don't be surprised if there are moments when no one is writing, as participants take in what they see. Take at least 15 minutes for this activity and take time afterwards to look for dominant themes/ the range of opinions/ clusters of similar ideas/and anything that was a surprise to participants.	This is extremely helpful when the reading focuses on an issue that's emotionally charged or when the group is deeply divided in its opinion. Somehow the silence frees people to write what they're honestly thinking, without the fear of being judged. Here are some question prompts: *[REAL]* *[2], pages 55-59]* "After the reading on community, what kinds of structures, activities, and opportunities would you like to see in your faculty learning community?" *[4], pages 99-103]* "After reading about dominant culture and privilege in high school, what are your thoughts about how your school supports equity and access for ALL students?" *[7], pages 139-154]* "After the reading on grading and assessment, what are you thinking, questioning, doubting, wondering?" Or "What thoughts do you want to share your school leadership team?" *[RIGHT, Introduction, [1], [2], [7]* "After the reading on discipline what are you thinking about the current discipline practices in your school?"
32. Kid Talk Protocol **(RIGHT, (7), pages 254-256)**	*[RIGHT], [7], page 254-256* Practice using this protocol (choose a real student to discuss) in conjunction with readings about how to support struggling, angry, or discouraged students or students who engage in chronic unwanted behaviors.
33. Responsive Listening Protocols (REAL (15) All of these protocols enable participants to practice responsive listening. **Fish Bowl (page 354)** **Pair-Shares (page 350)** **Partner Paraphrasing (page 349)** **Paraphrasing Circles (page 353)** **Listening Lab (page 352)**	Generate your own questions for any topic OR you might want to use questions that participants have generated from **Protocol 21. Question Pairs.**

Small and Large Group Dialogue Protocols	Topic and Text Connections
34. Role Chairs: This protocol is about defending your practice and what you believe. It's a powerful rehearsal for participants who are ready to try on classroom practices that may contradict the dominant teaching and learning norms in their school. Divide into groups of four. Ask one volunteer to become the defender of specific ideas, strategies, or practices you've read about and discussed. The other three group members take on the roles of a skeptical administrator, parent, and faculty colleague. They engage in a lively dialogue in which the defender shares their reasons for introducing new practices in the classroom.	This protocol is especially useful when participants are rethinking and changing practices related to: **[REAL]** **[7], pages 139-154, [12], pages 228-237, and [16], pages 378-384,** Assessment **[12], pages 241-248,** Well Paced, Student-Centered Lessons **[12], pages 250-267,** Independent and Project-Based Learning
	[RIGHT] **[4], pages 119-134,** Procedures and Routines **[5], pages 141-146,** Teaching Life Skills **[6], pages 184-186,** Lesson Pacing and Engaging ALL Learners **[7], pages 226-231,** Accountable Consequences and Supportive Interventions
35. Save the Last Word: This works best in groups of three. 1) Each person first circles or underlines three passages in the reading that were particularly significant for them. 2) Person #1 reads one of her selected passages; 3) Persons #2 and #3 in the group share their thoughts and perspectives about that particular passage; 4) Person #1 gets the last word and shares why they chose this particular passage and the significance it has for them. 5) Repeat the protocol two more times so each person in the group has an opportunity to read their passage and have the "last word." (Daniels and Zemelman, 2004, Subjects Matter, Heinemann Press, p. 133)	Any topics and readings in **REAL** or **RIGHT**
36. Written Conversation: Each participant receives a 5" × 8" note card and works with a partner. 1) Each person writes a first reaction to the reading; 2) Partners exchange cards and read them; 3) Partners write a response to what they read; 4) Partners exchange cards, then read and respond two more times. (Daniels and Zemelman, 2004, Subjects Matter, Heinemann Press, p. 130)	
37. Author and Audience: In groups of five, ask a participant in each group to volunteer to serve in the role of author of the text. The other group members engage in a dialogue with the "author," asking clarifying questions, sharing their reactions, affirming what they agree with, and raising their cautions and concerns.	
38. Tools for Formative Assessment # 2, 21, 22 (REAL, (13) page 381-384)	

Products / Presentations / Report Outs	Topic and Text Connections
39. Summary Points **(REAL (15), page 351**	Invite one group to end their discussion early and prepare summary points for the whole group.
40. What's the Difference? Use this protocol when a clear understanding of two related, but different terms is essential for discussion of the topic and application in the classroom. Give small groups two different colored large post-it notes. After completing the reading, the group discusses and reaches agreement on definitions or mantras that precisely capture the distinguishing characteristics of the two related terms or concepts.	**[REAL]** **[3], pages 83-84,** Expectations vs. Standards **[16], pages 378-380,** Formative vs. Summative Assessment **[12], pages 241-246,** Student-Centered vs. Teacher-Directed Instruction
	[RIGHT] **[I], pages 20-24,** Punishment, Do Nothing vs. Guided Discipline **[I], pages 34- 37,** Punitive vs. Accountable Consequences **[I], pages 39,** Responsibility vs. Accountability **[3], pages 66-67,** Authoritarian vs. Authoritative
41. MI3 Presentations: **(REAL, (13), pages 272-273)** Use three intelligences to present what you read to the rest of the group. Groups must post bullet points or a visual chart that highlights what the group agrees were the most significant ideas in the reading. Be sure to have plenty of props and materials around for the dramatically, artistically, and musically inclined.	This protocol is a good choice when different groups are responsible for sharing different readings on the same topic with the whole group.
42. Core Practice Trio Share **(REAL, Appendix, pages 444)**	This is useful to do the following topics: The first day of school; The first week of school; Grading and assessment; Classroom discipline.
43. Dos and Don'ts: Generate a list of Dos and Don'ts that reflect your reading and discussion about a specific topic.	**[REAL] [8], pages 159-169,** The First Day of School
	[RIGHT, [7], pages 196-205, Responding to Provocative Speech
44. Elevator Speech Give participants 10 minutes to write a one minute "elevator speech" that captures beliefs, rationale, and commitment that they associate with a specific practice. Present speeches to table group and solicit feedback and suggestions from table mates.	This is a useful protocol when participants perceive a change in practice as a risk that they need to confidently defend to other colleagues, an administrator, parents, or students.
45. Your Two Best Ideas: (REAL, Appendix, page 444)	These protocols provide a variety of ways to sum up and close small group discussions that follow any reading on any topic.
46. Golden Nuggets: (REAL, Appendix, page 444) After groups have mined their golden nuggets, do a quick whip around the room and invite each group to share one or two of their nuggets.	
47. A Text to Remember: A group chooses one sentence from the text that affirms the most important idea the group wants to take away from the reading. Write it on chart paper and post it.	
48. Going Further: (REAL, Appendix, page 444) Ask groups to generate questions that emerge from their discussion. Write questions on large sentence strips to post or chart further questions that the whole group generates together.	
49. Prioritizing Ideas: What Matters Most? **(REAL, Appendix, page 444)**	
50. Tools for Formative Assessment #1, 4, 8, 10, 11, 12, 14, 15, 17, 20 (REAL, (13) page 381-385)	

Products / Presentations / Report Outs

Your Two Best Ideas

① **What is it?**	② **What is it?**
I. What are the benefits?	I. What are the benefits?
2. What do you need to make it happen?	2. What do you need to make it happen?
3. Who makes it happen?	3. Who makes it happen?
4. When?	4. When?

Prioritizing Ideas — What Matters Most?

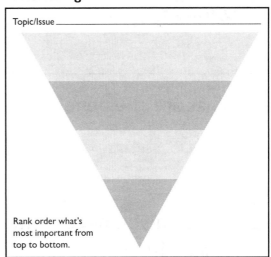

Topic/Issue _____

Rank order what's most important from top to bottom.

Core Practice Trio Share

Practice # _____

page _____ to page _____

Brief Description of Activities/Strategies

_____

Why and when would you use this?

What would be the benefits of using this with your students?

How might you modify or expand this activity for your groups?

Golden Nuggets

From your discussion what two or three "nuggets" feel most important to share with the whole group?

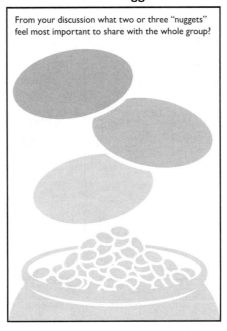

Going Further

I wonder…

What would it take to…? I

If I couldn't fail I (we) would…

How come …?

Why do we…?

What if…?

Why couldn't we…?

What would happen if…?

I'm still puzzled by…

I'm curious about…

What if we tried…?

How could we…?

I'm still not sure about…

If_____ then_____

YOUR TWO BEST IDEAS

What is it?	**What is it?**
1. What are the benefits?	1. What are the benefits?
2. What do you need to make it happen?	2. What do you need to make it happen?
3. Who makes it happen?	3. Who makes it happen?
4. When?	4. When?

PRIORITIZING IDEAS — WHAT MATTERS MOST?

Topic/Issue _____

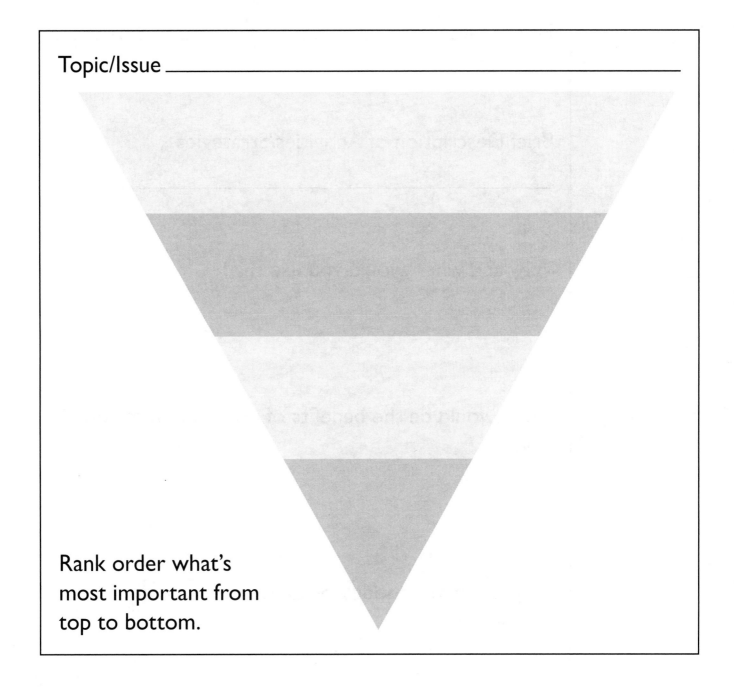

Rank order what's most important from top to bottom.

CORE PRACTICE TRIO SHARE

Practice # _____

page _____ to page _____

Brief Description of Activities/Strategies

_____

Why and when would you use this?

What would be the benefits of using this with your students?

How might you modify or expand this activity for your groups?

GOLDEN NUGGETS

From your discussion what two or three "nuggets" feel most important to share with the whole group?

GOING FURTHER

I wonder…

What would it take to…? I

If I couldn't fail I (we) would…

How come …?

Why do we…?

What if…?

Why couldn't we…?

What would happen if…?

I'm still puzzled by…

I'm curious about…

What if we tried…?

How could we…?

I'm still not sure about…

If_____ then_____

Assessment / Feedback / Planning / Closings / Final Thoughts	Topic and Text Connections
51. Self-Assessment: **Question Prompts: (REAL, (12) pages 233-237)** **Exit Cards: (REAL, (15), pages 315-317)** **Ticket Out: (REAL, Appendix B, page 446)** **4 – 3 – 2 – 1: (REAL, Appendix B, page 446)** **Two Glows and a Grow: (REAL, (12) pages 234)** **STOP Before You GO: (REAL, Appendix B, page 446)** **New Directions: (REAL, Appendix B, page 446)**	All of these protocols provide opportunities for self-reflection and feedback at the end of a PD session.
52. Learning Journey: Invite participants to use words, symbols, images, and other graphics to describe and map their learning journey during the course (Where you started / What you learned / What you gained / What you want to remember/ Where you want to go)	This is a meaningful protocol to use at the end of a series of PDs or at the end of a course.
53. Group Assessment: **(REAL, (15) pages 276-277, 320-326)**	These protocols are useful when it's essential for participants to assess the performance and accomplishments of the whole group or small groups.
54. Letter to the Principal: Write letters to the principal in small groups that communicate: a) your experiences in this course or series of PD sessions; b) practices you would like to try out; c) issues and policies you would like to discuss with the leadership team; and/or d) the support you need to continue the work you started.	These protocols invite participants to think about how they want to continue their work as a group.
55. Next Steps: (REAL, Appendix B, page 446)	
56. Stick With It: Pass out large post-it notes and invite participants to write down 1) practices they want to stick with and use regularly; or 2) issues they want to continue discussing within their team or professional learning community; or 3) consistent practices the group wants to establish across a team, grade level, or department.	
57. Banner Headlines: Share your big take-away from the PD session using seven words or less.	All of these closings invite participants to share their responses out loud at the end of a PD session.
58. Goodbye.....Hello!!: Say "goodbye" to habits and practices you want to stop and say "hello" to practices you want to try out or do more often.	
59. I Can Do It!! I Can: Pass out note cards and invite people to write one thing that they can do in the next week to improve their practice and reach and support more students. Share them with the group.	
60. Connections: (REAL, (15) page 314	
61. Appreciations: (REAL, (15) page 334	

Assessment / Feedback / Planning / Closings / Final Thoughts

Ticket Out

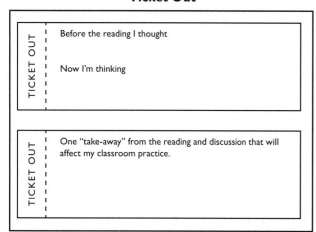

TICKET OUT

Before the reading I thought

Now I'm thinking

TICKET OUT

One "take-away" from the reading and discussion that will affect my classroom practice.

Next Steps

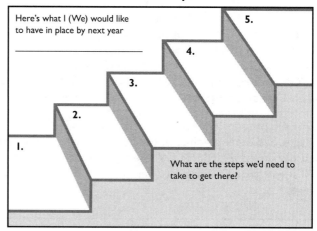

Here's what I (We) would like to have in place by next year

5.
4.
3.
2.
1.

What are the steps we'd need to take to get there?

Stop Before You GO

What actions do you want to take or what practices do you want to try out?

What will you need to stop doing or do less often to make this happen?

What reminder will help you keep your commitment?

New Directions

In relation to the reading and the issue of

_____

Where are you now?

Where do you want to be?

What would you need to get there?

4~3~2~1

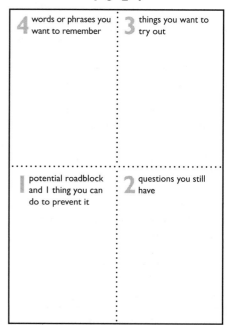

4 words or phrases you want to remember

3 things you want to try out

1 potential roadblock and 1 thing you can do to prevent it

2 questions you still have

TICKET OUT

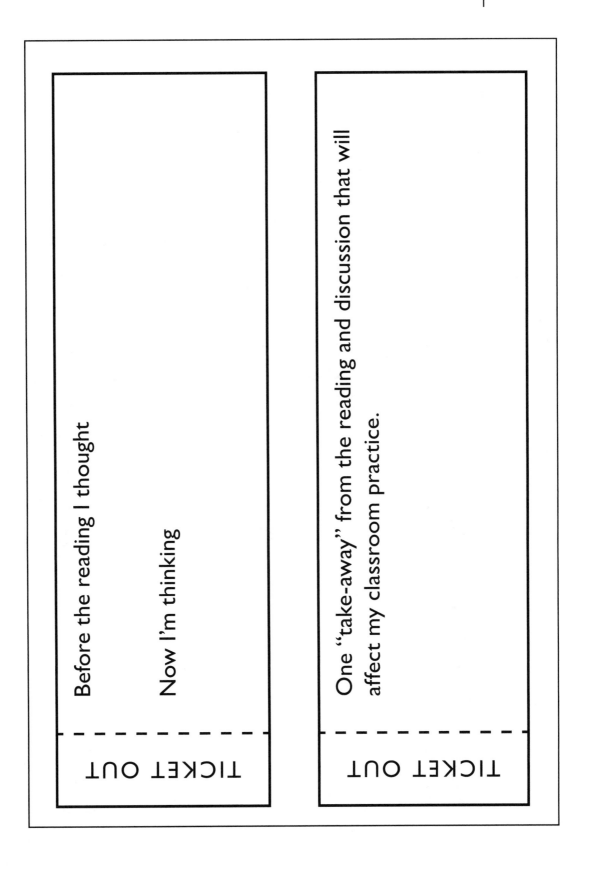

Before the reading I thought

Now I'm thinking

TICKET OUT

One "take-away" from the reading and discussion that will affect my classroom practice.

TICKET OUT

NEXT STEPS

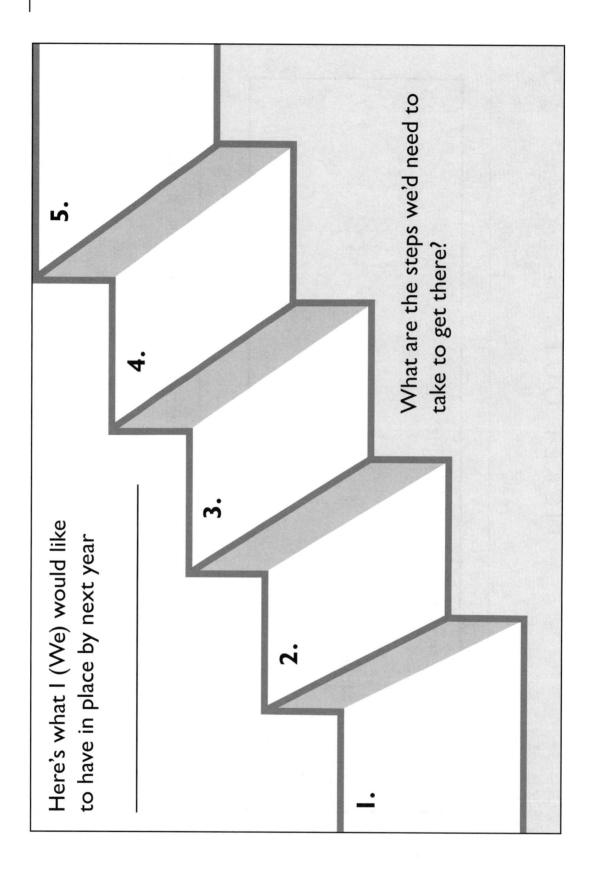

Here's what I (We) would like to have in place by next year

What are the steps we'd need to take to get there?

1.

2.

3.

4.

5.

STOP BEFORE YOU GO

What actions do you want to take or what practices do you want to try out?

What will you need to stop doing or do less often to make this happen?

What reminder will help you keep your commitment?

NEW DIRECTIONS

In relation to the reading and the issue of

_____

Where are you now?

Where do you want to be?

What would you need to get there?

4 ~ 3 ~ 2 ~ 1

4 words or phrases you want to remember

3 things you want to try out

1 potential roadblock and 1 thing you can do to prevent it

2 questions you still have

APPENDIX C

Bibliography & Suggested Resources

Bibliography

Chapter 1

[1] Adelman, H. & Taylor, L. (2001). *Enhancing classroom approaches for addressing barriers to learning.* Washington, DC: UCLA Center for Mental Health in Schools.

[2] McNeely, C., Nonnemaker, J. & Blum, R. (2002). Promoting school connectedness: Evidence from the National Longitudinal Study of Adolescent Health. *Journal of School Health, 4(72),* 138-146.

[3] Adelman, H. and Taylor, L. (2001). Ibid.

[4] Daniels, Bizar & Zemmelman (Eds.). (2001). *Rethinking high school: Best practice in teaching, learning, and leadership* Portsmouth, NH: Heinemann.

[5] Scales, P. & Leffert, N. (Eds.). (1999). *Developmental assets: A synthesis of the scientific research on adolescent development.* Minneapolis, MN: The Search Institute.

[6] Clarke, J. & Frazer, E. (2003). Making learning personal: Educational practices that work. In J. Clarke, J. DiMartino & D. Wolk, Eds. *Personalized learning: Preparing high school students to create their futures* (pp. 173-194). Lanham, MD: Scarecrow Education Press.

[7] Clarke, J. & Frazer, E. (2003). Ibid.

[8] Clarke, J. & Frazer, E. (2003). Ibid.

[9] Fredrichs, A. & Gibson, D. (2003). Personalization and secondary school renewal. In J. Clarke, J. DiMartino & D. Wolk, Eds. *Personalized learning: Preparing high school students to create their futures* (pp. 41-67). Lanham, MD: Scarecrow Education Press.

[10] Frey, J. (2001, March 21). Education's golden door for Brown U's new president, school was an opening full of possibilities. *Washington Post.*

[11] NASSP. (2005). *Breaking Ranks II: Strategies for leading high school reform.* Reston, VA: National Association of Secondary School Principals.

[12] Worsley, D. (2003). *Changing systems to personalize learning: Teaching to each student.* Providence, RI: The Education Alliance at Brown University.

[13] Meier, D. (2002). *The power of their ideas: Lessons for America from a small school in Harlem.* Boston, MA: Beacon Press.

Chapter 2

[1] Adelman, H. & Taylor, L. (2001). *Enhancing classroom approaches for addressing barriers to learning.* Washington, DC: UCLA Center for Mental Health in Schools.

[2] Sergiovanni, T. (1999). *Building community in schools.* San Francisco, CA: Jossey-Bass.

Chapter 3

[1] Darling-Hammond, L. (1997). *The right to learn: A blueprint for creating schools that work.* San Francisco, CA: Jossey-Bass.

[2] American Psychological Association (APA). *Developing adolescents: A reference for professionals.* Washington, DC: APA, 2002.

[3] Pruitt, D. (Ed.). (2000). *Your adolescent.* New York, NY: Harper Resource.

[4] APA. Ibid.

[5] Dacey, J., Margolis, D. & Kenny, M. (2006). *Adolescent development.* Custom Publishing.

[6] Elkind, D. (1981). *Children and adolescents.* USA: Oxford University Press.

[7] Sources include: American Psychological Association (APA). *Developing adolescents: A reference for professionals.* Washington, DC: APA, 2002.; Begley, S. (2000, February 28). Getting inside a teen brain. *Newsweek, 135,* 9., pp. 58-59.; Bostic, J. & Miller, C. (2005, April 25). Teen depression: When should you worry? *Newsweek.* Retrieved July 2009, from http://www.newsweek.com/id/51835; Yurgelun-Todd, D. Frontline: Inside the teenage brain. *PBS Frontline.* Retrieved June 2009, from http://www.pbs.org/wgbh/pages/frontlin e/shows/ teenbrain/interviews/todd.html; And National Institute of Mental Health. Teenage brain: A work in progress. *National Institute of Mental Health.* Retrieved June 2009, from www.nimh.nih.gov/publicat/teenbrain.cfm.

[8] Brendtro, L., Brokenleg, M. & Van Bockern, S. (2001). *Reclaiming Youth at Risk: Our Hope for the Future.* Bloomington, IN: Solution Tree Press.

[9] McCarthy, B. & McCarthy, D. (2005). *Teaching around the 4MAT® Cycle: Designing instruction for diverse learners with diverse learning styles.* Thousand Oaks, CA: Corwin Press.

[10] Vigotsky, L. (1986). *Thought and language.* In (A. Kozulin, Trans.). Cambridge, MA: MIT University Press.

[11] Gardner, H. (2000). *Intelligence reframed.* New York, NY: Basic Books.

[12] Sources include: Steward, L. G. & White, M. A. (1976). Teacher Comments, Letter Grades, and Student Performance. *Journal of Educational Psychology,* 68(4), 488-500.;

[12] Striggins, R. J. (1994). Communicating with Report Card Grades. *In Student-Centered Classroom Assessment* (pp. 363-396). New York, NY: Macmillan.; Guskey, T. R. (2000). Grading policies that work against standards … and how to fix them. *NASSP Journal, 84*(620), 20-29.; And Guskey, T. R. & Bailey, J. M. (2001). *Developing grading and reporting systems for student learning.* Thousand Oaks, CA: Corwin Press.

[13] Werner, E. & Smith, R. (1992). *Overcoming the odds: High-risk children from birth to adulthood.* New York, NY: Cornell University Press.

[14] Bandura, A. (1997). *Self-efficacy: The exercise of control.* New York, NY: Freeman.

[15] Sylwester, R. (2000). *A celebration of neurons: An educator's guide to the human brain.* Alexandria, VA: Association for Supervision and Curriculum Development.

[16] Wlodkowski, R. & Ginsberg, M. (1995). *Diversity and Motivation.* San Francisco, CA: Jossey-Bass.

[17] Adelman, H. & Taylor, L. (2006). *The implementation guide to student learning supports in the classroom and schoolwide.* Thousand Oaks, CA: Corwin Press.

[18] Akey, T. Student Context, Student Attitudes and Behavior and Academic Achievement: An Exploratory Analysis. *Manpower Demonstration Research Corporation (MDRC)* Retrieved 2009, from http://www.mdrc.org/publications/419/o verview.html

[19] Mendler, A. (2001). *) Motivating students who don't care: Successful techniques for educators.* Bloomington, IN: Solution Tree Press.

Chapter 4

[1] CASEL. (2002). *Social and emotional competencies.* Chicago, IL: CASEL at University of Illinois.

[2] Rasool, J. & Curtis, C. (2000). *Multicultural education in middle and high school classrooms: Meeting the challenge of diversity and change.* Belmont, CA: Wadsworth/Thompson Learning.

[3] Bandler, R. (1989). *Reframing: Neuro-linguistic programming and the transformation of meaning.* Moab, UT: Real People Press.

[4] Palmer, P. (1998). *The courage to teach: Exploring the inner landscape of a teachers life.* San Francisco, CA: Jossey-Bass.

[5] Rasool, J. & Curtis, C. Ibid.

[6] Kohl, H. (1994). *"I won't learn from you" and other thoughts on creative maladjustments.* New York, NY: The New Press.

[7] Nieto, S. (2000). *Affirming diversity: The socio-political context of multicultural education.* New York, NY: Addison Wesley Longman.

[8] (pg 97) Ibid.

[9] Delpit, L. (2006). *Other people's children: Cultural conflict in the classroom, Updated Edition.* New York, NY: The New Press.

[10] Rasool, J. & Curtis, C. Ibid.

[11] Abdal-Haqq, I. "Culturally responsive curriculum." *ERIC Clearinghouse on Teaching and Teacher Education.* ERIC Identifier: ED370936. Washington, DC: US Department of Education, June 1994.

[12] Ohanion, S. (1999). *One size fits few: The folly of educational standards*. Portsmouth, NH: Heinemann.

Chapter 5

[1] Payton, J., Wardlaw, D., Graczyk, P., Bloodworth, M., Tampsett, C. & Weissberg, R. (May 2000). Social and emotional learning: A framework for promoting mental health and reducing risk behaviors in children and youth. *Journal of School Health, 5*(70).

[2] Goleman, D. (2006). *Emotional intelligence: 10th anniversary edition; Why it can matter more than IQ*. New York, NY: Bantam.

[3] Adelman, H. & Taylor, L. (2006). *The implementation guide to student learning supports in the classroom and schoolwide*. Thousand Oaks, CA: Corwin Press.

[4] Zins, J. & Elias, M. (2000). Educating the mind and heart. *CASEL Collections*. Chicago, IL: CASEL at University of Illinois.

[5] Adelman, H., and Taylor, L. Ibid.

[6] Duckworth, A. L. & Seligman, M. P. (2005). Self-discipline outdoes IQ in predicting academic performance of adolescents. *Psychological Science, 16*(12), 939-944.

[7] Benard, B. & Marshall, K. (1997). A framework for practice: tapping innate resilience. *Research/Practice: Center for Applied Research and Educational Improvement, 5*(1).

Chapter 6

[1] Fried, R. (1995). *The passionate teacher*. Boston, MA: Beacon Press.

Chapter 7

[1] Silverman, S. & Casazza, M. (2000). *Learning and development: Making connections to enhance teaching*. San Francisco, CA: Jossey-Bass.

[2] Walberg, H. & Haertel, G. (Eds.). (1997). *Psychology and educational practice*. Berkeley, CA: McCutchen Publishing Corporation.

[3] Ibid.

[4] Brooks, D. (2001, April). The organization kid. *The Atlantic*. Retrieved 2009, from http://www. theatlantic.com/doc/200104/ brooks.

Chapter 10

[1] Senge, P. (2000). *Schools that learn: A fifth discipline field book for educators, parents, and everyone who cares about education*. New York, NY: Currency Doubleday.

[2] Silverman, S. & Casazza, M. (2000). *Learning and development: Making connections to enhance teaching*. San Francisco, CA: Jossey-Bass.

[3] Pruitt, D. (Ed.). (2000). *Your adolescent.* New York, NY: Harper Resource.

[4] Partnership for 21st Century Skills. Framework for 21st century learning: life and career skills. *Partnership for 21st Century Skills.* Retrieved 2009, from http://www.21stcenturyskills.org/ index .php?Itemid=120&id=254&option=com_conte nt&task=view. And US Department of Labor. What work requires of schools: A SCANS report for America. *US Department of Labor.* Retrieved 2009, from http://wdr.doleta.gov/SCANS/whatwork/w hatwork.pdf.

[5] Gardner, H. (2000). *Intelligence reframed.* New York, NY: Basic Books.

[6] Csikszentmihalyi, M. & Schneider, B. (2000). *Becoming adult: How teenagers prepare for the world of work.* New York, NY: Basic Books.

[7] Perry Jr., W. G. (1981). Cognitive and ethical growth: The making of meaning. In A. W. Chickering & Associates, Ed. *The Modern American College* (pp. 76-116). San Francisco, CA: Jossey-Bass.

Chapter 12

[1] Evertson, C. M. & Weinstein, C. S. (Eds.). (2006). *Handbook of classroom management.* Philadelphia, PA: Erlbaum Associates.

[2] Ibid.

[3] Sage, S. & Torp, L. (2002). *Problems as possibilities: problem-based learning for K-16 education.* Alexandria, VA: Association of Supervision and Curriculum Development.

[4] Jones, B., Rasmussen, C. & Moffitt, M. (1997). *Real-life problem solving: A collaborative approach to interdisciplinary learning.* Washington, DC: American Psychological Association.

[5] Sage, S. & Torp, L. Ibid.

[6] Steinberg, A., Cushman, K. & Riordan, R. (1999). *Schooling for the real world: the essential guide to rigorous and relevant learning.* San Francisco, CA: Jossey-Bass.

[7] Wagner, T. (2008, October). Rigor redefined. *Educational Leadership, 66,* 2.

[8] Wagner, T. (2008). *The global achievement gap: why even our best schools don't teach the new survival skills our children need and what we can do about it.* New York, NY: Basic Books.

[9] Educational Development Corporation. The I-search unit. *Make It Happen!* Retrieved 2009, from http://www.edc.org/FSC/MIH/. And Clarke, J. (2003). *Changing systems to personalize learning: personalized learning.* Providence, RI: The Education Alliance at Brown University.

Chapter 13

[1] Gardner, H. (2000). *Intelligence reframed.* New York, NY: Basic Books.

[2] Aronson, E. (2000). *Nobody left to hate: teaching compassion after Columbine.* New York, NY: Worth Publishers.

[3] Johnson, D., Johnson, R. & Holubec, E. (1994). *Cooperative learning in the classroom.* Alexandria, VA: Association of Supervision and Curriculum Development.

Chapter 15

[1] Harmony Education Center. *National School Reform Faculty.* Retrieved 2009, from http://www. nsrfharmony.org.

Chapter 16

[1] Ramaprasad, A. (1983). On the definition of feedback. *Behavioral Science, 28* (1), 4-13.

[2] Sadler, D. R. (1989). Formative assessment and the design of instructional systems. Instructional Science, 18 (2): p. 119-144.

[3] Bangert-Drowns, Kulick, & Morgan. (1991) The instructional effect of feedback in test-like events. Review of Educational Research, 61 (2): p. 213-238.

[4] Chappuis, S. & Chappuis, J. The best value in formative assessment. Educational Leadership. December 2007/January 2008. Alexandria, VA: Association of Supervision and Curriculum Development.

[5] Black, P., & Wiliam, D. (1998) Inside the black box: Raising standards through classroom assessment. Phi Delta Kappan, 80 (2): p. 139-148.

[6] Boston, Carol. (2002) The concept of formative assessment. ERIC Digest (ED470206). Washington, DC: US Department of Education.

Recommended Resources

In addition to the books and articles referred to throughout the book, these resources offer additional perspectives on adolescence and teaching and learning in high schools.

Adolescent Development

Adams, G. (2000). *Adolescent Development: Essential Readings*. Oxford, UK: Blackwell Publishers.

Csikszentmihali, M. & Larson, R. (1984). *Being Adolescent: Conflict and Growth in the Teenage Years*. New York: Basic Books.

Gauvain, M. (2001). *The Social Context of Cognitive Development*. New York: Guildford Press.

Levy-Warren, M. (1996). *The Adolescent Journey: Development, Identity Formation, and Psycholtherapy*. Northvale, NJ: Jason Aronson Inc.

Sadowski, M. (2003). *Adolescents at School: Perspectives on Youth, Identity, and Education*. Cambridge, MA: Harvard Education Press.

Scales, P. & Leffert, N. (1999). *Developmental Assets: A Synthesis of the Scientific Research on Adolescent Development*. Minneapolis, MN: The Search Institute.

Case Studies and Portraits of Adolescents

Cushman, K. (2003). *Fires in the Bathroom: Advice for Teachers from High School Students*. Providence, RI: What Kids Can Do/Next Generation Press.

Cushman, K. (2005). *Sent to the Principal: Students Talk About Making High Schools Better*. Providence, RI: Next Generation Press.

Hersch, P. (1998). *A Tribe Apart: A Journey in the Heart of American Adolescence*. New York: Ballantine Books.

Olsen, L. (1997). *Made in America: Immigrant Students in Our Public Schools*. New York: The New Press.

Suskind, R. (1998). *A Hope in the Unseen: An American Odyssey from the Inner City to the Alvy League*. New York: Broadway Books.

Community Building and Reflection in the Classroom

Butler, S. (1995). *Quicksilver: Adventure Games, Initiative Problems, Trust Activities, and a Guide to Effective Leadership*. Project Adventure. Dubuque, Iowa: Kendall/Hunt Publishing.

Chappelle, S. & Bigman, L. (1998). *Diversity in Action*. Beverly, MA: Project Adventure.

Jones, A. (1999). *Teambuilding Activities for Every Group*. Rec Room Pub.

MacGregor, M. (1997). *Leadership 101: Developing Leadership Skills for Resilient Youth – Facilitator's Guide*. (www.youthleadership.org).

McFarlane, E. & Saywell, J. (1995). *If (Questions for the Game of Life)*. New York: Villard Books.

Rohnke, Karl. (1984). *Silver Bullets: A Guide to Initiative Problems, Adventure Games, and Trust Activities*. Project Adventure. Dubuque, Iowa: Kendall/Hunt Publishing.

Sakofs, M. & Armstrong, G. (1996). *Into the Classroom: Outward Bound Resources for Teachers*. Dubuque, Iowa: Kendall/Hunt Publishing.

Van Linden, J. and Fertman, C. (1998). *Youth Leadership: A Guide to Understanding Leadership Development in Adolescents*. San Francisco: Jossey-Bass.

Written by and for Youth Leaders. (1995). *Youth Leadership in Action: A Guide to Cooperative Games and Group Activities.* Project Adventure Dubuque, Iowa: Kendall/Hunt Publishing.

High School Culture

Appleby, J., Dowd J., Grant, J., Hole, S., McEntee, G., & Silva, P. (2003). *At the Heart of*

Teaching: A Guide to Reflective Practice. New York, Teachers College Press.

Daniels, H., Bizsar, M., & Zemelman, S. (2000). *Rethinking High School: Best Practice in Teaching, Learning, and Leadership.* Portsmouth, NH: Heinemann.

Deal, T. (1999). *Shaping School Culture*. San Francisco: Jossey-Bass.

Delpit, L. (1996). *Other People's Children: Cutlural Conflict in the Classroom*. New York: The New Press.

Maran, M.(2000). *Class Dismissed: A Year in the Life of an American High School, A Glimpse into the Heart of a Nation*. New York: St. Martin's Press.

Perrotti, J. & Westheimer, K. (2001). *When the Drama Club Is Not Enough: Lessons from the Safe Schools Program for Gay and Lesbian Students*. Boston: Beacon Press.

Sizer, T. (1984).*Horace's Compromise: The Dilemma of the American High School*. New York: Houghton Mifflin.

Sizer, T. (1992). *Horace's School: Redesigning the American High School*. New York: Houghton Mifflin.

Sizer, T. & N. (1999). *The Students are Watching: Schools and the Moral Contract*. Boston: Beacon Press.

Tatum, B. (1997). *Why Are All the Black Kids Sitting Together in the Cafeteria? And Other Conversations About Race*. New York: Basic Books.

High School Teaching and Learning

Baloche, L. (1998). *The Cooperative Classroom: Empowering Learning*. New York: Prentiss-Hall.

Brookfield, S. & Preskill, S. (1999). *Discussion as a Way of Teaching: Tools and Techniques for Democratic Classrooms*. San Francisco: Jossey-Bass.

Brown, J., Benard, B., & D'Emidio-Caston, M. (2000). *Resilience Education*. Thousand Oaks, CA: Corwin Press.

Kohn, A. (1996). *Beyond Discipline: From Compliance to Community*. Alexandria, VA: Association of Supervision and Curriculum Development.

Krovetz, M. (1999). *Fostering Resiliency: Expecting All Students to Use Their Minds and Hearts Well*. Thousand Oaks, CA: Corwin Press.

Muse, D. (Ed.) (1995). *Prejudice: A Story Collection*. New York: Hyperion Books.

Newman, J. (1998). *Tensions of Teaching: Beyond Tips to Critical Reflection*. New York: Teachers' College Press.

Tomlinson, C. (1999). *The Differentiated Classroom: Responding to the Needs of All Learners*. Alexandria, VA: Association of Supervision and Curriculum Development.

Schmuck and Schmuck. (1988). *Group Processes in the Classroom*. Dubuque, Iowa: Wm. C. Brown.

Zemelman, S., Daniels, H., & Hyde, A. (1998). *Best Practice: New Standards for Teaching and Learning in America's Schools*. Portsmouth, NH: Heinemann Press.

Social and Emotional Learning

Cohen, J. (Ed.) (1999). *Educating Minds and Hearts: Social Emotional Learning and the Passage into Adolescence*. New York: Teachers' College Press.

Goleman, D. (1997). *Emotional Intelligence: Why it Can Matter More Than IQ*. New York: Bantam.

Goleman, D. (2006). *Social Intelligence: The New Science of Human Relationships*. New York: Bantam.

Lieber, C. (1998). *Conflict Resolution in the High School*. Cambridge, MA: ESR.

Love, P. & Love, Anne (1995). *Enhancing Student Learning: Intellectual, Social, and Emotional Integration*. ASHE-ERIC High Education Report #4. Washington, DC: The George Washington Graduate School of Education and Human Development.

Salovey, P. & Sluyter, D. (Eds.) (1997). *Emotional Development and Emotional Intelligence: Educational Implications*. New York: Basic Books.

Vorrath, H. & Brendtro, L. (1985). *Positive Peer Culture*. Hawthorne, NY: Aldine De Gruyter.

INDEX

About the Author

CAROL MILLER LIEBER got the call to teach as a teenager and never stopped. Exploration of the art, craft, and science of teaching and learning has been her driving passion for over forty years as an educator—in the roles of middle and high school teacher; school founder; principal; curriculum writer; clinical professor of teacher education; and professional development consultant, author, and program designer for Educators for Social Responsibility. Carol supports principals, leadership teams, and faculty in large and small high schools in their efforts to embed the five Rs (rigor, relevance, relationships, responsibility, and readiness for college and career) into every aspect of schooling: school climate, culture, and student development initiatives; classroom practice; professional learning communities; and schoolwide and classroom systems of discipline and student support.

She is the author of many books and articles, including, most recently, *Increasing College Access through School-Based Models of Postsecondary Preparation, Planning, and Support*. An unrepentant Deweyan, Carol holds two unwavering hopes for education in the 21st century: that schools will nurture the mind, heart, and spirit of every student within democratic learning communities and that teachers and learners will recapture the qualities of joy, meaning, and imagination in their classrooms. These are the things that make learning REAL.

About Educators for Social Responsibility

Educators for Social Responsibility (ESR), founded in 1982, is a national leader in school reform. We work directly with educators to implement systemic practices that create safe, caring, and equitable schools so that all young people succeed in school and life, and help shape a safe, democratic and just world. ESR provides professional development, consultation and publications for adults who teach children and young people from preschool through high school.

ESR creates, disseminates, and teaches core practices that:

1. Reduce educational disparities and facilitate equal access to quality instruction, supports, and opportunities for [remove the word "all" from here] secondary students. ESR helps schools build positive school climates and personalized learning communities that promote healthy development and academic success for *all* students.

2. Help students develop and strengthen social skills, emotional competencies and qualities of character that increase interpersonal effectiveness and cultivate social responsibility. ESR helps schools build high quality social and emotional learning programs and initiatives that also help to reduce intolerance, harassment and bullying, and risky and aggressive student behaviors.

ESR has a long history and a wealth of experience facilitating the change process and much practical expertise in how to create positive learning environments in today's schools. Our work with principals, school leadership teams, faculty, students, and families is informed by current research and the "best practices" in educational leadership, instructional reform, prevention, and youth development.

Visit our website (*www.esrnational.org*) for more information or to sign up for our free monthly e-newsletter.

We can be reached at:
Educators for Social Responsibility
23 Garden Street
Cambridge, MA 02138
617-492-1764
617-864-5164 fax
educators@esrnational.org